BRITISH RAILWAY STATIONS
1825 - 1900
A COMPREHENSIVE GAZETTEER

Manchester Liverpool Road Station viewed on 23 September 2013. It was opened by the Liverpool & Manchester Railway on 15 September 1830 as the eastern terminus of the line and was closed 4 May 1844 when the line was extended to join the Manchester & Leeds Railway at Hunt's Bank. It saw further use as a goods station and is now a Grade I listed building forming part of the Manchester Museum of Science and Industry.

PAUL SMITH AND SALLY SALMON

UNIQUE BOOKS

THIS BOOK IS DEDICATED TO
SALLY'S HUSBAND
PHILIP MARK SALMON

"Thank you for showing me the meaning of love and support. You will always be the best choice I ever made – my safe place." Sally Salmon

---

British Railway Stations 1825 - 1900 An Essential Gazetteer
Paul Smith and Sally Salmon
First published in the United Kingdom by Unique Books 2023
© Text: Authors 2023
© Photographs: As credited
ISBN: 978 1 913555 15 3
A CIP record for this book is available from the British Library
Unique Books is an imprint of Unique Publishing Services Ltd, 3 Merton Court, The Strand, Brighton Marina Village, Brighton BN2 5XY.
www.uniquebooks.pub
Printed in India

All rights reserved. No part of this book may be reproduced or transmitted in any form or by any means electronic or mechanical, including photocopying, recording or by any information storage without permission from the Publisher in writing. All enquiries should be directed to the Publisher.

THE COMPANION VOLUME TO THIS PUBLICATION;

BRITISH RAILWAY STATIONS SINCE 1901 - AN ESSENTIAL GAZETTEER

by Paul Smith and Sally Salmon
Softback; 208 Pages with colour photographs throughout. ISBN 978-1-913555-11-5
Price £19.99
Available from the publishers
Unique Books, 3 Merton Court, Brighton BN2 5XY
www.uniquebooks.pub. e-mail: uniquepublishingservicesltd@gmail.com. Tel: 01273 622205

This looks at the 9,000 or so stations that operated on the British railway system between 1901 and 2021 and, where possible, gives the Ordnance Survey ten-digit National Grid Reference for each one and the site status of those that are closed.

CONTENTS

Introduction	3
Notes and National Grid	4 - 5
Part One - National Rail Lines	6 - 146
Part Two - Independent Lines	147 - 151
Appendix Additional Stations	152 - 157
Abbreviations	158 - 160
With Thanks to, Bibliography and Websites Accessed	160

Cover Photograph;

The Grade II listed **Hampton Station** viewed on 7 May 2023. It was opened by the London & Birmingham Railway 9 April 1838 and the Birmingham & Derby Junction line from Whitacre was accommodated from 12 August 1839 when it joined the main line. After closure by the L&NWR 1 September 1884, when a new station was opened 660 yards east, the L&NWR platforms were removed but the station remained in use for the Whitacre line until closure by the MR 1 January 1917.

INTRODUCTION

The Wycombe Railway station and engine shed at **High Wycombe**, viewed on 2 July 2017. It was built to a design by Isambard Kingdom Brunel and opened 1 August 1854 as the terminus for the line from Maidenhead and closed 1 October 1864 when the currently-sited station opened on the through line.

The station found further use as a goods shed and over the years a number of additions were added to the fabric of the building but these were removed to restore it to its near-original condition when it received Grade II listed status in 1999.

This book could be considered to be a prequel, and companion volume, to our *British Railway Stations Since 1901* where the 9,000 or so in existence in that period were identified and located. As assumed from the title of this offering, a look is taken of those that opened from the birth of passenger carrying railways and failed to survive before the end of the 19thC.

Whilst the opening of the Railway Age was a pioneering period in our history, the two resources that help us to depict and locate the stations, photography and mapmaking, were also passing through their own periods of early development and these are briefly discussed on the following page. So, for the very early days of railway history there is much reliance on drawings, company minutes and contemporary newspaper reports to assist us.

In establishing just what stations existed, and when, chronologists who have compiled the lists that we work from today scoured contemporary timetables and train times published in newspapers. These timetables listed all the stops that a train would make on a journey - however, of course, these did not necessarily indicate that there was a "station". And many of these did not last long, as the railways progressed so the "railhead" stations at the end of the line were dispensed with, some only lasting for a few days or weeks!

Some 1,200 or so have been covered in the main body of this volume which, as well as having a small map of each, gives the Ordnance Survey Ten-Digit National Grid Reference, where known, for each one, and the site status

The Appendix (pages 152-157) lists some of those that only had the briefest of existences and were thus excluded plus a large majority of those which were rebuilt on the same site (and thus had continuous use into the 20thC) but even these additional sites do not embrace all of those that the timetables showed.

We hope that this volume can be a useful companion book to the many atlases and station chronologies and assist those who like to visit railway archæology or enjoy walking or cycling along the many converted trackbeds that we now have in Britain.

Paul Smith *and* Sally Salmon, **Redditch,** Worcestershire 2023

The information in this edition has been collated up to 1 January 2023.
The authors would be pleased to receive any comments, updates or corrections.
Please communicate through the publisher.

Unless stated all photographs are by the authors

EARLY HISTORY OF THE ORDNANCE SURVEY AND NOTES ON THE MAPS

The Ordnance Survey (OS) was "born" in 1784 when William Roy was commissioned to geodetically connect the Royal Observatories at Greenwich with Paris. This London/Paris triangulation required a highly accurate theodolite and in accumulating the series of accurately measured triangles he established a five-mile baseline on flat ground on Hounslow Heath, and this subsequently formed the basis of the Principal Triangulation of Great Britain. Following the successful completion of his mission the Ordnance Survey was officially formed on 21 June 1791.

With Europe in turmoil and England under threat of invasion from France the Board of Ordnance commanded that maps be radically improved and enhanced to show as many features as possible so that the army was able to gauge the terrain in advance. This was of primary importance along the south coast and these areas were dealt with first.

Following the establishment of peace, the first Ordnance Survey map was published in 1801 and featured the most south eastern county - Kent. It had taken three years to complete and followed the military specification of elaborate hill shading and identifying communication routes. The surveyors worked to two inches to the mile but were printed at one inch to the mile and cost three guineas per county survey. Essex followed four years later and within 20 years about a third of England and Wales had been covered.

However almost the entire staff of the OS was ordered to Ireland in 1824 to produce six inch scale maps of the country for taxation purposes and this was not completed until 1846, during which time the early railways were beginning to take shape and the engineers and surveyors bemoaned the fact that the maps, where available, were only one inch to the mile and virtually useless.

Thus the OS started to produce six inch maps of the mainland and these are the ones that became available, some twenty years or so following the first railways.

We have "cleaned up" those that we have used by erasing superfluous information, bench marks etc, but what will be easily observed about them is the shear differences, even of those from the same period, depending on the teams involved. Bearing in mind that those prior to about 1880 are scaled six inch to the mile all of them require a great deal of skill but some are just sublime in their style and cartography (Durham, Northumberland and other northern counties) whilst in others (south Wales for example) the annotations had taken over and in some areas virtually obliterated the maps! It appears that it was a few years before some sort of uniformity was arrived at.

LITHOGRAPHS, ENGRAVINGS AND EARLY PHOTOGRAPHY

The other assistant to the historian in the quest for information and clarity are visual images. Photography was still being developed during the early years of the railways. At the commencement of the 19thC numerous pioneers were working with various chemicals and substrates to attempt to capture a permanent image and great strides were made by the 1830s with the daguerreotype method and Fox Talbot's paper-based calotype negative and salt print process. However, practical use of photography was not achieved until the end of the 19thC and too late to be used to record the early railway stations.

So we are indebted to the artists, lithographers and engravers who recorded images of those early days. Many were commissioned by the railway companies themselves to add positive publicity as the lines were constructed across the country.

The first station at **Swinton**, depicted in a tinted lithograph.
It was opened by the Midland Railway 1 July 1840 and closed 2 July 1899.
Unfortunately the names of the artist and lithographer are unrecorded

SOME NOTES ON THE TERMINOLOGY USED

Demolished: Where the station was of conventional construction with buildings and platforms etc., unless otherwise stated this term includes total removal and site clearance. With reference to stopping off points and similar locations, where there were no fixed facilities - perhaps merely utilising portable steps to gain access to a carriage - this refers to the facility being removed and unused.

No access: On operational lines this indicates that the site is generally fenced off.

In agricultural use: The site may be in use as a field or a location for farm buildings etc.

In commercial use: A general term covering uses from storage areas through to industrial and retail parks.

(a): Although not precisely established by mapping, the site may be assumed to be within 100 yards of the point specified and these are indicated as "Assumed Locations" on the maps.

(e): The authors have not, thus far, found any anecdotal or mapping information to accurately assess the location. This is particularly relevant for short-lived or temporary stations, and in some instances, "Possible Locations" are indicated.

* Private/untimetabled stations, employee's platforms and stopping points.

Subterranean (a): Where a station is totally underground the OS Reference is for the street-level building. Where the location of the station is known then the name is highlighted in RED.

ANOMALIES

Readers may observe that some of the maps used pre-date the opening of the particular station. The dates used are those noted on the maps as to when the survey was carried out so it might be safe to assume that they were in existence at that point. There may be two or three suggested answers to this situation;

a) The station was under construction at the time and was inserted onto the map in anticipation of its completion.

b) The assumed opening date was inaccurate (particularly if extracted from timetables)

or, the least likely, c) The surveyors were aware that a station was to be built and it was added to the map based on the plans submitted.

FIRST CASUALTIES

And finally, it is probably worth noting that the first casualties of those listed in this book (although short term temporary stations were inevitably closed earlier) were Stockton 1st S&DR [27 December 1830] and Woodley M&KR [c1830].

THE NATIONAL GRID

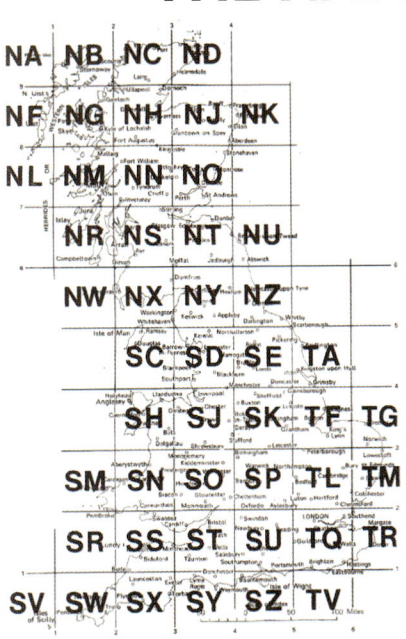

DISPOSITION OF THE SQUARES ACROSS THE COUNTRY

The country is divided into 100km (62.13 miles) squares, each one given a two letter code and then numerically into 10km (6.213 miles) squares. These are further divided into smaller and smaller units depending upon the accuracy of the co-ordinates required.

In this book the stations are given 10-figure references which pinpoint them to within a metre.

Those readers who prefer to use latitude/longitude (decimal) co-ordinates are advised that these can easily be obtained on the
UK Grid Reference Finder Website.
(https://gridreferencefinder.com/)
Example; Belper (1st) (MR)
Insert **SK34750 46653** where indicated and the relevant co-ordinates; 53.016057, -1.4834670 will be shown.
Latitude/longitude co-ordinates in degrees, minutes and seconds are also available.

PART ONE
NATIONAL RAIL LINES

This part details the stations that closed prior to 1901 on the lines that genealogically led to British Railways in 1948. Those that did not, the independent lines, are dealt with in Part Two, commencing on Page 149.

ABBOTSFORD FERRY (1st) (NBR)
May 1856 - ?
Line lifted – Demolished – Station site used as a domestic parking area **NT49672 33376**

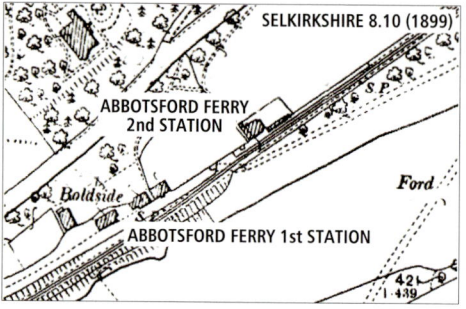

ABBOT'S WOOD JUNCTION (MR)
November 1850 - 1 October 1855
Line Operational – Demolished – No access
SO88947 50085 (a)

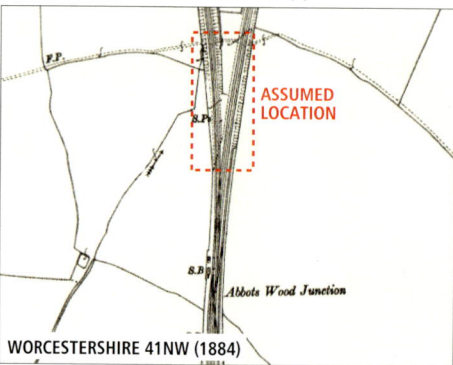

ABDIE (Ed&NR)
20 September 1847 - 9 December 1847
Line Operational – Demolished – No access
NO25720 16701 (a)

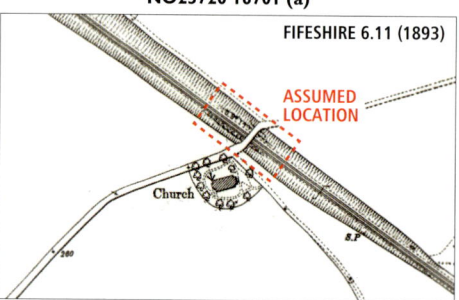

ABERAMAN (1st) (TVR)
5 April 1847 - 12 July 1856
Location unknown but near Treaman (1st) (qv)
SO02378 00788 (e)

ABERDEEN FERRYHILL (AberdeenR)
1 April 1850 - 2 August 1854
Line Operational – Demolished – No access
NJ94193 05007 (a)

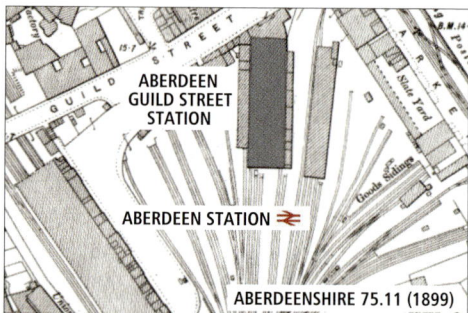

ABERDEEN GUILD STREET (CR)
2 August 1854 - 4 November 1867
Line lifted – Demolished – Station site in commercial use
NJ94247 05948

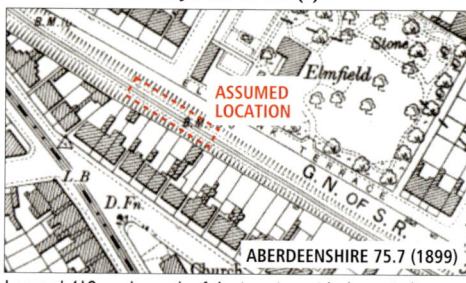

ABERDEEN KITTYBREWSTER (GNofSR)
20 September 1854 - 1 April 1856
Line Operational for Freight – Demolished
NJ93466 07499 (a)

Located 418 yards south of the junction with the main line.

ABERDEEN WATERLOO (GNofSR)
1 April 1856 - 4 November 1867
Line lifted – Demolished – Station site in commercial use
NJ94849 06227

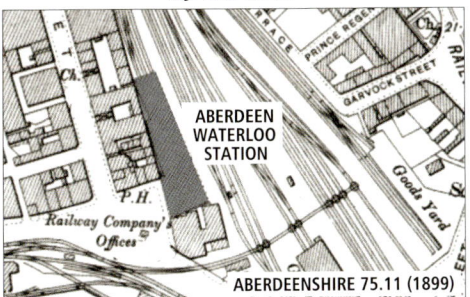

ABERDEEN WATERLOO STATION

ABERDEENSHIRE 75.11 (1899)

ABERCARN (1st) (GWR)
23 December 1850 - August 1867
Precise location unknown
ST21500 95261 (a)

ABERDOVEY HARBOUR (CamR)
24 October 1863 - 14 August 1867
Line lifted – Demolished – Station site occupied by a car park
SN61220 95963 (a)

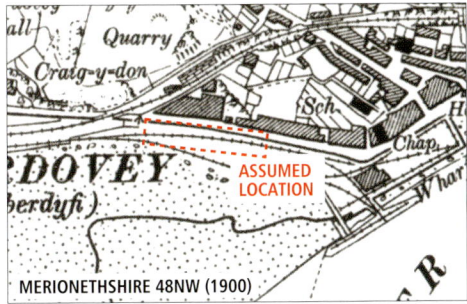

ASSUMED LOCATION

MERIONETHSHIRE 48NW (1900)

ABERGAVENNY JUNCTION (1st)
(GWR/L&NWR)
1 October 1862 - 20 June 1870
Line Operational – Demolished – No access
SO30865 14704 (a)

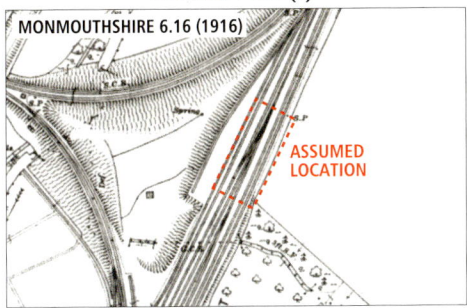

MONMOUTHSHIRE 6.16 (1916)

ASSUMED LOCATION

Sited 552 yards south of *Abergavenny Junction 2nd [GWR/L&NWR]* (20 June 1870 - 9 June 1958)

ABERDEEN WATERLOO - ABINGDON JUNCTION
ABERNETHY ROAD (Ed&NR)
17 May 1848 - 25 July 1848
Line Operational – Demolished – Station site unused
NO18968 16671

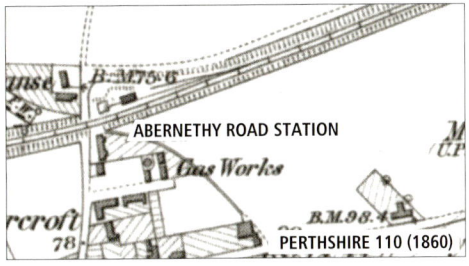

ABERNETHY ROAD STATION

PERTHSHIRE 110 (1860)

ABERTILLERY (1st) (GWR)
23 December 1850 - 7 December 1890
Line lifted – Demolished – Station site unused
SO21645 03985 (a)

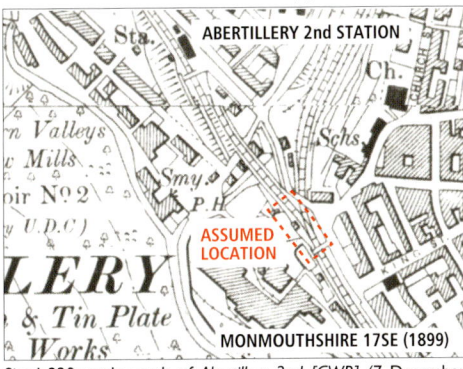

ABERTILLERY 2nd STATION

ASSUMED LOCATION

MONMOUTHSHIRE 17SE (1899)

Sited 220 yards south of *Abertillery 2nd [GWR]* (7 December 1890 - 30 April 1962)

ABINGDON JUNCTION (GWR)
2 June 1856 - 8 September 1863
Main Line Operational – Demolished – No access (Wik)
SU52582 97678 (a)

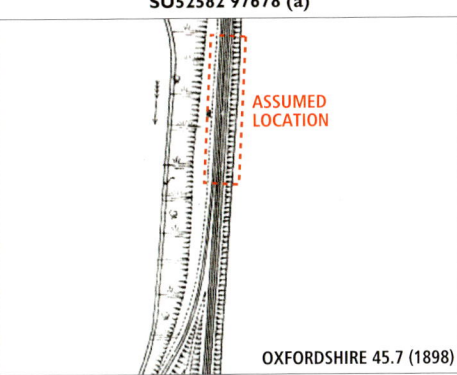

ASSUMED LOCATION

OXFORDSHIRE 45.7 (1898)

This was located where the Abingdon Branch left the main line. As it was only used as an exchange station no road access was provided.

ABINGTON - ALDERMINSTER [TRAMWAY STATION]

ABINGTON (NewmarketR)
4 April 1848 - 9 October 1851
Line lifted – Demolished – Station site unused
TL52104 50170 (a)

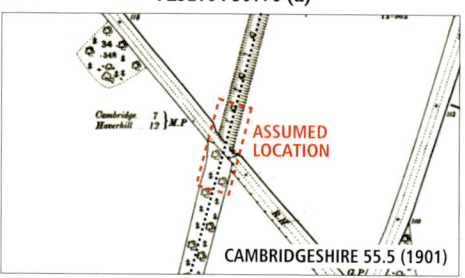

CAMBRIDGESHIRE 55.5 (1901)

ADVIE (1st) (GNofSR)
1 July 1863 - 1 September 1868
Line lifted – Demolished – A roadway passes through the station site. **NJ13637 34773 (a)**

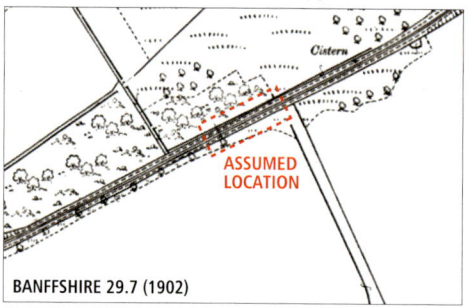

BANFFSHIRE 29.7 (1902)

Sited about 1,323 yards east of Advie 2nd [GNofSR] (1 September 1868 - 18 October 1965)

AGECROFT BRIDGE (L&YR)
29 May 1838 - January 1861
Line Operational – Demolished – No access
SD80489 00972 (a)

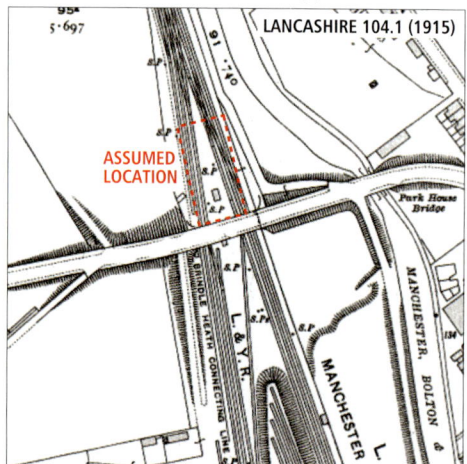

LANCASHIRE 104.1 (1915)

AIKBANK (M&CR)
10 February 1845 - 2 February 1848
Line Operational – Demolished – No access
NY21260 46103 (a)

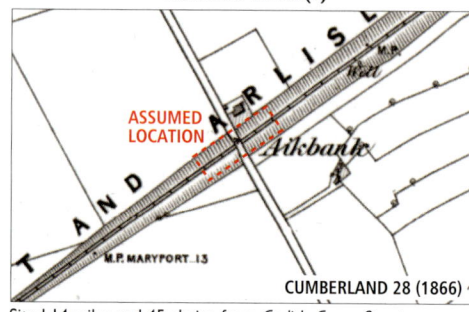

CUMBERLAND 28 (1866)

Sited 14 miles and 45 chains from Carlisle Crown Street

AIRDRIE HALLCRAIG STREET (NBR)
26 December 1844 - 1 June 1871
Line lifted – Demolished – Station site occupied by "Hallcraig Street Car Park" **NS76276 65558**

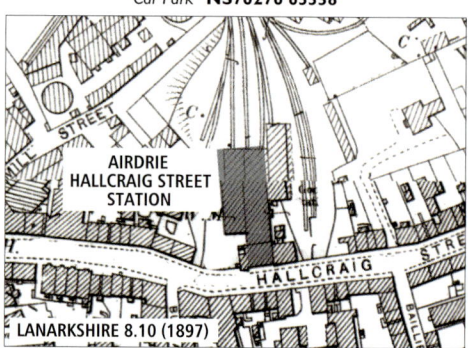

LANARKSHIRE 8.10 (1897)

ALDERMINSTER [TRAMWAY STATION] (OW&WR)
1834 - 30 September 1858
Line lifted – Demolished – Trackbed absorbed by Shipston Road
SP23025 48675 (a)

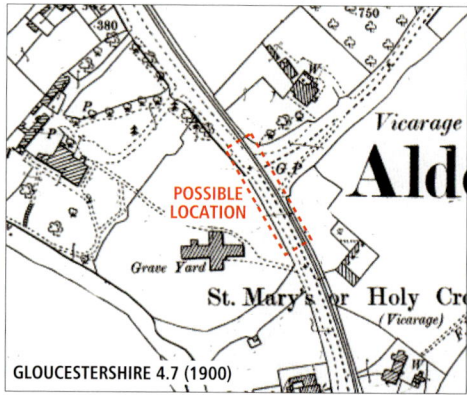

GLOUCESTERSHIRE 4.7 (1900)

ALLOA FERRY (St&DunfR)
3 June 1851 - July 1852
Line lifted – Demolished – Station site in commercial use
NS88159 92419 (a)

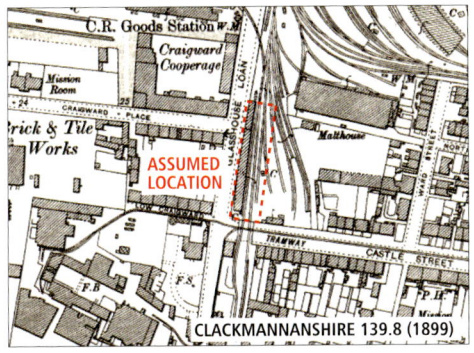

CLACKMANNANSHIRE 139.8 (1899)

ALLOA JUNCTION (CR)
2 September 1850 - November 1865
Main Line Operational – Demolished – Station site unused
NS85195 85987

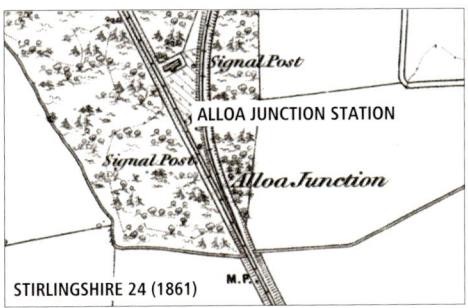

STIRLINGSHIRE 24 (1861)

ALLOA NORTH (CR)
? - 1 October 1885
Demolished - Station site in commercial use
NS88112 92297 (a)
THIS WAS A FERRY-ONLY STATION AND NOT RAIL CONNECTED

ALNWICK (1st) (NER)
19 August 1850 - 5 September 1887
Line lifted – Demolished – Station site in commercial use
NU19143 12913

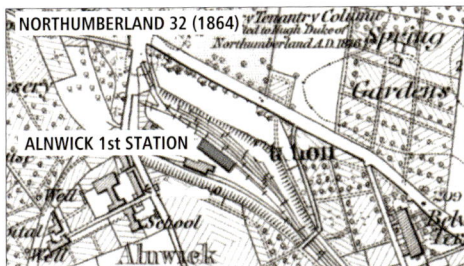

NORTHUMBERLAND 32 (1864)

ALLOA FERRY - AMBERGATE (1st)
ALTON (1st) (L&SWR)
28 July 1852 - 2 October 1865
Line lifted – Demolished – Station site partially in use as the station car park **SU72374 39779 (a)**

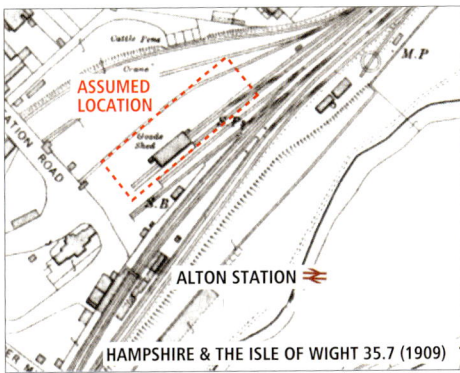

HAMPSHIRE & THE ISLE OF WIGHT 35.7 (1909)

ALTRINCHAM (MSJn&AR)
20 July 1849 - 3 April 1881
Line Operational – Demolished – No access
SJ77077 88138

CHESHIRE 18 (1876)

AMBERGATE (1st) (MR)
11 May 1840 - 1 June 1863
Line Operational – Demolished – Station site in commercial use
SK35060 51619

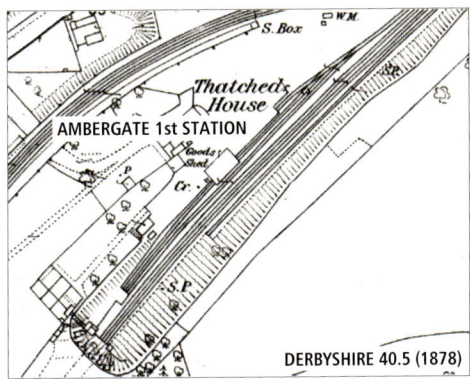

DERBYSHIRE 40.5 (1878)

AMBERGATE (2nd) - ARKLEBY

AMBERGATE (2nd) (MR)
1 June 183 - 10 December 1876
Line Operational – Demolished – Station site in private use
SK34824 51323

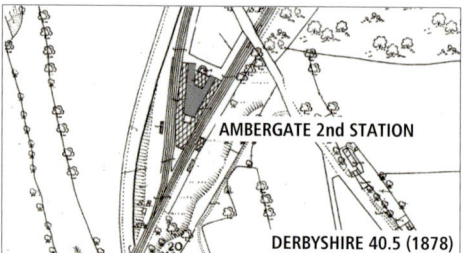

AMBERGATE 2nd STATION
DERBYSHIRE 40.5 (1878)

ANGARRACK (1st) (WCwallR)
23 May 1843 - 16 February 1852
Line lifted – Demolished – Station site unused
SW57936 38416 (a)

ANGARRACK (2nd) (WCwallR)
11 March 1852 - October 1853
Line Operational – Demolished – No access
SW58016 38023 (a)

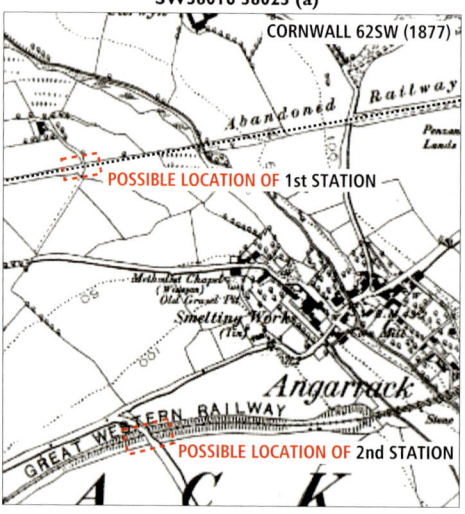

CORNWALL 62SW (1877)
POSSIBLE LOCATION OF 1st STATION
POSSIBLE LOCATION OF 2nd STATION

ANSTRUTHER (1st) (NBR)
1 September 1863 - 1 September 1883
Line lifted – Demolished – Station site occupied by housing in Dreelside **NO56145 03475**

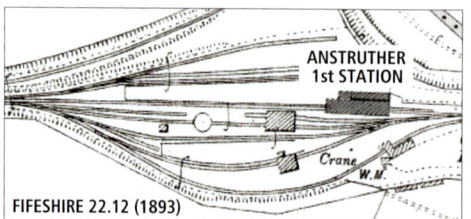

ANSTRUTHER 1st STATION
FIFESHIRE 22.12 (1893)

ARBROATH CATHERINE STREET
(AberdeenR)
3 January 1839 - 1 February 1848
Line lifted – Demolished – Station site in commercial use
NO63917 40971

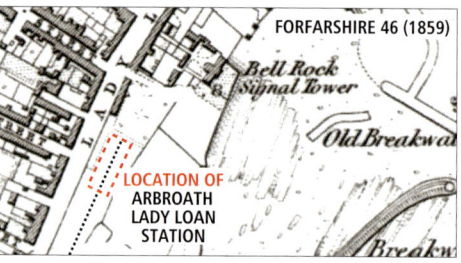

ARBROATH STATION
LOCATION OF ARBROATH CATHERINE STREET STATION
FORFARSHIRE 46.15 (1904)

ARBROATH LADY LOAN (D&AR)
8 October 1838 - 1 February 1848
Line lifted – Demolished – Station site landscaped
NO63981 40382

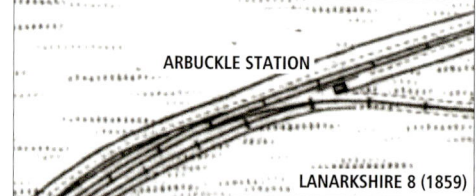

FORFARSHIRE 46 (1859)
LOCATION OF ARBROATH LADY LOAN STATION

ARBUCKLE (MonklandR)
July 1848 - October 1862
Line lifted – Demolished – Station site unused **NS78946 68565**

ARBUCKLE STATION
LANARKSHIRE 8 (1859)

ARKLEBY (M&CR)
1840 - 1 January 1852
Line Operational – Demolished – No access
NY13116 40231 (a)

ASSUMED LOCATION
Ellen Villa
CUMBERLAND 35 (1866)

10

ARTHINGTON (NER)
10 July 1849 - 1 February 1865
Line Operational – Demolished – Station site unused
SE25968 44800

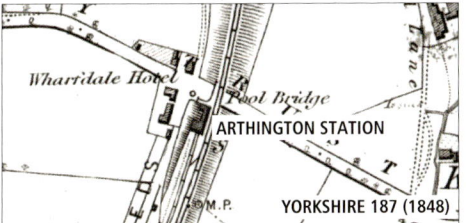

ASHFORD WEST (LC&DR)
ARTHINGTON - ASTLEY BRIDGE
1 July 1884 - 1 January 1899
Line lifted – Demolished – HS1 passes through the station site
TR00490 42639

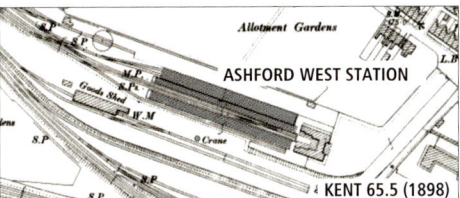

ARUNDEL AND LITTLEHAMPTON (LB&SCR)
16 March 1846 - 1 September 1863
Line Operational - Demolished - No access
TQ02866 03849

ASHINGTON COLLIERY JUNCTION (NER)
December 1871 - July 1878
Main Line Operational – Demolished – No access
NZ23562 88077

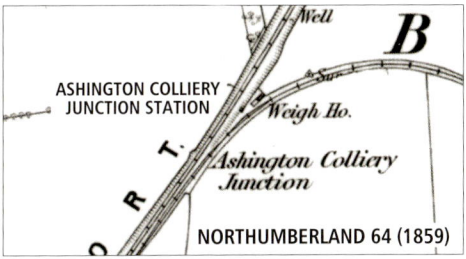

ASHBOURNE (NSR)
31 May 1852 - 1 August 1899
Line lifted – Demolished – Station site occupied by buildings in Leisure Way **SK17695 46276**

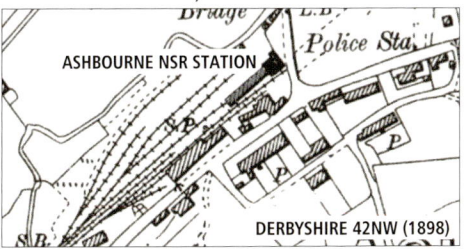

ASHTON (B&ER)
21 July 1852 - 1 February 1856
Line Operational – Demolished – No access
ST54988 69996 (a)

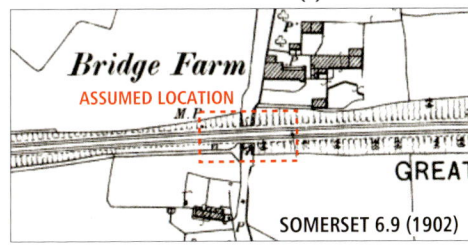

ASHFORD BOWDLER (S&HR)
1 December 1854 - 1 November 1855
Line Operational – Demolished – No access
SO51776 70634

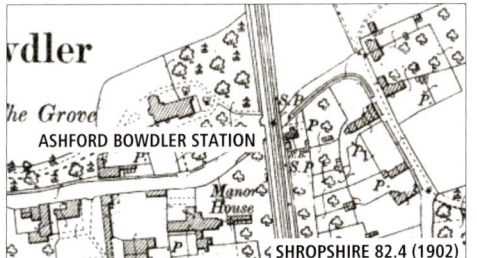

ASTLEY BRIDGE (L&YR)
15 October 1877 -1 October 1879
Line lifted – Demolished – Station site occupied by the "Waters Meeting Health Centre" **SD71592 11133 (a)**

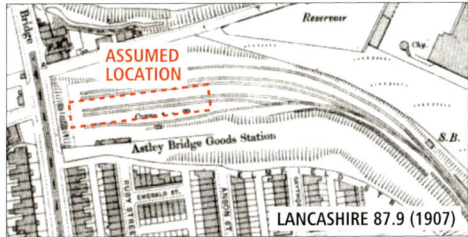

ATHERSTONE-ON-STOUR
[TRAMWAY STATION] (OW&WR)
1834 - 30 September 1858
Line lifted – Demolished – Trackbed absorbed by the A3400, Shipston Road **SP20958 51125 (a)**

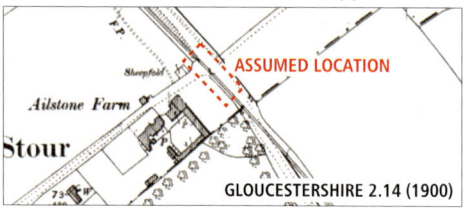

GLOUCESTERSHIRE 2.14 (1900)

AUCHNAGOOL* (HR)
6 August 1874 - ?
Line Operational - Demolished **NC92979 42814**

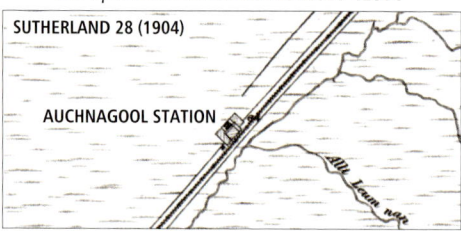

AUCHTERHOUSE (D&NR)
16 December 1831 - 16 October 1860
Line lifted – Demolished – Station site in agricultural use as part of a field **NO33256 37657**

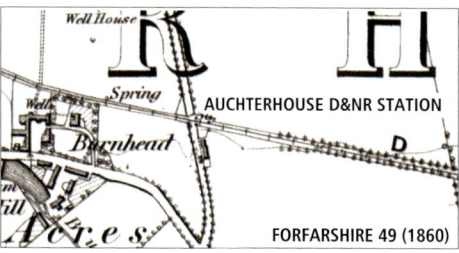

FORFARSHIRE 49 (1860)

AYLESBURY (1st) (L&NWR)
11 June 1839 - 16 June 1889
Line lifted – Demolished – Upper Hundreds Way crosses part of the station site, remainder in commercial use
SP82245 13943

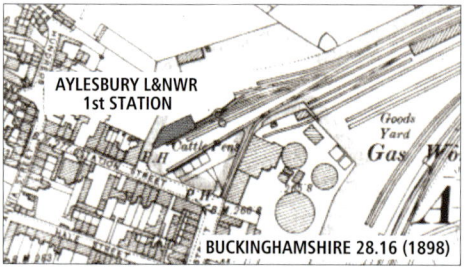

BUCKINGHAMSHIRE 28.16 (1898)

AYLESBURY BROOK STREET (MetR)
1 September 1892 - 1 January 1894
Line lifted – Demolished – Station site in use as Aylesbury Station car park **SP81886 13435**

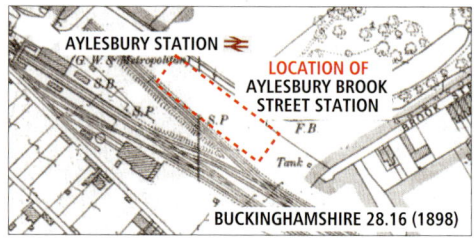

BUCKINGHAMSHIRE 28.16 (1898)

AYR (1st) (G&SWR)
5 August 1839 - 1 July 1857
Line lifted – Demolished – Station site in commercial use
NS33715 22319

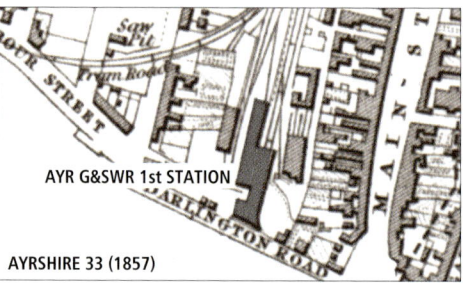

AYRSHIRE 33 (1857)

AYR NEWTONHEAD (G&SWR)
1 October 1864 - April 1868
Line Operational – Demolished **NS34140 23081 (a)**

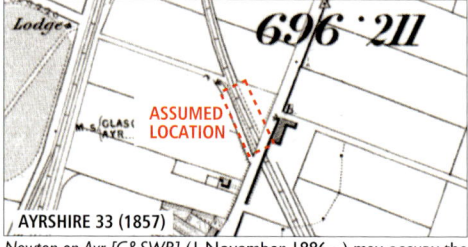

AYRSHIRE 33 (1857)

Newton-on-Ayr [G&SWR] (1 November 1886 -) may occupy the north end of the station site.

BACK OF LAW (DP&AJR)
May 1833 - July 1855
Line lifted – Demolished – Station site unused
NO39199 32225

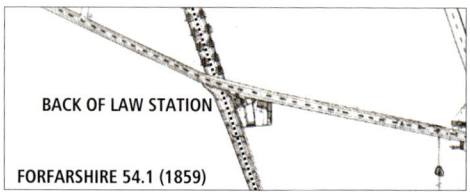

FORFARSHIRE 54.1 (1859)

BACKWORTH - BALBEUCHLY TOP

BACKWORTH (B&TR)
28 August 1841 - 27 June 1864
Line Operational for Freight – Demolished – No access
NZ30548 72328

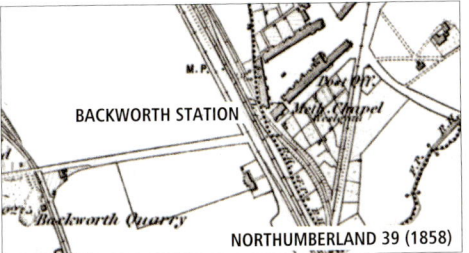

NORTHUMBERLAND 39 (1858)

BADGWORTH (MR)
22 August 1843 - 1 November 1846
Line Operational – Demolished – No access
SO90282 20654 (a)

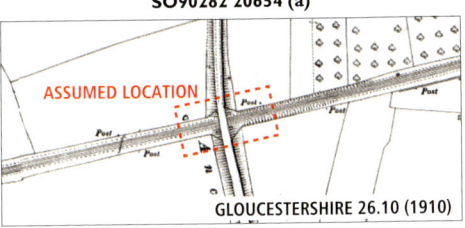

GLOUCESTERSHIRE 26.10 (1910)

BAGILLT (1st) (L&NWR)
1841 - 1871
Line Operational – Demolished – Degraded platforms extant
SJ22181 75371

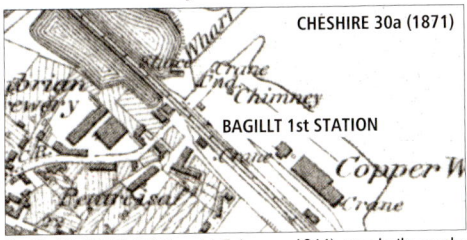

CHESHIRE 30a (1871)

Bagillt [L&NWR] (1871 – 14 February 1966) was built on the same site.

BAGWORTH (1st) (MR)
18 July 1832 - 27 March 1848
Line lifted – Demolished – Station site unused
SK4547908421 (a)

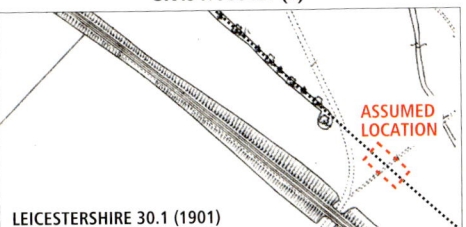

LEICESTERSHIRE 30.1 (1901)

BAINTON GATE (MR)
1 November 1854 - 1 August 1856
Line Operational – Platforms demolished – Crossing Keepers Cottage (which may have also been the station house) in private use **TF09308 06499**

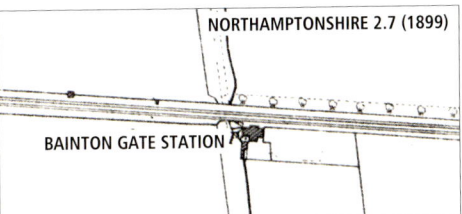

NORTHAMPTONSHIRE 2.7 (1899)

BALA (1st) (GWR)
1 April 1868 - 1 November 1882
Line Operated by the 1ft 11.625in gauge Bala Lake Railway – Demolished – One platform extant **SH92926 34967**

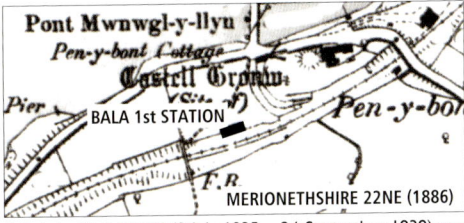

MERIONETHSHIRE 22NE (1886)

Bala Lake Halt [GWR] (8 July 1935 – 24 September 1939) was built on the station site. *Bala Pen-y-Bont* was subsequently opened on here by the Bala Lake Railway (25 March 1976 -)

BALBEUCHLY FOOT (DP&AJR)
16 December 1831 - July 1855
Line lifted – Demolished – Station site unused
NO36101 35554 (a)

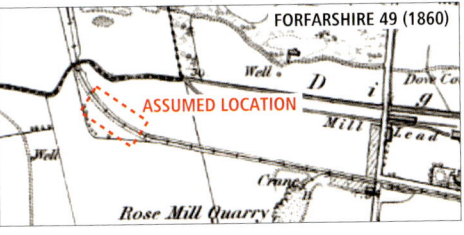

FORFARSHIRE 49 (1860)

BALBEUCHLY TOP (DP&AJR)
16 December 1831 - 1 November 1860
Line lifted – Demolished – Station site unused
NO35757 37367 (a)

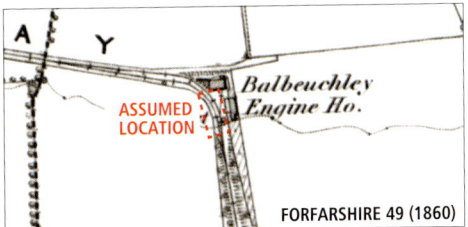

FORFARSHIRE 49 (1860)

BALHAM HILL - BARNARD CASTLE (1st)

BALHAM HILL (LB&SCR)
1 December 1856 - 1863
Line Operational – Demolished – No access
TQ28275 73243

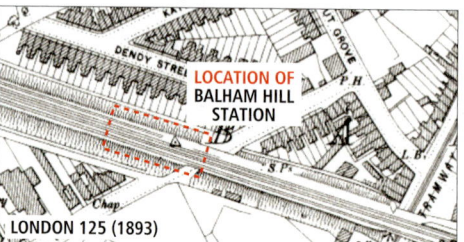

LONDON 125 (1893)

BALLATHIE (CR)
2 August 1848 - July 1868
Line lifted – Demolished – A road track passes through the station site **NO13440 36423**

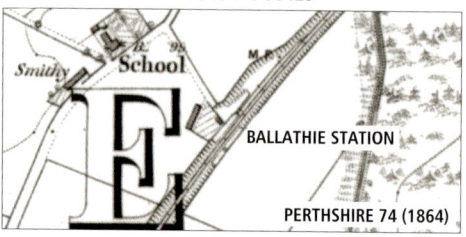

BALLATHIE STATION

PERTHSHIRE 74 (1864)

BALLENCRIEFF (NBR)
22 June 1846 - 1 November 1847
Line Operational – Demolished – No access
NT48441 78330

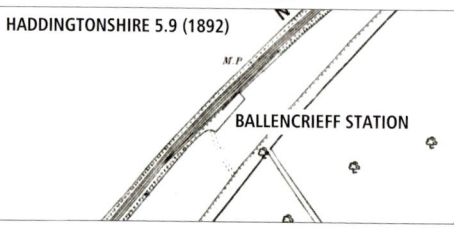

HADDINGTONSHIRE 5.9 (1892)

BALLENCRIEFF STATION

BALSHAM ROAD (NewmarketR)
4 April 1848 - 9 October 1851
Line lifted – Demolished – Station site in agricultural use
TL53976 53899

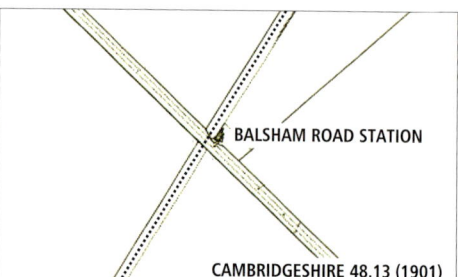

BALSHAM ROAD STATION

CAMBRIDGESHIRE 48.13 (1901)

BANCHORY (1st) (DeesideR)
8 September 1853 - 2 December 1859
Line lifted – Demolished – Station site occupied by housing in Glebe Park **NO70380 95581**

BANCHORY (2nd) (DeesideR)
2 December 1859 - c1902
Line lifted – Demolished – Station site occupied by housing in Glebe Park **NO70514 95648**

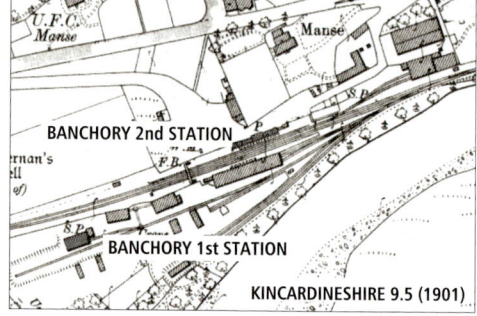

BANCHORY 2nd STATION

BANCHORY 1st STATION

KINCARDINESHIRE 9.5 (1901)

BANFF AND MACDUFF (GNofSR)
4 June 1860 - 1 July 1872
Line lifted – Demolished – Station site unused
NJ69737 63432

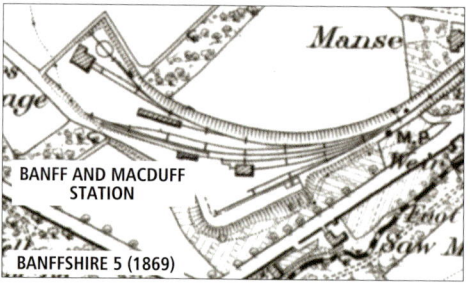

BANFF AND MACDUFF STATION

BANFFSHIRE 5 (1869)

BARLASTON (1st) (NSR)
17 April 1848 - 21 September 1852
Precise location unknown but near Barlaston 2nd [NSR]
(21 September 1852 -) **SJ88797 38367 (a)**

BARNARD CASTLE (1st) (S&DR)
9 July 1856 - 1 May 1862
Line lifted – Platforms demolished – Station building incorporated into "Strathmore Court" **NZ05254 17002**

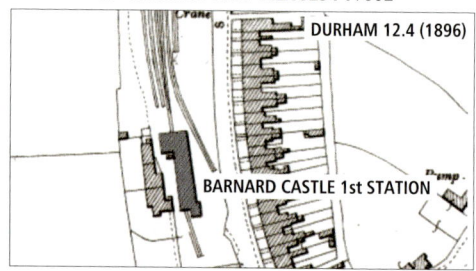

DURHAM 12.4 (1896)

BARNARD CASTLE 1st STATION

BARNBY DUN (MS&LR)
1 July 1856 - 1 October 1866
Line lifted – Demolished – Station site occupied by a car park
SE61287 09532

YORKSHIRE 277 (1850)

BARNHILL (DP&AJR)
24 May 1847 - 1 March 1849
Line Operational – Demolished – No access
NO12355 22789 (a)

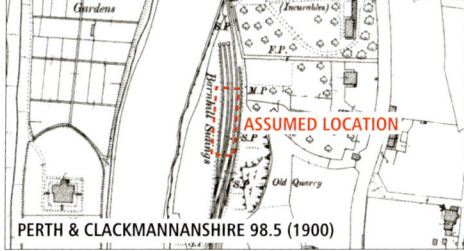

PERTH & CLACKMANNANSHIRE 98.5 (1900)

BARNSBURY (1st) (NLR)
18 June 1852 - 21 November 1870
Line Operational – Demolished – No access
TQ30568 84306

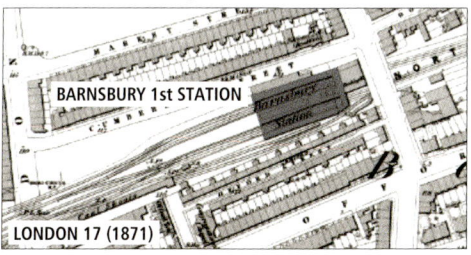

LONDON 17 (1871)

BARNSTAPLE TOWN (1st) (L&SWR)
20 July 1874 - 16 May 1898
Line lifted – Demolished – Station site landscaped
SS55707 33087

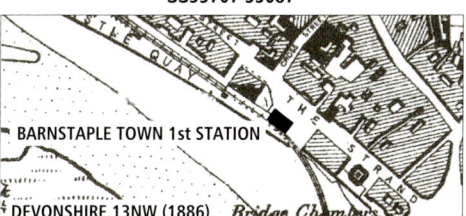

DEVONSHIRE 13NW (1886)

BARNBY DUN - BARTON MOSS (1st)
BARROW PIER (FurnR)
24 August 1846 - 6 May 1863
Site unknown but possibly replaced on same site by Barrow Town (qv) **SD20210 68664 (e)**

BARROW TOWN (FurnR)
6 May 1863 - 1 June 1882
Line lifted – Station building Grade II Listed
SD20210 68664

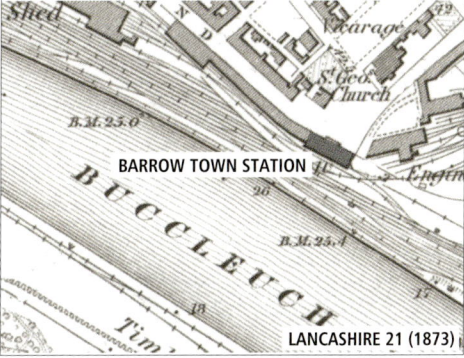

LANCASHIRE 21 (1873)

BARRS COURT JUNCTION* (S&HR)
September 1864 - July 1873
Line Operational – Demolished – No access
SO51184 41542 (a)

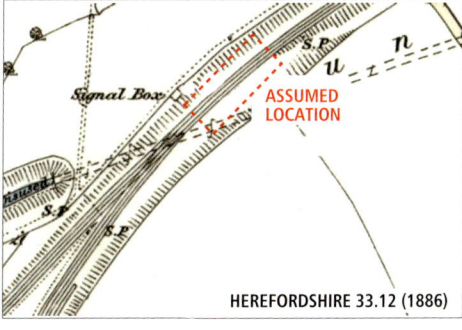

HEREFORDSHIRE 33.12 (1886)

BARTON MOSS (1st) (L&NWR)
1832 - 1 May 1862
Line Operational – Demolished – No access **SJ72100 97607**

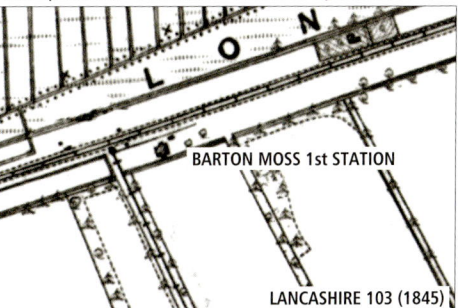

LANCASHIRE 103 (1845)

BASFORD - BEIGHTON (1st)

BASFORD (L&NWR)
8 August 1838 - 1 July 1875
Line Operational – Demolished – No access
SJ72276 51343 (a)

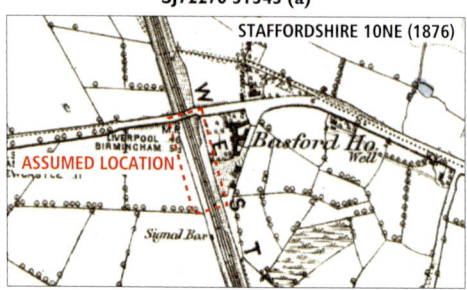
STAFFORDSHIRE 10NE (1876)

BATTERSEA PARK (LB&SCR)
1 October 1860 - 1 November 1870
Line Operational – Demolished – No access **TQ28726 77653**

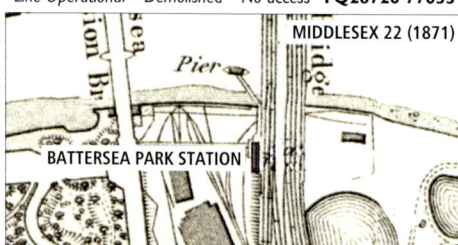
MIDDLESEX 22 (1871)

BEAG FAIR SIDING (R&FR)
April 1878 - 1 January 1883
Line lifted – Demolished – Station site unused **SN10156 20637**

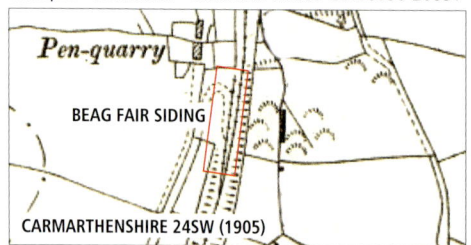
CARMARTHENSHIRE 24SW (1905)

BECK HOLES (NER)
? - 1 July 1865
Line lifted – Demolished – A pathway passes through the station site **NZ82010 02185**

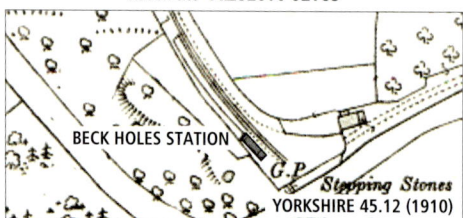
YORKSHIRE 45.12 (1910)

BEDFORD (1st) (L&NWR)
18 November 1846 - 1 August 1862
Line lifted – Demolished – Station site unused **TL05275 48909**

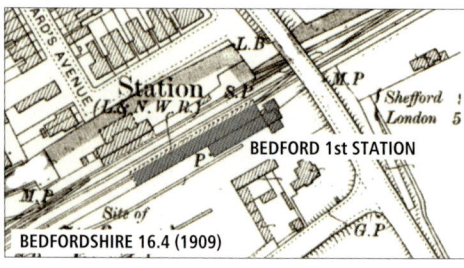
BEDFORDSHIRE 16.4 (1909)

BEDMINSTER (1st) (GWR)
Prior to 1869 - 27 May 1884
Line Operational – Demolished – No access **ST59042 71588**

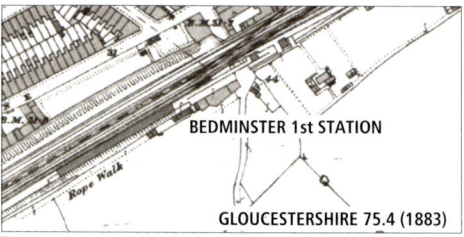
GLOUCESTERSHIRE 75.4 (1883)

This was opened as an Excursion Platform

BEDMINSTER (2nd) (GWR)
1 August 1869 - c1874
Line Operational – Demolished – No access **ST58723 71378**

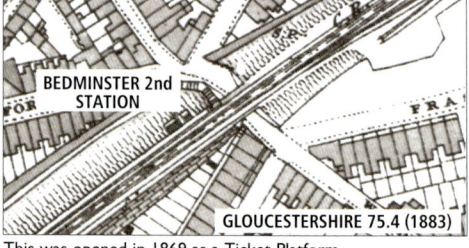
GLOUCESTERSHIRE 75.4 (1883)

This was opened in 1869 as a Ticket Platform

BEIGHTON (1st) (MS&LR)
12 February 1849 - 1 November 1893
Line Operational – Demolished – No access **SK44377 83954**

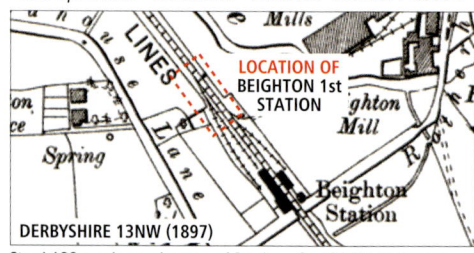
DERBYSHIRE 13NW (1897)

Sited 132 yards north west of Beighton 2nd [GCR] (1 November 1893 - 1 November 1954)

BEIGHTON (NMidR)
11 May 1840 - May 1843
Line Operational – Demolished – No access
SK44574 84353 (a)

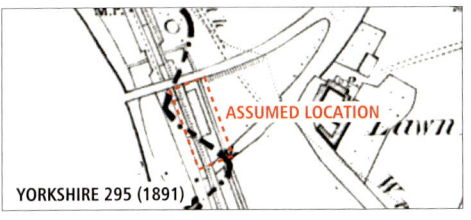

BELMONT (NER)
15 April 1844 – 1 April 1857
Line lifted – Demolished – Station site unused **NZ30919 44810**

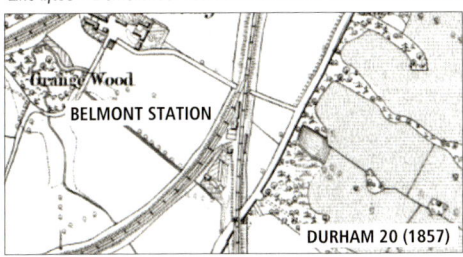

BELPER (1st) (MR)
11 May 1840 – 10 March 1878
Line Operational – Demolished – Station site in commercial use
SK34750 46653

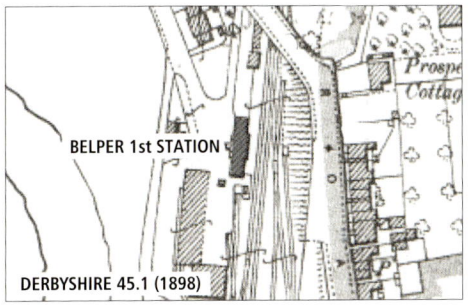

BENTLEY (MR)
1 November 1872 – 1 October 1898
Line lifted – Demolished – Station site crossed by the M6 (just north of Junction 10) **SO99002 99821**

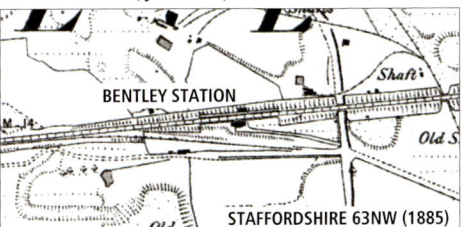

BENTLEY CHURCH (EUnionR)
October 1853 – December 1853
Line lifted – Demolished – Crossing Gatekeeper's cottage in private use **TM11930 38276 (a)**

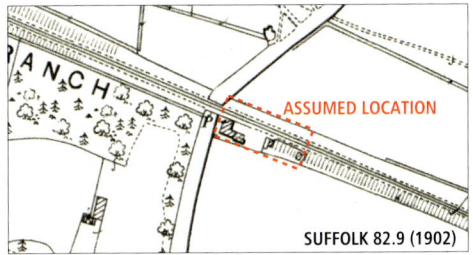

BENTON (1st) (NER)
27 June 1864 – 1 March 1871
Line Operated by T&WM – Demolished – No access
NZ27033 68470

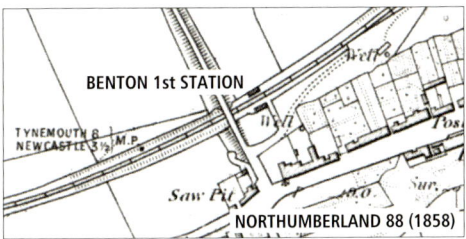

BERKHAMPSTEAD (1st) (L&NWR)
16 October 1837 – c1875
Line Operational – Demolished – No access
SP99564 08053 (a)

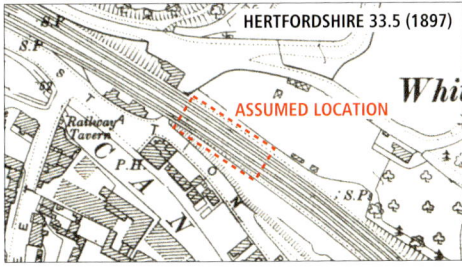

BESFORD (MR)
November 1841 – 1 September 1846
Line Operational – Demolished – No access
SO90462 45111 (e)

BIDDICK LANE - BIRKDALE (2nd)

BIDDICK LANE (NER)
February 1864 - January 1869
Line lifted – Demolished – Station site unused **NZ30894 54793**

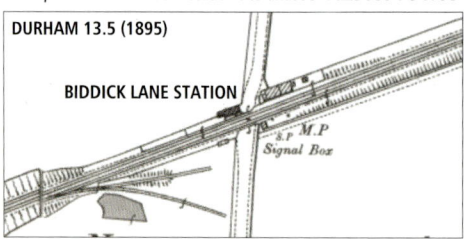

DURHAM 13.5 (1895)

BIDEFORD (1st) (L&SWR)
2 November 1855 - 10 June 1872
Line lifted – Demolished – The Tarka Trail passes through the station site **SS45825 26791 (a)**

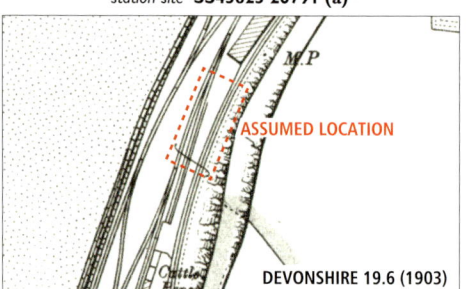

DEVONSHIRE 19.6 (1903)

BIGBY ROAD BRIDGE HALT (MS&LR)
March 1852 - August 1882
Line Operational – Demolished – No access
TA03916 07181 (a)

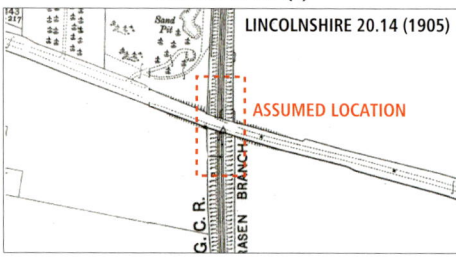

LINCOLNSHIRE 20.14 (1905)

BILNEY (GER)
27 October 1846 - 1 August 1866
Line lifted – Demolished – Station site in private use
TF72378 15222

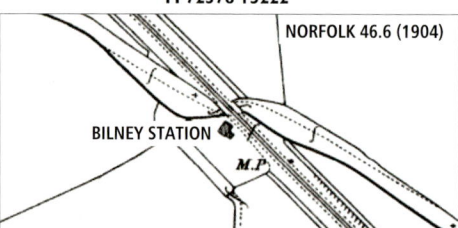

NORFOLK 46.6 (1904)

BILSON ROAD PLATFORM (S&WyeR)
1 September 1876 - 5 August 1878
Line lifted – Demolished – Station site unused **SO64004 14531**

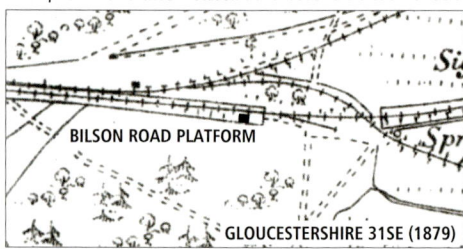

GLOUCESTERSHIRE 31SE (1879)

BINGLEY (1st) (MR)
16 March 1847 - 24 July 1892
Line Operational – Platforms demolished – A period building, possibly a goods shed, built on the site of the station is extant
SE10672 39385

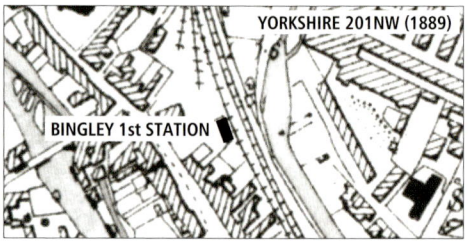

YORKSHIRE 201NW (1889)

BIRCHGROVE (MR)
7 April 1866 - 1 March 1875
Line lifted – Demolished – A pathway passes through the station site **SS69680 98804 (a)**

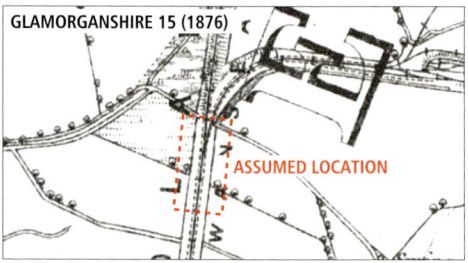

GLAMORGANSHIRE 15 (1876)

BIRKDALE (2nd) (L&YR)
October 1848 - 1852
Line Operational – Demolished **SD32473 14749**

LANCASHIRE 83 (1846)

BIRKENHEAD BRIDGE ROAD (SH&DR)
2 July 1866 - 2 January 1888
Line lifted – Demolished – Station site in commercial use
SJ29682 90574

BIRKENHEAD GRANGE LANE
(C&BheadR)
23 September 1840 - 23 October 1844
Line lifted – Derelict frontage still extant – Station site unused
SJ32494 88554

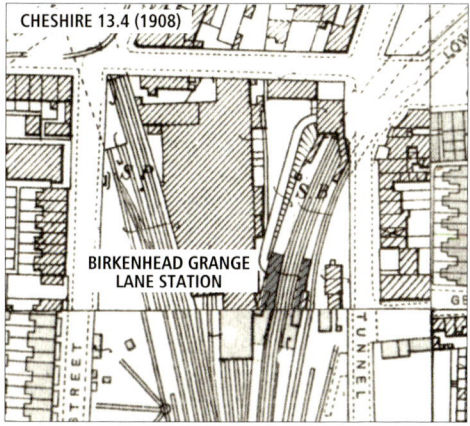

BIRKENHEAD MONK'S FERRY (BheadR)
23 October 1844 - 1 April 1878
Line lifted – Demolished – Station site occupied by dwellings in Priory Wharf **SJ32970 88774**

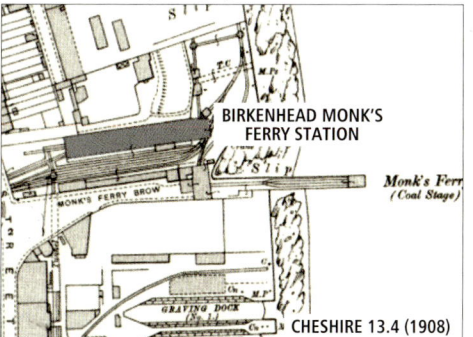

BIRMINGHAM CURZON STREET
Line lifted – Station Entrance building Grade I listed – Station site being rebuilt as "Birmingham Curzon" the HS2 terminus
LONDON & BIRMINGHAM RAILWAY (L&NWR)
1 October 1838 - 1 June 1854
SP07915 87067
GRAND JUNCTION RAILWAY (L&NWR)
19 November 1838 - 1 June 1854
SP08010 87132
EXCURSION PLATFORMS (L&NWR)
3 April 1874 - 3 April 1893
SP07820 87006

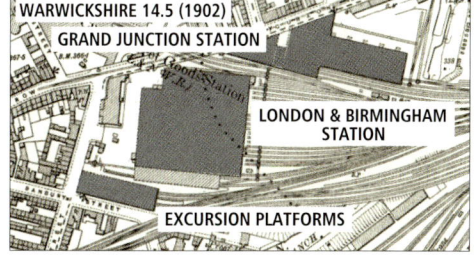

BIRMINGHAM LAWLEY STREET
(L&NWR)
4 July 1837 - 1 March 1869
Line Operational – Demolished – No access
SP08352 87181 (a)

BIRMINGHAM LAWLEY STREET (MR)
10 February 1842 - 1 March 1851
Line lifted – Demolished – Station site in commercial use
SP08420 87126

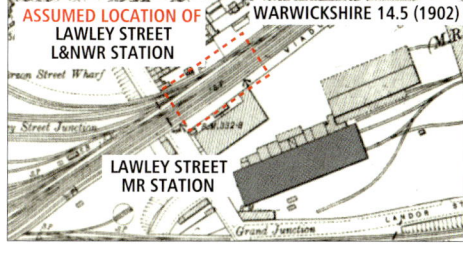

BISHOP AUCKLAND TENTER STREET
(NER)
1 April 1857 - 21 December 1867
Line lifted – Demolished – The A689, Bob Hardisty Drive, passes through the station site **NZ20884 29846**

BISHOPSGATE (1st) - BLAKENEY

BISHOPSGATE (1st) (GER)
1 July 1840 - 1 November 1875
Line lifted – Demolished – Station site unused **TQ33557 82195**

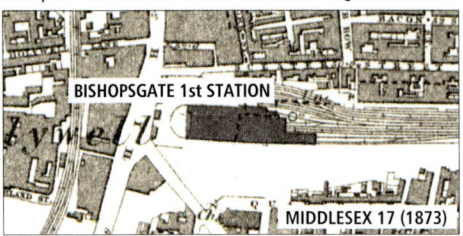

BLACKBURN DARWEN STREET
(ELancsR)
3 August 1847 - 1 December 1852
Line Operational – Demolished – No access **SD68225 27514**

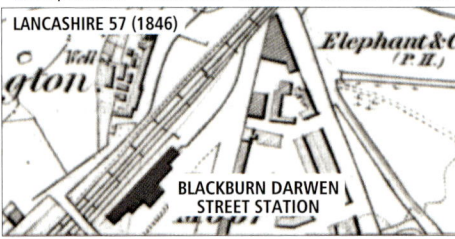

BLACKFRIARS (SER)
11 January 1864 - 1 January 1869
Line Operational – Demolished – No access **TQ31746 80062**

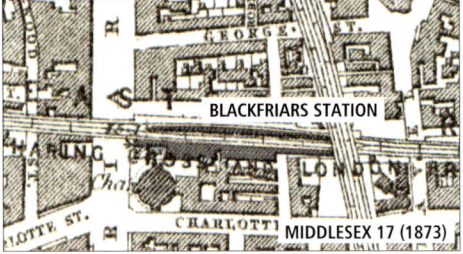

BLACKFRIARS BRIDGE (LC&DR)
1 June 1864 - 1 October 1885
Line Operational – Demolished – Part of station site in commercial use **TQ31708 80572**

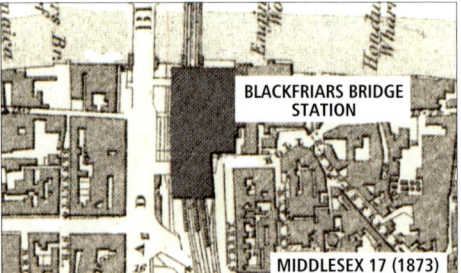

BLACKHALL (NBR)
19 September 1864 - 1 November 1893
Line lifted – Demolished – Station site unused **NS88317 57657**

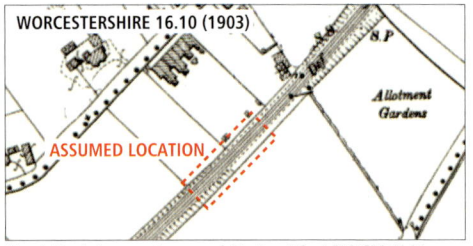

BLACKWELL (1st) (B&GR)
5 June 1841 - 4 November 1844
Line Operational – Demolished – No access
SO99841 72409 (a)

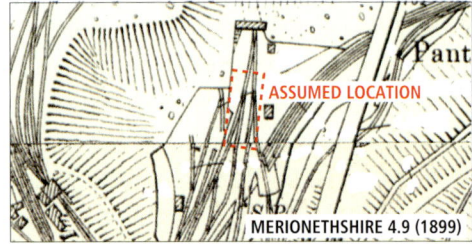

Sited 41 chains north east of *Blackwell 2nd [B&GR]* (4 November 1844 -18 April 1966)

BLAENAU FESTINIOG (1st) (L&NWR)
22 July 1879 - 1 April 1881
Line Operational – Demolished **SH69690 46902 (a)**

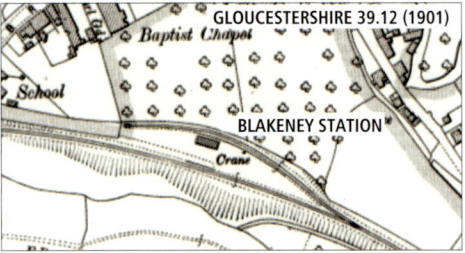

BLAKENEY (GWR)
1887 - 1895
Line lifted – Demolished – Station site occupied by housing in Old Station Close **SO67073 06810**

BLANDFORD ST MARY (DsetCR)
1 November 1860 - 31 August 1863
Line lifted – Demolished – Station site landscaped
ST88837 05539 (a)

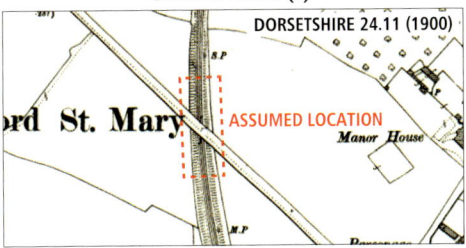

Sited 924 yards south of Blandford Forum [DsetCR] (31 August 1863 - 7 March 1966)

BLENKINSOPP HALL HALT* (NER)
18 June 1838 - 1875
Line Operational – Demolished – No access **NY67583 63873**

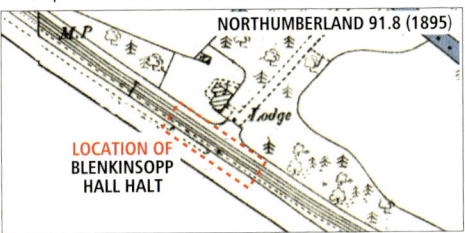

BLISWORTH (1st) (L&NWR)
17 September 1838 - 1851
Line Operational – Demolished – No access
SP72780 54172 (a)

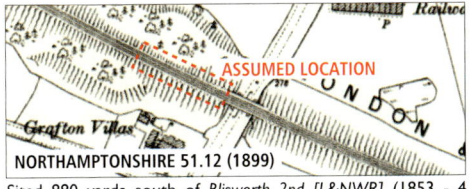

Sited 880 yards south of Blisworth 2nd [L&NWR] (1853 - 4 January 1960)

BLOOMSBURY AND NECHELLS (L&NWR)
1 August 1856 - 1 March 1869
Line Operational – Demolished – No access
SP08992 88640 (a)

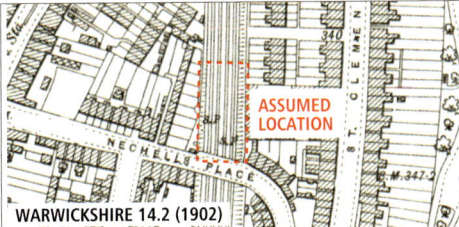

BLYTH (1st) (B&TR)
3 May 1847 - 1 May 1867
Line lifted – Demolished – The B1329 passes through the station site **NZ31413 81729**

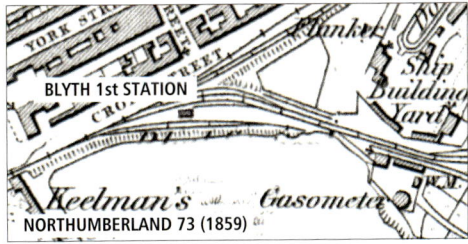

BODMIN (1st) (L&SWR)
1 October 1834 - 1 November 1886
Line lifted – Demolished – Station site occupied by a car park – Brownlee Place passes through the station site
SX06876 67242

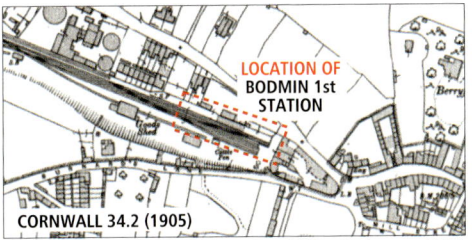

Bodmin North [L&SWR] (1 November 1895 – 31 January 1967) was built on the same site.

BOGSIDE* (G&SWR)
7 May 1844 – 27 August 1858
Line Operational – Demolished – No access **NS31052 40229**

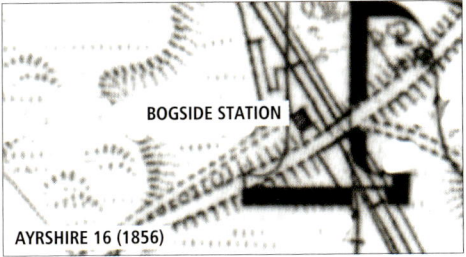

BOLD (StHC&RC)
November 1856 - January 1858
Line lifted – Demolished – A roadway passes through the station site **SJ52355 89454 (e)**

21

BOLDON - BOROUGHBRIDGE (1st)

BOLDON (YN&BR)
August 1841 - December 1853
Line lifted – Demolished – Station site occupied by
A184/B1298 roundabout **NZ34268 60924**

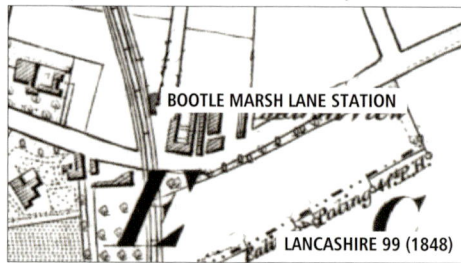
DURHAM 7.8 (1896)

BOLTON CROOK STREET (L&NWR)
1 August 1871 - 28 September 1874
Line lifted – Demolished – Station site occupied by part of "Bolton Shopping Park" **SD71533 08626**

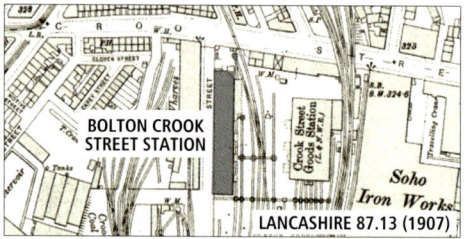
LANCASHIRE 87.13 (1907)

BOLTON GREAT MOOR STREET (1st) (L&NWR)
13 June 1831 - 1 April 1875
Line lifted – Demolished – Station site in commercial use
SD71576 08842

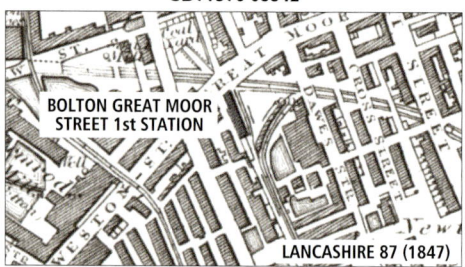
LANCASHIRE 87 (1847)

BONT NEWYDD (NantleR)
11 August 1856 - 12 June 1865
Line Operated by the 1ft 11½in gauge Welsh Highland Railway – Demolished – Station rebuilt as a halt **SH47791 60134**

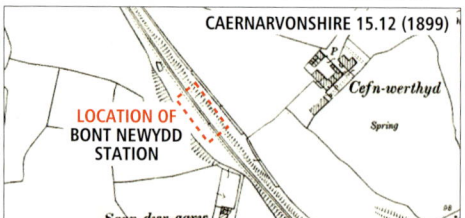
CAERNARVONSHIRE 15.12 (1899)

BOOTLE MARSH LANE (L&YR)
1 October 1850 - 11 April 1886
Line Operational – Demolished – No access **SJ34045 95726**

LANCASHIRE 99 (1848)

BOOTLE VILLAGE (L&YR)
1 October 1850 - April 1876
Line Operational – Demolished – No access **SJ33952 95035**

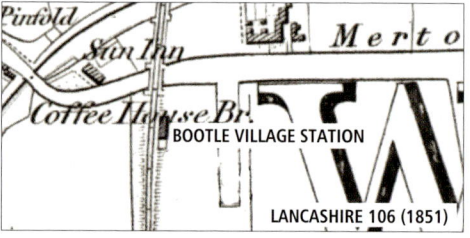
LANCASHIRE 106 (1851)

BOREHAM HOUSE* (GER)
c1859 - 19 September 1877
Line Operational – Demolished – No access **TL74081 09650**

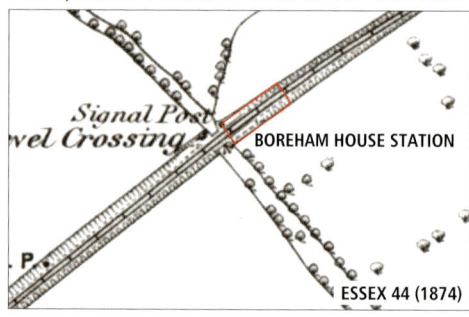
ESSEX 44 (1874)

BOROUGHBRIDGE (1st) (NER)
17 June 1847 - 1 April 1875
Line lifted – Demolished – One station building extant, remainder of station site in commercial use **SE39698 67302**

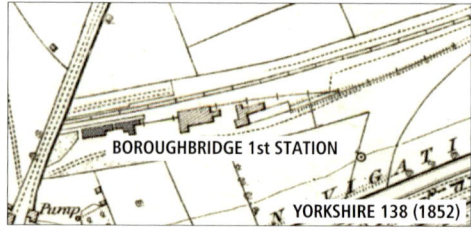
YORKSHIRE 138 (1852)

BORROWASH (1st) (MR)
4 June 1839 – 1 May 1871
Line Operational – Demolished – Station building in private use
SK41686 34114

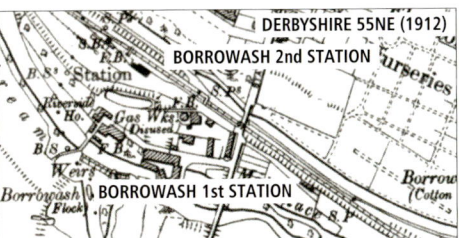

BOTTESFORD SOUTH (GNR/L&NWR)
15 December 1859 – 1 May 1882
Line lifted – Demolished – A pathway passes through the station site **SK79796 38890**

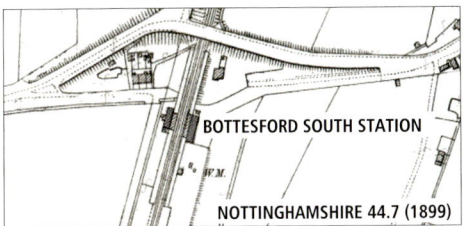

BOURNE BRIDGE (1st) (NewmarketR)
4 April 1848 – 1 July 1850
Line lifted – Demolished – Station building in private use
TL51853 49049

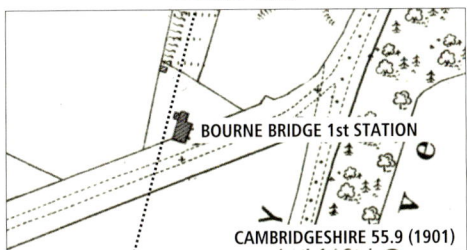

BOURNE BRIDGE (2nd) (NewmarketR)
9 September 1850 – 9 October 1851
Line lifted – Demolished – Station site unused alongside of the A11
TL51790 48764

BOURNEMOUTH EAST (1st) (L&SWR)
14 March 1870 – 20 July 1885
Line Operational – Demolished – Station site in commercial use
SZ09922 91902

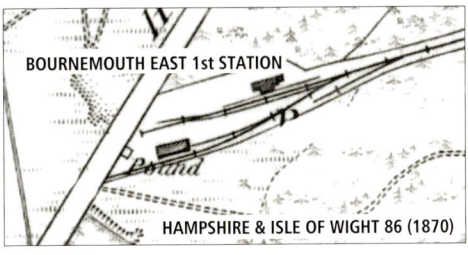

BOW & BROMLEY (L&BwallR)
31 March 1849 – 26 September 1850
Line Operational – Demolished – No access **TQ37249 82798**

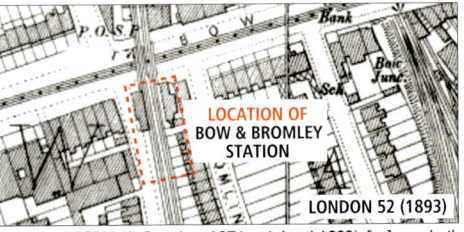

Bow Road [GER] (1 October 1876 – 4 April 1892) [qv] was built on the same site

BOWDON (MSJn&AR)
January 1850 – 3 April 1881
Line lifted – Demolished – Station site in commercial use
SJ76772 87615

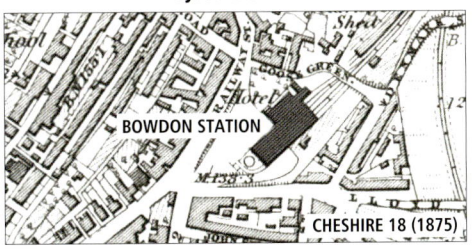

BOWES BRIDGE (BlingJnR)
18 June 1842 – August 1844
Line Operated by the Tanfield Railway – Demolished – The Tanfield Walkway also passes through the station site
NZ20755 57901

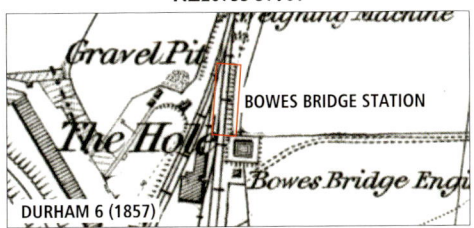

BOWLING (C&DumbtnJR) - BRAMCOTE

BOWLING (C&DumbtnJR)
15 July 1850 - 1 May 1858
Line Operational – Demolished – Station site in use as a landing and car park for adjacent canal basin **NS45003 73574**

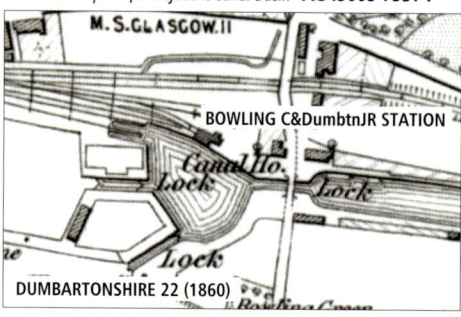

BOWLING (GNR)
1 August 1854 - 1 February 1895
Line lifted – Demolished – Station site unused **SE17392 32256**

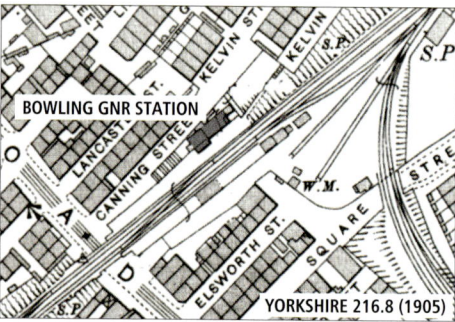

BOW ROAD (1st) (GER)
1 October 1876 - 4 April 1892
Line Operational – Demolished – No access
This station occupies the same site as Bow & Bromley [L&BwallR] (2 April 1849 - 26 September 1850) – See page 23

BRADFORD ADOLPHUS STREET (GNR)
1 June 1855 - 7 January 1867
Line lifted – Demolished – Wakefield Street crosses the west end of the station site, remainder unused or in commercial use
SE16863 32658

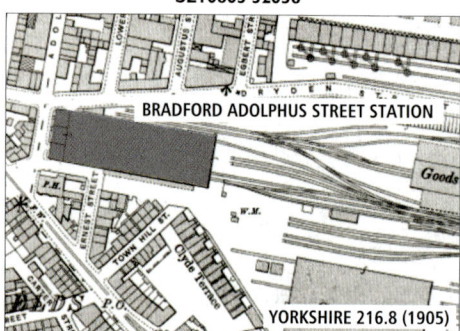

BRADFORD MARKET STREET (MR)
1 July 1846 - 2 March 1890
Line lifted – Demolished – Station site occupied by dwellings in Blaze Square **SE16411 33359**

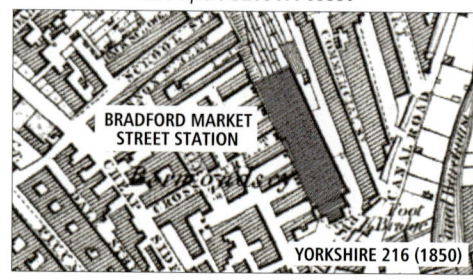

BRADLEY (1st) (L&NWR)
2 August 1847 - July 1849
Line Operational – Demolished – Station site in commercial use
SE16924 19645

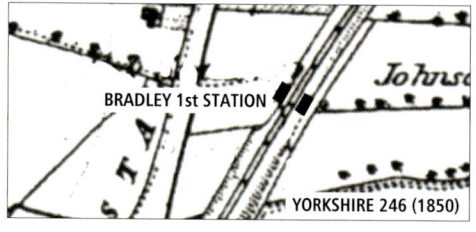

BRAINTREE (1st) (GER)
2 October 1848 - 22 February 1869
Line lifted – Demolished – Station site occupied by dwellings
TL76291 22868

BRAMCOTE* (MR)
? - c1892
Line Operational – Demolished – No access **SK50777 39474**

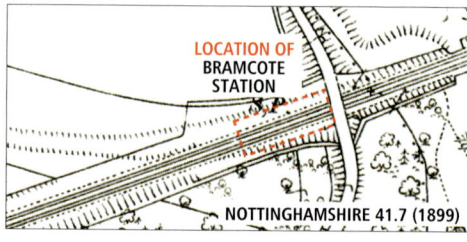

24

BRAMPTON FELL (N&CR)
1836 - c1867
Line Operational – Demolished **NY53955 59124**

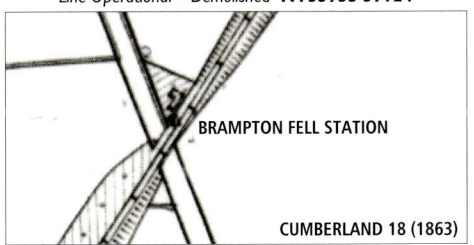

BRECON WATTON (B&MTJR)
January 1863 - 1 March 1871
Line lifted – Demolished – Station site in commercial use
SO05260 28124 (a)

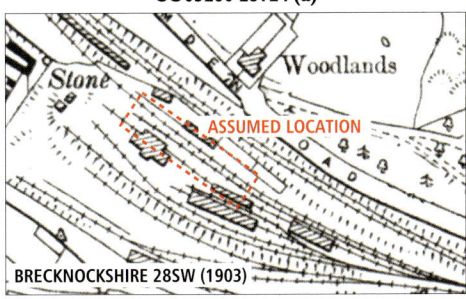

BRAMWITH (MS&LR)
1 July 1856 - 1 October 1866
Line lifted – Demolished – A pathway passes through the station site **SE62076 11475**

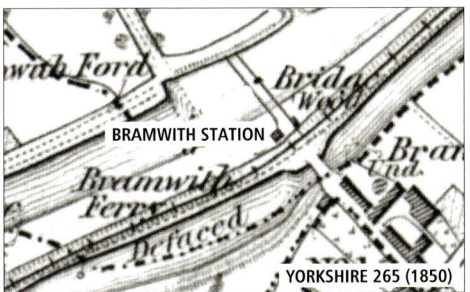

BREDICOT (MR)
November 1845 - 1 October 1855
Line Operational – Demolished – No access
SO90547 54889 (a)

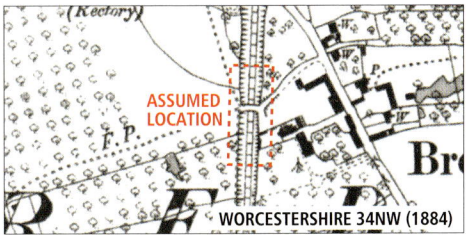

BRAUNSTON (MR)
1 June 1850 - 1 July 1859
Line Operational – Demolished – No access
SK52459 03527 (a)

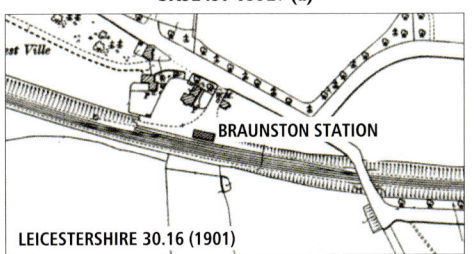

BRENDON HILL* (WSsetMinR)
c1860 - 7 November 1898
Line lifted – Station building in private use **ST02239 34351**

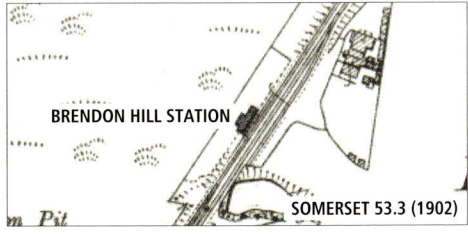

BRECON MOUNT STREET (N&BR)
3 June 1867 - 6 March 1872
Line lifted – Demolished – Heol Gouesnou passes through the station site **SO04603 28707**

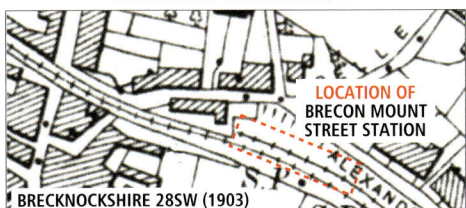

BRIDGEFORD (GJnR)
4 July 1837 - 10 September 1840
Line Operational – Demolished – No access
SJ87929 27478 (e)

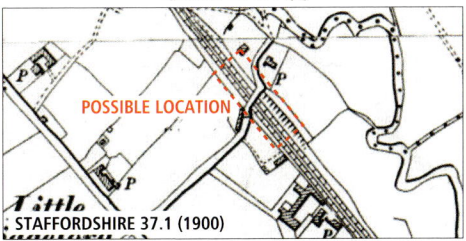

BRIDGEND - BRISTOL (GWR)

BRIDGEND (Ll&OR)
25 February 1864 - 1 July 1873
Line Operational SS90780 79882

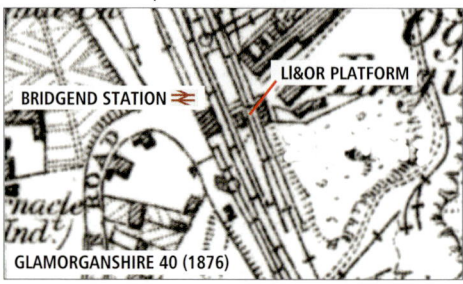

The terminus adjoined the east side of Bridgend [GWR] Station

BRIDGE OF EARN (1st) (NBR)
18 July 1848 - 1 February 1892
Line Operational – Demolished – No access NO13226 18076

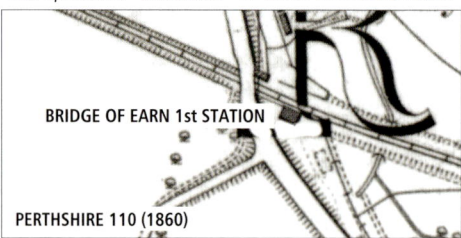

BRIDGE OF WEIR (1st) (G&SWR)
20 June 1864 - 18 May 1868
Line lifted – Demolished – Station site unused
NS39103 65405

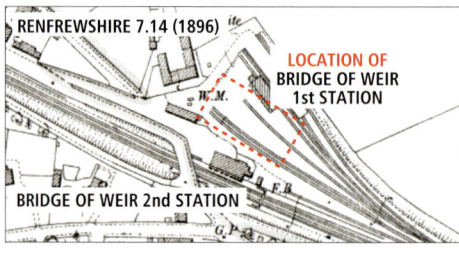

BRIDGETON (CR)
1 April 1879 - 1 November 1895
Line lifted – Demolished – A728, The Clyde Gateway, passes through the station site NS61277 63265

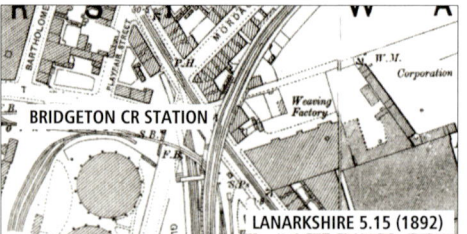

BRIGHOUSE FOR RASTRICK (1st) (L&YR)
5 October 1840 - 1 May 1893
Line Operational – Demolished – Station site in commercial use
SE14916 22352

BRISCO (L&CR)
December 1846 - November 1852
Line Operational – Station House in private use
NY43117 51259

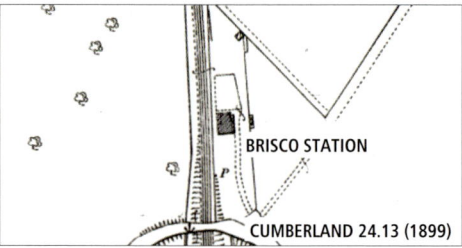

BRISTOL (B&ER)
1845 - June 1874
Line lifted – B&ER headquarters building and office extant
ST59693 72369

BRISTOL (GWR)
31 August 1840 - June 1874
Line lifted – Station building Grade I listed
ST59679 72474

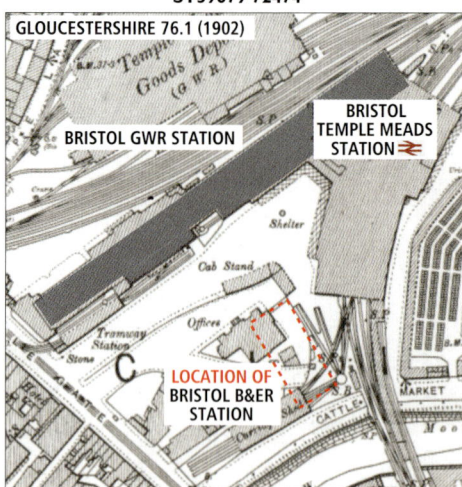

26

BRITANNIA BRIDGE (C&HR)
July 1851 - 1 October 1858
Line Operational – Demolished – No access **SH54333 70779**

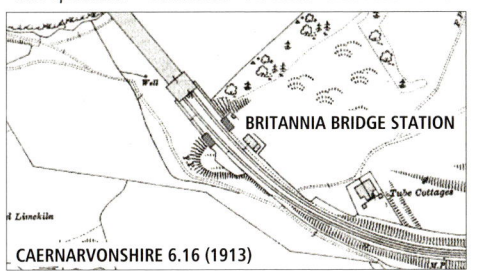

BROUGHTON (1st) (FurnR)
15 February 1848 - 18 June 1859
Line lifted – Demolished – Station site occupied by dwellings in Station Yard and Copper Rigg **SD21278 87428 (a)**

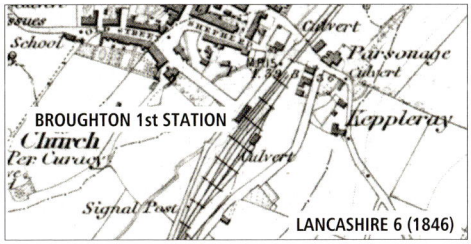

BROMLEY (1st) (LT&SR)
31 March 1858 - 1 March 1894
Line Operational – Demolished – No access **TQ38127 82541**

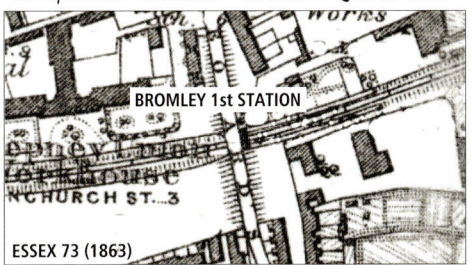

BROUGHTON SKEOG (WigtownshireR)
May 1878 - 6 August 1885
Line lifted – Demolished – Station site in agricultural use
NX45564 44086

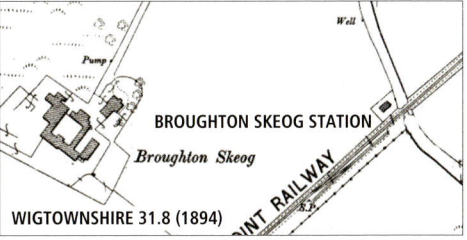

BROMSHALL (NSR)
1 November 1848 - 1 January 1866
Line Operational – Demolished – Station building in private use
SK05473 33094

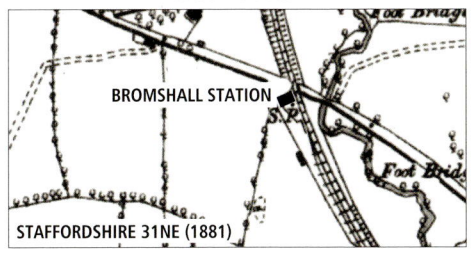

BROUGHTY PIER (D&AR)
17 May 1848 - 19 June 1887
Line lifted – Demolished – Station site in pier use
NO46367 30540

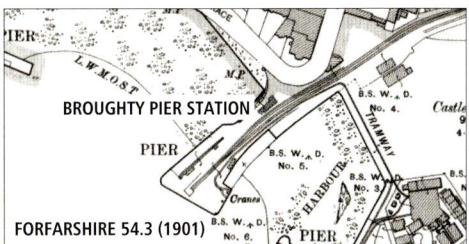

BROOMFIELD JUNCTION (NBR)
1 November 1865 - November 1877
Line lifted – Demolished – Station site landscaped
NO71735 59237

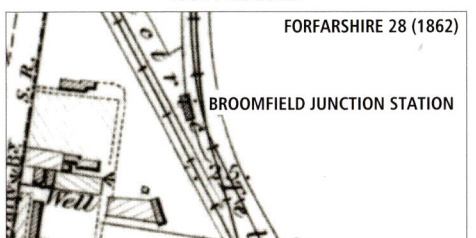

BROXBURN (E&GR)
August 1843- 12 November 1849
Line Operational – Demolished – No access
NT09838 73552 (e)

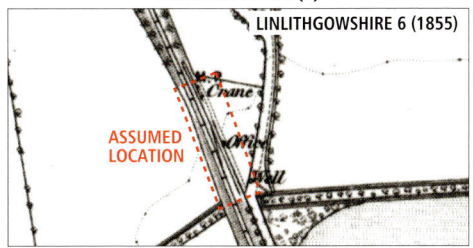

BUCHANSTONE - BUSBY (1st)

BUCHANSTONE (GNofSR)
1 December 1854 - September 1866
Line Operational – Demolished – No access **NJ65918 26120**

ABERDEENSHIRE 44 (1867)

BUCKLEY OLD (WM&CQR)
1 May 1866 - February 1895
Line lifted – Demolished – Station site unused **SJ29006 64407**

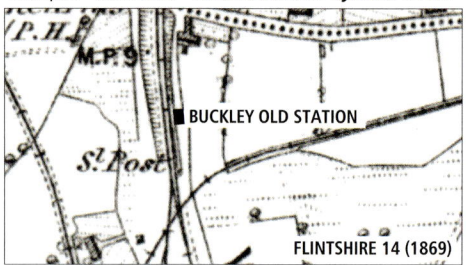
FLINTSHIRE 14 (1869)

BUITTLE (G&SWR)
July 1862 - 1 August 1894
Line lifted – Demolished – Station site unused **NX81110 64073**

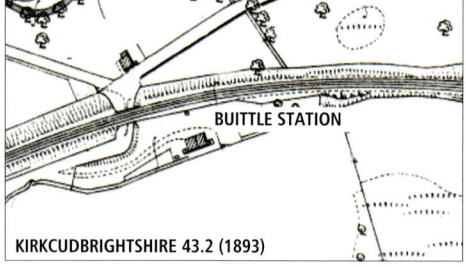
KIRKCUDBRIGHTSHIRE 43.2 (1893)

BURGHEAD (1st) (HR)
22 December 1862 - 10 October 1892
Line lifted – Demolished – Station site landscaped
NJ11200 68833

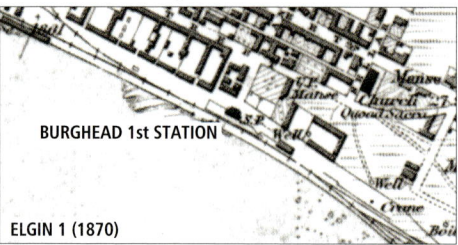
ELGIN 1 (1870)

BURNLEY THORNEYBANK (L&YR)
12 November 1849 - 1 November 1866
Line Operational – Demolished **SD83750 32039**

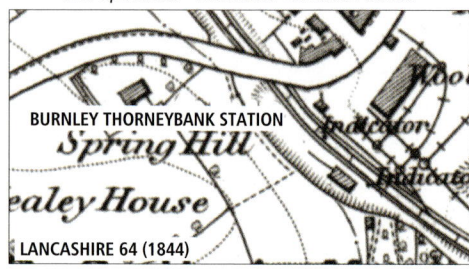
LANCASHIRE 64 (1844)

BURNTISLAND (1st) (NBR)
20 September 1847 - 2 June 1890
Line lifted – Demolished – Station buildings extant
NT23252 85599

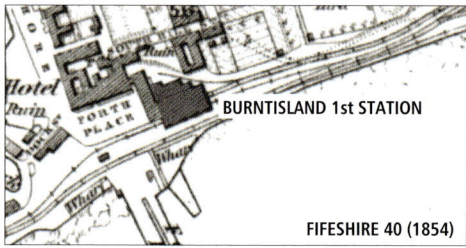
FIFESHIRE 40 (1854)

BURNGULLOW (1st) (GWR)
1 March 1863 – 1 February 1896
Line Operational – Demolished – A dwelling occupies part of the station site **SW98329 52413**

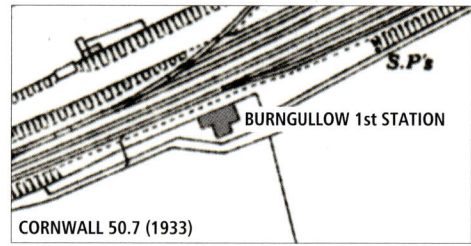
CORNWALL 50.7 (1933)

BUSBY (1st) (G&SWR)
September 1848 – 15 April 1850
Line Operational – Demolished **NS39967 39694**

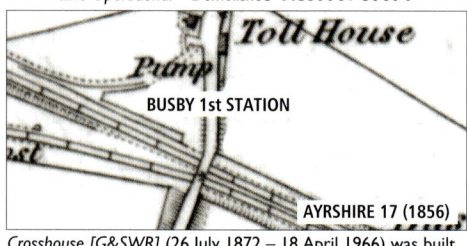
AYRSHIRE 17 (1856)

Crosshouse [G&SWR] (26 July 1872 – 18 April 1966) was built on the station site.

BURTON (1st) (MR)
12 August 1839 - 29 April 1883
Line Operational – Demolished – No access
SK24300 23336 (a)

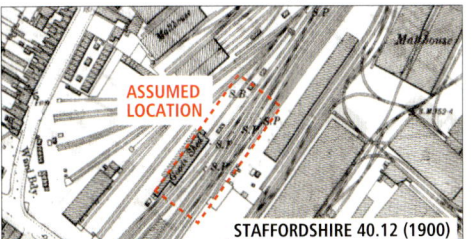

STAFFORDSHIRE 40.12 (1900)

BYERS GREEN (1st) (NER)
November 1845 - April 1867
Line lifted – Demolished – Station site unused
NZ22296 33505 (a)

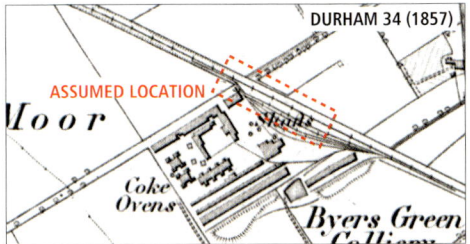

DURHAM 34 (1857)

BYERS GREEN (2nd) (NER)
November 1845 - 1 December 1885
Line lifted – Demolished – Station site in commercial use
NZ21394 33980

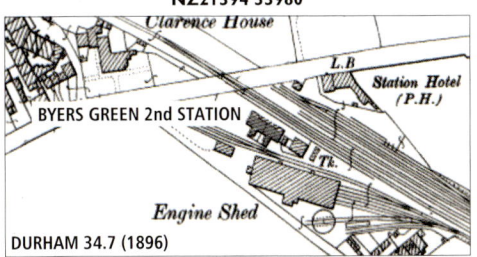

DURHAM 34.7 (1896)

CADISHEAD (1st) (CLC)
1 September 1873 - 1 August 1879
Line lifted – Demolished – A pathway passes through the station site **SJ71038 92425**

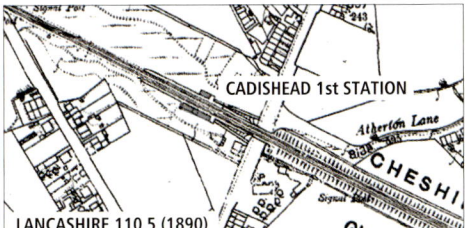

LANCASHIRE 110.5 (1890)

CADOXTON (TVR)
8 July 1889 - 22 May 1890
Line lifted – Demolished – Station site occupied by "The Business Centre" **ST14406 69210 (a)**

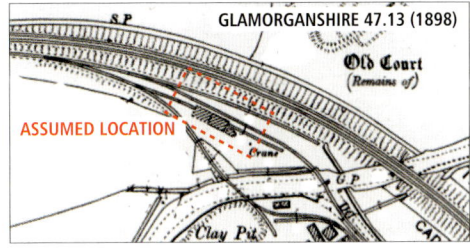

GLAMORGANSHIRE 47.13 (1898)

CAERPHILLY (1st) (RhyR)
31 March 1858 - 1 April 1871
Line lifted – Demolished – Station site in commercial use
ST14719 87122

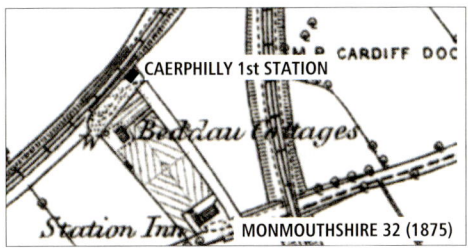

MONMOUTHSHIRE 32 (1875)

CAERSWS (VanR)
1 December 1873 - July 1879
Line lifted – Demolished – Station site in commercial use
SO02884 91801

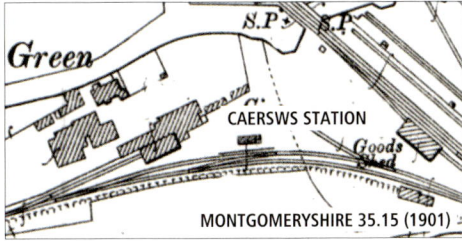

MONTGOMERYSHIRE 35.15 (1901)

CAIRNEY (NBR)
June 1832 - 1849
Line Operational – Demolished – Station site absorbed into Millerhill Marshalling Yard **NT32405 70569 (e)**

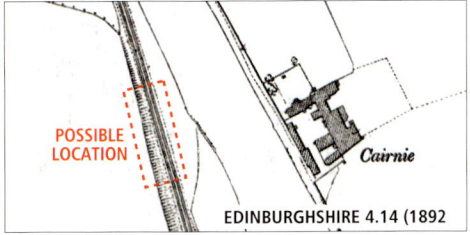

EDINBURGHSHIRE 4.14 (1892)

CAIRNHILL BRIDGE - CANNING TOWN

CAIRNHILL BRIDGE (NBR)
10 December 1849 - 1 January 1850
Line lifted – Demolished – Station site unused [or in commercial use] **NS75203 63837** (a)

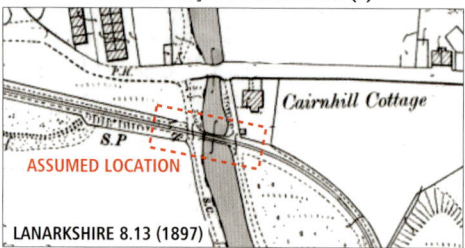

LANARKSHIRE 8.13 (1897)

CALLANDER (CR)
1 July 1858 - 1 June 1870
Line lifted – Demolished – Station site occupied by housing in Murdiston Avenue **NN63364 07698**

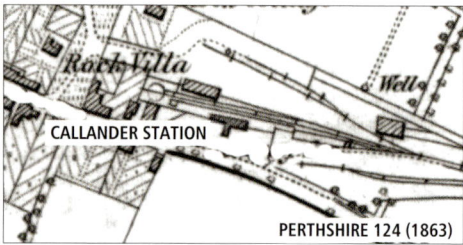

PERTHSHIRE 124 (1863)

CAMDEN (1st) (L&NWR)
1 November 1851 - 1 May 1852
Line Operational – Demolished – No access
TQ28229 84217 (a)

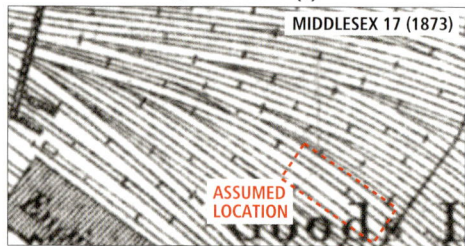

MIDDLESEX 17 (1873)

CAMDEN CHALK FARM (1st) (L&NWR)
1 May 1852 - 1 April 1872
Line Operational – Demolished – No access
TQ28017 84290 (a)

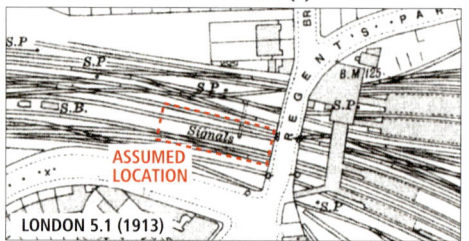

LONDON 5.1 (1913)

CAMDEN TOWN (1st) (NLR)
7 December 1850 - 5 December 1870
Line Operational – Demolished – No access **TQ29262 84176**

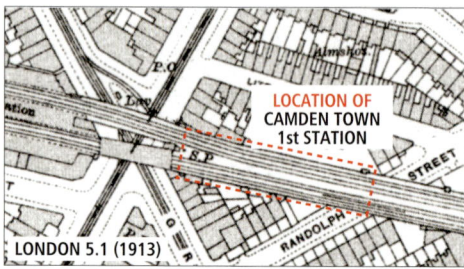

LONDON 5.1 (1913)

CAMP HILL (B&GR)
17 December 1840 - 17 August 1841
Line lifted – Demolished – Station site partially in commercial use
SP08276 85532

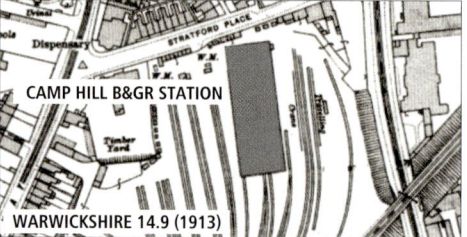

WARWICKSHIRE 14.9 (1913)

CAMP HILL (1st) (MR)
4 November 1844 - 1 April 1862
Line Operational – Demolished – No access
SP08110 85051 (a)

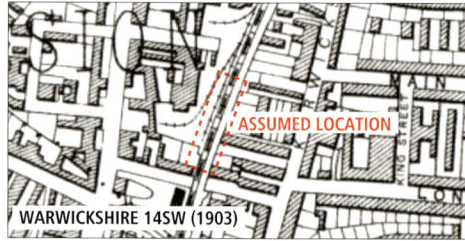

WARWICKSHIRE 14SW (1903)

CANNING TOWN (GER)
14 June 1847 - 1888
Line Operated by DLR – Demolished **TQ39364 81469**

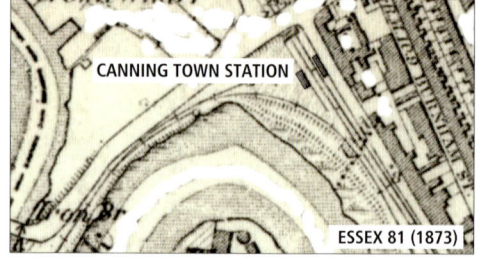

ESSEX 81 (1873)

CANNON STREET ROAD (L&BwallR)
21 August 1842 - November 1848
Line lifted – Demolished – No access **TQ34585 80954**

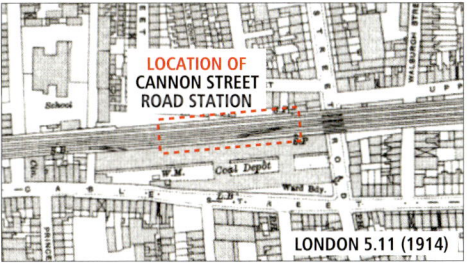
LONDON 5.11 (1914)

CANONBURY (NLR)
1 September 1858 - 1 December 1870
Line Operational – Demolished – No access **TQ32777 85074**

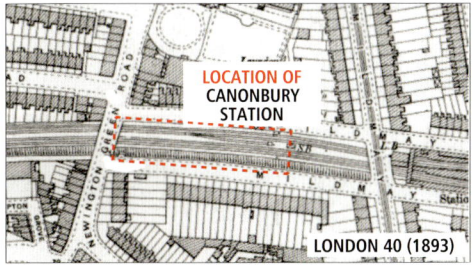
LONDON 40 (1893)

CANTERBURY (1st) (SER)
4 May 1830 - 6 April 1846
Line lifted – Demolished – Station site occupied by housing in Orient Place **TR14691 58381**

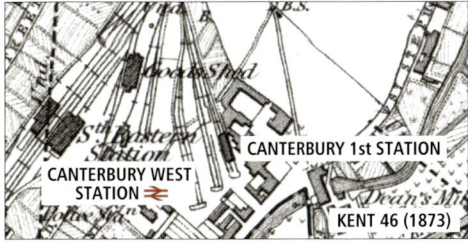
KENT 46 (1873)

CARDIFF ADAM STREET (RhyR)
31 March 1858 - 1 April 1871
Line lifted – Demolished – Station site occupied by "Knox Street Car Park" **ST19016 76567**

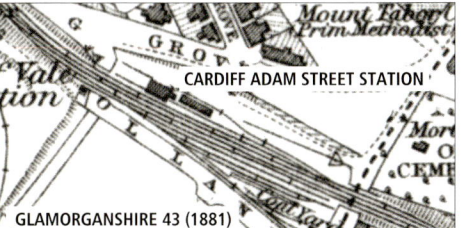
GLAMORGANSHIRE 43 (1881)

CANNON STREET ROAD - CARLISLE CANAL

CARDIFF LOW WATER PIER (RhyR)
9 July 1870 – c1888
Line lifted – Demolished – Station site occupied by "Cardiff Sailing Centre" **ST19275 73497**

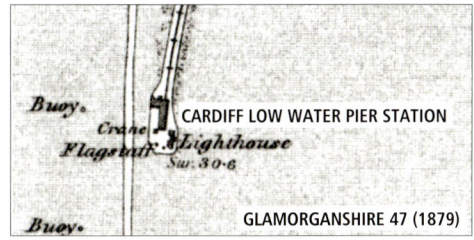
GLAMORGANSHIRE 47 (1879)

CARGO FLEET (1st) (NER)
September 1847 - 9 November 1885
Line Operational – Demolished – Station site unused **NZ51671 20540 (a)**

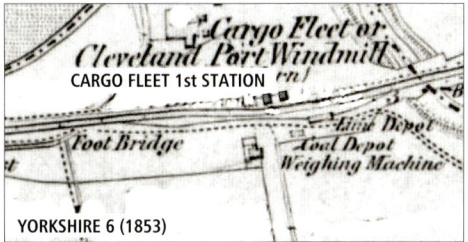
YORKSHIRE 6 (1853)

CARLISLE BOGFIELD (M&CR)
10 May 1843 - 30 December 1844
Line lifted – Demolished – Station site unused **NY40260 55034 (a)**

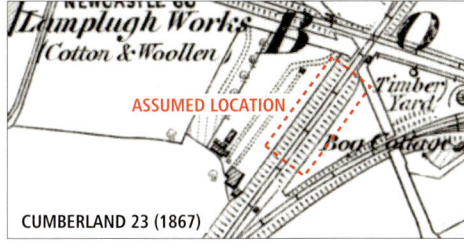
CUMBERLAND 23 (1867)

CARLISLE CANAL (NBR)
22 June 1854 - 1 July 1864
Line lifted – Demolished – Station site in commercial use **NY39065 55958**

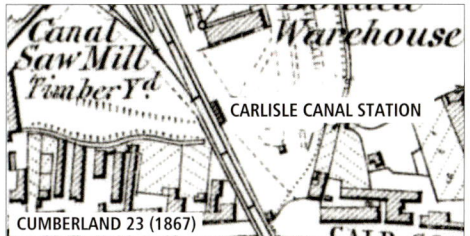
CUMBERLAND 23 (1867)

CARLISLE CANAL STREET - CARNFORTH (FurnR&MR)

CARLISLE CANAL STREET (N&CR)
9 March 1837 - 1 September 1847
Line lifted – Demolished – Station site landscaped
NY39127 55832 (a)

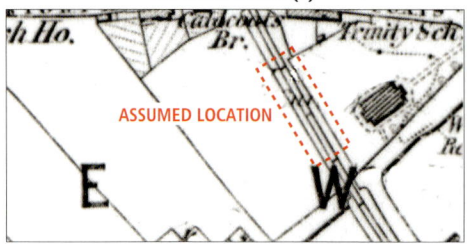

CARLISLE CROWN STREET (M&CR)
30 December 1844 - 17 March 1849
Line lifted – Demolished – Station site absorbed into Carlisle Citadel Station **NY40385 55372 (a)**

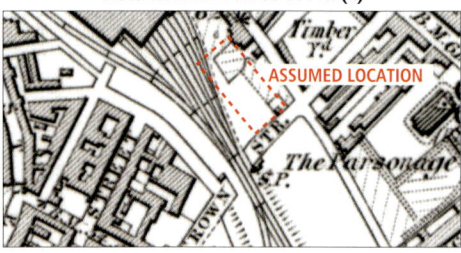

CARLISLE LONDON ROAD (NER)
20 July 1836 - 17 March 1849
Line lifted – Demolished – Station site in commercial use
NY41132 54992

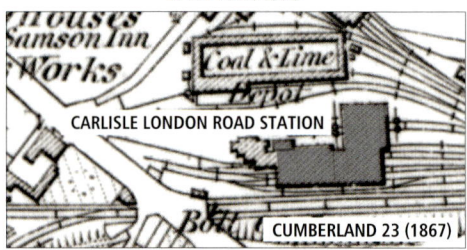

CARLUKE & LANARK (CR)
8 May 1843 - c1853
Line lifted – Demolished – Station site unused **NS82807 54206**

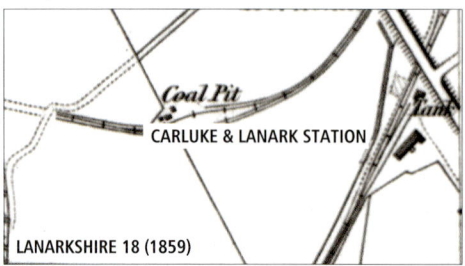

CARNARVON CASTLE (NantlleR)
11 August 1856 - 12 June 1865
Line lifted – Demolished – Station site occupied by a car park
SH47802 62626

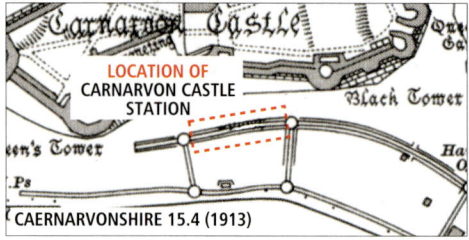

CARNBROE IRON WORKS (W&Cness)
5 May 1843 - 1847
Line Operational – Demolished – No access **NS74270 63465**

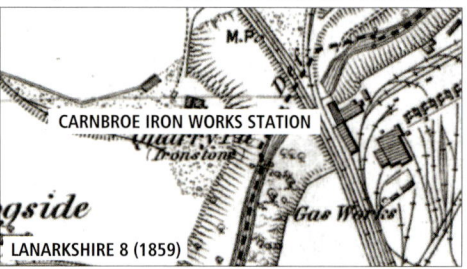

CARNBROE TUNNEL (W&Cness)
? - 1847
Line Operational – Demolished – No access
NS74547 62364 (a)

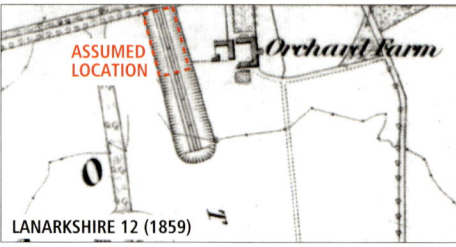

CARNFORTH (FurnR&MR)
6 June 1867 - 2 August 1880
Line Operational – Demolished – No access
SD49238 71412 (a)

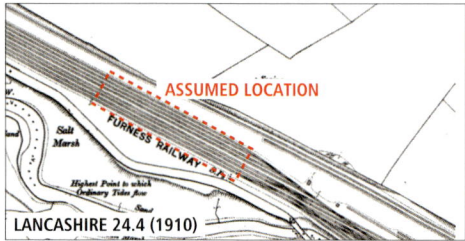

CARNFORTH (L&NWR)
22 September 1846 - 2 August 1880
Line Operational **SD49684 70662**

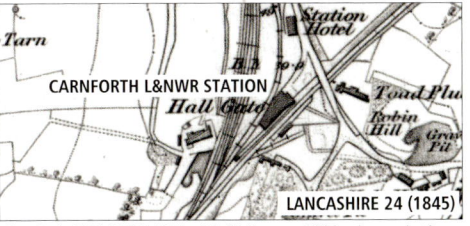

Carnforth [L&NWR/MR/FurnR] (2 August 1880 -) was built on the station site

CARR HOUSE (NER)
1 July 1858 - 1 October 1868
Line lifted – Demolished – Station site occupied by housing
NZ11474 51135 (a)

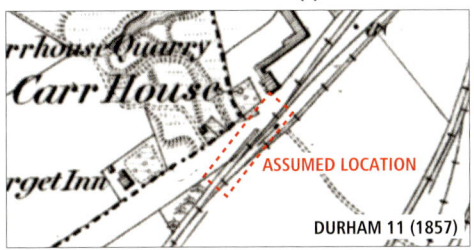

CASTLE DOUGLAS St ANDREW STREET (G&SWR)
7 March 1864 - 1 December 1867
Line lifted – Demolished – A pathway passes through the station site **NX76169 62388**

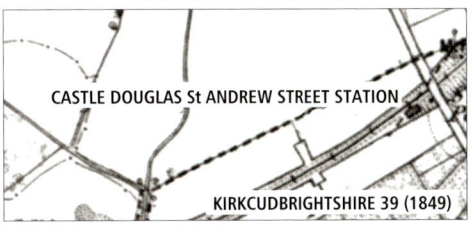

CASTLEFORD (1st) (NER)
1 July 1840 - 1871
Line Operational – Demolished – No access **SE43172 25749**

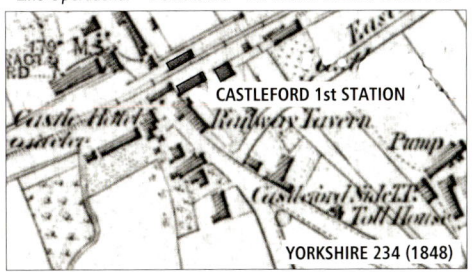

CARNFORTH (L&NWR) - CAUSEWAYEND (WigtownshireR)
CATERHAM (1st) (SE&CR)
5 August 1856 - 1 January 1900
Line Operational – Demolished – Station site occupied by Caterham Station Car Park
TQ34123 55459

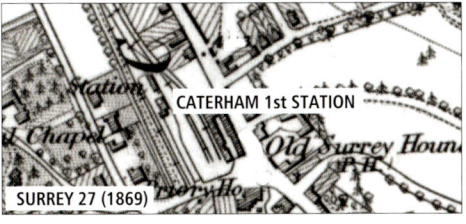

CATHCART (1st) (CR)
25 May 1886 - 18 March 1894
Line Operational – Demolished – Station site occupied by dwellings in Old Castle Gardens **NS58602 60743 (a)**

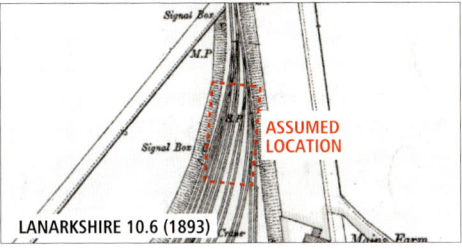

CAUSEWAYEND (1st) (NBR)
5 August 1840 - c1865
Line lifted – Demolished – Station site unused
NS95903 76090 (e)

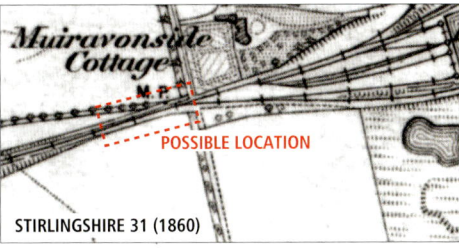

CAUSEWAYEND (WigtownshireR)
May 1875 - November 1885
Line lifted – Demolished – Station site unused **NX42030 59603**

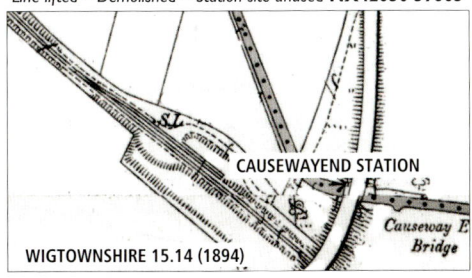

CAUSEWAY HEAD - CHEADLE (M&BR)

CAUSEWAY HEAD (C&SBR)
4 October 1856 - April 1859
Line lifted – Demolished – Level Crossing Keeper's Cottage in private use **NY12425 52879**

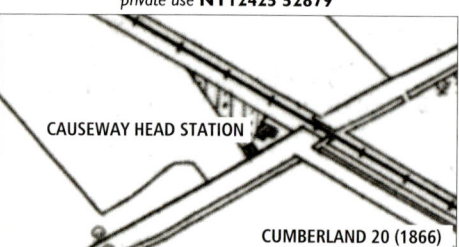

CHAPEL BRIDGE (GWR)
May 1855 - 1 July 1876
Line Operational – Demolished – No access **ST21584 93611**

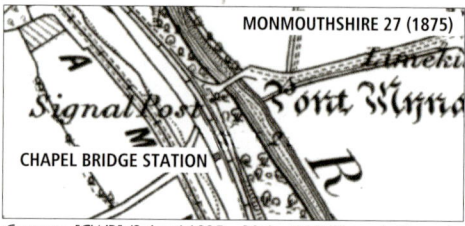

Cwmcarn [GWR] (2 April 1925 – 30 April 1962) was built on the station site

CEFN CRIB (WMidR)
February 1860 - October 1860
Line lifted – Demolished – Station site unused **ST23430 98916 (a)**

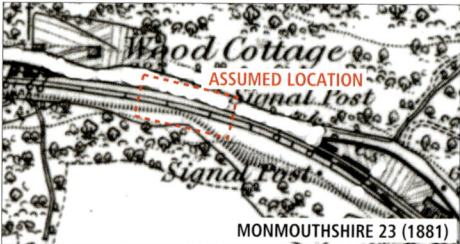

CHARLTON (NBR)
1 February 1861 - 1 October 1862
Line lifted – Demolished – Station site unused **NY80887 84720**

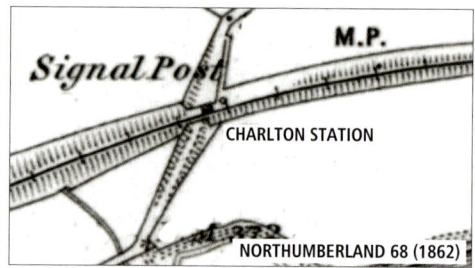

CEMETERY* (RhyR)
1872 - 1898
Line Operational – Demolished – Station House in private use **ST18451 78529**

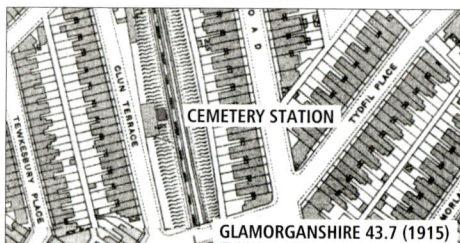

CHATBURN (1st) (L&YR)
22 June 1850 - 2 June 1879
Line Operational – Demolished – No access **SD76540 43682**

CERIST (VanR)
1 December 1873 - July 1879
Line lifted – Demolished – Station site in private use and occupied by a dwelling **SN96443 88065**

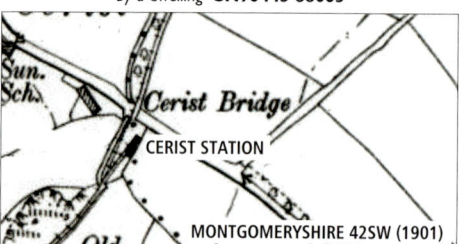

CHEADLE (M&BR)
10 May 1842 - 24 November 1845
Line Operational – Platforms demolished – Station building in private use **SJ87275 86177**

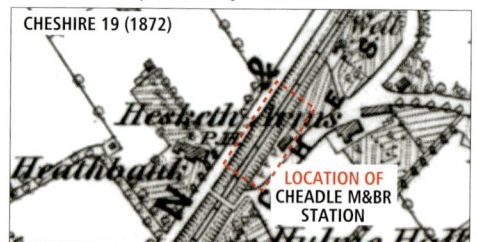

CHEESEWRING QUARRIES* (L&CdnR)
1860 - 1886
Line lifted – Demolished – Station site unused
SX26104 72329 (e)

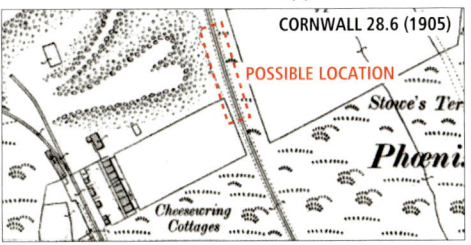

CHEEESEWRING QUARRIES - CHESTER (L&NWR)

CHERRYHINTON (ECR)
August 1852 - 1 May 1854
Line Operational – Station building in private use
TL48872 56874

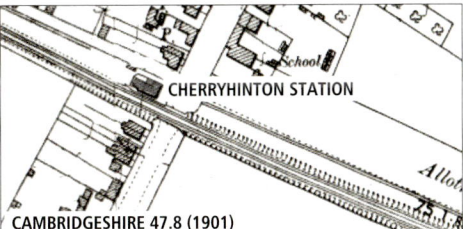

CHELMSFORD (1st) (GER)
29 March 1843 - 1856
Line Operational – Demolished – No access **TL70823 07225**

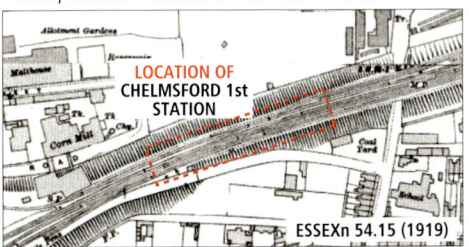

Sited 202 yards north east of *Chelmsford 2nd [GER]* (1856 -)

CHERTSEY (1st) (L&SWR)
14 February 1848 - 1 October 1866
Line Operational – Demolished – Part of station site in commercial use **TQ03903 66330**

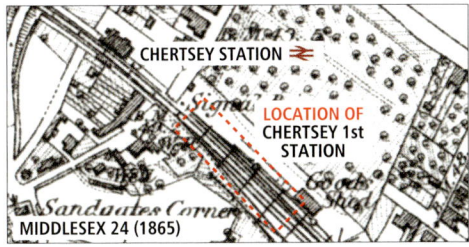

CHELTENHAM (1st) (GWR)
23 October 1947 - 9 September 1894
Line lifted – Demolished – Station site in commercial use
SO94345 22569

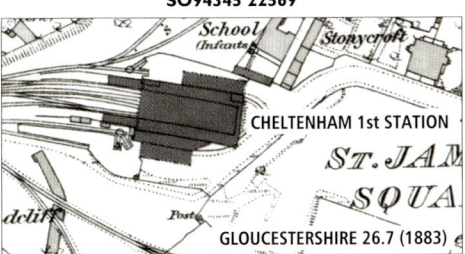

CHESHUNT (1st) (GER)
31 May 1846 - 1 October 1891
Line Operational – Demolished **TL36659 02376**

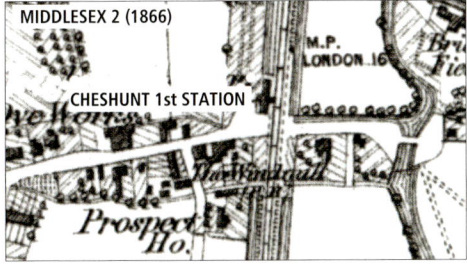

CHEQUERBENT (1st) (L&NWR)
cOctober 1835 - 2 February 1885
Line lifted – Demolished – Station site in private use
SD67417 06078

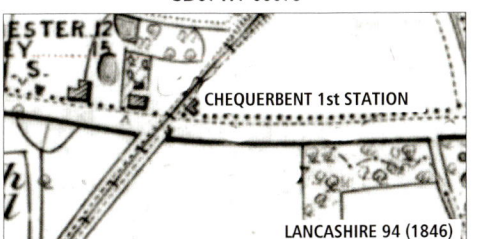

CHESTER (L&NWR)
1 October 1840 - 1 August 1848
Line Operational - Demolished **SJ41152 67088 (a)**

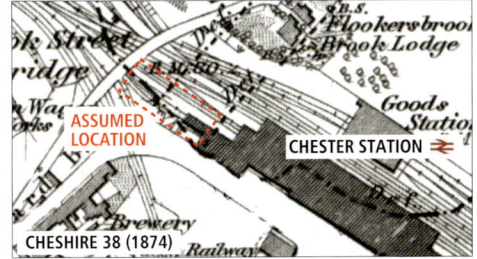

CHESTER BROOK STREET - CHIPPING NORTON (1st)

CHESTER BROOK STREET
(BLcs&ChshJnR)
23 September 1840 - 1 August 1848
Line Operational – Demolished – Station site occupied by part of Chester Depot **SJ41035 67268 (a)**

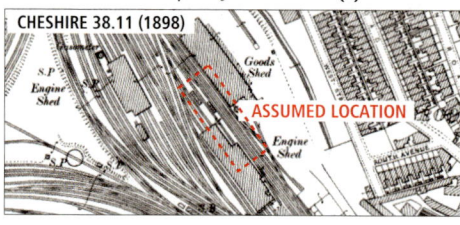
CHESHIRE 38.11 (1898)

CHESTERFIELD (1st) (MR)
11 May 1840 - 2 May 1870
Line Operational – Demolished – No access
SK38801 71230 (a)

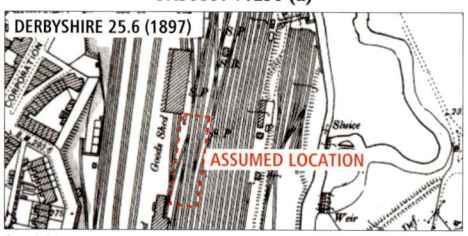
DERBYSHIRE 25.6 (1897)

Sited 98 yards south of *Chesterfield 2nd [MR]* (2 May 1870 -)

CHESTER GOLF CLUB PLATFORM*
(MS&LR)
1891 - 1895
Line Operational – Demolished – No access **SJ31249 69614**

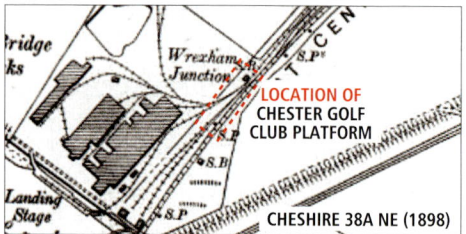
CHESHIRE 38A NE (1898)

CHESTER-LE-STREET (1st) (NER)
March 1862 - 1 December 1868
Line lifted – Demolished – A cycle/walkway passes through the station site **NZ26642 52453**

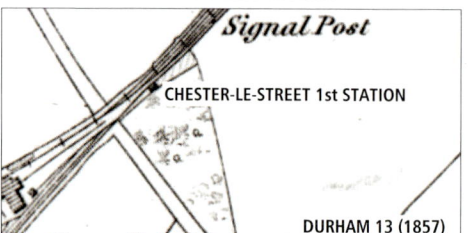
DURHAM 13 (1857)

CHESTERTON (ECR)
19 January 1850 - 1 February 1851
Line Operational – Demolished – No access **TL47437 60319**

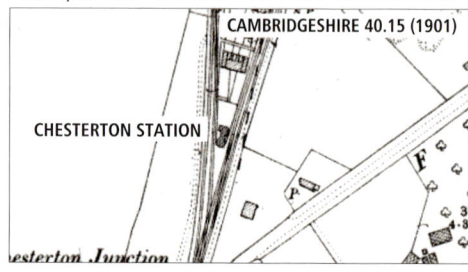
CAMBRIDGESHIRE 40.15 (1901)

CHEW MOOR (L&YR)
January 1851 - July 1851
Line Operational – Demolished – No access **SD66423 07378**

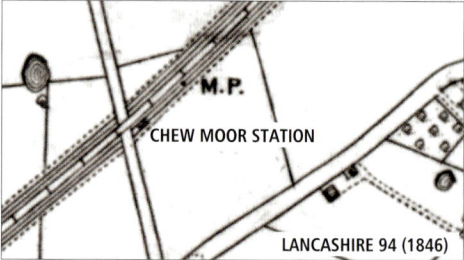
LANCASHIRE 94 (1846)

CHINGFORD (1st) (GER)
17 November 1873 - 2 September 1878
Line lifted – Demolished – Station site occupied by dwellings in Larkshall Road **TQ38821 94002**

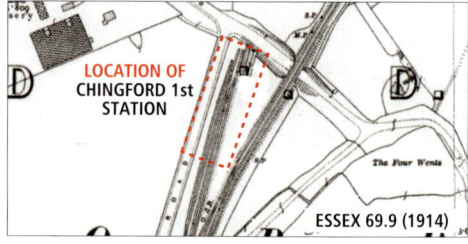
ESSEX 69.9 (1914)

CHIPPING NORTON (1st) (GWR)
10 August 1855 - 6 April 1887
Line lifted – Demolished – Station site in commercial use
SP30742 26892

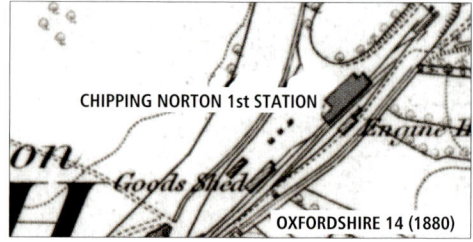
OXFORDSHIRE 14 (1880)

CHISLEHURST (1st) (SER)
1 July 1865 - 2 March 1868
Line Operational – Demolished – Station site occupied by dwellings in Oakhurst Close **TQ42829 69810 (a)**

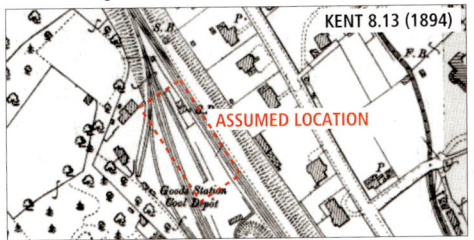
KENT 8.13 (1894)
ASSUMED LOCATION

CHRISTCHURCH (1st) (L&SWR)
13 November 1862 - 30 May 1886
Line lifted – Demolished – Station site in commercial use
SZ15473 93390

CHRISTCHURCH 1st STATION
HAMPSHIRE & ISLE OF WIGHT 86 (1870)

CHRYSTON (MonklandR)
1 October 1826 - 10 December 1851
Line lifted – Demolished – Station site unused **NS68946 70813**

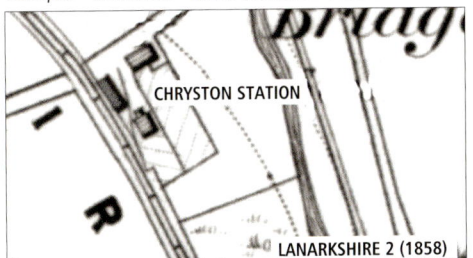
CHRYSTON STATION
LANARKSHIRE 2 (1858)

CHURCH SIDING (Wotton [Brill] Tramway)
March 1872 - August 1894
Line lifted – Demolished – A track passes through the station site
SP69051 15695

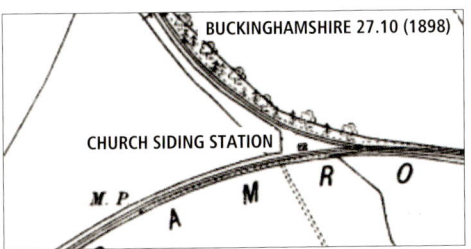
BUCKINGHAMSHIRE 27.10 (1898)
CHURCH SIDING STATION

CHISLEHURST (1st) - CLARKSTON (1st)

CILFREW PLATFORM (N&BR)
December 1888 - 1 May 1895
Line Operational for Freight - Demolished **SN77304 00220**

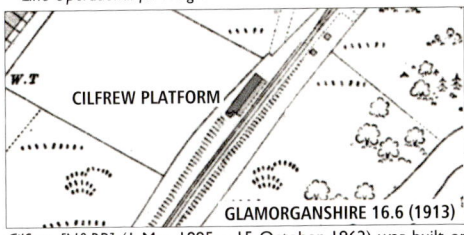
CILFREW PLATFORM
GLAMORGANSHIRE 16.6 (1913)

Cilfrew [N&BR] (1 May 1895 – 15 October 1962) was built on the station site

CINDERFORD (S&WyeR)
5 August 1878 - 2 July 1900
Line lifted – Demolished – A trail passes through the station site
SO64981 12679

CINDERFORD STATION
GLOUCESTERSHIRE 31SE 1879

Ruspidge Halt [GWR] (3 August 1907 – 3 November 1958) was built on the station site

CLAPHAM COMMON (L&SWR)
21 May 1838 - 2 March 1863
Line Operational – Demolished – No access **TQ27009 74988**

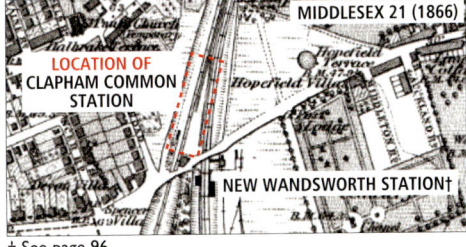
MIDDLESEX 21 (1866)
LOCATION OF CLAPHAM COMMON STATION
NEW WANDSWORTH STATION†

† See page 96

CLARKSTON (1st) (CR)
1 January 1866 - 1881
Line Operational – Demolished – No access
NS57307 57593 (a)

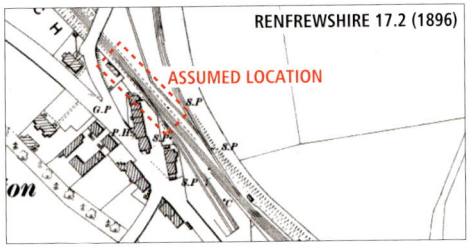
RENFREWSHIRE 17.2 (1896)
ASSUMED LOCATION

CLAUGHTON (L&NWR)
June 1850 - 1 August 1853
Line lifted – Demolished – Station House in private use
SD56453 66807

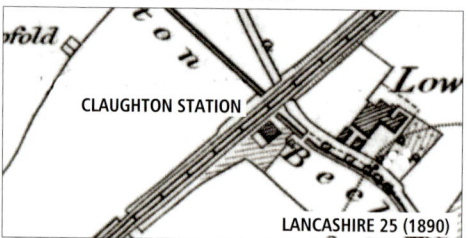
LANCASHIRE 25 (1890)

CLIFFE VALE (NSR)
March 1865 - 31 July 1865
Line Operational – Demolished – No access
SJ87042 46396 (a)

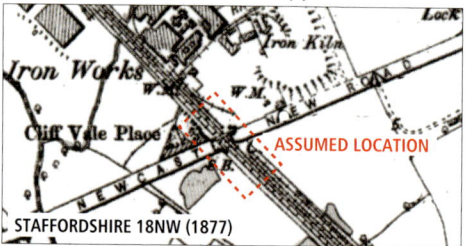
STAFFORDSHIRE 18NW (1877)

CLITHEROE (1st) (L&YR)
22 June 1850 - 1893/4
Line Operational – Demolished – Part of station site in commercial use
SD74088 41817

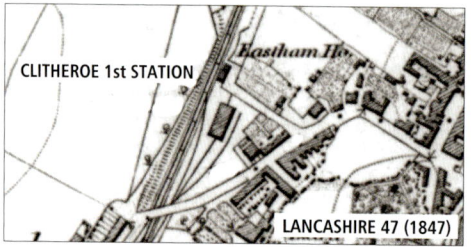
LANCASHIRE 47 (1847)

COATBRIDGE (MonklandR)
10 December 1849 - 10 December 1851
Line Operational – Demolished – No access
NS73020 65175

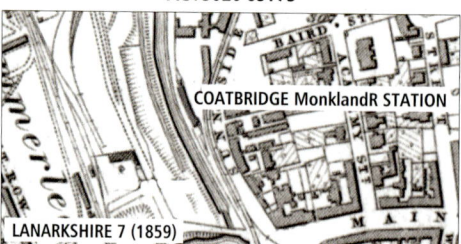
LANARKSHIRE 7 (1859)

COATHAM LANE* (NER)
1865 – c1899
Line Operational – Demolished – No access
NZ59215 24856

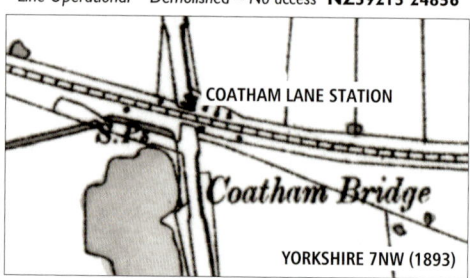
YORKSHIRE 7NW (1893)

COBBINSHAW (1st) (CR)
October 1874 - 4 October 1875
Line Operational – Demolished – No access
NT01624 58445

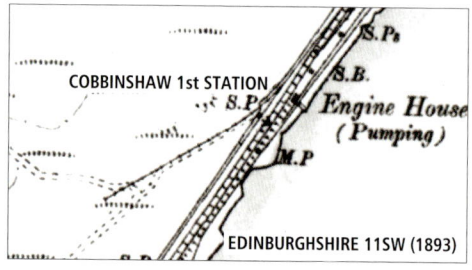
EDINBURGHSHIRE 11SW (1893)

COBORN ROAD (GER)
1 February 1865 - 2 December 1883
Line Operational – Demolished – No access
TQ36663 82979

ESSEX 73 (1863)

COCKER BAR (L&YR)
September 1851 - October 1859
Line Operational – Demolished
SD50159 21778

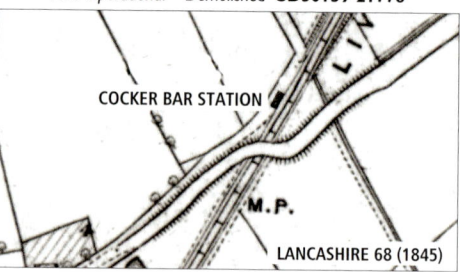
LANCASHIRE 68 (1845)

COCKERMOUTH -COMBE ROW

COCKERMOUTH (L&NWR)
28 April 1847 - 2 January 1865
Line lifted – Demolished – Station site occupied by "Lakes Home Centre" and car park **NY11387 30757**

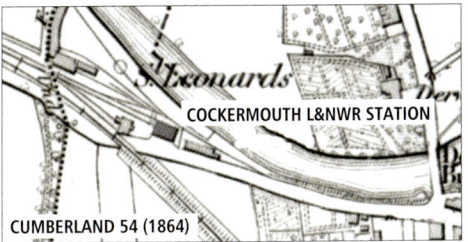

COLLEGE (CofGUR)
1 February 1871 - 15 March 1886
Line lifted – Demolished – Station site in commercial use
NS59885 65137

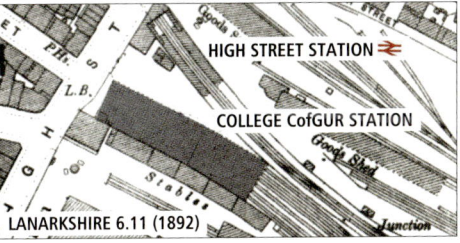

COFTON (B&GR)
November 1841 - December 1843
Line Operational – Demolished – No access
SP01079 76447 (a)

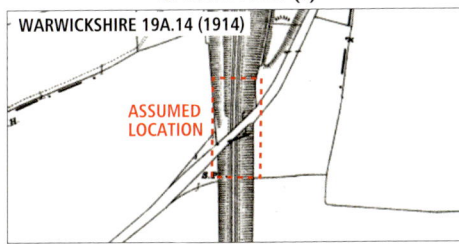

COLNEY HATCH CEMETERY* (GNR)
10 July 1861 - 3 April 1863
Line lifted – Demolished – Station site in commercial use
TQ27985 93300

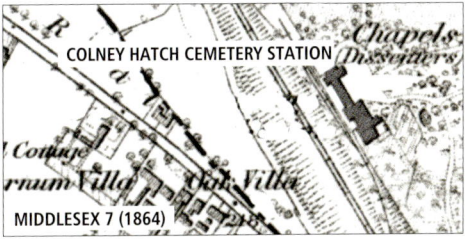

COLD BLOW (LB&SCR)
1 October 1847 - 30 April 1849
Line Operational – Demolished – No access **TQ35867 77634**

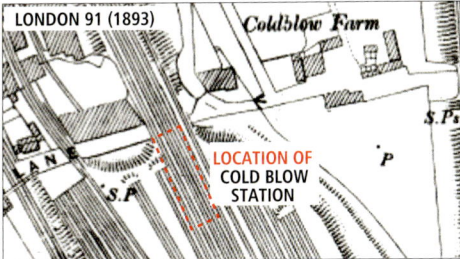

COLWYN (1st) (C&HR)
October 1849 - Prior to 1875
Line Operational – Demolished – No access
SH86270 78740 (a)

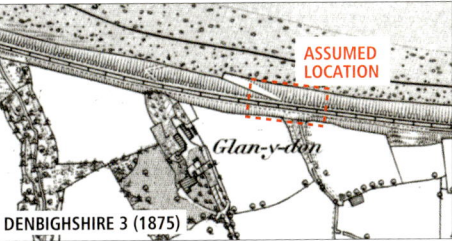

COLD ROWLEY (WrVyR)
1 September 1845 - 1847
Line lifted – Demolished – Subsequent station rebuilt at Beamish Museum – Station site occupied by a picnic area
NZ08698 47877

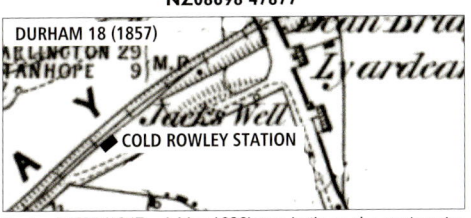

Rowley [NER] (1847 – 1 May 1939) was built on the station site

COMBE ROW (WSetMinR)
4 September 1865 - 7 November 1898
Line lifted – Demolished – Station Masters House in private use
ST02976 35321

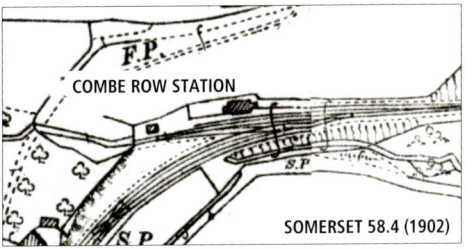

COMMERCIAL DOCK - COPPULL (1st)

COMMERCIAL DOCK (SER)
1 May 1856 - 1 January 1867
Line Operational – Demolished – No access **TQ35198 78543**

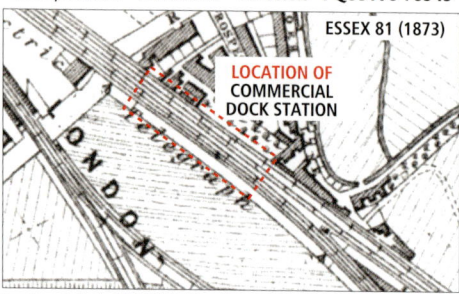
ESSEX 81 (1873)

Southwark Park [SECR] (1 October 1902 – 21 September 1925) was built on the station site

COMPSTALL (MS&LR)
5 August 1862 - 1 October 1865
Line Operational – Demolished
Location unknown but was a temporary station opened whilst a viaduct was being constructed
SJ95542 90098 (e)

CONISBROUGH (MS&LR)
10 November 1849 - c1895
Line Operational – Demolished – No access **SK51027 99419**

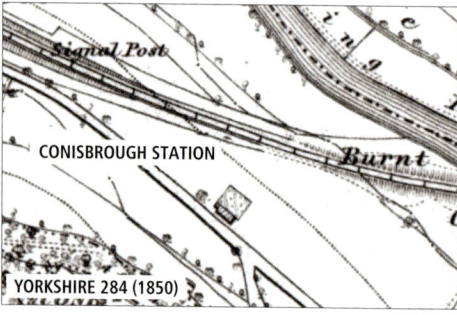
YORKSHIRE 284 (1850)

CONNAH'S QUAY (WM&CQR)
31 March 1890 - 1897
Line lifted – Demolished – Station site occupied by dwellings in Leighton Court **SJ29235 69896 (a)**

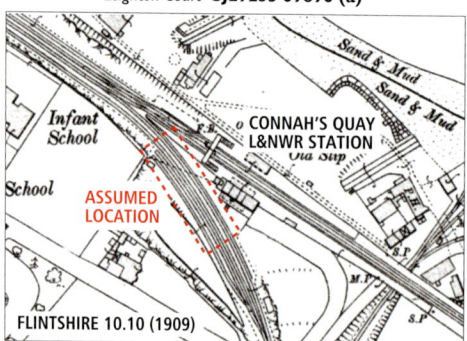
FLINTSHIRE 10.10 (1909)

CONSETT (1st) (NER)
1 September 1862 - 2 December 1867
Line lifted – Demolished – Station site grassed and wooded area
NZ09731 49935

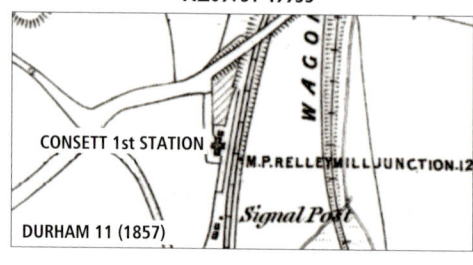
DURHAM 11 (1857)

COPPENHALL (GJnR)
4 July 1837 - 10 September 1840
Line Operational – Demolished – No access **SJ70220 57392**

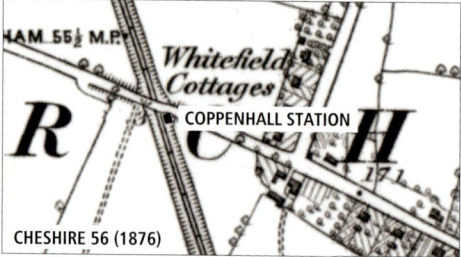
CHESHIRE 56 (1876)

COPPERHOUSE (WCwallR)
23 May 1843 - 16 February 1852
Line lifted – Demolished – A pathway passes through the station site **SW57127 38295 (a)**

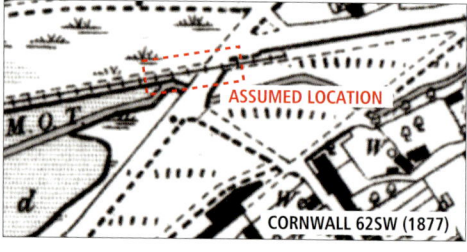
CORNWALL 62SW (1877)

COPPULL (1st) (L&NWR)
31 October 1838 - 2 September 1895
Line Operational – Demolished - No access **SD56472 14406**

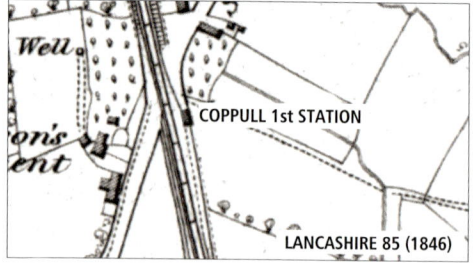
LANCASHIRE 85 (1846)

CORNBROOK (CLC)
2 September 1873 - 9 July 1877
Line Operational – Demolished - No access
SJ82270 96972 (a)

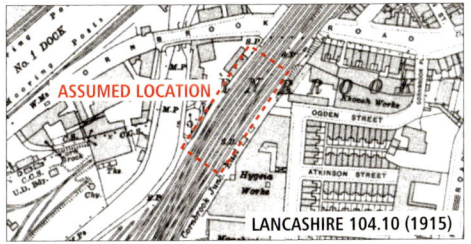

LANCASHIRE 104.10 (1915)

COSSINGTON GATE (MR)
December 1845 - 27 September 1873
Line Operational – Demolished - No access
SK61027 13705

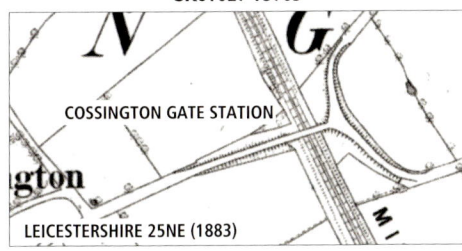

LEICESTERSHIRE 25NE (1883)

COUNTESS PARK (NBR)
1 December 1859 - 1 February 1861
Line lifted – Demolished – Station site unused
NY87131 80463 (a)

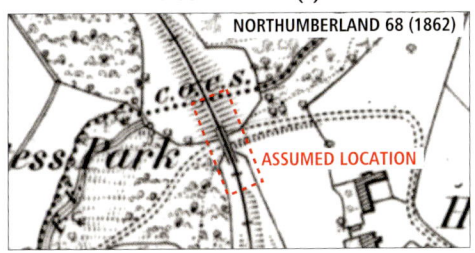

NORTHUMBERLAND 68 (1862)

COWBRIDGE (1st) (TVR)
18 September 1865 - 1 October 1892
Line lifted – Demolished – Station site occupied by dwellings
in Druids Green and Grays Walk **SS99917 74510**

GLAMORGANSHIRE 45 (1877)

CORNBROOK - CRATHES CASTLE HALT

CRABLEY CREEK (NER)
c1844 - 1864
Line Operational – Demolished – No access
SE90526 27342 (a)

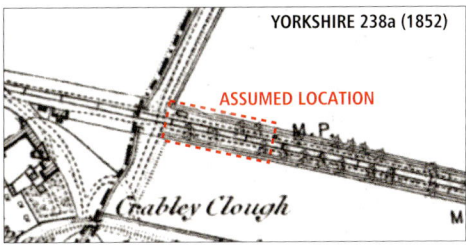

YORKSHIRE 238a (1852)

CRAGG MILL (NER)
February 1849 - October 1877
Line Operational – Demolished **NU11598 34925**

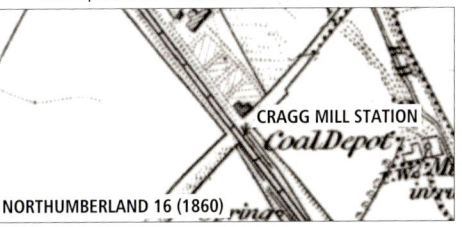

NORTHUMBERLAND 16 (1860)

This station was originally opened as *Belford 1st [NER]* (March – August 1847)

CRAIGMYLE* (GNofSR)
? - 1887
Line lifted – Demolished – Station site in use as part of a field
NJ63751 00717

ABERDEENSHIRE 83 (1866)

CRATHES CASTLE HALT* (DsideR)
8 September 1853 - 1 January 1863
Line lifted – Demolished – Station site unused
NO74285 96243 (a)

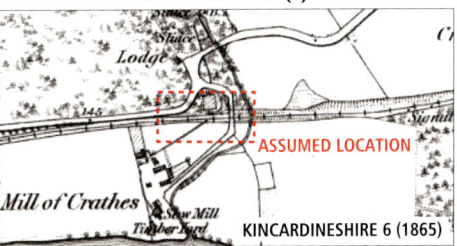

KINCARDINESHIRE 6 (1865)

CRAWLEY FOR STANHOPE - CROOK (S&DR)

CRAWLEY FOR STANHOPE (W&DwtJnR)
1 September 1845 - 31 December 1846
Line lifted – Demolished – A track passes through the station site
NY99311 40607

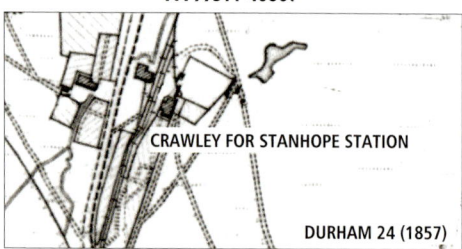

CRIMPLE (NER)
November 1867 - May 1869
Line Operational – Demolished – No access **SE32141 52840**

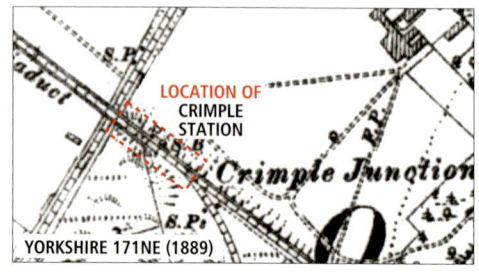

CREDITON (B&ER)
12 May 1851 - 1 August 1854
Line lifted – Demolished – Station site occupied by dwellings in Joseph Locke Way **SX84092 99497**

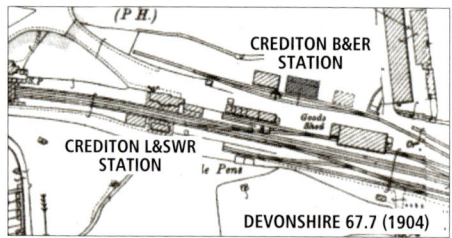

CROFT (S&DR)
27 October 1829 - 30 March 1841
Line lifted – Demolished – Station site occupied by dwellings in Linden Road **NZ29126 10037**

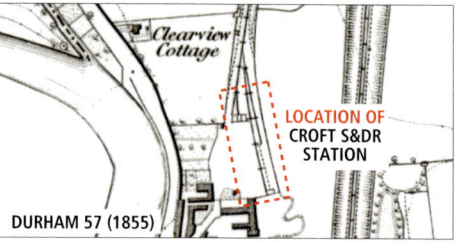

CREWE (M&BR)
10 August 1842 - c1846
Line lifted – Demolished – Station site in railway use
SJ71060 54969

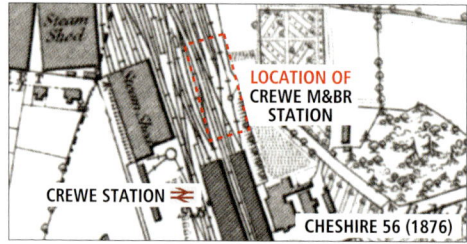

CROMFORD (L&NWR)
June 1833 - December 1877
Line lifted – Demolished – Station site in commercial use
SK31275 55996 (a)

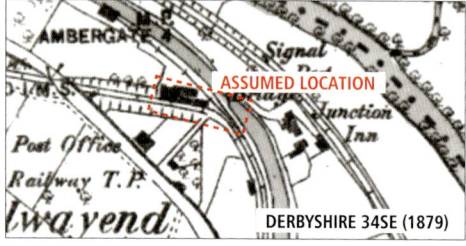

CRIEFF (1st) (CR)
14 March 1856 - 1 June 1893
Line lifted – Demolished – Station site occupied by "Crieff Medical Centre" **NN86165 21306**

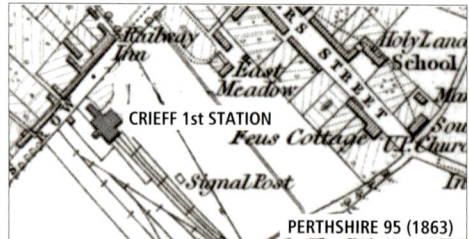

CROOK (S&DR)
1844 - 1 September 1845
Line lifted – Demolished – Station site landscaped
NZ16021 35303

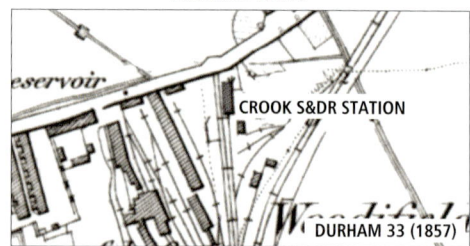

CROSSHILL - CULLERCOATS (1st)

CROSSHILL (G&SWR)
24 May 1860 - 1 March 1862
Line Operational – Demolished – No access **NS30944 07146**

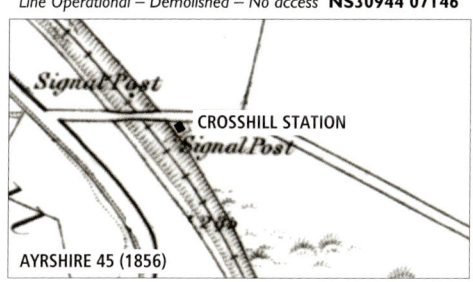

AYRSHIRE 45 (1856)

CROSSROADS (DP&AJnR)
3 April 1832 - 1861
Line lifted – Demolished – Station building in private use
NO39208 32238

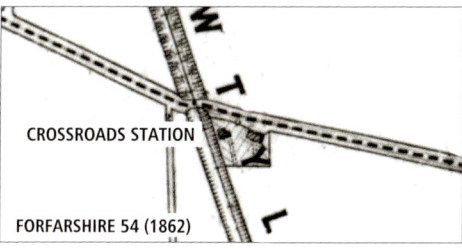

FORFARSHIRE 54 (1862)

CROSS SLACK (P&WR)
June 1870 - November 1873
Line Operational – Demolished **SD31102 31004 (e)**

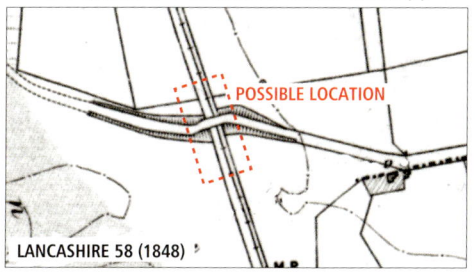

LANCASHIRE 58 (1848)

CROYDON CENTRAL (L&SWR)
1 January 1868 - 1 September 1890
Line lifted – Demolished – Station site occupied by Queens Gardens and Croydon Town Hall **TQ32432 65394**

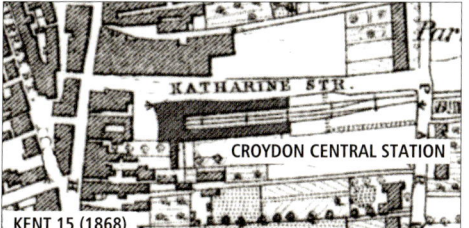

KENT 15 (1868)

CRUMSTANE (NBR)
15 August 1849 - May 1852
Line lifted – Demolished – Station site unused **NT80932 53537**

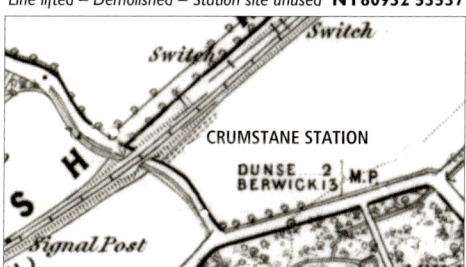

CUDWORTH FOR BARNSLEY (MR)
1 July 1840 - c1854
Line lifted – Demolished – A pathway passes through the station site **SE38265 08264**

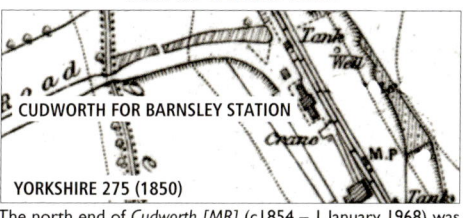

YORKSHIRE 275 (1850)

The north end of *Cudworth [MR]* (c1854 – 1 January 1968) was built on the station site

CUERDLEY (StHC&RC)
March 1856 - January 1858
Line Operational – Demolished – No access **SJ54745 85824**

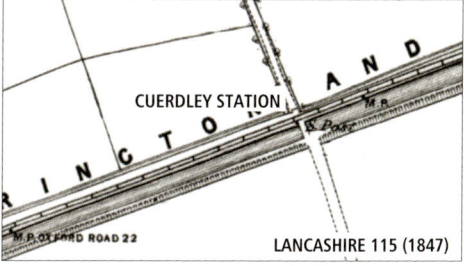

LANCASHIRE 115 (1847)

CULLERCOATS (1st) (NER)
27 June 1864 - 7 July 1882
Line lifted – Demolished – Station site occupied by housing in Sedbergh Road **NZ35566 70875**

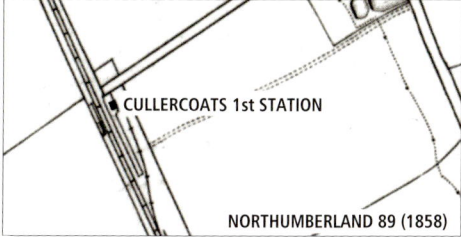

NORTHUMBERLAND 89 (1858)

CULTS (DeesideR)
8 September 1853 - 1855
Line lifted – Demolished – The Deeside Way passes through the station site **NJ89256 02716 (a)**

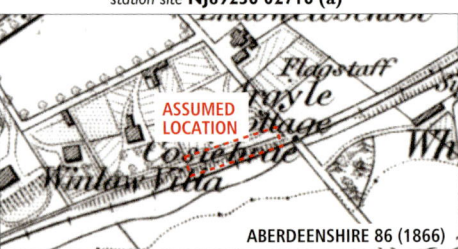
ABERDEENSHIRE 86 (1866)

CWMBRAN (1st) (GWR)
1 July 1852 - 11 March 1880
Line lifted – Demolished – Station site unused **ST29289 94814**

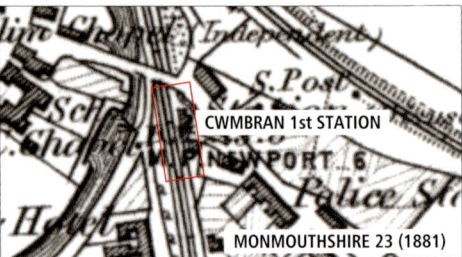
MONMOUTHSHIRE 23 (1881)

DALMARNOCK (1st) (CR)
24 June 1841 - 1 November 1895
Line lifted – Demolished – Station site occupied by dwellings **NS61312 63110**

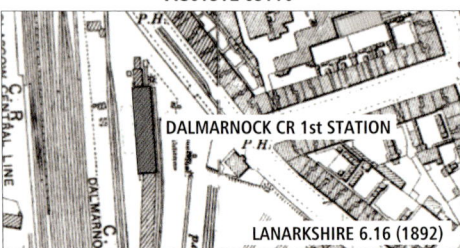
LANARKSHIRE 6.14 (1892)

DALMENY (NBR)
1 March 1866 - 5 March 1890
Line Operational – Demolished – Station site occupied by a caravan park **NT14275 76969**

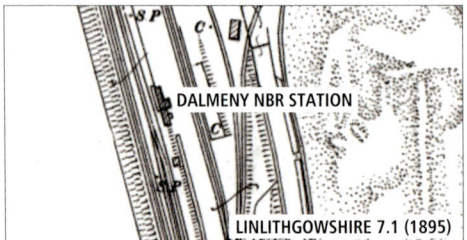
LINLITHGOWSHIRE 7.1 (1895)

DALMUIR (1st) (NBR)
31 May 1858 - 17 May 1897
Line Operational – Demolished – Station site partially in use as a car park for Dalmuir Station **NS48621 71301**

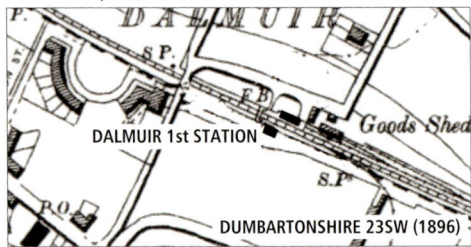
DUMBARTONSHIRE 23SW (1896)

DALRY (1st) (G&SWR)
21 July 1840 - 10 July 1878
Line Operational – Demolished – No access **NS29766 49232**

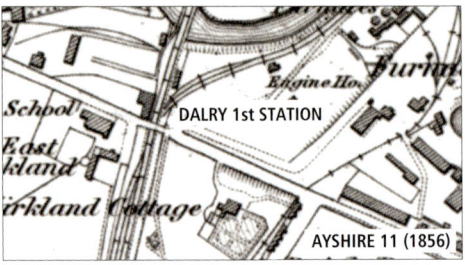
AYSHIRE 11 (1856)

DALRY JUNCTION (G&SWR)
4 April 1843 - 2 January 1860
Line Operational – Demolished – No access **NS29782 48261**

AYSHIRE 11 (1856)

DALVEY (GNofSR)
1 July 1863 - 1 September 1868
Line lifted – Demolished – The Speyside Way passes through the station site **NJ11543 32257 (a)**

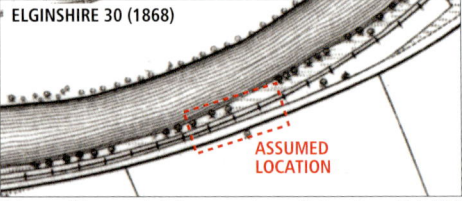
ELGINSHIRE 30 (1868)

This possibly occupied the same site as *Dalvey Farm Halt [BR]* (15 June 1959 – 18 October 1965)

DANYGRAIG (1st) (R&SBR)
14 March 1895 – 7 May 1899
Line lifted – Demolished – Station site unused
SS67584 93054 (a)

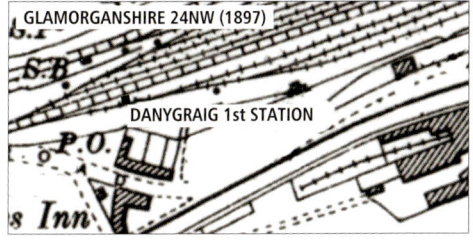

DAUBHILL (1st) (L&NWR)
13 June 1831 – 2 February 1885
Line lifted – Demolished **SD70054 07423 (e)**

DANYGRAIG (1st) - DENBIGH (VoCR)

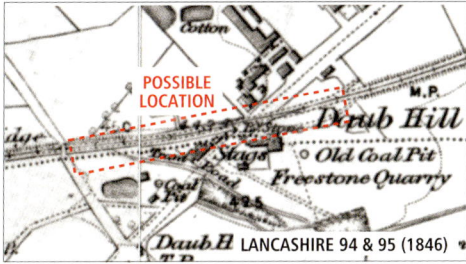

DARLASTON (2nd) (L&NWR)
14 September 1863 – 1 November 1887
Line lifted – Demolished – A footpath passes through the station site **SO97805 96520**

DAVIE'S DYKE (WM&CR)
2 June 1845 – May 1848
Line lifted – Demolished – Station site in agricultural use
NS85557 55821

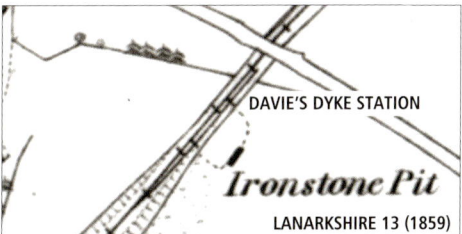

DARLINGTON BANK TOP (1st) (NER)
31 March 1841 – 1 July 1887
Line Operational – Demolished – No access **NZ29503 14142**

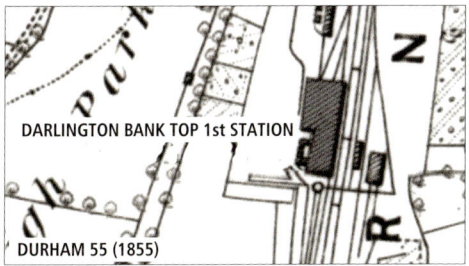

DECHMONT (E&GR)
October 1850 – 1 January 1862
Line Operational – Demolished – No access **NT03983 68987**

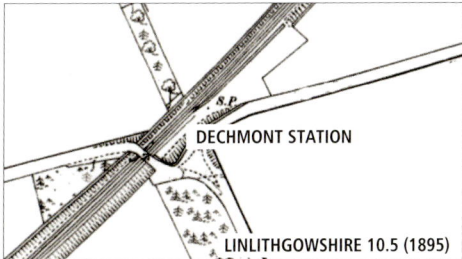

DARLINGTON NORTH ROAD (S&DR)
10 October 1825 – 1842
Line Operational – Demolished **NZ29072 15631 (a)**

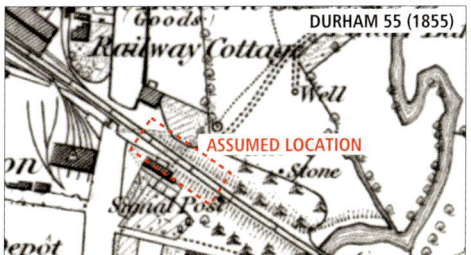

DENBIGH (VoCR)
5 October 1858 – 1 March 1862
Line lifted – Demolished – Station site occupied by an Aldi Supermarket **SJ05699 66503**

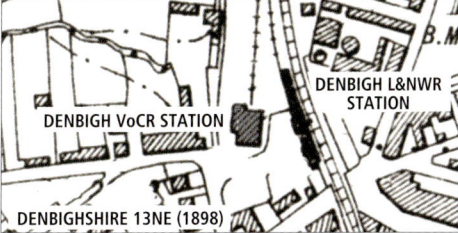

DEREHAM (EAnglianR) - **DINTING** (MS&LR)

DEREHAM (EAnglianR)
11 September 1848 - Prior to March 1850
*Line lifted – Demolished – Station site occupied by
"Lynn Hill Guest House"* **TF99188 12713**

NORFOLK 49SW (1882)

DERWENTHEUGH (NER)
11 June 1836 - February 1868
Line Operational – Demolished – No access **NZ20366 63268**

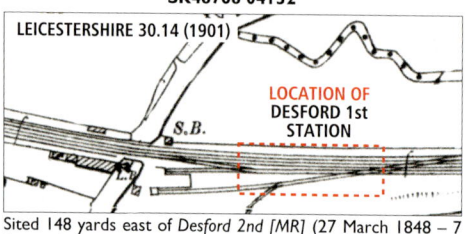
DURHAM 2 (1856)

DESFORD (1st) (MR)
18 July 1932 - 27 March 1848
Line Operational for Freight – Demolished – No access
SK48768 04132

LEICESTERSHIRE 30.14 (1901)

Sited 148 yards east of Desford 2nd [MR] (27 March 1848 – 7 September 1964)

DEVONSHIRE STREET, MILE END (ECR)
20 June 1839 - January 1841
Line Operational – Demolished – No access **TQ36021 82745**

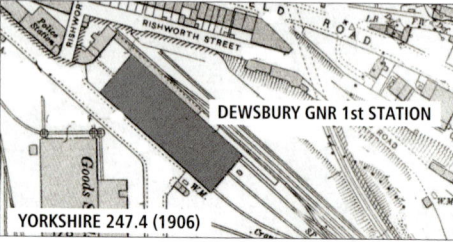
LONDON 52 (1893)

DEWSBURY (1st) (GNR)
9 September 1874 - 12 April 1880
Line lifted – Demolished – Station site in commercial use
SE24834 21658

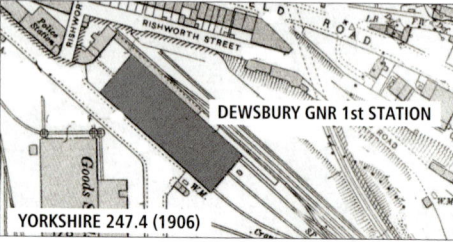
YORKSHIRE 247.4 (1906)

DEYHOUSE (D&AR)
1843 - August 1847
Line Operational – Demolished **NO54187 33711**

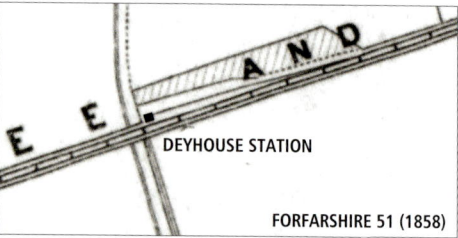
FORFARSHIRE 51 (1858)

Barry Links [D&AR] (31 July 1851 -) was built on the station site

DILSTON* (N&CR)
10 March 1835 - c1836
Line Operational – Demolished - No access **NY98333 63640**

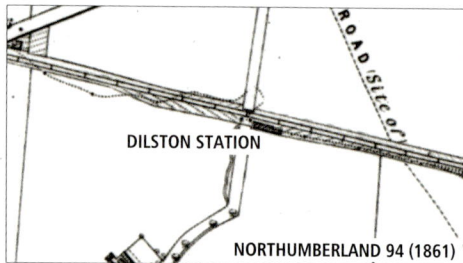
NORTHUMBERLAND 94 (1861)

DINTING (MS&LR)
25 December 1842 - 1 February 1847
Line Operational – Demolished **SK01384 94103**

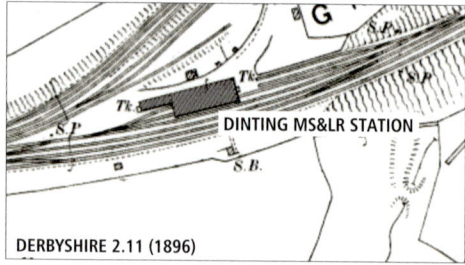
DERBYSHIRE 2.11 (1896)

DITTON MILL (L&NWR)
1 July 1852 - 1 May 1871
Line Operational – Demolished – No access **SJ48922 84669**

LANCASHIRE 114 (1846)

DITTON MILL - DUDLEY HILL (1st)
DOWLAIS TOP (L&NWR)
1 January 1873 - 4 May 1885
Line lifted – Demolished – The A465, Heads of the Valleys Road, passes through the station site **SO08338 08598**

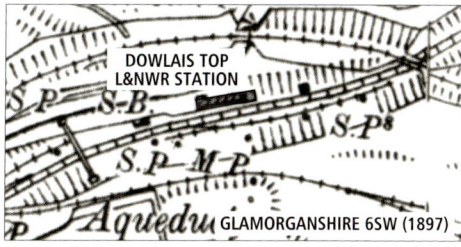
GLAMORGANSHIRE 6SW (1897)

DODDERHILL (B&GR)
November 1841 - 5 March 1844
Line Operational – Demolished – No access
SO93574 65078 (a)

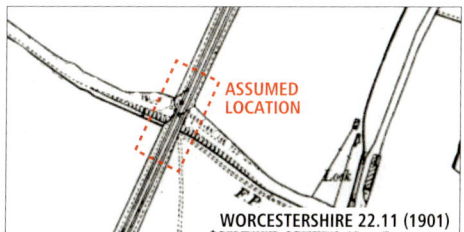
WORCESTERSHIRE 22.11 (1901)

DROITWICH ROAD (MR)
24 June 1840 - 1 October 1855
Line Operational – Demolished – No access **SO92758 62873**

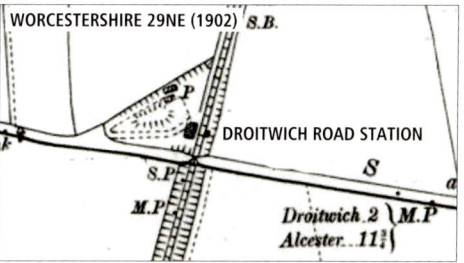

DOVER HARBOUR (1st) (LC&DR)
1 November 1861 - February 1865
Line Operational – Demolished **TR31644 40379 (a)**

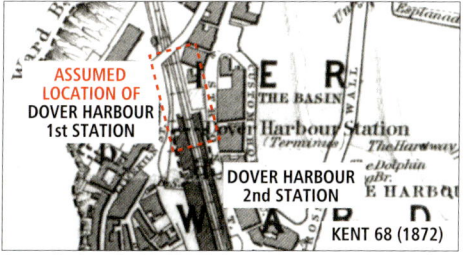
KENT 68 (1872)

Dover Harbour 2nd [LC&DR] (June 1863 – 10 July 1927) was either built on the same site or adjacent to it

DUDLEY COLLIERY (NER)
April 1860 - 8 July 1878
Line Operational – Demolished – No access **NZ25749 73908**

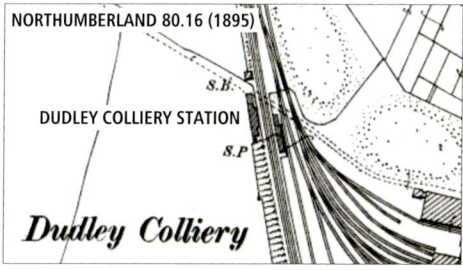

DOWLAIS JUNCTION (TVR)
21 August 1851 - May 1854
Line lifted – Demolished – Station site unused
SO06897 07152 (e)

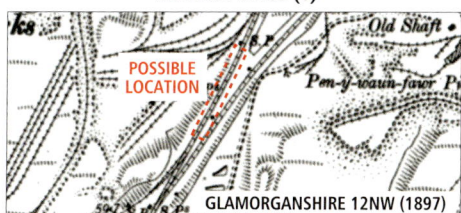
GLAMORGANSHIRE 12NW (1897)

DUDLEY HILL (1st) (GNR)
20 August 1856 - 1 October 1875
Line lifted – Demolished – Station site in commercial use by "Applelec Ltd" **SE18821 30228**

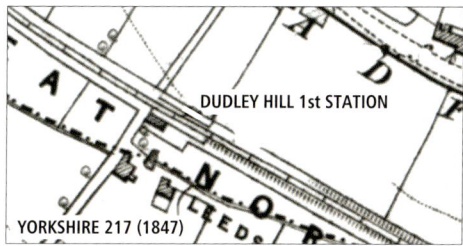
YORKSHIRE 217 (1847)

DUFFIELD (1st) - DUNDEE WARD

DUFFIELD (1st) (MR)
6 April 1841 - 1 October 1867
Line Operational – Demolished – No access
SK34521 43795 (a)

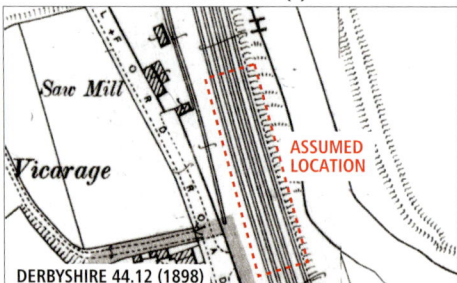
ASSUMED LOCATION
DERBYSHIRE 44.12 (1898)

DUFFIELD GATE (NER)
June 1849 - 1 May 1890
Line lifted – Demolished – Station building in private use
SE67743 34336

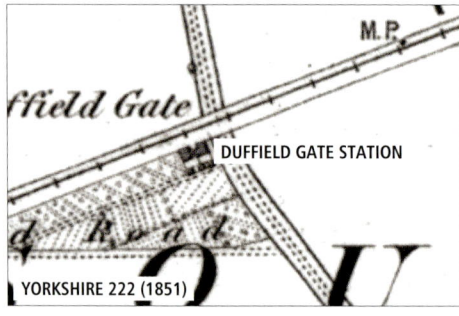
DUFFIELD GATE STATION
YORKSHIRE 222 (1851)

DUKINFIELD (MS&LR)
23 December 1845 - March 1863
Line Operational – Demolished – No access
SJ93308 97458 (a)

DUKINFIELD DOG LANE (SAuL&MR)
17 November 1841 - 23 December 1845
Line Operational – Demolished – No access
SJ93340 97448 (a)

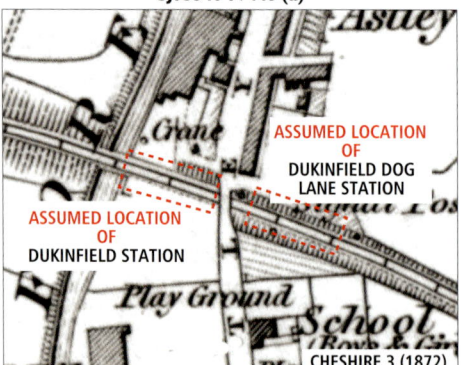
ASSUMED LOCATION OF DUKINFIELD DOG LANE STATION
ASSUMED LOCATION OF DUKINFIELD STATION
CHESHIRE 3 (1872)

DUMFRIES (GD&CR)
23 August 1848 - 15 October 1849
Line lifted – Demolished – Station site in commercial use
NX97849 761895

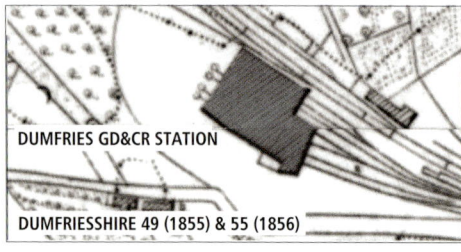
DUMFRIES GD&CR STATION
DUMFRIESSHIRE 49 (1855) & 55 (1856)

DUMFRIES (1st) (G&SWR)
15 October 1849 - March 1859
Line Operational – Demolished – No access
NX97770 76281

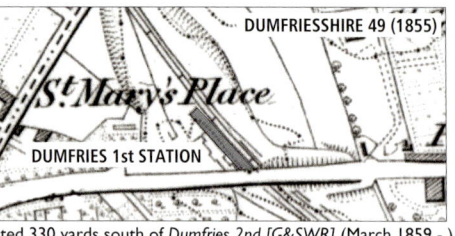
DUMFRIESSHIRE 49 (1855)
DUMFRIES 1st STATION

Sited 330 yards south of *Dumfries 2nd [G&SWR]* (March 1859 -)

DUNDEE TRADES LANE (D&AR)
2 April 1840 - 14 December 1857
Line lifted – Demolished – Station site occupied by a car park
NO40741 30365

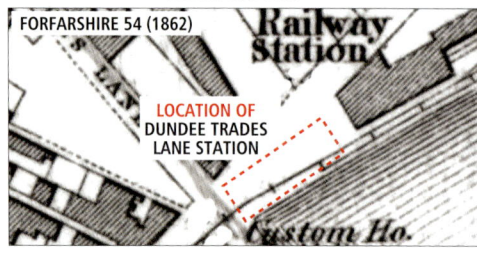
FORFARSHIRE 54 (1862)
LOCATION OF DUNDEE TRADES LANE STATION

DUNDEE WARD (DP&AJR)
3 April 1832 - 10 June 1861
Line lifted – Demolished – Station site occupied by a BT building
NO39939 30377

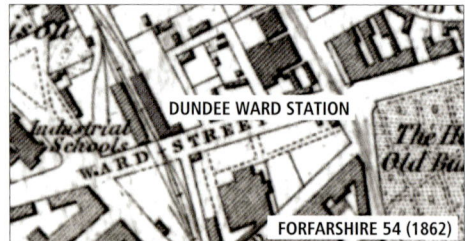
DUNDEE WARD STATION
FORFARSHIRE 54 (1862)

DUNHAMPSTEAD (MR)
November 1841 - 1 October 1855
Line Operational – Demolished – No access **SO91882 59935**

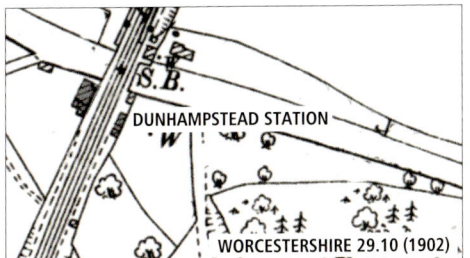

DUNNERHOLME GATE (FurnR)
Not known
Line Operational – Demolished – Probable station site occupied by a dwelling **SD21674 79622**

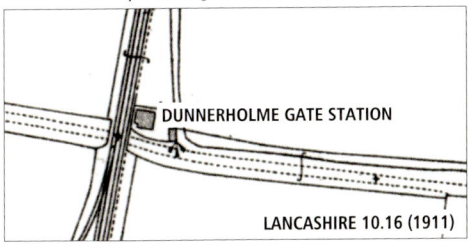

DUNSTABLE (1st) (L&NWR)
29 May 1848 - January 1866
Line lifted – Demolished – Station site occupied by council offices
TL01167 22578 (a)

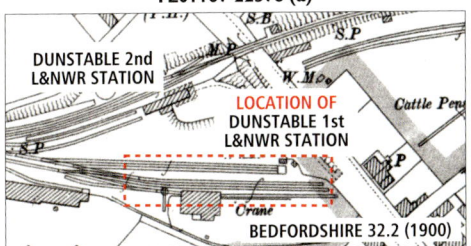

DURHAM GILESGATE (NER)
15 April 1844 - 1 April 1857
Line lifted – Demolished – Station building in use as a "Travelodge"
NZ28230 42791

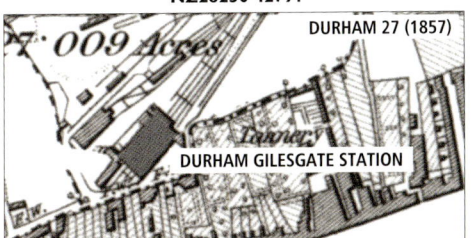

DUNHAMPSTEAD - EASTBOURNE (1st)
DURHAM TURNPIKE (S&TR)
16 April 1835 - 9 March 1840
Line lifted – Demolished – A walkway passes through the station site **NZ27321 53547**

DYCE (1st) (GNofSR)
20 September 1854 - 18 June 1861
Line Operational – Demolished – No access
NJ88287 13200 (a)

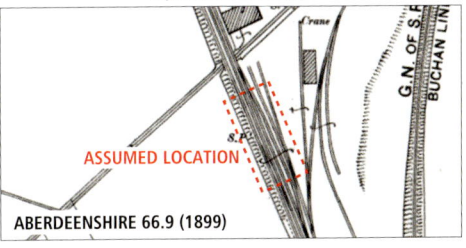

EARL'S COURT (1st) (MDR)
30 October 1871 - 30 December 1875
Line Operational – Demolished – No access **TQ25576 78621**

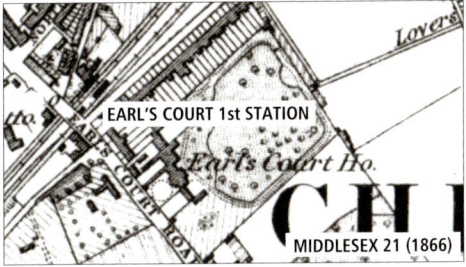

EASTBOURNE (1st) (LB&SCR)
15 May 1849 - 1866
Line lifted – Demolished – Station site occupied by housing in Wharf Road **TV60860 99208 (a)**

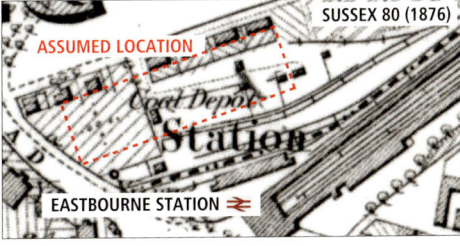

EAST GRINSTEAD (1st) - EDINBURGH LOTHIAN ROAD

EAST GRINSTEAD (1st) (LB&SCR)
9 July 1855 - 1 October 1866
Line lifted – Demolished – Station building in commercial use – Beeching Way passes through the station site **TQ39166 38281**

EAST GRINSTEAD (2nd) (LB&SCR)
1 October 1866 - 15 October 1883
Line lifted – Demolished – Beeching Way passes through the station site **TQ39168 38311**

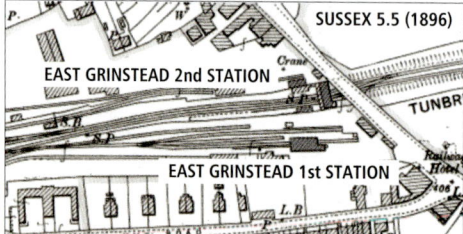

EASTREA (GER)
October 1847 - 1 August 1866
Line Operational – Demolished **TL29950 96504**

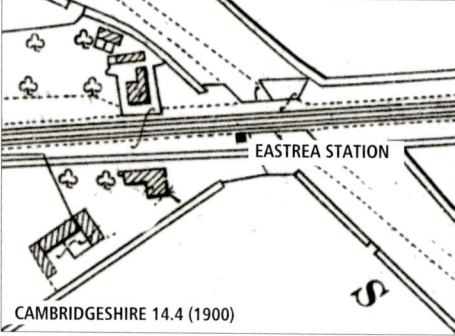

EBBW VALE (MonmouthsR)
19 April 1852 - 1 November 1859
Line Operational – Demolished – No access
SO17303 08918 (a)

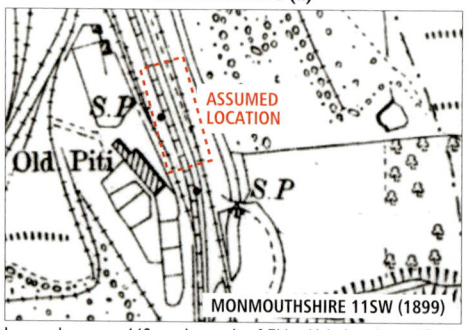

Located approx 440 yards south of *Ebbw Vale Low Level [GWR]* (19 April 1852 - 30 April 1962). *Tyllwyn Halt [GWR]* (20 November 1943 – 30 April 1962) may have been constructed on the station site

ECKINGTON (1st) (MR)
11 May 1840 - 13 September 1874
Line Operational – Demolished – No access
SK44227 78337 (a)

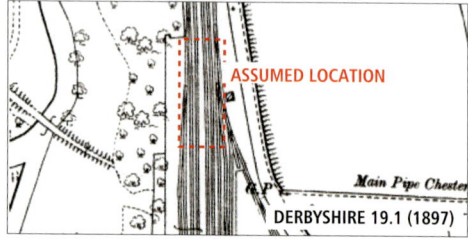

EDENHAM (E&LBR)
8 December 1857 - 17 October 1871
Line lifted – Demolished – Station site in commercial use
TF05856 22100

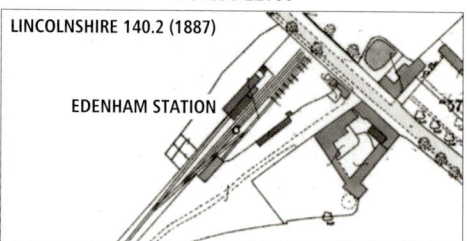

EDINBURGH CANAL STREET (NBR)
17 May 1847 - 2 March 1868
Line lifted – Demolished – Station site occupied by a public square
NT25722 73925

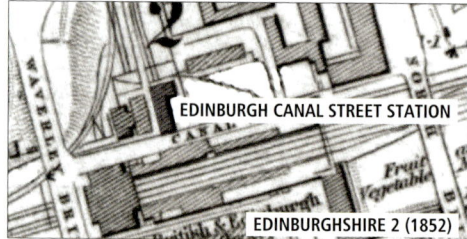

EDINBURGH LOTHIAN ROAD (CR)
15 February 1848 - 2 May 1870
Line lifted – Demolished – Station site in commercial use
NT24717 73340

EGGINTON (NSR)
13 July 1849 - 1 July 1878
Line Operational – Demolished – No access
SK25429 29464 (a)

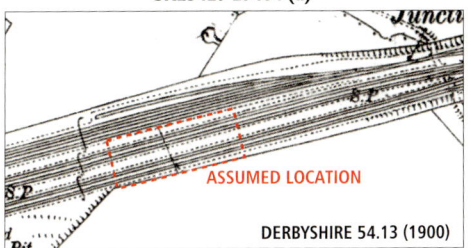

DERBYSHIRE 54.13 (1900)

ELLAND (1st) (L&YR)
12 April 1841 - 1 August 1865
Line Operational – Demolished – No access **SE10672 21561**

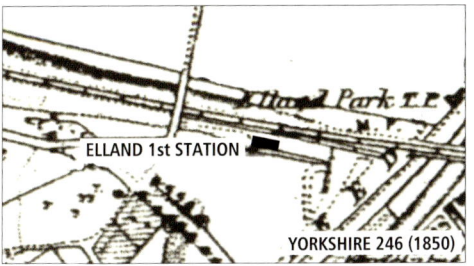

YORKSHIRE 246 (1850)

ELSECAR* (GCR)
1870 - c1871
Line lifted – Demolished – A pathway passes through the station site **SE38796 00163 (e)**

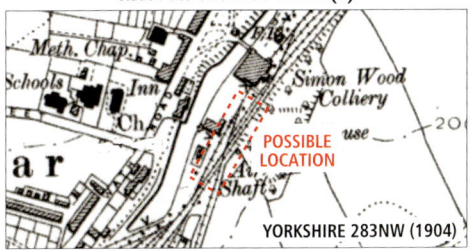

YORKSHIRE 283NW (1904)

ENFIELD LOCK (1st) (GER)
2 April 1855 - c1891
Line Operational – Demolished – No access **TQ36424 98804**

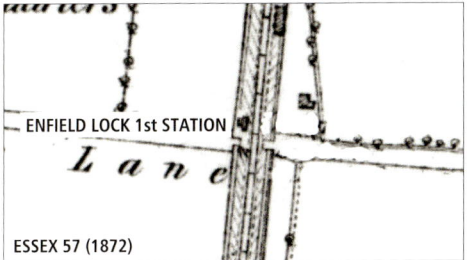

ESSEX 57 (1872)

EGGINTON - ETRURIA (1st)

ESKETT (WC&ER)
1 February 1864 - 11 June 1872
Line lifted – Demolished – Station site unused
NY04760 16420 (a)

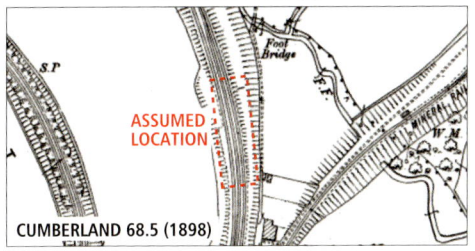

CUMBERLAND 68.5 (1898)

ESTON (1st) (NER)
June 1853 - 22 November 1885
Line Operational – Demolished – No access
NZ53688 21380 (a)

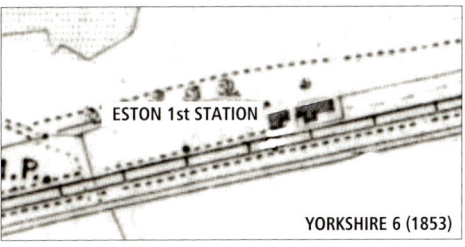

YORKSHIRE 6 (1853)

ETHERLEY (1st) (NER)
1844 - Prior to October 1867
Line Mothballed – Demolished **NZ17329 30335**

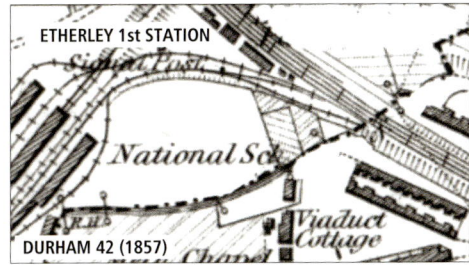

DURHAM 42 (1857)

ETRURIA (1st) (NSR)
9 October 1844 - 2 August 1874
Line Operational – Demolished – No access
SJ86489 47069 (a)

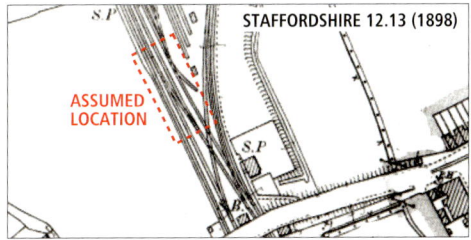

STAFFORDSHIRE 12.13 (1898)

ETTERIDGE CROSSING - FALKIRK CAMELON

ETTERIDGE CROSSING (HR)
Not known
Line Operational – Demolished – No access **NN68404 92675**

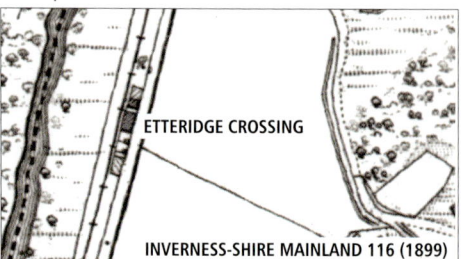

INVERNESS-SHIRE MAINLAND 116 (1899)

EUXTON (1st) (L&NWR)
31 October 1838 - 2 September 1895
Line Operational – Demolished – No access **SD55540 19557**

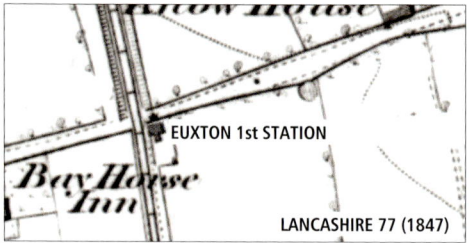

LANCASHIRE 77 (1847)

EVENWOOD (1st) (NER)
13 October 1858 - May 1864
Line lifted – Demolished – A pathway passes through the station site **NZ15164 26204**

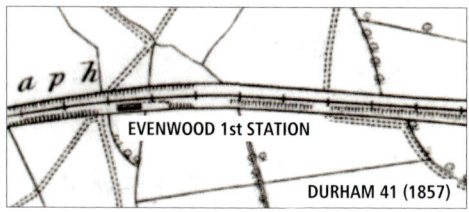

DURHAM 41 (1857)

EXETER TERMINUS (B&ER)
1 May 1844 - c1862
Line Operational - Demolished **SX91152 93382 (a)**

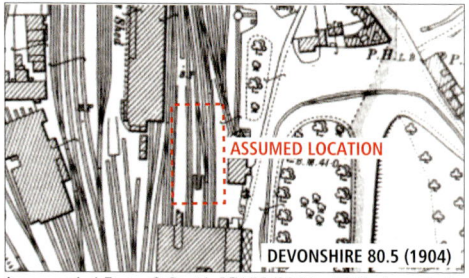

DEVONSHIRE 80.5 (1904)

An expanded *Exeter St Davids [GWR]* (30 May 1846 -) was built on the station site.

EXHIBITION (MSJn&AR)
May 1857 - October 1887
Line Operated by Manchester Metrolink - Demolished **SJ81186 95544**

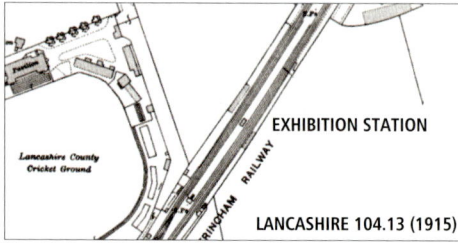

LANCASHIRE 104.13 (1915)

Warwick Road [MSJn&AR] (11 May 1931 – 25 December 1991) was built on the same site. This was subsequently demolished and replaced by *Old Trafford Metrolink* (15 June 1992 -).

FAIRFIELD (MS&LR)
17 November 1841 - 2 May 1892
Line Operational – Demolished – No access **SJ90161 97147**

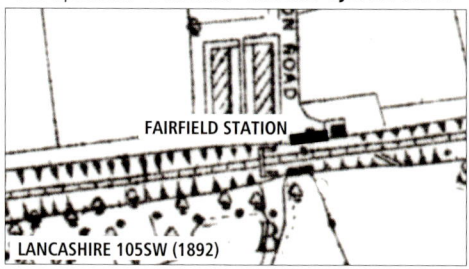

LANCASHIRE 105SW (1892)

FAIRFIELDS SIDING (NBR)
June 1861 - c1867
Line lifted – Demolished – The A811 passes through the station site **NS64036 95503**

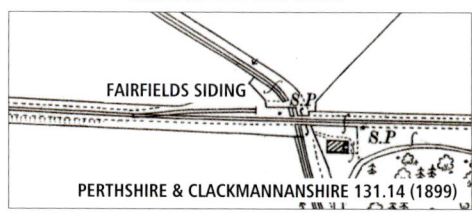

PERTHSHIRE & CLACKMANNANSHIRE 131.14 (1899)

FALKIRK CAMELON (E&GR)
November 1843 - October 1844
Line Operational – Demolished – No access
NS86497 79553 (a)

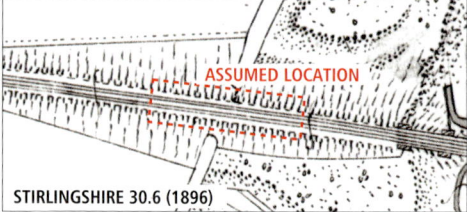

STIRLINGSHIRE 30.6 (1896)

FALMER (1st) (LB&SCR)
8 June 1846 – 1 August 1865
Line Operational – Demolished – No access
TQ35822 08917 (a)

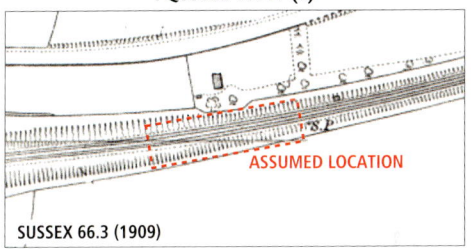

FIGHTING COCKS (NER)
November 1846 – 1 July 1887
Line lifted – Demolished – A footpath passes through the station site **NZ34248 14183**

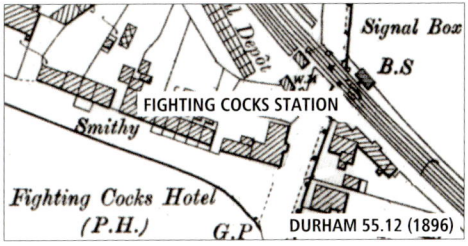

FARRINGDON STREET (1st) (MetR)
10 January 1863 – 1 March 1866
Line Operational – Demolished **TQ31571 81777**

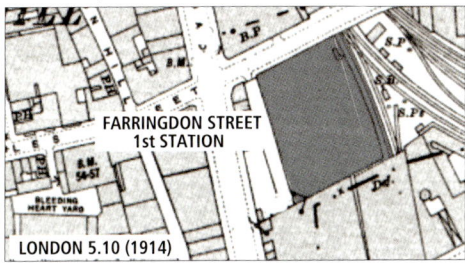

FILTON (1st) (GWR)
8 September 1863 – 4 October 1886
Line Operational – Demolished – No access **ST61132 78871**

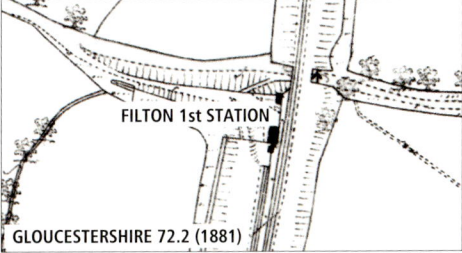

FELLING (1st) (NER)
12 October 1839 – 18 November 1896
Line Operated by Tyne and Wear Metro – Demolished – Station building extant **NZ27633 62110**

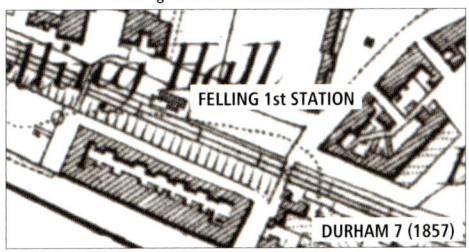

FINCHLEY ROAD (1st) (MR)
13 July 1868 – 3 February 1884
Line Operational – Demolished – No access **TQ26152 84858**

FERNIEGAIR (CR)
1 December 1866 – 2 October 1876
Line lifted – Demolished – Station site occupied by housing in O'Donnell Gardens **NS74107 54564**

FINDHORN (HR)
18 April 1860 – 1 February 1869
Line lifted – Demolished – Station site landscaped
NJ03887 64399

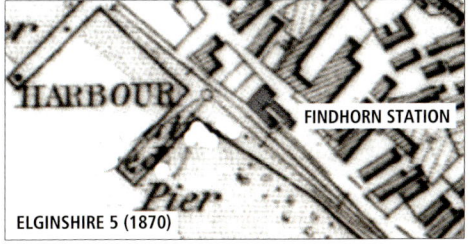

FISHERROW - FOREST HALL

FISHERROW (NBR)
1831 - 1 February 1847
Line lifted – Demolished – Station site partially landscaped and partially occupied by a filling station **NT33419 72885**

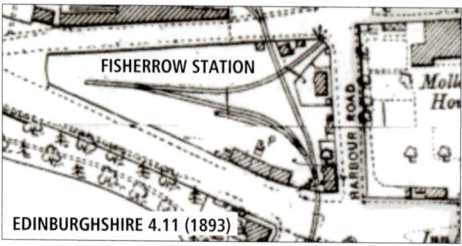
EDINBURGHSHIRE 4.11 (1893)

FLAX BOURTON (1st) (GWR)
1 September 1860 - 2 March 1893
Line Operational – Demolished – No access **ST51755 69711**

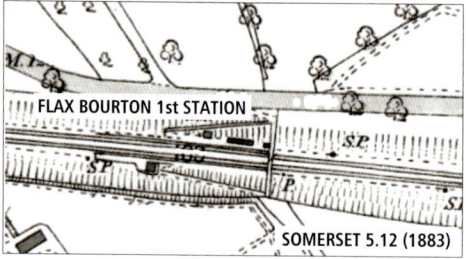
SOMERSET 5.12 (1883)

FLEETWOOD (1st) (P&WR)
16 July 1840 - 15 July 1883
Line lifted – Demolished – Station site in commercial use
SD33918 47769

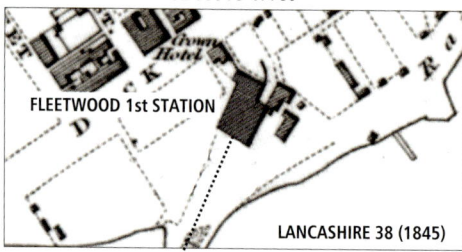
LANCASHIRE 38 (1845)

FLOW MOSS (L&MR)
Prior to September 1838 - 29 October 1842
Line Operational – Demolished – No access **SJ69060 97085**

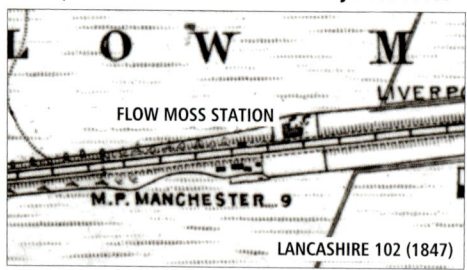
LANCASHIRE 102 (1847)

FLUSHDYKE (1st) (GNR)
2 April 1864 - 1867
Line lifted – Demolished – Station site in commercial use
SE28879 21156

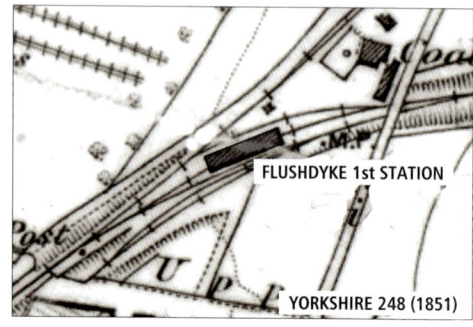
YORKSHIRE 248 (1851)

FOLKESTONE HARBOUR (SER)
1 January 1849 - 1856
Line Operational – Demolished **TR23341 35839**

FOLKESTONE PIER (SER)
4 March 1876 - 1883
Line lifted – Demolished – Station site in dockyard use

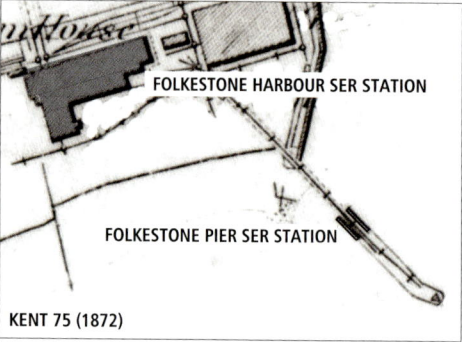
KENT 75 (1872)

FOREST HALL (B&TR)
27 June 1864 - 1 March 1871
Line Operated by Tyne & Wear Metro – Demolished
NZ28548 69344

NORTHUMBERLAND 89 (1858)

FORFAR (AberdeenR) - FRANKLAND

FORFAR (AberdeenR)
4 December 1838 - 2 August 1848
Line lifted – Demolished – Station site occupied by housing in Victoria Street **NO45804 51023**

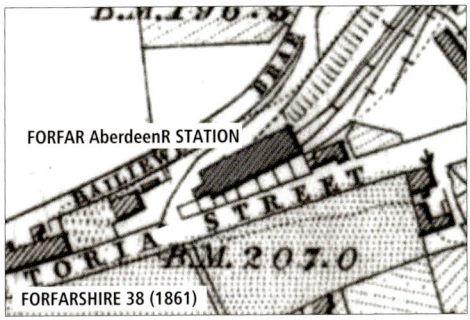

FORYD PIER* (VoCR)
August 1859 - 1 October 1865
Line lifted – Demolished – Station site occupied by boat storage area for the "Rhyl Yacht Club" **SH99372 80704 (a)**

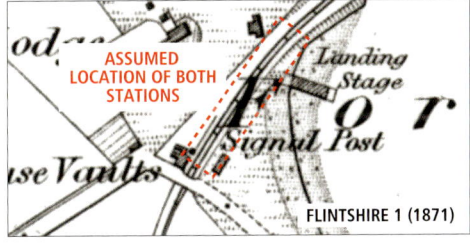

FOTHERBY GATE HOUSE (GNR)
September 1863 - 28 June 1872
Line lifted – Demolished – Station site unused **TF32074 91645**

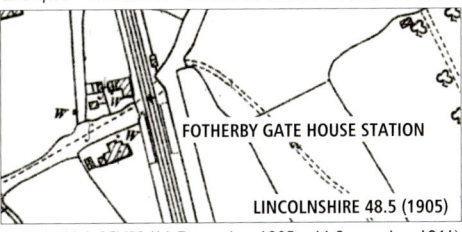

Fotherby Halt [GNR] (11 December 1905 – 11 September 1961) was built on the same site

FORRES (I&AJnR)
25 March 1858 - 3 August 1863
Line Operational – Demolished – The approach road to Forres Station passes through the station site **NJ03203 59128**

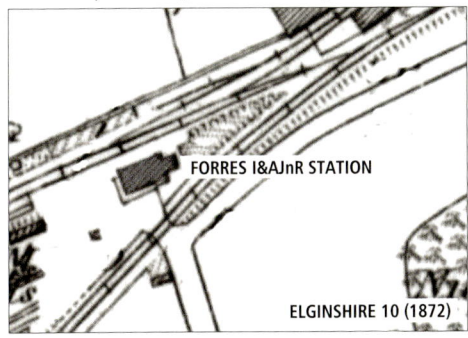

FOULSHIELS* (E&BR)
May 1850 - 1852
Line lifted – Demolished – A pathway passes through the station site **NS97141 63689**

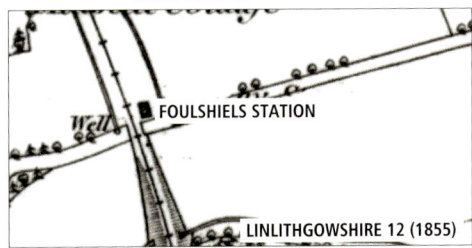

FORYD (1st) (L&NWR)
5 October 1858 - 20 April 1885
Line lifted – Demolished – A track passes through the station site **SH99503 79753**

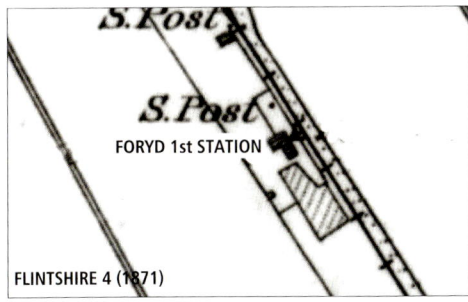

FRANKLAND (NER)
March 1861 - July 1877
Line lifted – Demolished – Station site unused **NZ28937 45226 (a)**

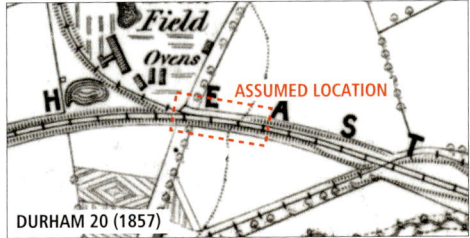

FORYD PIER* (L&NWR)
1 October 1865 - 20 April 1885
Line lifted – Demolished – Station site occupied by boat storage area for the "Rhyl Yacht Club" **SH99372 80704 (a)**
SEE MAP IN NEXT COLUMN

FRIDEN – GARTSHERRIE (MonklandR)

FRIDEN (L&NWR)
June 1833 – December 1877
Line lifted – Demolished – The High Peak Trail passes through the station site **SK17115 60804**

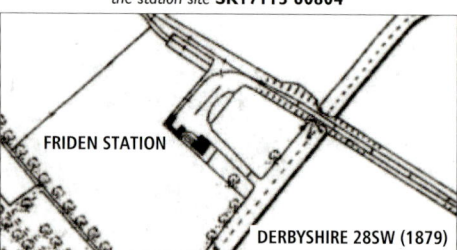

FRODINGHAM (MS&LR)
1 October 1866 – 2 January 1888
Line Operational – Demolished – No access **SE90443 11196**

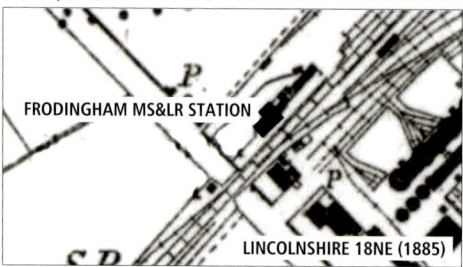

FUGAR BAR (BlingJnR)
18 June 1842 – August 1844
Line lifted – Demolished – Station site unused
NZ21853 59706 (a)

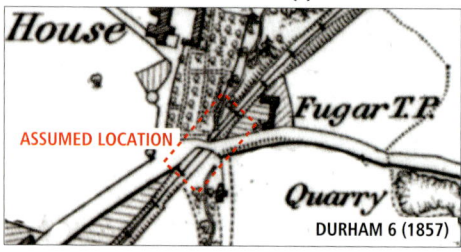

FULLERTON (1st) (L&SWR)
6 March 1865 – 1 June 1885
Line lifted – Demolished **SU37965 39485**

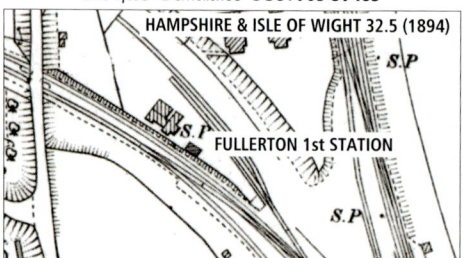

GARNANT (1st) (GWR)
1 May 1850 – 20 March 1865
Line lifted – Demolished – Station site in the rear garden of a dwelling in Cwmamman Road **SN69329 13089**

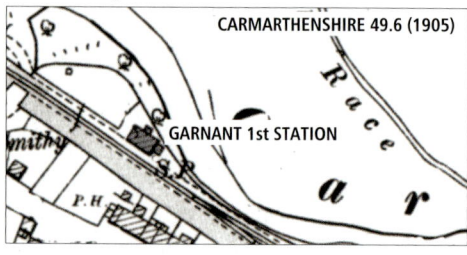

GARNQUEEN (MonklandR)
10 December 1849 – 10 December 1851
Line lifted – Demolished – The Inchneuk Path passes through the station site **NS71999 68578 (a)**

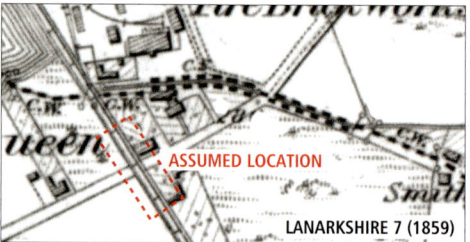

GARTH AND VAN ROAD (VanR)
1 December 1873 – July 1879
Line lifted – Demolished – A driveway passes through the station site **SN95044 87405**

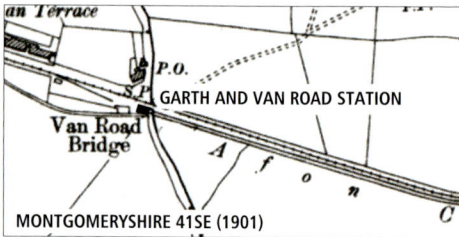

GARTSHERRIE (MonklandR)
1 October 1826 – 10 December 1851
Line lifted – Demolished – Station site unused **NS72245 66715**

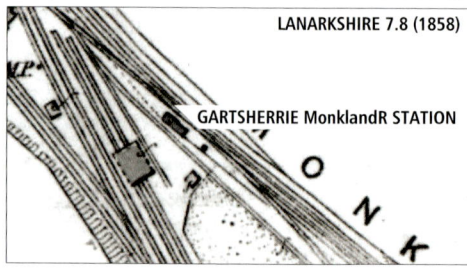

GATCOMBE (PURTON PASSAGE) (GWR)
August 1852 – 1 April 1869
Line Operational – Demolished **SO67110 04584**

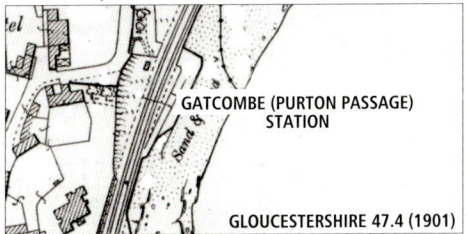

GATCOMBE (PURTON PASSAGE) - GLASGOW TOWNHEAD

GLASGOW DUNLOP STREET (CoGUR)
12 December 1870 – 17 October 1876
Line lifted – Demolished – Station site occupied by the "St Enoch Shopping Centre" **NS59129 64939**

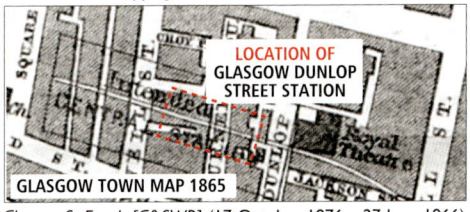

Glasgow St Enoch [G&SWR] (17 October 1876 – 27 June 1966) was built on the station site

GELLY-CEIDRIM (LlnyR)
November 1851 – December 1861
Line Operational for Freight – Demolished **SN68204 13504 (a)**

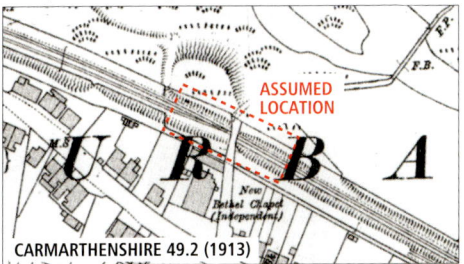

GLASGOW MAIN STREET (G&SWR)
1871 – 20 August 1900
Line Operational – Demolished – No access **NS58976 64036**

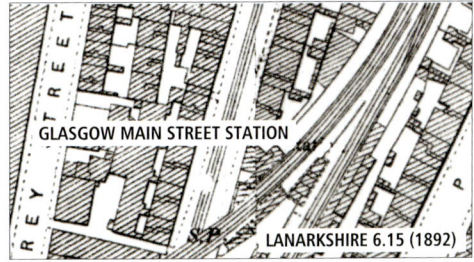

GIRVAN (OLD) (G&SWR)
24 May 1860 – 1 April 1893
Line lifted – Demolished – Station site unused **NX18603 98379**

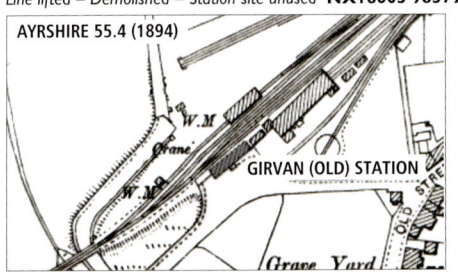

GLASGOW SOUTH SIDE (CR)
20 September 1848 – 1 July 1879
Line lifted – Demolished – Station site in commercial use
NS58833 63797

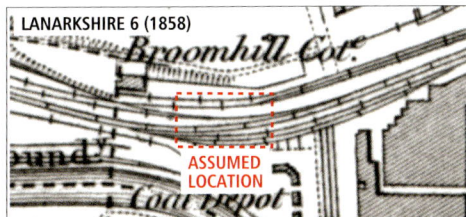

GLAIS (1st) (MR)
21 February 1860 – 1 March 1875
Line lifted – Demolished – Station site in domestic use
SN70362 00551

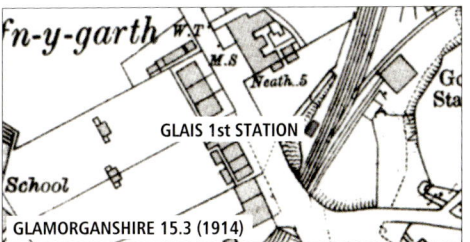

GLASGOW TOWNHEAD (CR)
1 June 1831 – 1 November 1849
Line lifted – Demolished – Station site partially occupied by the eastbound carriageway of the M8 and partially landscaped
NS59871 66302 (a)

GLENELLRIG (MonklandR)
c1848 - 1 January 1850
Line lifted – Demolished – Station site in agricultural use
NS88818 73365 (a)

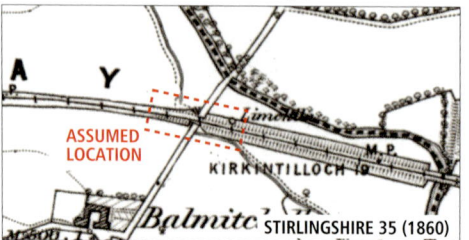
STIRLINGSHIRE 35 (1860)

GLENESK (NBR)
October 1855 - Post 1886
Line Operational – Demolished – No access
NT32371 67094 (a)

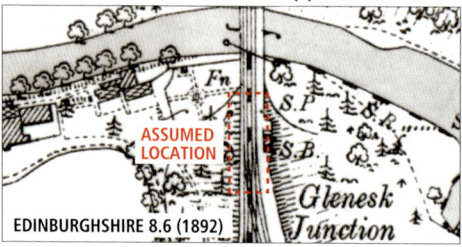
EDINBURGHSHIRE 8.6 (1892)

GLENFIELD (1st) (MR)
18 July 1832 - 1875
Line lifted – Demolished – A pathway passes through the station site **SK54208 06522 (a)**

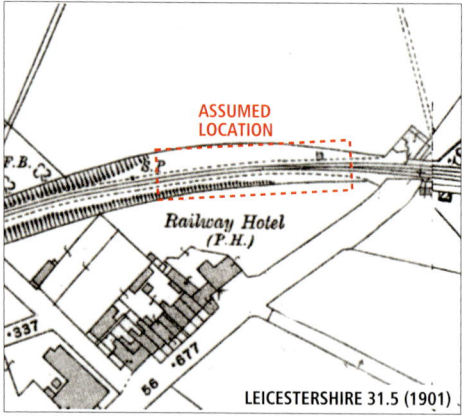
LEICESTERSHIRE 31.5 (1901)

GLOUCESTER (1st) (GWR)
8 July 1844 - 22 May 1854
Line Operational – Demolished **SO83740 18515 (a)**

GLOUCESTER (2nd) (GWR)
19 September 1851 - cSeptember 1852
Line Operational – Demolished **SO83751 18528 (a)**

GLOUCESTER (1st) (MR)
4 November 1840 - 12 April 1896
Line lifted – Demolished – Station site occupied by car park for Gloucester Station **SO83700 18499**

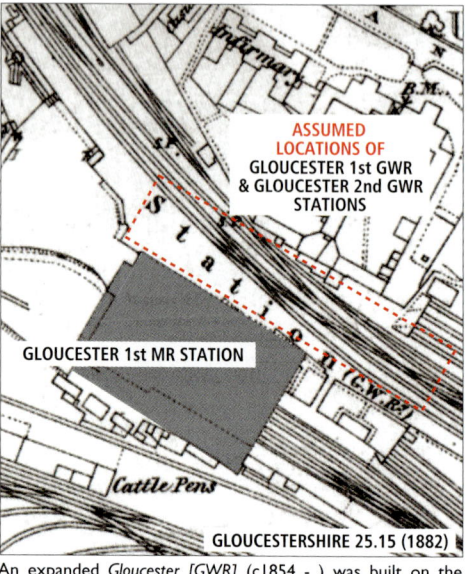
GLOUCESTERSHIRE 25.15 (1882)

An expanded *Gloucester [GWR]* (c1854 -) was built on the station sites of *Gloucester 1st* and *2nd [GWR]*

GLOUCESTER (T-STATION) (GWR)
23 October 1847 - 19 September 1851
Line lifted – Demolished – Station site partially in commercial use **SO84659 17771**

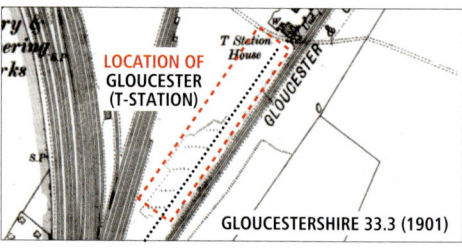
GLOUCESTERSHIRE 33.3 (1901)

GLYNRHONWY (L&NWR)
April 1870 - c1874
Line lifted – Demolished – Station site in commercial use **SH57214 60988 (a)**

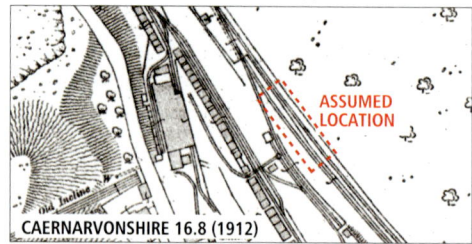
CAERNARVONSHIRE 16.8 (1912)

GOATHLAND (1st) (NER)
26 May 1836 - 1 July 1865
Line lifted – Demolished – A pathway passes through the station site **NZ83254 01556**

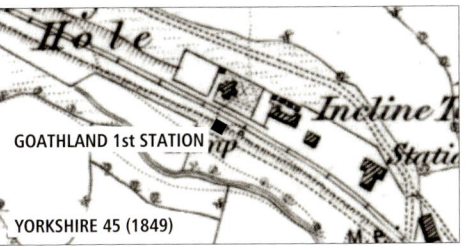

GOATHLAND (1st) - GRANVILLE STREET
GOOSEHOUSE (BBC&WYorksR)
3 August 1847 - 1849
Line Operational – Demolished – No access
SD69080 23676 (a)

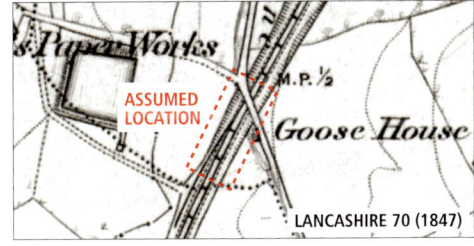

GODALMING OLD (L&SWR)
15 October 1849 - 1 May 1897
Line lifted – Demolished – Station site partially occupied by dwellings in Old Station Way and partially in commercial use
SU97393 44459

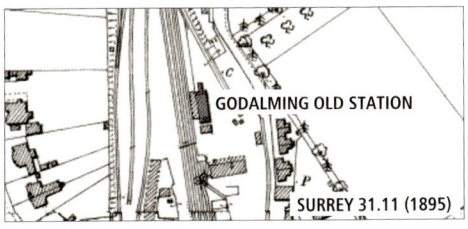

GORING (1st) (GWR)
1 June 1840 - 29 February 1892
Line Operational – Demolished – No access **SU60215 80747**

GODLEY TOLL BAR (SAuL&MR)
17 November 1841 - 11 December 1842
Line Operational – Demolished – No access
SJ96474 94997 (a)

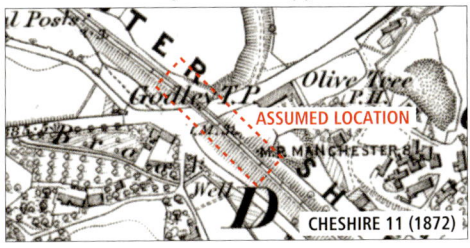

GRANTHAM OLD WHARF (AN&B&EJnR)
15 July 1850 - 2 August 1852
Line lifted – Demolished – Station site in commercial use
SK90847 35611

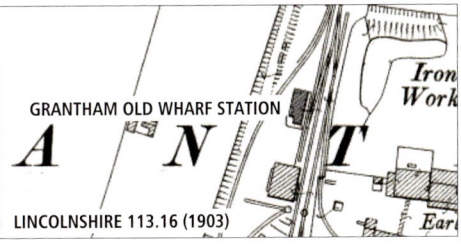

GOOLE (L&YR)
1 April 1848 - 1 October 1879
Line lifted – Demolished – Station site absorbed into docks
SE74635 23418

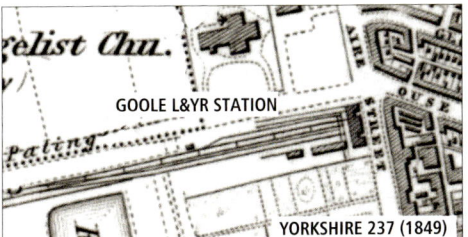

GRANVILLE STREET (MR)
3 April 1876 - 1 July 1885
Line lifted – Demolished – Station site unused
SP06254 86285 (a)

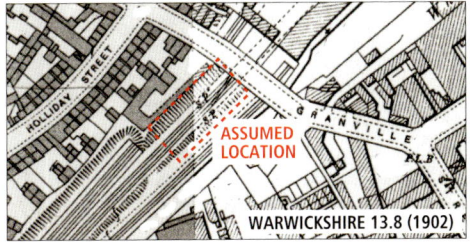

GRAVESEND CANAL BASIN - GREENWICH (L&GrR)

GRAVESEND CANAL BASIN (SER)
10 February 1845 - 30 July 1849
Line lifted – Demolished – Station site in commercial use
TQ65701 74231 (a)

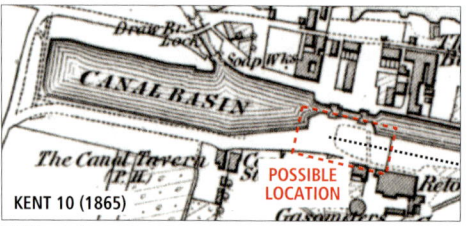

NB Track disposition also unknown

GRAYRIGG (L&CR)
8 July 1848 - 1 November 1849
Line Operational – Demolished – No access **SD57011 95840**

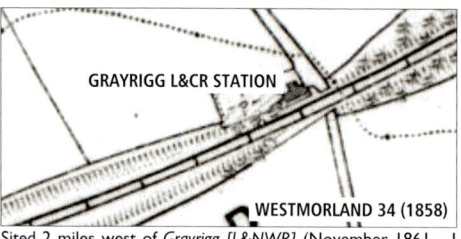

Sited 2 miles west of Grayrigg [L&NWR] (November 1861 - 1 February 1954)

GREAT BARR (1st) (L&NWR)
1 October 1862 - 25 March 1899
Line Operational – Demolished – No access **SP04858 92493**

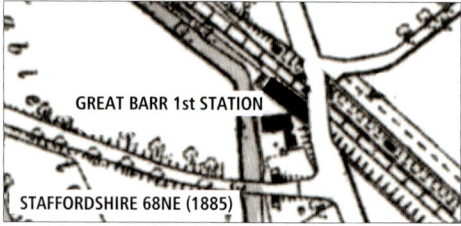

GREENESFIELD (YN&BR)
15 January 1839 - 30 August 1850
Line lifted – Demolished – Station site occupied by dwellings
NZ25190 63354

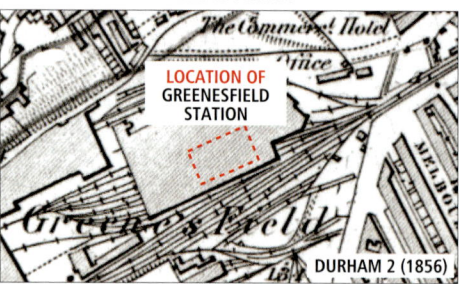

GREENOCK CATHCART STREET (CR)
31 March 1841 - 1 June 1889
Line lifted – Demolished – Station Avenue passes through the station site **NS28199 75996**

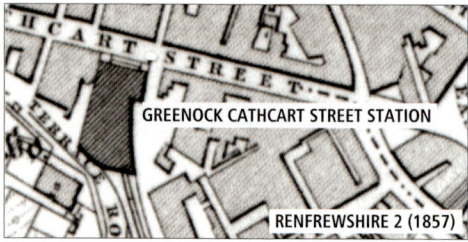

GREENOCK PRINCES PIER (1st) (G&SWR)
23 December 1869 - 25 May 1894
Line lifted – Demolished – Station site part of "Clydeport Container Terminal" **NS27411 77014**

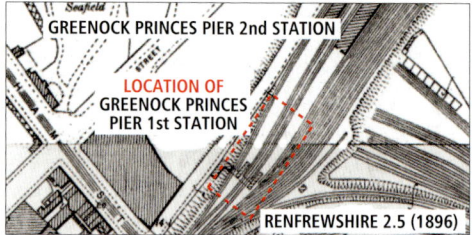

The south west end of Greenock Princes Pier 2nd [G&SWR] (25 May 1894 – 2 February 1959) occupied the station site

GREENS OF DRAINIE (MorayshireR)
4 June 1853 - 1898
Line lifted – Demolished – Station site unused **NJ23501 68120**

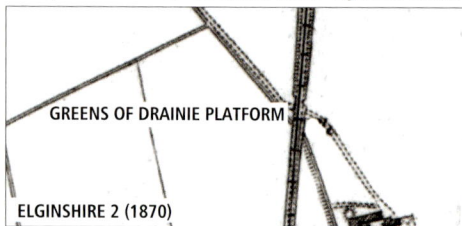

GREENWICH (L&GrR)
24 December 1838 - 12 April 1840
Line Operational – Demolished – No access
TQ37725 77316 (a)

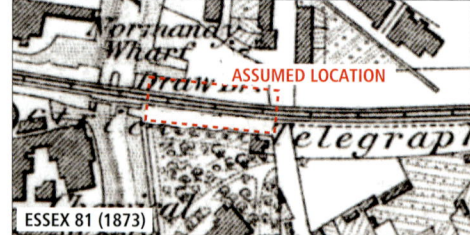

GREENWICH (SER)
12 April 1840 - 11 January 1877
Line Operational – Demolished – Part of station site occupied by current Greenwich Station building and forecourt
TQ38048 77320

GRESLEY (MR)
1 March 1849 - c1869
Line Operational – Demolished – No access
SK28250 17789 (a)

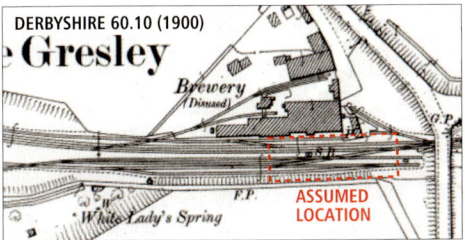

GRIMESTHORPE BRIDGE (S&RR)
24 November 1838 - 1 February 1843
Line Operational – Demolished – No access
SK37925 90013 (a)

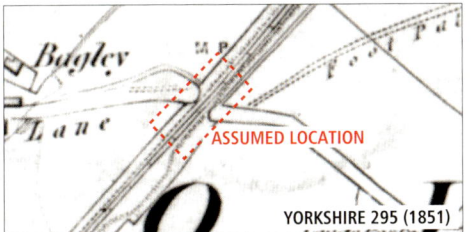

GUPWORTHY* (WSsetMinR)
4 September 1865 - 7 November 1898
Line lifted – Demolished – Station building in private use
SS96251 35556

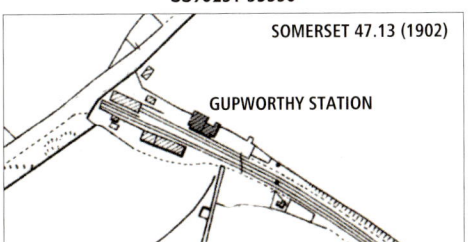

GREENWICH (SER) - HALIFAX SHAW SYKE
HACKNEY (NLR)
26 September 1850 - 1 December 1870
Line Operational – Demolished – No access **TQ34988 84932**

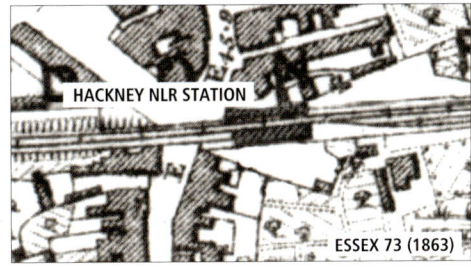

HAFOD (TVR)
30 August 1861 - 17 October 1892
Line Operational – Demolished – No access **ST04100 91163**

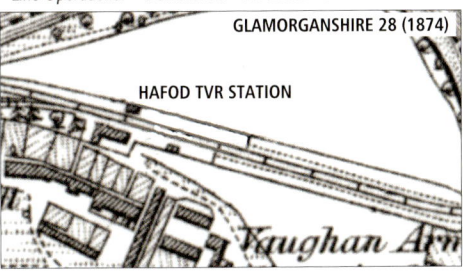

HALESWORTH (1st) (GER)
4 December 1854 - June 1856
Line Operational – Demolished – No access
TM38840 77945 (a)

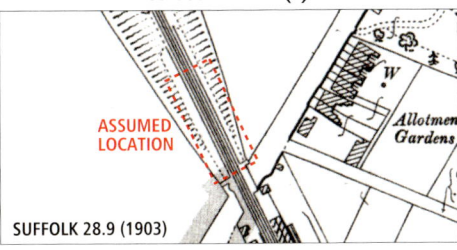

HALIFAX SHAW SYKE (L&YR)
1 July 1844 - 7 August 1850
Line lifted – Demolished – Station site occupied by the car park for a "B&M Homestore" **SE09548 24504**

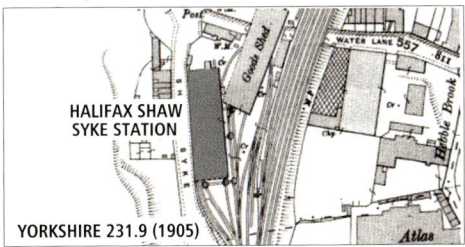

HALLILOO PLATFORM - HARPUR HILL

HALLILOO PLATFORM* (SE&CR)
1856 - 1 January 1900
Line Operational – Demolished – No access **TQ34422 57354**

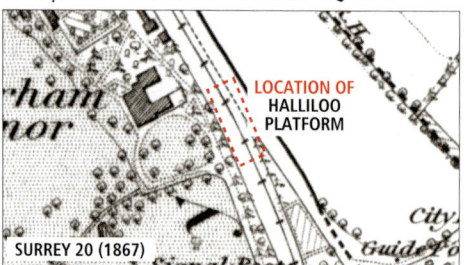

HAMPTON (1st) (L&NWR)
17 September 1838 - 1 September 1884
Main Line Operational – Demolished - Station building and ticket and parcels building Grade II listed **SP20280 81592**

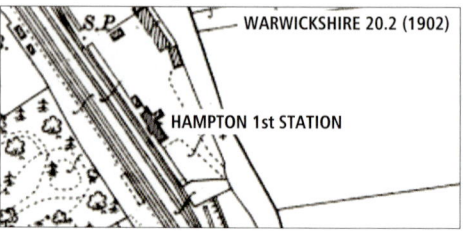

The B&DJR line from Whitacre was accommodated at the station from 12 August 1839 and, after the L&NWR platforms were removed in 1884, continued to use it until closed by the MR 1 January 1917

HALLIWELL (L&YR)
15 October 1877 - 1 October 1879
Line lifted – Demolished – Station site occupied by the Waters Meeting Road/Hereford Street roundabout and commercial premises **SD71871 10425 (a)**

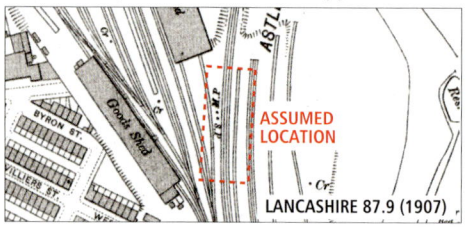

HAMWORTHY (L&SWR)
1 June 1847 - 1 July 1896
Line Operational for Freight – Demolished **SZ00363 90114**

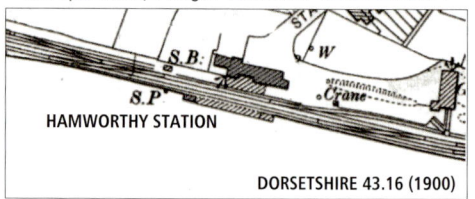

HALTON DIAL (NER)
January 1851 - February 1864
Line Operational – Demolished – No access
SE33926 33981 (a)

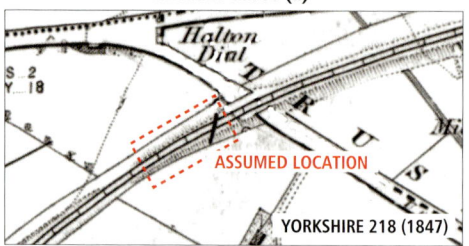

HANLEY (1st) (NSR)
13 July 1864 - 1 November 1873
Line lifted – Demolished – Station site in commercial use
SJ88033 47568

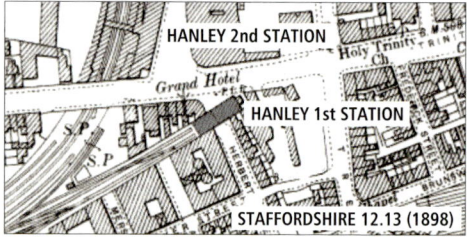

HAMPSTEAD ROAD (1st) (NLR)
9 June 1851 - 5 May 1855
Line Operational – Demolished – No access
TQ28251 84280 (a)

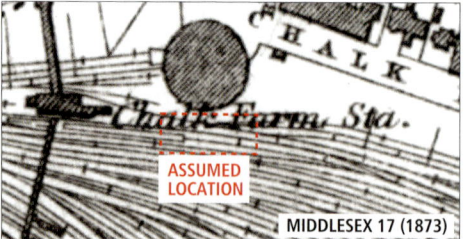

HARPUR HILL (L&NWR)
June 1833 - December 1877
Line lifted – Demolished – The High Peak Trail passes through the station site **SK06508 70893 (a)**

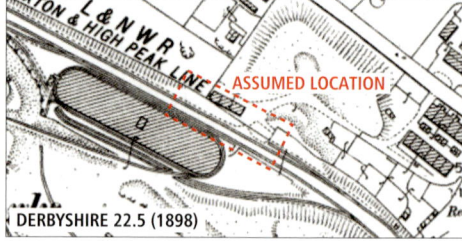

HARROGATE BRUNSWICK (NER)
20 July 1848 - 1 August 1862
Line lifted – Demolished – Station site landscaped (A plaque and stone mark the site) **SE30282 54636**

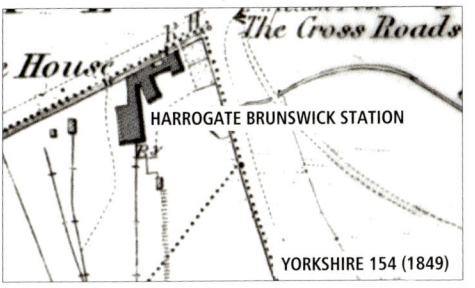

HARROGATE BRUNSWICK - HAWICK (1st)
HASWELL (2nd) (NER)
30 August 1836 - 1 November 1877
Line lifted – Demolished – Station site unused
NZ37541 43662 (e)

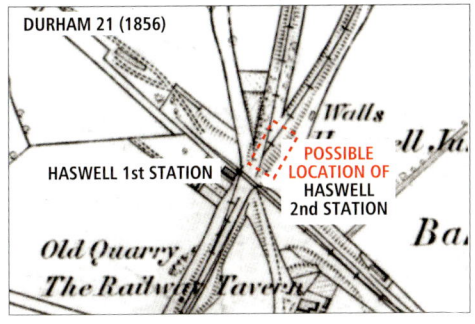

HARTLEY PIT (B&TR)
3 May 1847 - 1851
Line Operational for Freight – Demolished **NZ31162 76714**

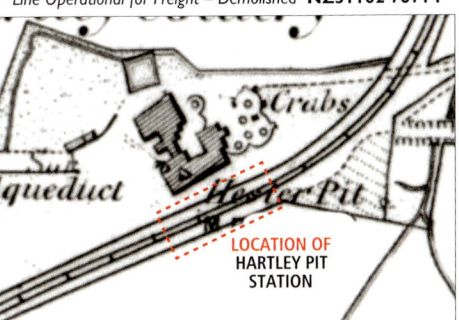

HATTON (CR)
16 December 1831 - October 1865
Line lifted – Demolished – A farm track passes through the station site **NO30684 40608**

HAUGHLEY ROAD (EUnionR)
24 December 1846 - 9 July 1849
Line Operational – Demolished – Part of station building possibly extant **TM02907 63342**

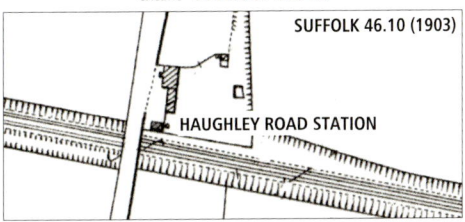

HARWICH TOWN (1st) (GER)
15 August 1854 - March 1865
Line lifted – Demolished – Station site unused
TM25950 32522 (a)

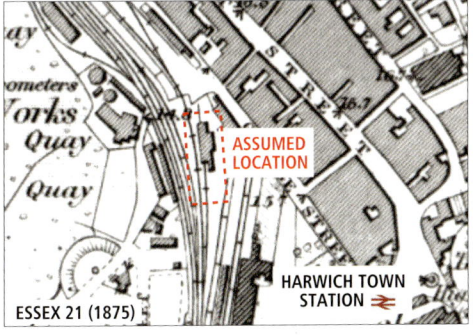

HAWICK (1st) (NBR)
29 October 1849 - 1 July 1862
Line lifted – Demolished – The A7, Dovermount Place, passes through the station site **NT50437 15253**

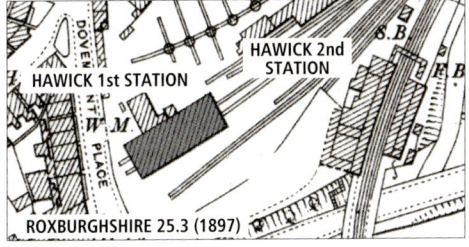

HASWELL (1st) (NER)
23 November 1835 - 1 November 1877
Line lifted – Demolished – Station site unused
NZ37506 43661
SEE MAP IN NEXT COLUMN

63

HAYBURN WYKE (1st) (NER)
16 July 1885 - 1900
Line lifted – Demolished – The Scarborough to Whitby Rail Trail passes through the station site **TA00703 96828**

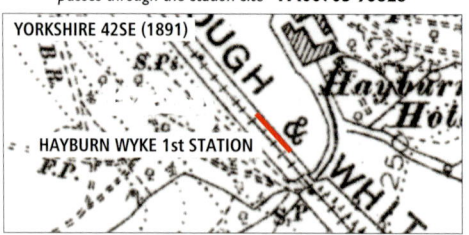

Hayburn Wyke 2nd [NER] (1900 – 8 March 1965) was built on the opposite side of the track

HAY LANE (GWR)
17 December 1840 - 31 May 1841
Line Operational – Demolished – No access
SU10892 82434 (a)

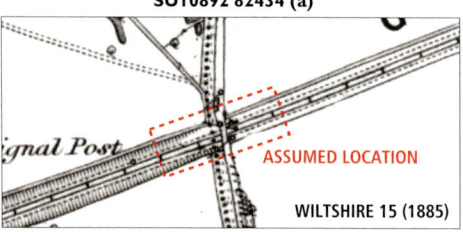

HAYLE (WCwallR)
23 May 1843 - 16 February 1852
Line lifted – Demolished – Station site occupied by the "RNLI Memorial Gardens" **SW55856 37198**

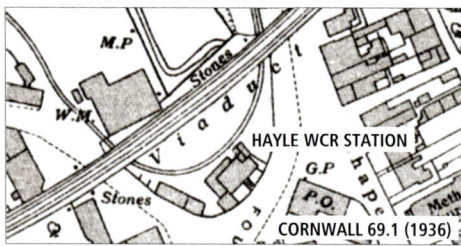

HAYLE RIVIERE BRIDGE (WCwallR)
23 May 1843 - 16 February 1852
Line lifted – Demolished – The King George V Memorial Walk passes through the station site **SW55854 37778 (a)**

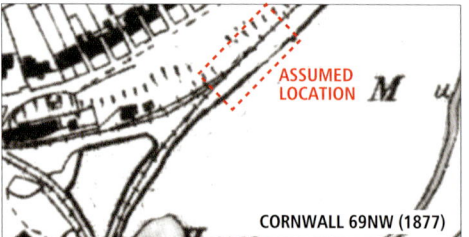

HAY PARK LANE, KNARESBOROUGH (Y&NM)
30 October 1848 - 21 July 1851
Line Operational – Demolished – No access **SE35935 57533 (a)**

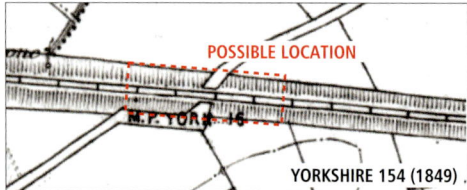

The line crossed Hay Park Lane at two points, the one indicated above and one further east at **SE36863 57461**. The location of the station is not known

HEADLESS CROSS (E&GR)
2 June 1845 - December 1852
Line lifted – Demolished – Station site unused **NS90718 58795**

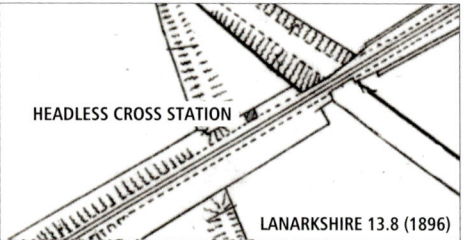

HEATHFIELD (M&CR)
30 November 1844 - c1846
Line Operational – Demolished – No access
NY17314 44035 (a)

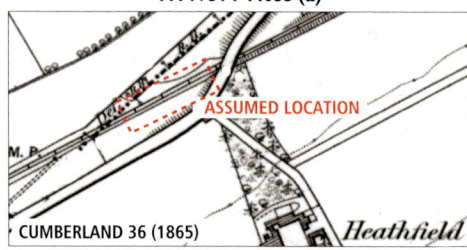

HEATON (1st) (New&BR)
July 1847 - 1 April 1887
Line Operational – Demolished – No access **NZ26980 65177**

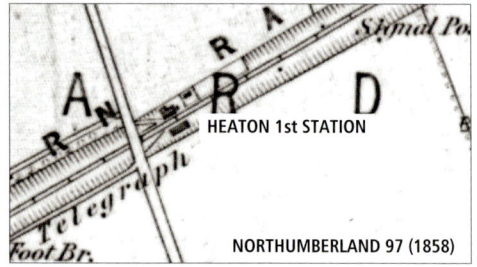

HEATON LODGE (L&NWR)
2 August 1847 - 31 October 1864
Lines Operational – Demolished – No access **SE18538 20493**

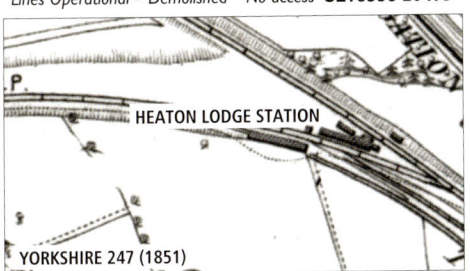

HENDON BURN (LderryS&SR)
HEATON LODGE - HERNE BAY (1st)
1 July 1855 - 1 October 1868
Line Operational – Demolished – No access **NZ40943 56503**

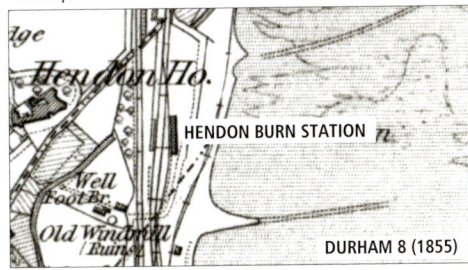

HECKMONDWIKE (1st) (L&YR)
18 July 1848 - 9 August 1888
Line lifted – Demolished – Station site occupied by housing in Carriage Way **SE21593 23120**

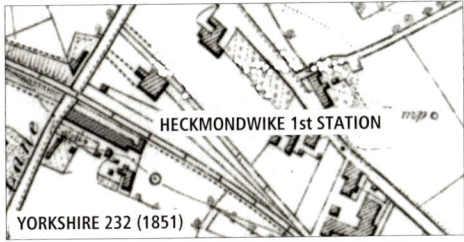

HEREFORD BARTON (GWR)
2 January 1854 - 2 January 1893
Line lifted – Demolished – Station Road passes over the station site **SO50417 40020**

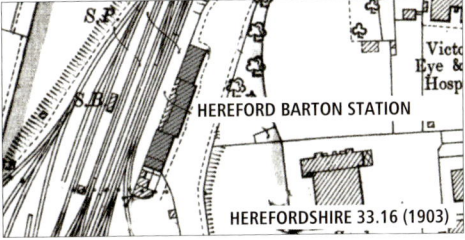

HELLIFIELD (1st) (MR)
30 July 1849 - 1 June 1880
Line Operational – Demolished – No access **SD85745 56789**

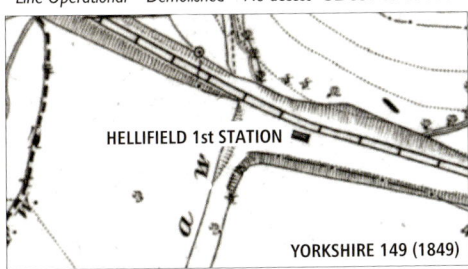

HEREFORD MOORFIELDS (HH&BR)
30 June 1863 - 1 April 1874
Line lifted – Demolished – Station site occupied by dwellings in Attlee Close **SO50507 40567**

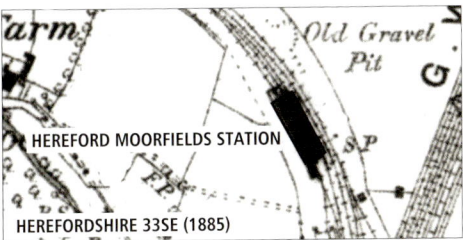

HENDON (NER)
1 May 1858 - 4 August 1879
Line Operational – Demolished – No access **NZ40915 56764**

HERNE BAY (1st) (L&CDR)
13 July 1861 - 5 October 1863
Line Operational – Demolished – No access
TR16430 67320 (a)

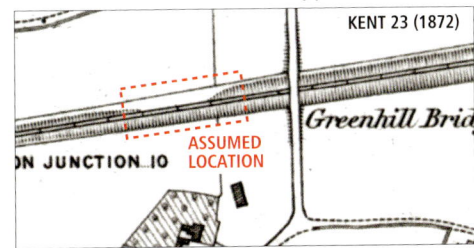

HERTFORD (1st) - HOGHTON TOWER

HERTFORD (1st) (GER)
31 October 1843 - 27 February 1888
Line lifted – Demolished – Station site occupied by dwellings in Holden Close **TL33255 13005**

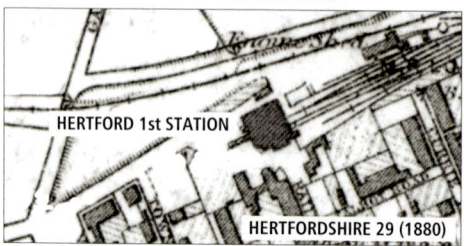
HERTFORDSHIRE 29 (1880)

HIGH STOOP (NER)
Not known
Line lifted – Demolished – Railway Cottages extant as dwellings **NZ10299 40116**

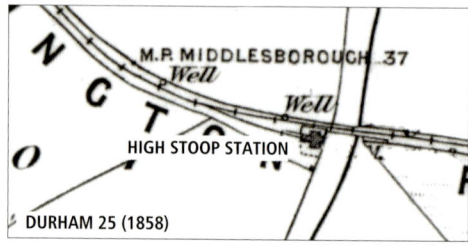
DURHAM 25 (1858)

HEXTHORPE (SYorks&RDNR)
1 February 1850 - February 1855
Line Operational – Demolished – No access **SE56171 01966 (a)**

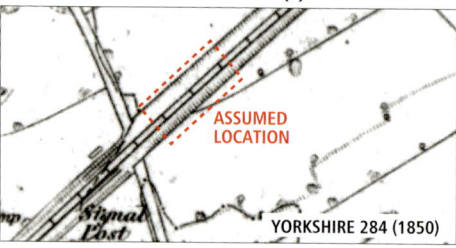
YORKSHIRE 284 (1850)

HIGH WYCOMBE (1st) (GWR/GCR)
1 August 1854 - 1 October 1864
Line lifted – Train shed and engine shed Grade II listed **SU86853 93050**

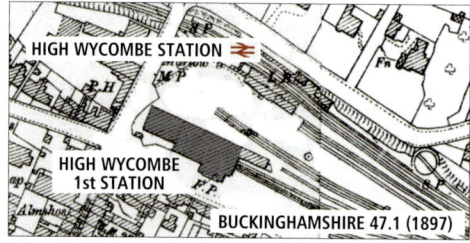
BUCKINGHAMSHIRE 47.1 (1897)

HEYWOOD (1st) (L&YR)
15 April 1841 - 1 May 1848
Line lifted – Demolished – Station site in commercial use **SD86296 10304**

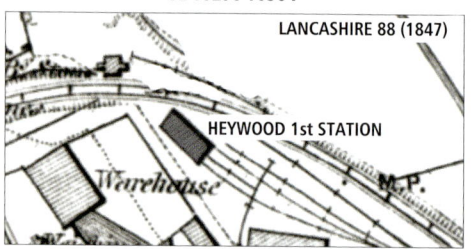
LANCASHIRE 88 (1847)

HINDHAUGH* (NBR)
c1866 - c1879
Line lifted – Demolished – Station site unused **NY88080 84603**

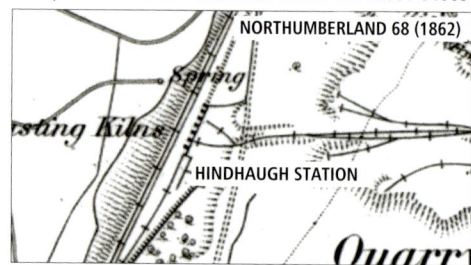
NORTHUMBERLAND 68 (1862)

HIGH SHIELDS (1st) (NER)
17 December 1842 - 2 June 1879
Line lifted – Demolished – Station site unused **NZ35860 66316**

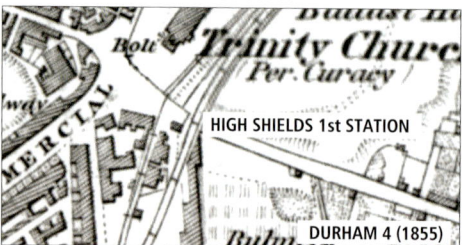
DURHAM 4 (1855)

HOGHTON TOWER (ELancsR)
May 1847 - October 1848
Line Operated by East Lancs Railway – Demolished **SD62290 26708**

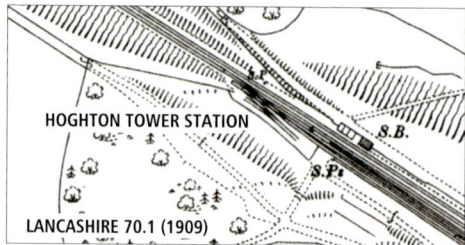
LANCASHIRE 70.1 (1909)

HOLBECK JUNCTION (NER)
2 July 1855 - 2 June 1862
Line lifted – Demolished – Station site unused **SE28812 33061**

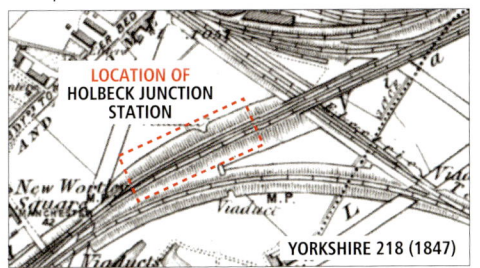

HOLYHEAD (C&HR)
HOLBECK JUNCTION - HOPTON TOP WHARF
1 August 1848 - 15 May 1851
Line lifted – Demolished – The A55 passes through the station site **SH24825 81844 (a)**

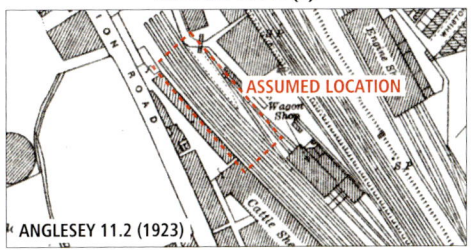

HOLLY BUSH (1st) (SirhowyR)
August 1871 - 31 August 1891
Line lifted – Demolished **SO16421 04229 (a)**

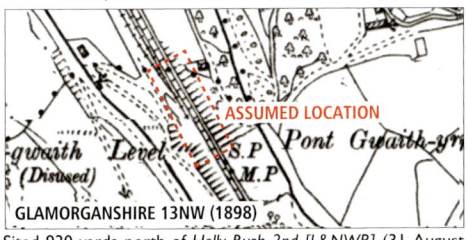

Sited 930 yards north of Holly Bush 2nd [L&NWR] (31 August 1891 – 13 June 1960)

HONINGTON (1st) (GNR)
1 July 1857 - 12 April 1867
Line Operational – Demolished – Station House in private use **SK94190 43693**

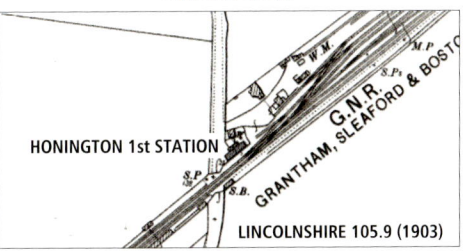

HOLLYM GATE (NER)
December 1854 - 1 September 1870
Line lifted – Demolished – A track passes through the station site **TA33110 25545**

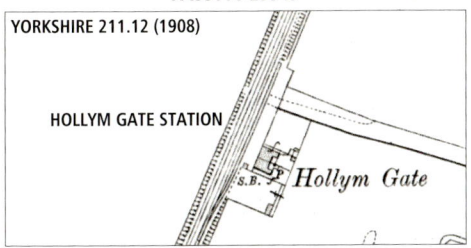

HOPESBROOK (GWR)
11 July 1853 - 2 June 1855
Line lifted – Demolished – Station site in private use **SO67786 20861 (e)**

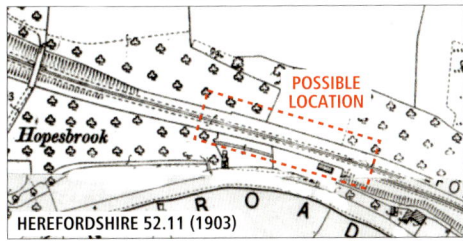

HOLME (ECR)
February 1847 - March 1853
Line Operational – Demolished **TF60951 09276**

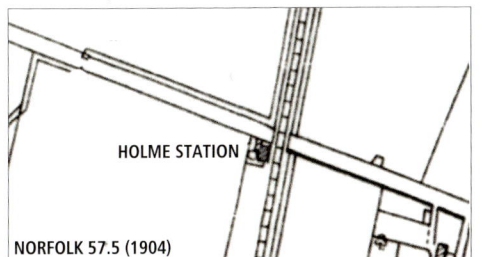

HOPTON TOP WHARF (L&NWR)
June 1833 - December 1877
Line lifted – Demolished – The High Peak Trail passes through the station site **SK25287 54643**

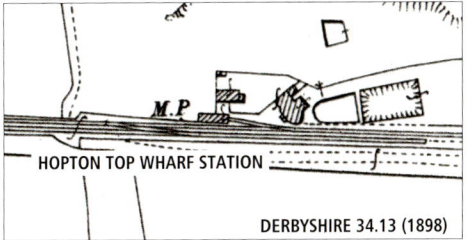

HORSFORTH WOODSIDE - HULL NEPTUNE STREET

HORSFORTH WOODSIDE (NER)
July 1850 - April 1864
Line Operational – Demolished – No access SE25546 37582

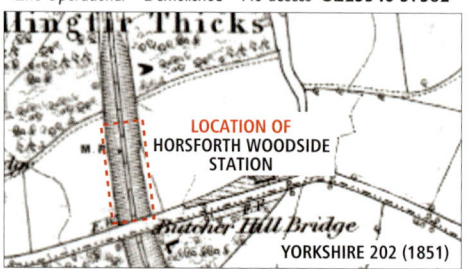
YORKSHIRE 202 (1851)

HULL ANLABY ROAD (NER)
8 May 1848 - 30 September 1854
Line Operational – Demolished – No access
TA07750 28715 (a)

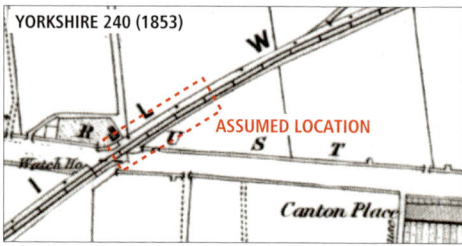
YORKSHIRE 240 (1853)

HOVE (1st) (LB&SCR)
12 May 1840 - 1 March 1880
Line lifted – Demolished – No access TQ29753 05321

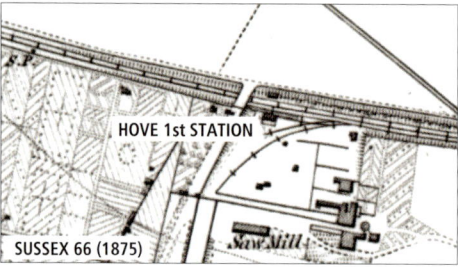
SUSSEX 66 (1875)

HULL HESSLE ROAD (Y&NMR)
8 May 1848 - October 1853
Line Operational – Demolished – No access
TA06832 27548 (a)

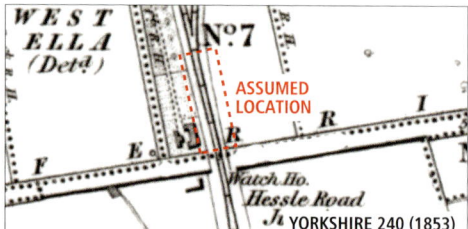
YORKSHIRE 240 (1853)

HOWNES GILL (S&DR)
January 1857 - 1 July 1858
Line lifted – Demolished – The Waskerley Way passes through the station site NZ09480 48885 (a)

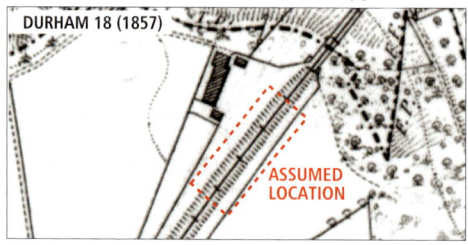

HULL MANOR HOUSE STREET (NER)
1 July 1840 - 1 June 1864
Line lifted – Demolished – Station site in commercial use and partially occupied by housing in Wellington Street West
TA09685 28204

YORKSHIRE 240 (1853)

HUCKNALL (1st) (MR)
2 October 1848 - 22 December 1895
Line Operational – Demolished – No access SK53954 49409

NOTTINGHAMSHIRE 33.9 (1879)

HULL NEPTUNE STREET* (H&BR)
Not known
Line lifted – Demolished – Station site in commercial use
TA08637 27738

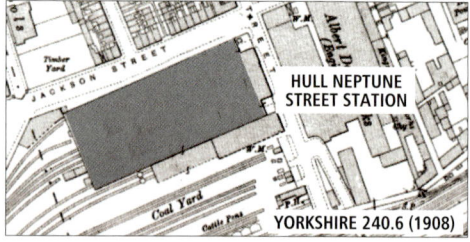
YORKSHIRE 240.6 (1908)

HULL NEWINGTON* (NER)
Not known
Line lifted – Demolished – A cycle/walkway passes through the station site **TA06451 29059**

HULL VICTORIA DOCK (NER)
1 June 1853 – 1 June 1864
Line lifted – Demolished – Station site in commercial use
TA11037 28997

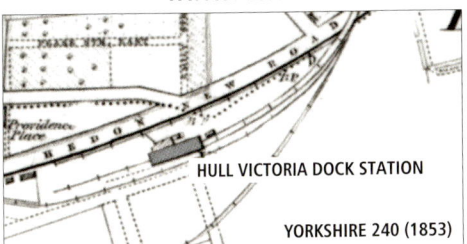

HUNCOAT (1st) (L&YR)
Not known
Line Operational – Demolished – No access **SD77748 31230**

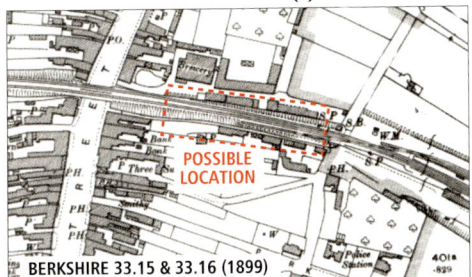

HUNGERFORD (1st) (GWR)
18 September 1848 – 11 November 1862
Line Operational – Demolished – No access
SU33930 68568 (a)

HULL NEWINGTON – HYDE (MS&LR)

HUNSLET (1st) (MR)
1 April 1850 – 14 September 1873
Line Operational – Demolished – No access
SE31041 31146 (a)

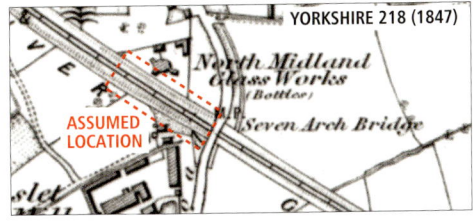

HUSKISSON (CLC)
13 July 1880 – 1 May 1885
Line lifted – Demolished – Station site in commercial use
SJ34269 92610

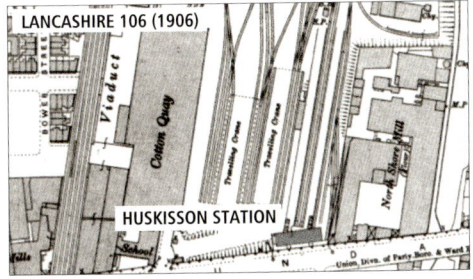

HUTTON JUNCTION (NER)
1 November 1878 – April 1891
Line lifted – Demolished – The Guisborough Branch Walkway passes through the station site
NZ61009 15177 (a)

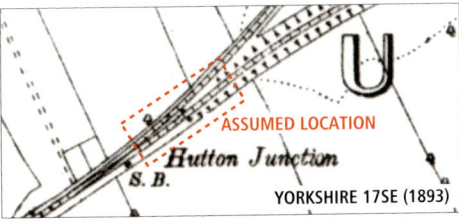

HYDE (MS&LR)
1 March 1858 – 5 August 1862
Line Operational – Demolished – No access
SJ94465 94750 (a)

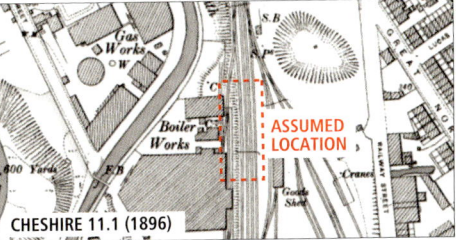

69

ICKNIELD PORT ROAD (1st) - INVERNESS HARBOUR

ICKNIELD PORT ROAD (1st) (L&NWR)
10 August 1874 - 1897
Line lifted – Demolished – Station site occupied by part of Barford Primary School **SP04485 87457**

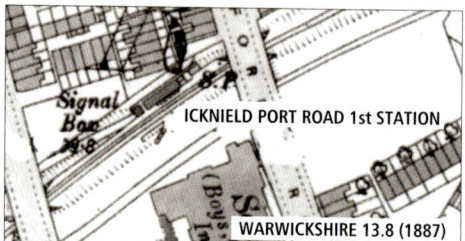
ICKNIELD PORT ROAD 1st STATION
WARWICKSHIRE 13.8 (1887)

IDLE (MR)
1 September 1847 - 1 October 1848
Line Operational – Demolished – No access **SE16913 38837**

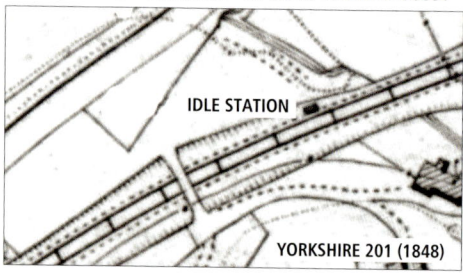
IDLE STATION
YORKSHIRE 201 (1848)

ILKESTON JUNCTION (1st) (MR)
6 September 1847 - 2 May 1870
Line Operational – Demolished – No access
SK47513 42359 (a)

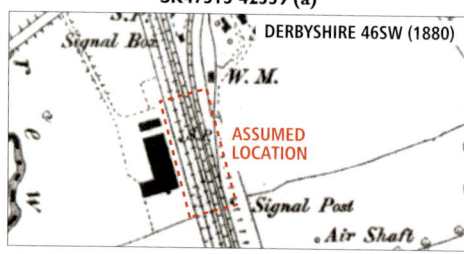
DERBYSHIRE 46SW (1880)
ASSUMED LOCATION

ILMINGTON [TRAMWAY STATION] (OW&WR)
c1833 - 30 September 1858
Line lifted – Demolished – Station site in private use
SP22062 43862 (a)

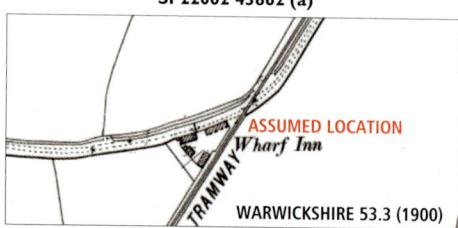
ASSUMED LOCATION
WARWICKSHIRE 53.3 (1900)

INCLINE TOP (TVR)
29 September 1841 - December 1857
Line Operational – Demolished – No access
ST08922 95500 (a)

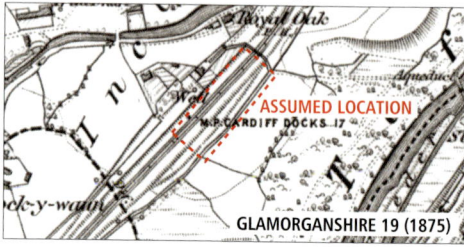
ASSUMED LOCATION
GLAMORGANSHIRE 19 (1875)

INGATESTONE (ECR)
December 1843 - 7 September 1846
Line Operational – Demolished – No access
TQ65370 99513 (a)

ASSUMED LOCATION
ESSEX 60 (1874)

INVERKEITHING (1st) (NBR)
1 November 1877 - 2 June 1890
Line lifted – Demolished – Station site partially occupied by a car park **NT13180 83084**

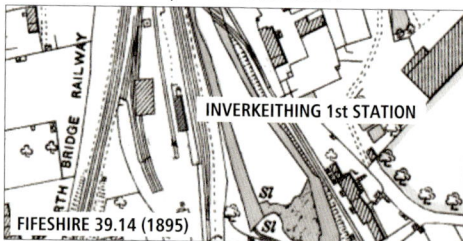
INVERKEITHING 1st STATION
FIFESHIRE 39.14 (1895)

INVERNESS HARBOUR (HR)
October 1863 - June 1867
Line lifted – Demolished – Station site in commercial use
NN66460 45926 (a)

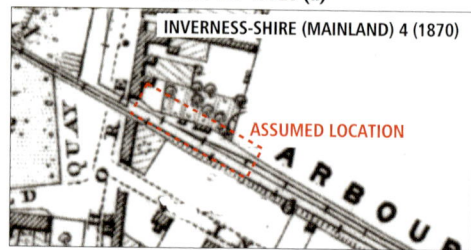
INVERNESS-SHIRE (MAINLAND) 4 (1870)
ASSUMED LOCATION

IPSWICH STOKE HILL (GER)
15 June 1846 - 1 July 1860
Line lifted – Demolished – Station site occupied by dwellings in Bruff Road **TM16349 43316 (a)**

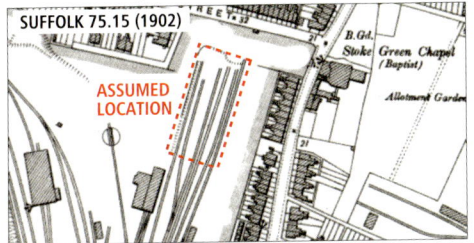

IRLAM AND CADISHEAD (1st) (CLC)
2 September 1873 - 26 March 1893
Line lifted – Demolished – Station site occupied by dwellings in Station Road **SJ71329 93175**

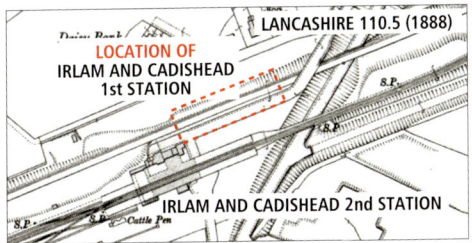

JARROW DOCKS (NER)
April 1844 - 1 March 1872
Line lifted – Demolished – Station site unused **NZ35782 64665**

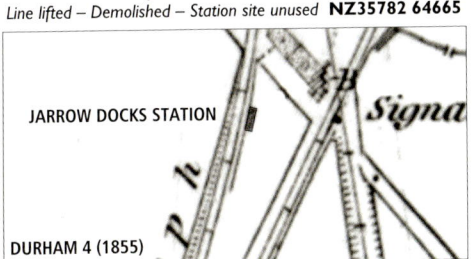

JOCKS LODGE (NBR)
1 September 1847 - 1 July 1848
Line Operational – Demolished – No access **NT28307 74307 (a)**

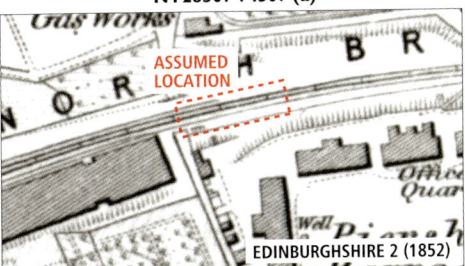

IPSWICH STOKE HILL - KEIGHLEY (1st)

JOPPA (1st) (NBR)
July 1846 - c1848
Line Operational – Demolished – No access **NT31259 72956 (a)**

JOPPA (2nd) (NBR)
1848 - 16 May 1859
Line Operational – Demolished – No access **NT31285 72897**

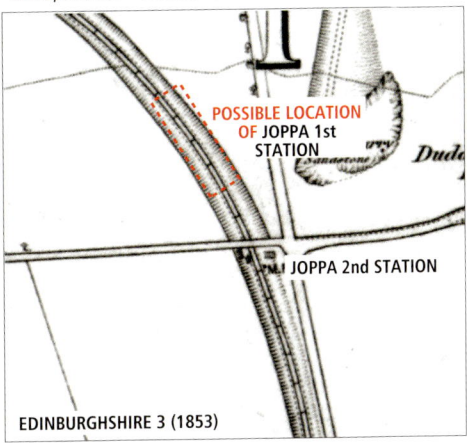

KEADBY FOR AMCOTTS & BURRINGHAM (MS&LR)
13 September 1859 - 2 November 1874
Line lifted – Demolished – Station site in commercial use **SE83489 11432**

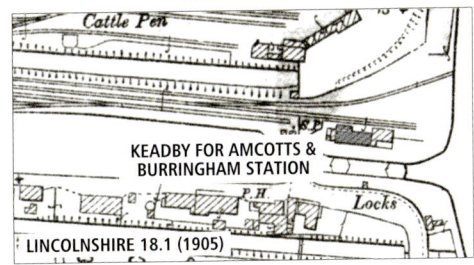

KEIGHLEY (1st) (MR)
16 March 1847 - 6 May 1883
Line Operational – Demolished – No access **SE06503 41360**

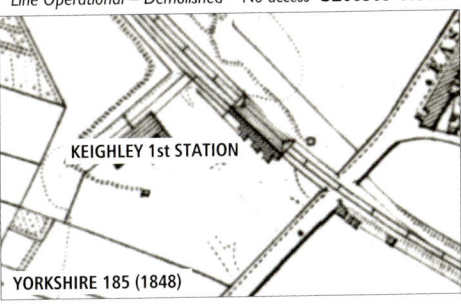

71

KENSAL GREEN AND HARLESDEN - KILMARNOCK (1st)

KENSAL GREEN AND HARLESDEN
(L&NWR)
1 November 1861 - 1 July 1873
Line Operational – Demolished – No access **TQ22615 83031**

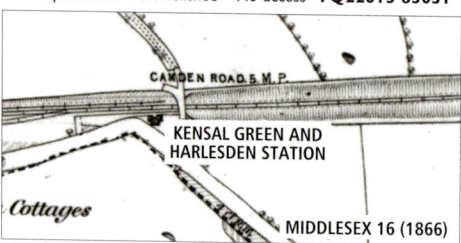

KEW (1st) (NLR)
1 August 1853 - October 1866
Line Operational – Demolished – No access **TQ18693 78221**

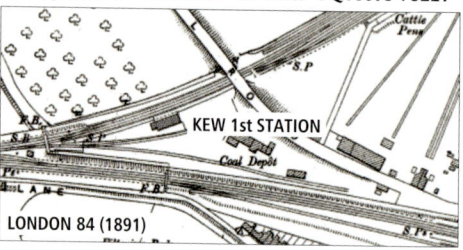

KEYMER JUNCTION (1st) (L&SWR)
1 October 1847 - 1 January 1862

KEYMER JUNCTION (2nd) (L&SWR)
1 January 1862 - 1 November 1883
Line Operational – Demolished – No access **TQ31918 19470**

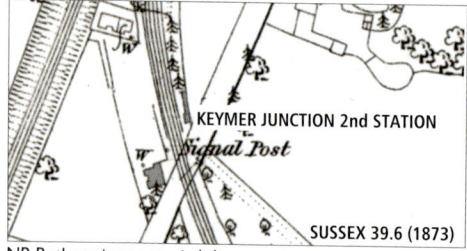

NB Both stations occupied the same site.

KIDWELLY QUAY* (BP&GVR)
Not known
Line lifted – Demolished – A pathway passes through the station site **SN39781 06361**

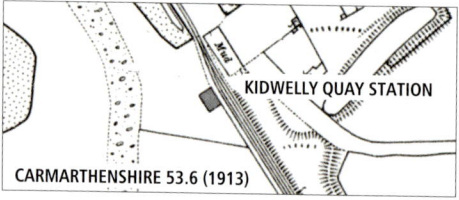

KILDRUMMIE PLATFORM* (HR)
1 December 1855 - 1 January 1858
Line Operational – Demolished – No access
NH84951 54299 (a)

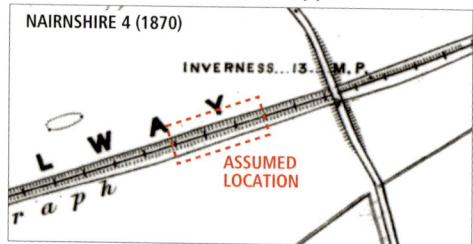

KILDWICK AND CROSSHILLS (1st) (MR)
April 1848 - 7 April 1889
Line Operational – Demolished – Station building in private use
SE01191 45280

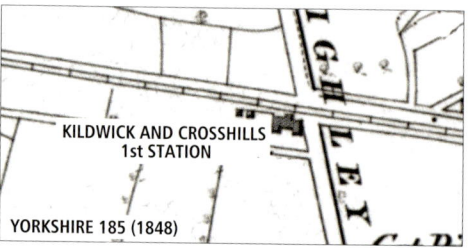

KILMARNOCK (St MARNOCKS)
(GPK&AR)
1818 - 4 April 1843
Line lifted – Demolished – Station site occupied by dwellings
NS42568 37731

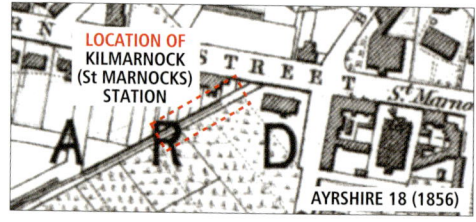

KILMARNOCK (1st) (GPK&AR)
4 April 1843 - 20 July 1846
Line Operational – Demolished – Station site partially occupied by the station car park **NS42661 38260**

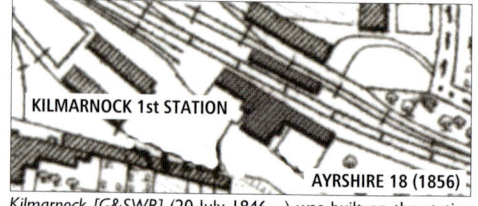

Kilmarnock [G&SWR] (20 July 1846 -) was built on the station site

KINGS CROSS (1st) - KINROSS JUNCTION (1st)

KINGS CROSS (1st) (GNR)
7 August 1850 - 14 October 1852
Line Operational – Demolished – Station site occupied by dwellings in Granary Square **TQ30237 83607**

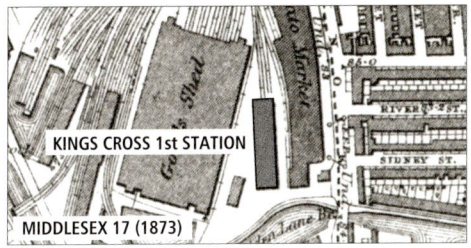

KINGS CROSS CEMETERY STATION*
(GNR)
1861 - 1873
Line lifted – Demolished – Station building partially extant and derelict? **TQ30299 83994**

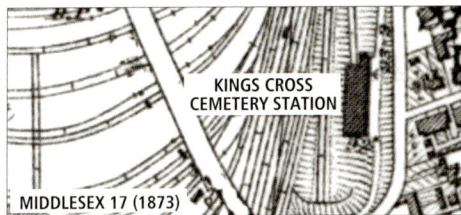

KINGSTON (1st) (L&SWR)
21 May 1838 - 1845
Line Operational – Demolished – No access **TQ18659 67675**

KINGSTON-ON-SEA (LB&SCR)
12 May 1840 - 1 April 1879
Line Operational – Demolished – No access **TQ23117 05084**

KINGTON (1st) (GWR)
20 August 1857 - 25 September 1875
Line lifted – Demolished – Station building in private use on "Hatton Gardens Industrial Estate" **SO30412 57007**

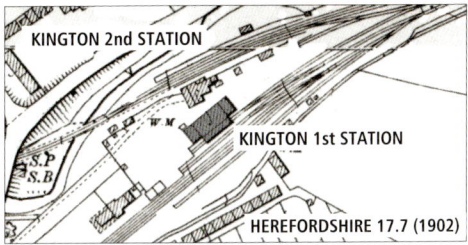

KING WILLIAM STREET (C&SLR)
18 December 1890 - 25 February 1900
Line lifted – Tunnels closed - Demolished
TQ32870 80760 (Subterranean) **(a)**

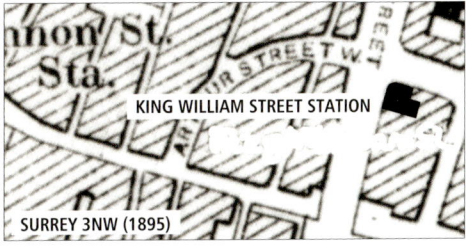

KINLOSS (I&AJnR)
25 March 1858 - 18 April 1860
Line Operational – Demolished – No access **NJ07066 61292**

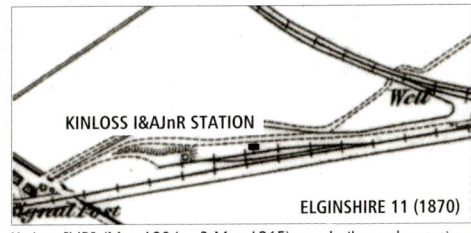

Kinloss [HR] (May 1904 – 3 May 1965) was built on the station site

KINROSS JUNCTION (1st) (NBR)
20 August 1858 - 1890
Line lifted – Demolished – Station site occupied by a Sainsbury's supermarket car park **NO11213 02552 (a)**

KIRBY (NER)
8 July 1845 - 1 October 1858
Line lifted – Demolished – Station House in private use
SE80331 81534

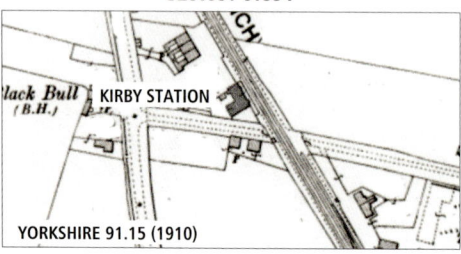

YORKSHIRE 91.15 (1910)

KIRKHAM (P&WR)
16 July 1840 - 1890
Line Operational – Demolished – No access **SD41784 32665**

LANCASHIRE 60 (1845)

KIRKINCH (D&PR)
4 June 1838 - October 1847
Line lifted – Demolished – Station Cottage in private use
NO31027 44216

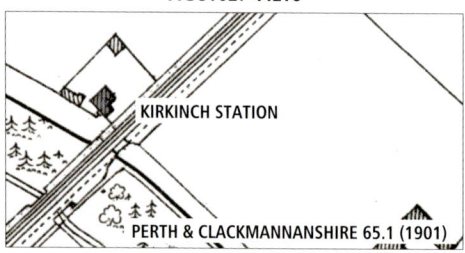

PERTH & CLACKMANNANSHIRE 65.1 (1901)

KIRKINTILLOCH (M&KR)
26 December 1844 - 28 July 1847
Line lifted – Demolished – Station site unused
NS66257 72178 (a)

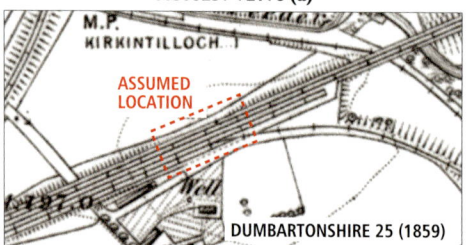

DUMBARTONSHIRE 25 (1859)

KIRKINTILLOCH BASIN (M&KR)
1 October 1826 - 6 March 1846
Line lifted – Demolished – Station site occupied by "New College Lanarkshire" **NS65357 73383 (a)**

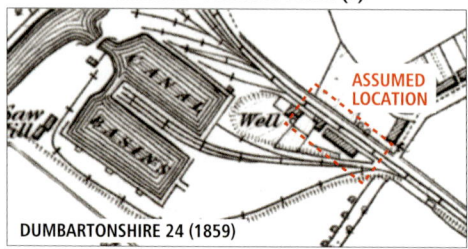

DUMBARTONSHIRE 24 (1859)

KIRKSANTON CROSSING (W&FJnR)
1 December 1850 - March 1861
Line Operational – Demolished **SD14222 80706**

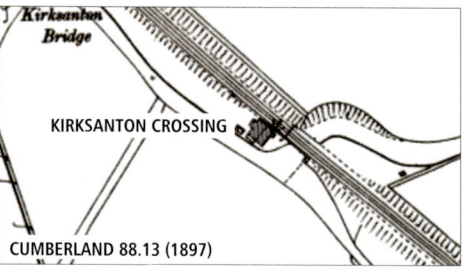

CUMBERLAND 88.13 (1897)

KIRKSTALL (1st) (MR)
July 1846 - 5 July 1905
Line Operational – Demolished – No access **SE25949 35533**

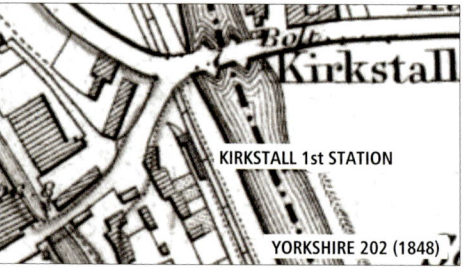

YORKSHIRE 202 (1848)

KIRRIEMUIR JUNCTION (SNER)
December 1854 - June 1864
Line lifted – Demolished – Degraded platforms partially extant
NO41579 50835

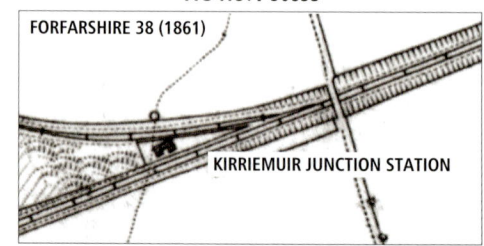

FORFARSHIRE 38 (1861)

KITTYBREWSTER (1st) - LANCASTER (L&CR)

KITTYBREWSTER (1st) (GNofSR)
20 September 1854 - 4 November 1867
Line Operational – Demolished – No access **NJ93220 07712**

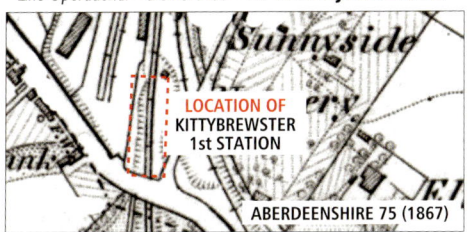

Kittybrewster 2nd [GNofSR] (4 November 1867 – 6 May 1968) was built on, or partially on, the station site

KNOCK (1st) (GNofSR)
30 July 1859 - c1894
Line lifted – Demolished – A track passes through the station site **NJ54578 52834**

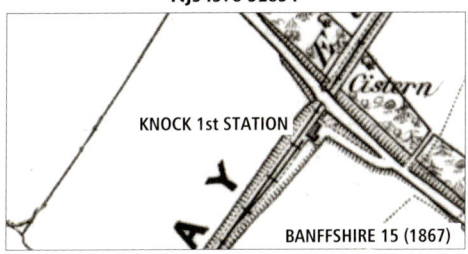

LACKENBY (S&DR)
5 June 1846 - c1872
Line Operational – Demolished – No access **NZ55342 22198**

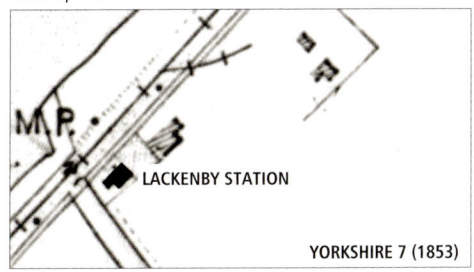

LADMANLOW (L&NWR)
June 1833 - December 1877
Line lifted – Demolished – Station site unused **SK04056 71792**

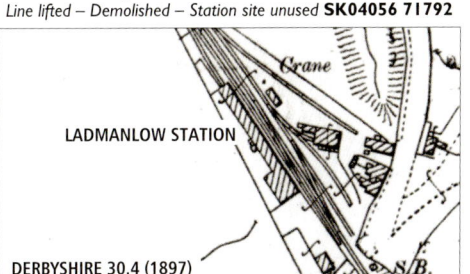

LAGGAN FARM HOUSE* (CR)
Not known
Line lifted – Demolished – Part of the Rob Roy Way passes through the station site **NN56145 14667 (a)**

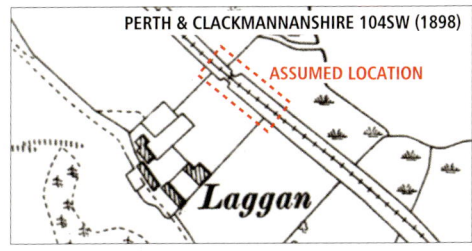

LAIRA GREEN (SDevonR)
5 May 1848 - 2 April 1849
Line Operational – Demolished – No access **SX50619 55817 (a)**

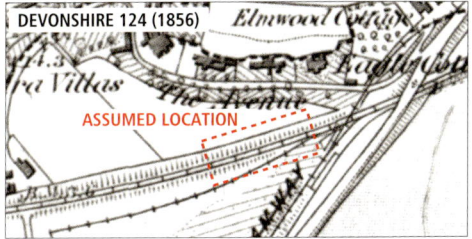

LAMB'S COTTAGE (L&MR)
Prior to September 1834 - October 1842
Line Operational – Demolished **SJ70924 97288**

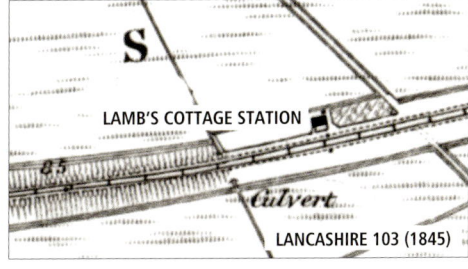

LANCASTER (L&CR)
26 June 1840 - 1 August 1849
Line lifted – Platform partially extant – Grade II listed Station building in use as part of the Royal Lancaster Infirmary **SD47819 61126**

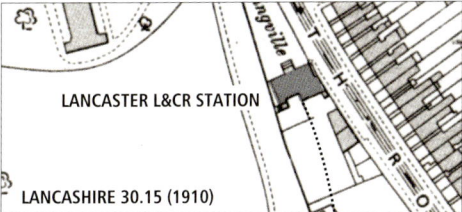

75

LANCASTER GREEN AYRE (1st) - LAZENBY

LANCASTER GREEN AYRE (1st) (MR)
12 June 1848 - 9 August 1873
Location unknown but "a little further down the line" from Lancaster Green Ayre 2nd [MR]
SD47912 62165 (e)

LANDORE (1st) (GWR)
19 June 1850 - 1876
Line Operational – Demolished – No access
SS65894 95441 (a)

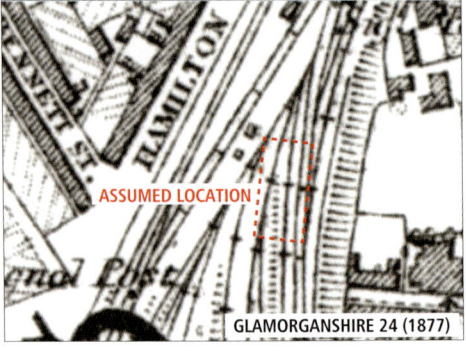
ASSUMED LOCATION
GLAMORGANSHIRE 24 (1877)

LANDS (NER)
13 October 1858 - 1 May 1872
Line lifted – Demolished – Station site unused
NZ13271 25111 (a)

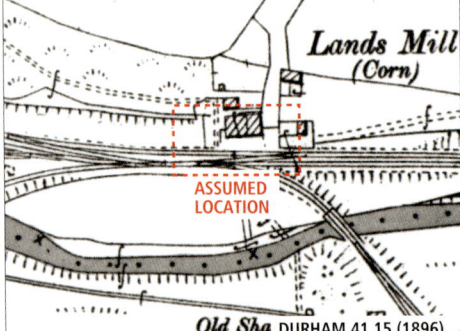
ASSUMED LOCATION
DURHAM 41.15 (1896)

LANGFORD (1st) (GWR)
30 June 1856 - October 1857
Line Operational – Demolished – No access
SU03291 36897 (a)

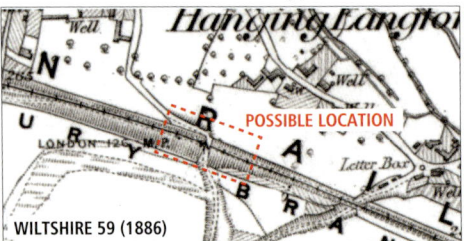
POSSIBLE LOCATION
WILTSHIRE 59 (1886)

LANGHAM HILL* (WSsetMinR)
4 September 1865 - 7 November 1898
Line lifted – Demolished – Station site unused **SS98164 35484**

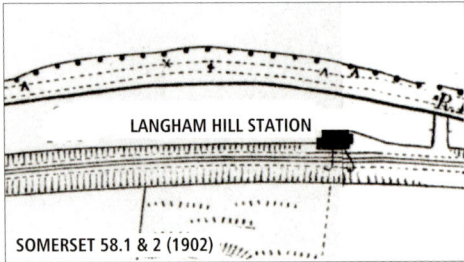
LANGHAM HILL STATION
SOMERSET 58.1 & 2 (1902)

LANGLEY GREEN (1st) (GWR)
1 April 1867 - 1 May 1885
Line Operational – Demolished – No access **SO99646 88198**

LANGLEY GREEN 1st STATION
WORCESTERSHIRE 5NW (1883)

Sited 220 yards south of *Langley Green 2nd [GWR]* (1 May 1885 -)

LATCHFORD (1st) (L&NWR)
December 1853 - 9 July 1893
Line lifted – Demolished – Station site in commercial use
SJ62646 86966

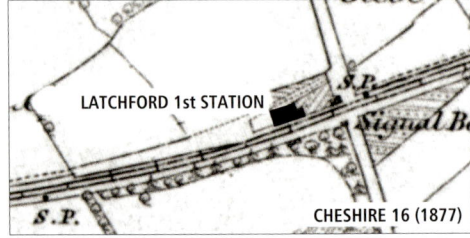
LATCHFORD 1st STATION
CHESHIRE 16 (1877)

LAZENBY (NER)
5 June 1846 - May 1864
Line Operational – Demolished – No access **NZ56226 23118**

LAZENBY STATION
YORKSHIRE 7 (1853)

LEAMSIDE (1st) - **LEICESTER WEST BRIDGE** (1st)

LEAMSIDE (1st) (NER)
15 April 1844 - c1857
Line lifted – Demolished – A pathway passes through the station site **NZ31383 46590**

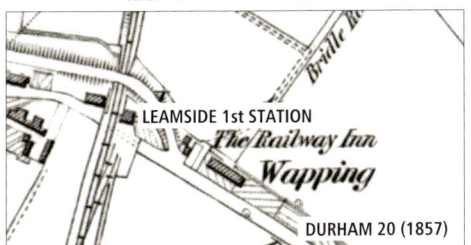

LEASINGTHORNE (NER)
c1852 - April 1867
Line lifted – Demolished – Station site unused/in agricultural use **NZ25601 30149 (a)**

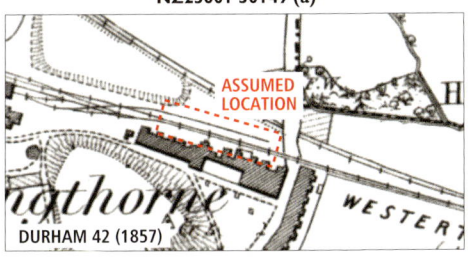

LEASON HILL (SMJR)
4 June 1838 - c1847
Line lifted – Demolished – Station site in agricultural use **NO33253 45919 (a)**

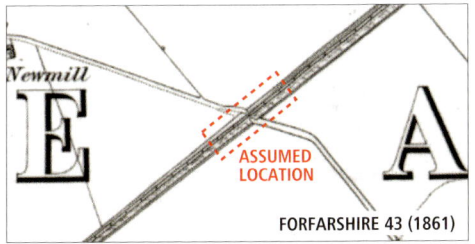

LEATHERHEAD (E&LR)
1 February 1859 - 2 February 1885
Line Operational – Demolished – No access **TQ16466 57569**

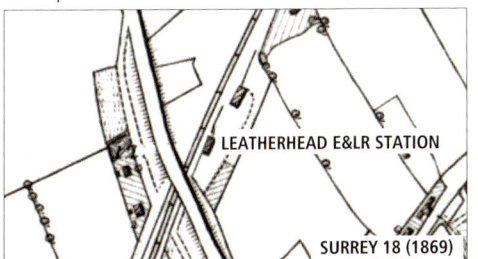

LEEDS HUNSLET LANE (MR)
1 July 1840 - 1 March 1851
Line lifted – Demolished – Station site occupied by "Crown Point Retail Park" **SE30303 32596**

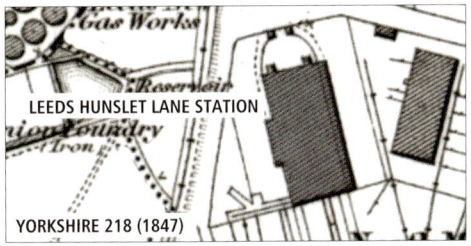

LEEDS MARSH LANE (1st) (NER)
22 September 1834 - 1 April 1869
Line lifted – Demolished – Station site partially occupied by a car park and partially unused **SE31160 33541**

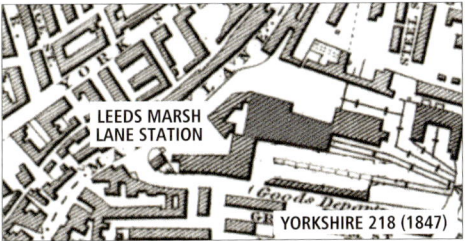

LEEDS WELLINGTON STREET (GNR)
14 May 1850 - 4 August 1854
Line lifted – Demolished – Station site in commercial use **SE29430 33423**

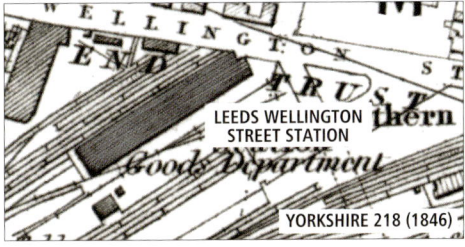

LEICESTER WEST BRIDGE (1st) (MR)
18 July 1832 - 13 March 1893
Line lifted – Demolished – Station site landscaped **SK58054 04458**

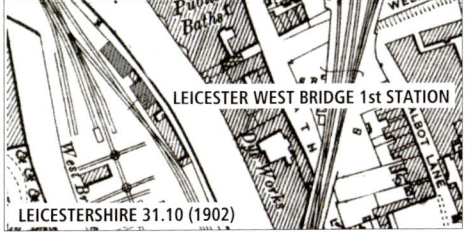

LEIGHTON (1st) - LICHFIELD (L&NWR)

LEIGHTON (1st) (L&NWR)
9 April 1838 - 14 February 1859
Line Operational – Demolished – No access
SP91125 25222 (a)

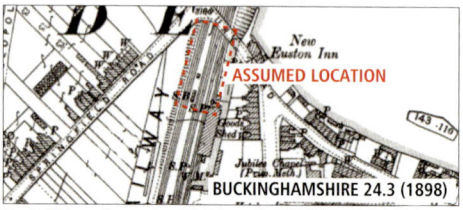

Sited 175 yards north of Leighton 2nd [L&NWR] (14 February 1859 -)

LENNOXTOWN OLD (NBR)
5 July 1848 - 1 October 1881
Line lifted – Demolished – Station site occupied by a warehouse for "The Highland Spirit Group" **NS62673 77818**

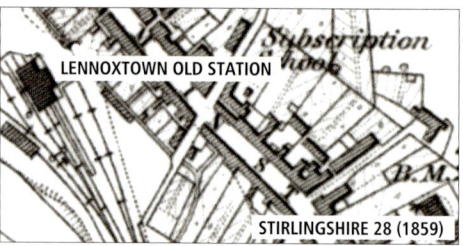

LESBURY (YN&BR)
1 July 1847 - 19 August 1850
Line Operational – Demolished – Station building in private use
NU23054 12505

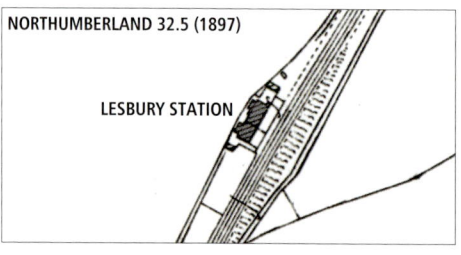

LEVEN (EP&DR)
7 August 1854 - 18 August 1857
Line lifted – Demolished – Station site in commercial use
NO37606 00958

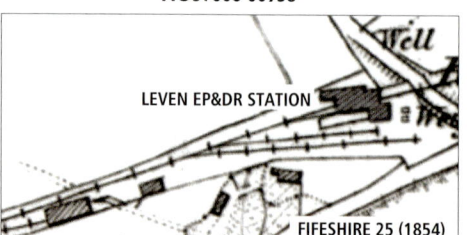

LEWES (1st) (LB&SCR)
1 November 1857 - 4 March 1889
Line Operational **TQ41653 09832**

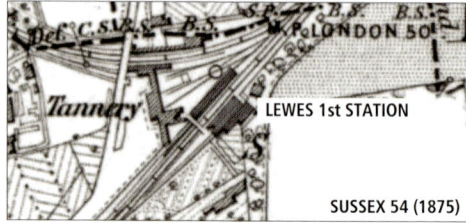

Lewes 2nd [LB&SCR] (4 March 1889 -) was built on the station site

LEWES FRIARS WALK (LB&SCR)
8 June 1846 - 1 November 1857
Line lifted – Demolished – Station site occupied by dwellings in Court Road **TQ41857 10153**

LEWES HAM (LB&SCR)
8 June 1846 - 1 November 1857
Line lifted – Demolished – Station site occupied by dwellings in Pinwell Road **TQ41738 09927**

LEWES PINWELL (LB&SCR)
1 October 1847 - 1 November 1857
Line lifted – Demolished – Station site occupied by dwellings in Greyfriars Court **TQ41927 10075**

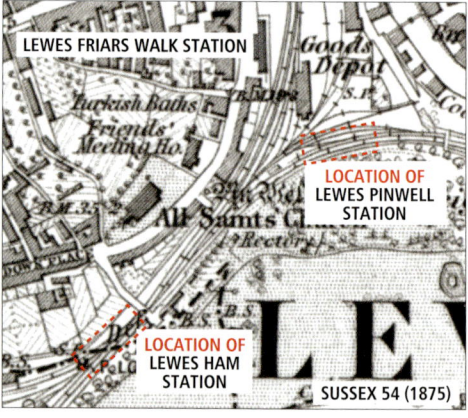

LICHFIELD (L&NWR)
15 September 1847 - 3 July 1871
Line Operational – Demolished – No access **SK13401 10098**

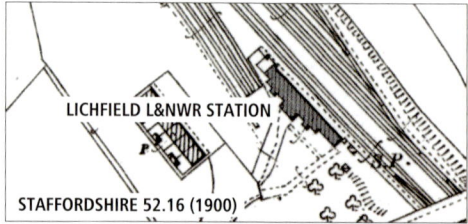

LICHFIELD CITY (1st) **- LITTLE BYTHAM** (E&LBR)

LICHFIELD CITY (1st) (L&NWR)
9 April 1849 - 3 November 1884
Line Operational – Demolished – No access **SK12022 09267**

LICHFIELD TRENT VALLEY JUNCTION (L&NWR)
July 1849 - 3 July 1871
Line Operational – Demolished – No access
SK13910 10037 (a)

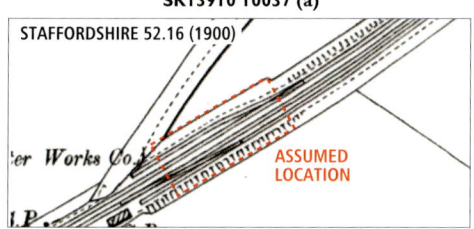

LIFFORD (B&GR)
17 December 1840 - 1 December 1844
Line Operational – Demolished – No access **SP05562 80125**

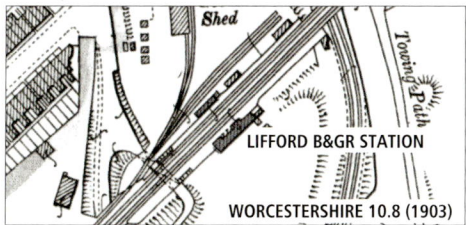

Lifford [MR] (28 September 1885 – 27 November 1946) was built on the station site

LIFFORD (1st) (MR)
1 June 1876 - 28 September 1885
Line lifted – Demolished – Station site occupied by part of "Kings Norton Business Centre" **SP05473 79873**

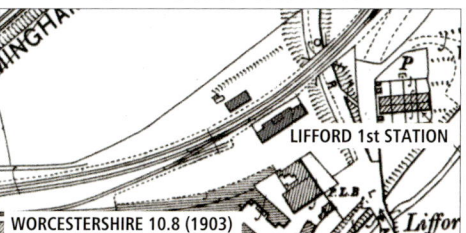

LIGHTMOOR (GWR)
2 May 1859 - 1 November 1864
Line Operational for Freight – Demolished – No access
SJ68071 05097 (a)

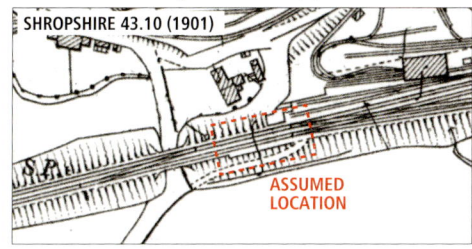

LINDAL EAST (FurnR)
27 May 1852 - 7 June 1854
Line Operational – Demolished – No access
SD26228 76376 (a)

LINKSFIELD LEVEL CROSSING (MorayshireR)
4 June 1853 - December 1859
Line lifted – Demolished – Station site unused **NJ23105 64652**

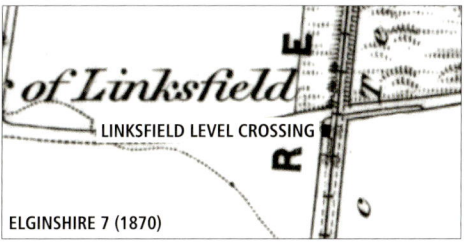

LITTLE BYTHAM (E&LBR)
8 December 1857 - 17 October 1871
Line lifted – Demolished – Station site unused **TF01901 17260**

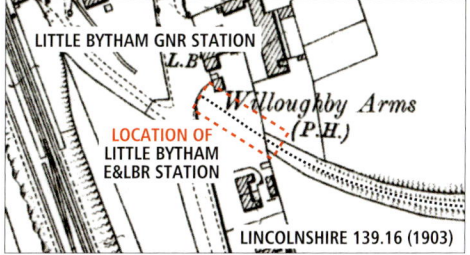

LIVERPOOL BRUNSWICK (CLC) - LLANGOLLEN ROAD

LIVERPOOL BRUNSWICK (CLC)
1 June 1864 - 1 March 1874
Line lifted – Demolished – Station site occupied by a Renault Dealership **SJ35001 88201**

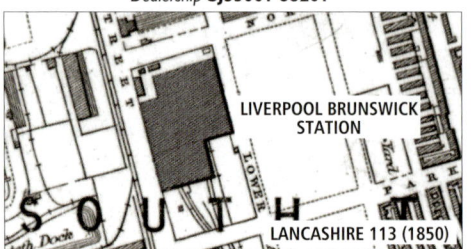

LIVERPOOL CROWN STREET (L&MR)
17 September 1830 - 15 August 1836
Line lifted – Demolished – Station site landscaped as "Crown Street Park" **SJ36616 89771**

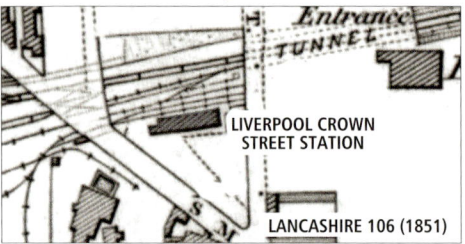

LIVERPOOL GREAT HOWARD STREET (L&YR/ELancsR)
20 November 1848 - 13 May 1850
Line Operational – Demolished – No access **SJ33925 91456**

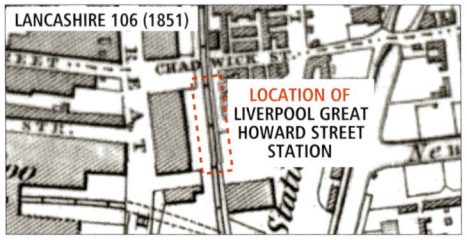

LLANDUDNO JUNCTION (1st) (L&NWR)
1 October 1858 - 1 November 1897
Line Operational – Demolished – No access **SH79063 77820**

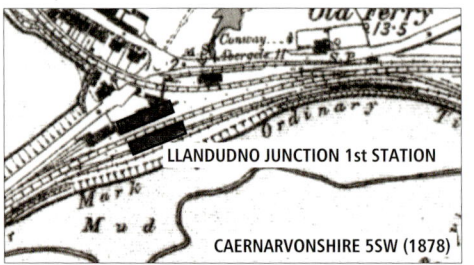

LLANELLY (LlnyR)
April 1853 - 1 September 1879
Line Operational **SS50659 99424**

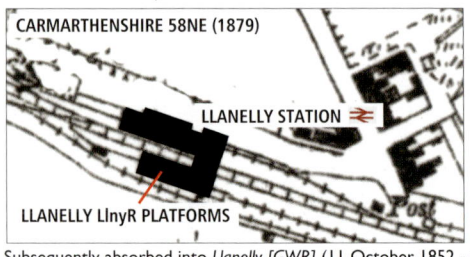

Subsequently absorbed into Llanelly [GWR] (11 October 1852 -)

LLANELLY DOCK (GWR)
1 May 1850 - 1 September 1879
Line lifted – Demolished – Station site in commercial use **SS51287 98951**

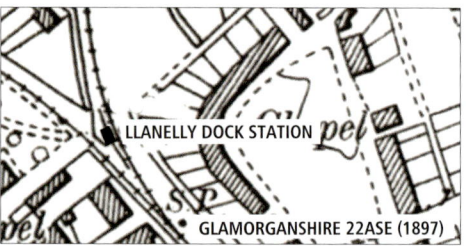

LLAN FESTINIOG (GWR)
30 May 1868 - 1 November 1882
Line Mothballed – Demolished **SH70442 41918**

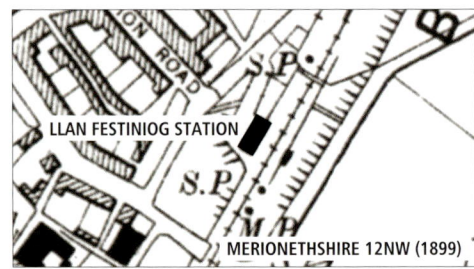

LLANGOLLEN ROAD (GWR)
14 October 1848 - 1 July 1862
Line Operational – Demolished – No access **SJ28666 39986**

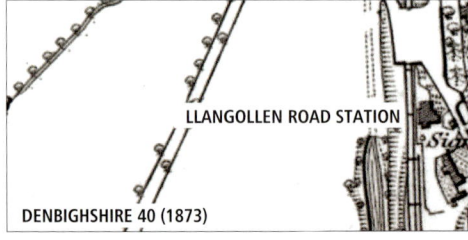

LLANGYNWYD (1st) (GWR)
September 1865 - 1897
Line Operational – Demolished – No access **SS87186 88929**

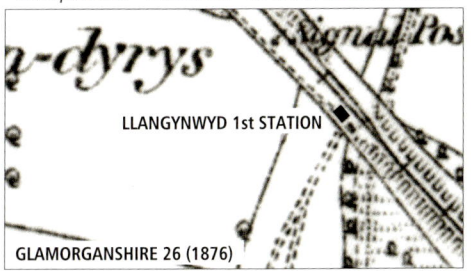

LLANGYNWYD (1st) - LLANSAMLET (MR)
LLANNERCH* (L&NWR)
5 October 1858 - December 1871
Line lifted – Demolished – Station site unused
SJ04702 72247 (a)

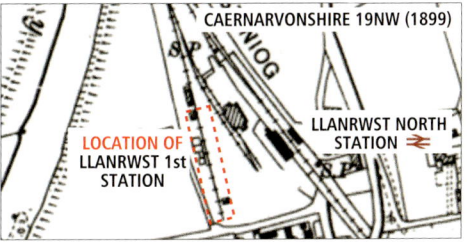

LLANHARRY (1st) (TVR)
July 1871 - 2 March 1891
Line lifted – Demolished – Station site unused **ST01840 80523**

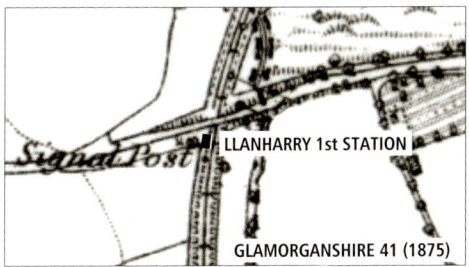

LLANRWST (1st) (L&NWR)
17 June 1863 - 6 April 1868
Line lifted – Demolished – Station site in commercial use
SH79448 62278 (a)

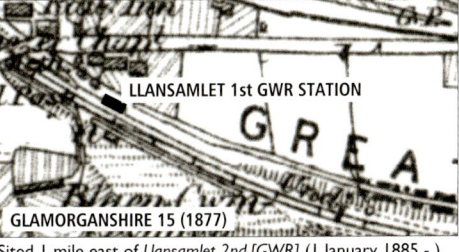

LLANHILLETH (MonmouthsR)
August 1853 - 1 November 1861
Line Operational – Demolished – No access
SO21514 00805 (a)

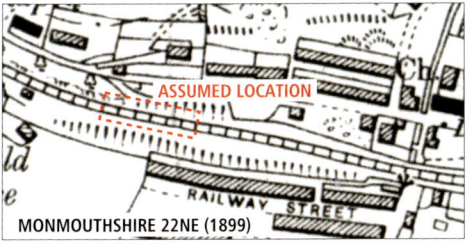

LLANSAMLET (1st) (GWR)
1 April 1852 - 1 June 1882
Line Operational – Demolished – No access **SS70544 97221**

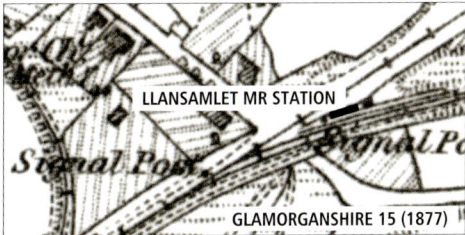

Sited 1 mile east of *Llansamlet 2nd [GWR]* (1 January 1885 -)

LLANIDLOES (L&NR)
11 August 1859 - Prior to January 1862
Line lifted – Demolished – Station site in commercial use
SN95866 84714

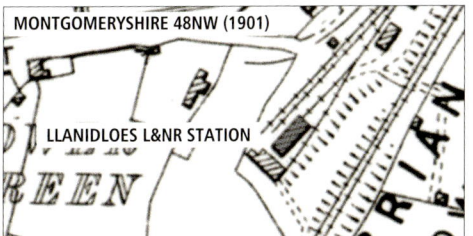

LLANSAMLET (MR)
21 February 1860 - 1 March 1875
Line lifted – Demolished – Station site occupied by dwellings in
Ffordd Cynghordy **SS68775 97346**

LLANTARNAM (1st) - LONG EATON JUNCTION

LLANTARNAM (1st) (GWR)
2 May 1853 - 11 March 1880
Line lifted – Demolished – The A4051, Cwmbran Drive, passes through the station site **ST29852 92333**

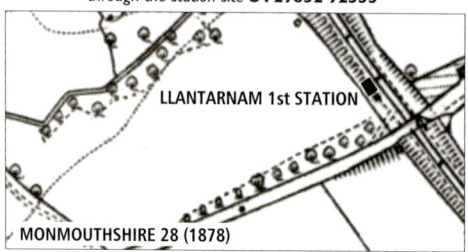

LONG BENTON (B&TR)
27 June 1864 - 1 March 1871
Line Operated by Tyne & Wear Metro – Demolished – No access
NZ27031 68466

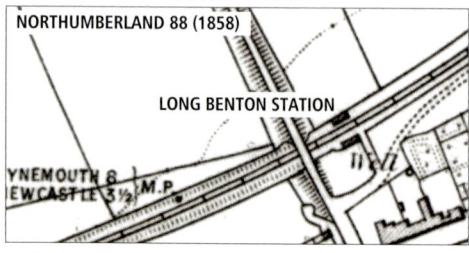

LOBLEY HILL (BlingJnR)
18 June 1842 - August 1844
Line lifted – Demolished – The Tanfield Railway Path passes through the station site **NZ23142 60689**

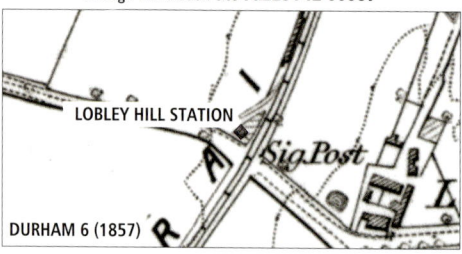

LONGCLIFFE (L&NWR)
June 1833 - December 1877
Line lifted – Demolished – The High Peak Trail passes through the station site **SK22546 55712**

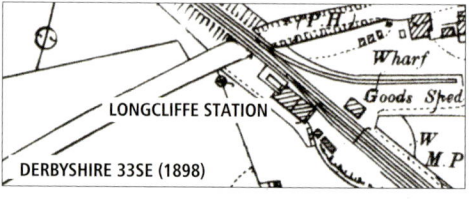

LONDESBOROUGH PARK* (NER)
? - January 1867
Line lifted – Demolished – Station site in agricultural use
SE84650 44268

LONG EATON (2nd) (MR)
6 September 1847 - July 1863
Line Operational – Demolished – No access
SK49321 33883 (a)

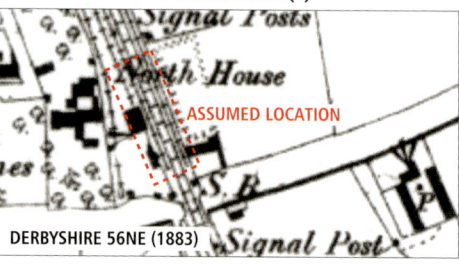

LONDON ROAD (GLASGOW) (CR)
1 April 1879 - 1 November 1895
Line lifted – Demolished – A728, The Clyde Gateway, passes through the station site **NS61728 63859**

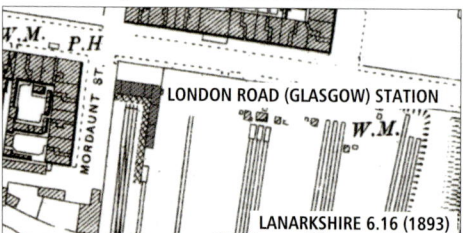

LONG EATON JUNCTION (MR)
4 June 1839 - 1 May 1862
Main line Operational – Demolished – No access
SK50102 32893

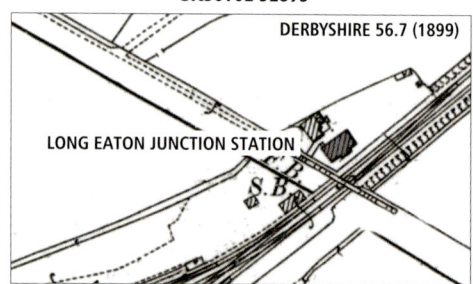

LONGRIDGE (1st) (WM&CR)
2 June 1845 - 1848
Line lifted – Demolished – Station site planted with trees
NS95329 61344

LONGRIDGE (2nd) (E&GR)
1848 - December 1852
Line lifted – Demolished – Station site unused **NS95315 61449**

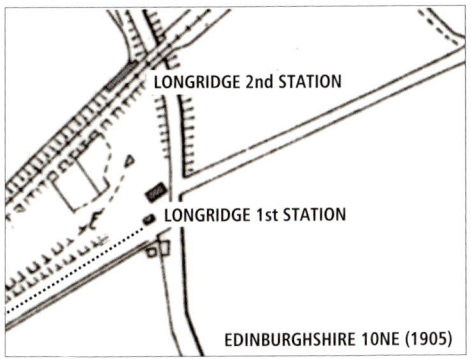

LOSTOCK LANE (L&YR)
November 1846 - 1 June 1879
Line Operational – Demolished **SD65149 08748**

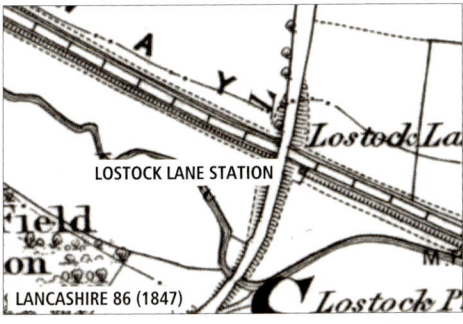

LOUGHBOROUGH (1st) (MR)
5 May 1840 - 13 May 1872
Line Operational – Demolished – No access
SK54450 20378 (a)

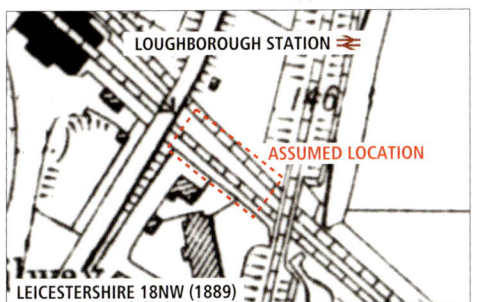

Loughborough 2nd [MR] (13 May 1872 -) was constructed just north of the station site

LONGRIDGE (1st) - LOW MARISHES
LOUGHTON (1st) (GER)
22 August 1856 - 24 April 1865
Line lifted – Demolished – Station site occupied by part of Sainsbury's supermarket car park
TQ42198 95781

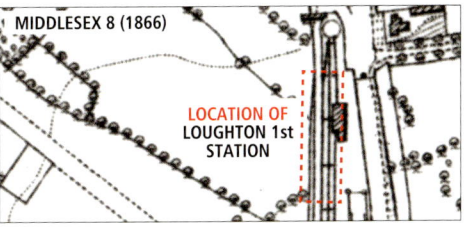

LOW BENTHAM (L&NWR)
2 May 1850 - 1 August 1853
Line Operational – Demolished – No access

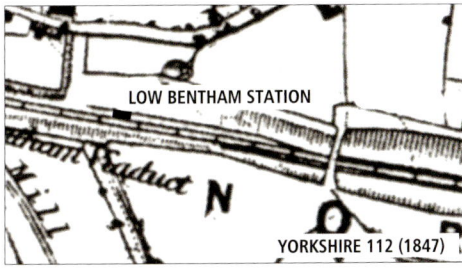

LOW GILL (1st) (L&NWR)
17 December 1846 - 15 September 1861
Line Operational – Demolished – No access **SD61651 96809**

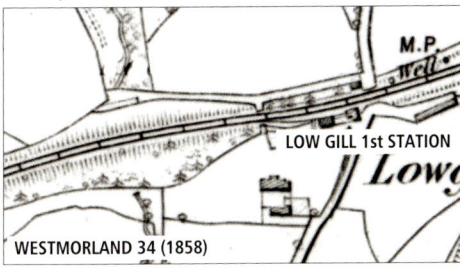

LOW MARISHES (Y&NMR)
5 July 1845 - 1847
Line lifted – Demolished – A track passes through the station site
SE82936 78050 (a)

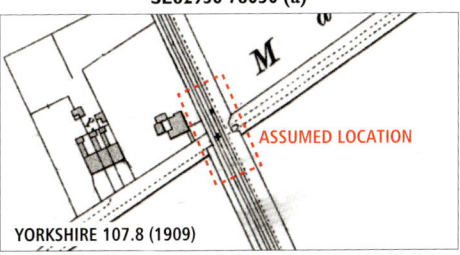

LOW ROW - MACCLESFIELD BEECH ROAD

LOW ROW (M&CR)
30 November 1844 - 2 February 1848
Line Operational – Demolished – No access
NY19061 44908 (a)

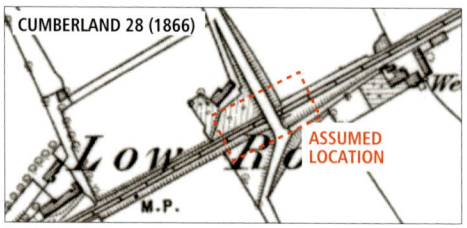

Sited 15 miles and 1,320 yards from *Carlisle Crown Street*

LYDNEY JUNCTION (S&WyeR)
23 September 1875 - 16 October 1879
Line lifted – Demolished – Station Road passes through the station site **SO63361 01910**

LYMINGTON (1st) (L&SWR)
12 July 1858 - 19 September 1860
Line Operational – Demolished – No access
SZ32637 96008 (a)

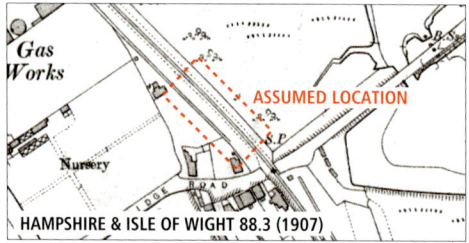

LYNN (1st) (GER)
27 October 1846 - 28 August 1871
Line lifted – Demolished – Station site occupied by an access road and a car park **TF62343 20100**

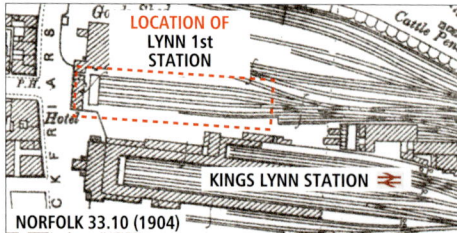

LYTHAM (1st) (P&WR)
16 February 1846 - 1 July 1874
Line lifted – Demolished – Station site occupied by Lytham St Annes Fire Station **SD37019 27318**

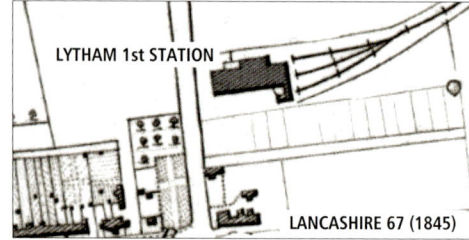

LYTHAM JUNCTION (P&WR)
June 1853 - November 1853
Line Operational – Demolished – No access
SD41353 32740 (a)

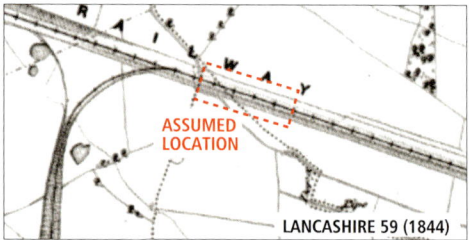

MACCLESFIELD (MaccCteeR)
2 August 1869 - 1 July 1873
Line lifted – Demolished – The A523, The Silk Road, crosses the station site **SJ91858 74143**

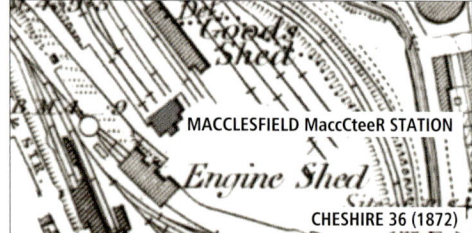

MACCLESFIELD BEECH ROAD (L&NWR)
24 November 1845 - 30 July 1849
Line Operational – Demolished – No access
SJ91443 74492 (a)

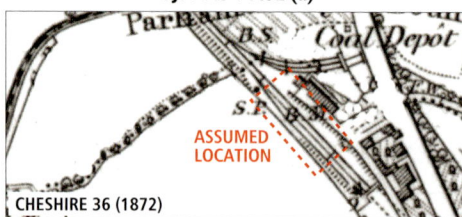

84

MACDUFF BANFF (GNofSR)
4 June 1860 - 1 July 1872
Line lifted – Demolished – Station site in agricultural use
NJ69772 63390

MAIDSTONE (1st) (SER)
1844 - 1856
Line lifted – Demolished - Station site in commercial use
TQ75646 55320

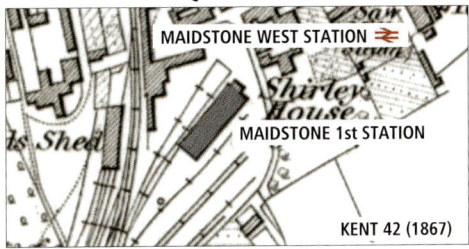

MACDUFF BANFF STATION
BANFFSHIRE 5 (1869)

MAIDSTONE WEST STATION
MAIDSTONE 1st STATION
KENT 42 (1867)

MAESMAWR (TVR)
30 October 1840 - July 1845
Line Operational – Demolished – No access
ST10548 86402 (a)

MAINS OF PENNINGHAME PLATFORM (WigtownshireR)
June 1875 - 6 August 1885
Line lifted – Demolished – A track passes through the station site
NX41098 61165 (a)

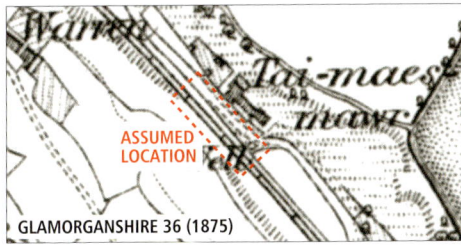
ASSUMED LOCATION
GLAMORGANSHIRE 36 (1875)

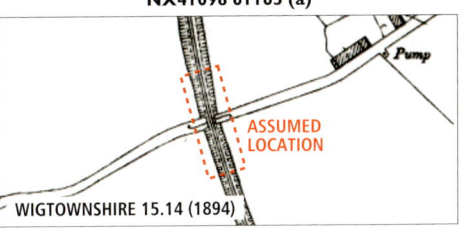
ASSUMED LOCATION
WIGTOWNSHIRE 15.14 (1894)

MAGDALEN GATE (GER)
July 1843 - 1 August 1866
Line lifted – Demolished – Station site unused **TF59199 10436**

MANCHESTER DUCIE BRIDGE (L&YR)
1855 - 30 March 1884
Line Operated by Manchester Metrolink – Demolished – Station site occupied by Manchester Victoria Tram Stop **SJ84070 99071**

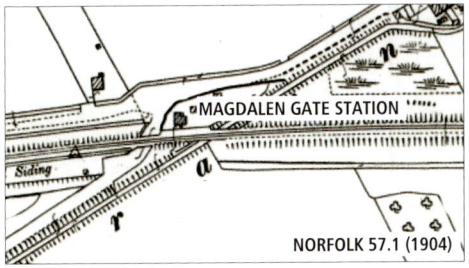
MAGDALEN GATE STATION
NORFOLK 57.1 (1904)

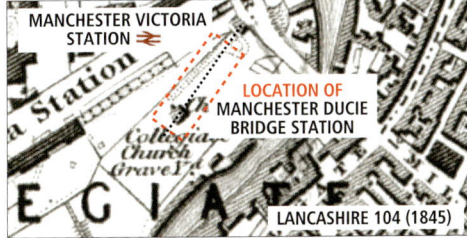
MANCHESTER VICTORIA STATION
LOCATION OF MANCHESTER DUCIE BRIDGE STATION
LANCASHIRE 104 (1845)

MAIDENHEAD BOYN HILL (GWR)
1 August 1854 - 1 November 1871
Line Operational – Demolished – No access **SU88280 81109**

MANCHESTER FREE TRADE HALL (CLC)
9 July 1877 - 1 July 1880
Line lifted – Demolished – Station site in commercial use
SJ83645 97813

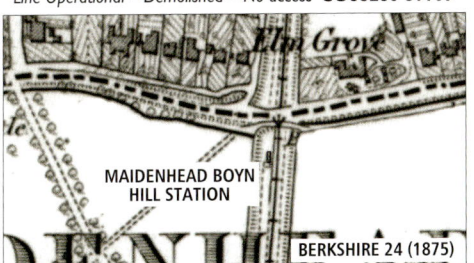
MAIDENHEAD BOYN HILL STATION
BERKSHIRE 24 (1875)

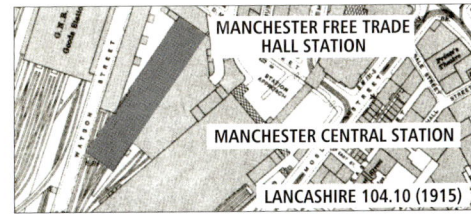
MANCHESTER FREE TRADE HALL STATION
MANCHESTER CENTRAL STATION
LANCASHIRE 104.10 (1915)

MANCHESTER LIVERPOOL ROAD - MARCH (1st)

MANCHESTER LIVERPOOL ROAD (L&MR)
17 September 1830 - 4 May 1844
Line lifted – Grade I listed station part of Manchester's Museum of Science & Industry **SJ82946 97873**

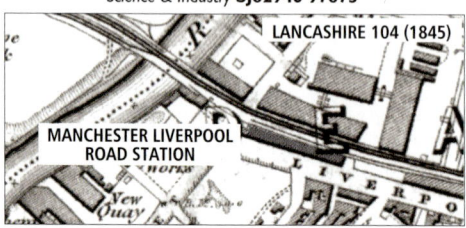
LANCASHIRE 104 (1845)

MANCHESTER OLDHAM ROAD (M&LR)
4 July 1839 - 1 January 1844
Line lifted – Demolished – Station site in commercial use
SJ84940 99005

LANCASHIRE 104 (1845)

MANCHESTER TRAVIS STREET (M&BR)
4 June 1840 - 6 May 1842
Line Operational – Demolished **SJ85070 97778 (a)**

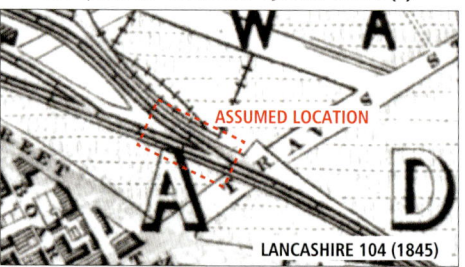
LANCASHIRE 104 (1845)

MANGOTSFIELD (1st) (MR)
21 August 1845 - 4 August 1869
Line lifted – Demolished – Station House in private use – A pathway passes through the station site **ST67247 75749**

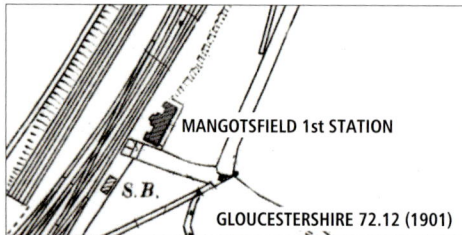
GLOUCESTERSHIRE 72.12 (1901)

MANLEY (CLC)
22 June 1870 - 1 May 1875
Line lifted – Demolished – Station building in private use
SJ49571 71957

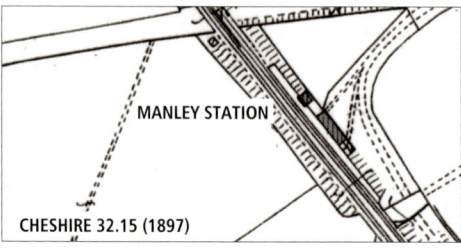
CHESHIRE 32.15 (1897)

MANSFIELD (1st) (MR)
1832 - 9 October 1849
Line lifted – Demolished – Station site in commercial use
SK53773 60862 (a)

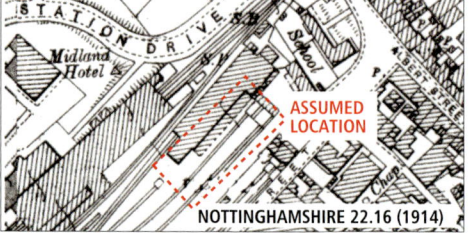
NOTTINGHAMSHIRE 22.16 (1914)

MANSTON (NER)
1850 - 1 April 1869
Line Operational – Demolished – No access **SE38052 34348**

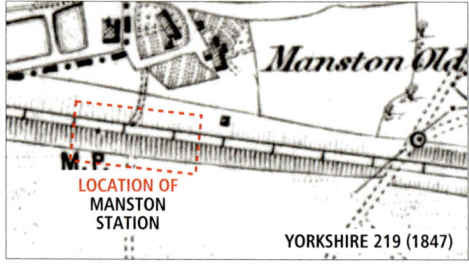
YORKSHIRE 219 (1847)

MARCH (1st) (GER)
14 January 1847 - 1886
Line Operational – Demolished – No access
TL42030 97791 (a)

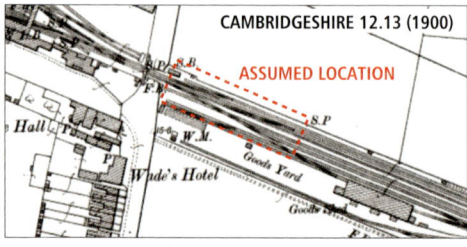
CAMBRIDGESHIRE 12.13 (1900)

MARYPORT (1st) (M&CR)
15 July 1840 - 4 June 1860
Line lifted – Demolished – Station site unused
NY03381 35981 (a)

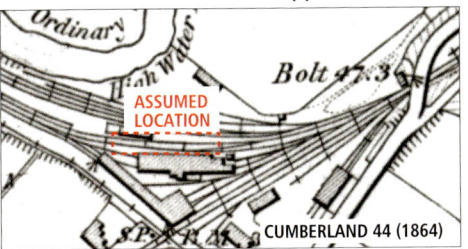

MARYPORT (1st) - MENSTON JUNCTION
MEIGLE JUNCTION (DP&AJnR)
2 August 1848 - 1 August 1861
Line lifted – Demolished – A track passes through the station site
NO30273 43556

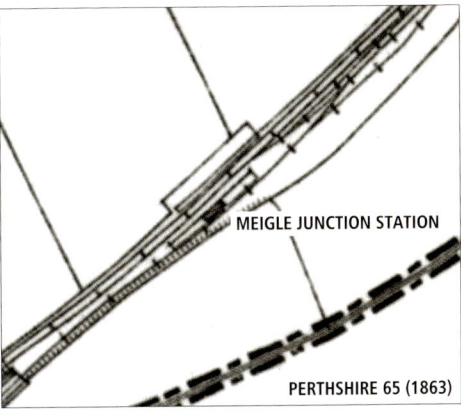

MAUD'S BRIDGE (MS&LR)
November 1859 - 1 October 1866
Line lifted – Demolished – Station site unused **SE71794 12223**

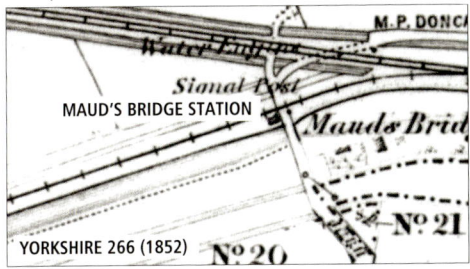

MEIKLE FERRY (HR)
1 June 1864 - 1 January 1869
Line Operational – Platform partially intact - Station building in private use as part of "Dornoch Firth Caravan Park"
NH74897 84396

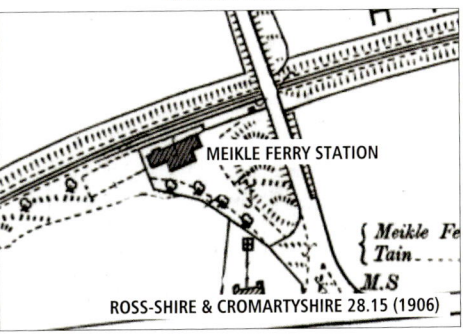

MAYBOLE (1st) (G&SWR)
13 October 1856 - 24 May 1860
Line lifted – Demolished – Station site in commercial use
NS30538 10424

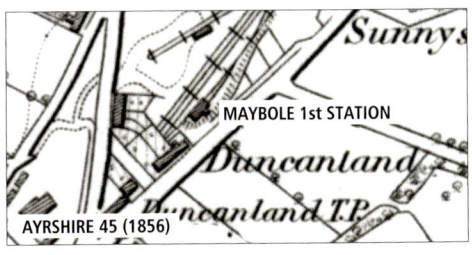

MENSTON JUNCTION (MR)
1 March 1873 - 1 March 1876
Main line Operational – Demolished – No access
SE16915 44454 (a)

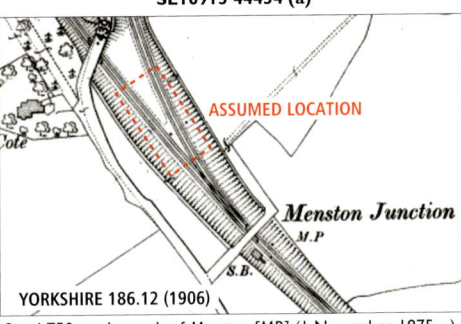

MAYBOLE JUNCTION (G&SWR)
7 August 1856 - 1 December 1859
Lines Operational – Demolished – No access **NS35689 16670**

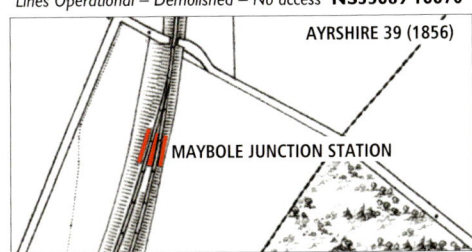

This was an exchange platform

Sited 750 yards north of Menston [MR] (1 November 1875 -)

MERRY LEES - MIDDLESBROUGH (1st) (S&DR)

MERRY LEES (MR)
18 July 1832 - 27 March 1848
Line Operational – Demolished **SK46999 05785**

MERRYLEES (MR)
27 March 1848 - 1 March 1871
Line Operational – Demolished **SK46966 05832**

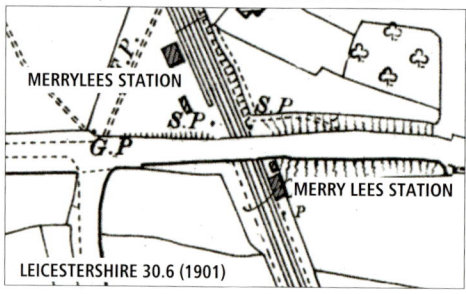
MERRYLEES STATION
MERRY LEES STATION
LEICESTERSHIRE 30.6 (1901)

MERSTHAM (SER)
12 July 1841 - 1845
Line Operational – Demolished – No access
TQ28764 52267 (a)

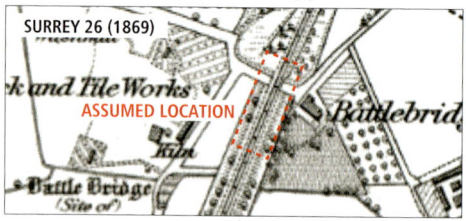
SURREY 26 (1869)
ASSUMED LOCATION

MERSTONE (1st) (IoWCR)
1 February 1875 - 20 July 1895
Line lifted – Demolished – Newlands and National Cycling Route No.20 pass through the station site **SZ52712 84445**

HAMPSHIRE & ISLE OF WIGHT 95 (1863)
MERSTONE 1st STATION

MERTHYR (TVR)
21 April 1841 - 1 August 1877
Line lifted – Demolished – Station site in commercial use
SO05063 05649

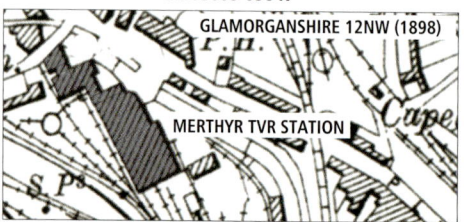
GLAMORGANSHIRE 12NW (1898)
MERTHYR TVR STATION

MERTHYR ROAD (VoNR)
24 September 1851 - 2 November 1853
Line Operational for Freight – Demolished – No access
SN97201 05541 (a)

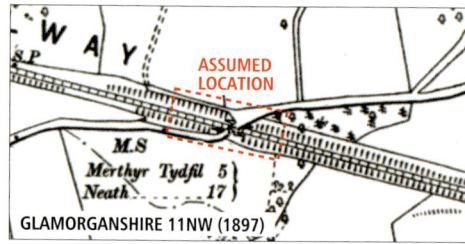
ASSUMED LOCATION
GLAMORGANSHIRE 11NW (1897)

MEXBOROUGH JUNCTION (MS&LR)
January 1850 - 3 April 1871
Line Operational – Demolished – No access **SK46765 99739**

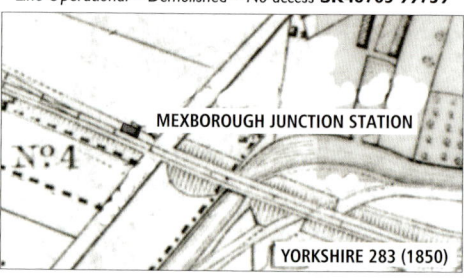
MEXBOROUGH JUNCTION STATION
YORKSHIRE 283 (1850)

MIDDLESBROUGH (1st) (NER)
4 June 1846 - 1 December 1877
Line Operational – Demolished – Station site partially incorporated into current Middlesbrough Station **NZ49515 20726**

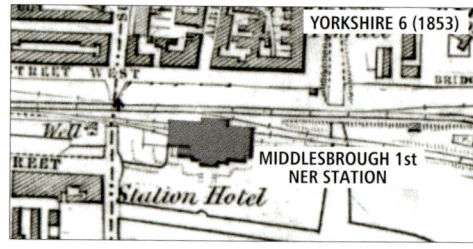
YORKSHIRE 6 (1853)
MIDDLESBROUGH 1st NER STATION

MIDDLESBROUGH (1st) (S&DR)
27 December 1830 - 1837
Line lifted – Demolished – Station site in commercial use
NZ49146 21366

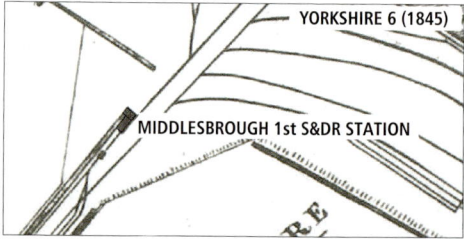
YORKSHIRE 6 (1845)
MIDDLESBROUGH 1st S&DR STATION

MIDDLESBROUGH (2nd) (S&DR)
1837 - 4 June 1846
Line lifted – Demolished – Station site in commercial use
NZ49574 21243

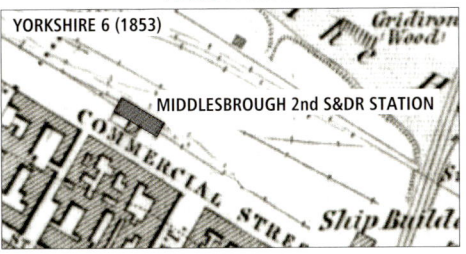

MIDDLETON* (L&NWR)
June 1833 - April 1876
Line lifted – Demolished – The High Peak Trail passes through the station site **SK27542 55183**

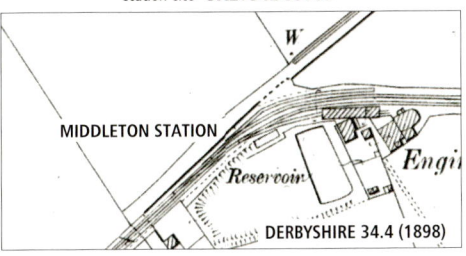

MIDHURST (1st) (LB&SCR)
15 October 1866 - 11 July 1881
Line lifted – Demolished – Station site occupied by housing in Oakwood Close **SU87950 21069**

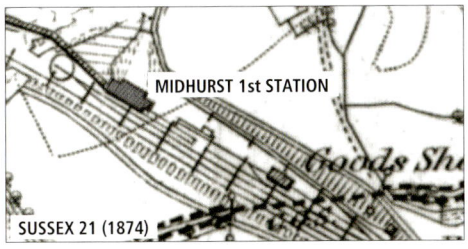

MILE END (GER)
1841 - 24 May 1872
Line Operational – Demolished – No access
TQ35030 82402 (a)

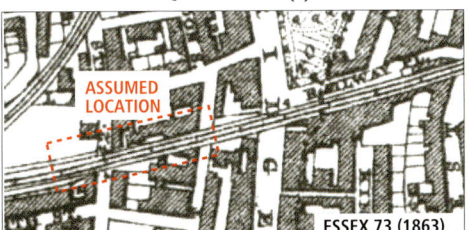

MIDDLESBROUGH (2nd) (S&DR) - MILLS HILL

MILLAGAN (GNofSR)
1 October 1859 - 4 November 1867
Line lifted – Demolished – The realigned B9117 crosses over the station site **NJ51615 50873**

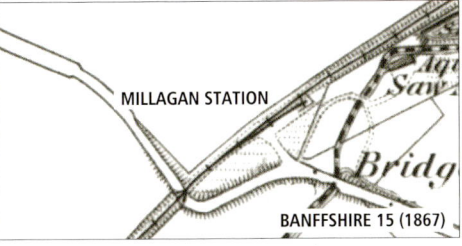

MILLER'S BRIDGE (L&YR)
October 1851 - April 1876
Line Operational – Demolished – No access
SJ33998 94625 (a)

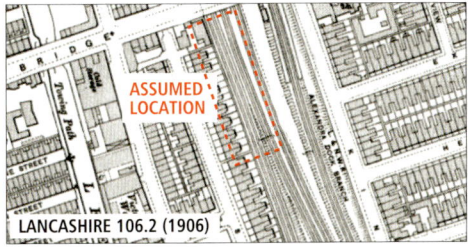

MILLFIELD (1st) (NER)
1 June 1853 - 1890
Line Operated by Tyne & Wear Metro – Demolished – Station site occupied by Millfield Metro Station **NZ38490 57046**

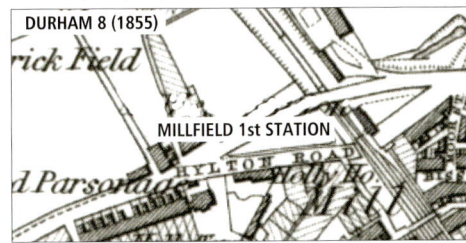

MILLS HILL (M&LR)
4 July 1839 - 11 August 1842
Line Operational - Demolished **SD88735 06077**

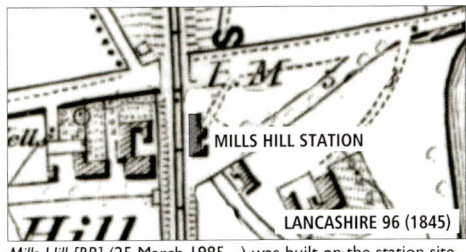

Mills Hill [BR] (25 March 1985 -) was built on the station site

MILLS OF DRUM - MONUMENT LANE (1st)

MILLS OF DRUM (DsideR)
8 September 1853 - 1 January 1863
Line lifted – Demolished – Station site unused **NO76090 96898**

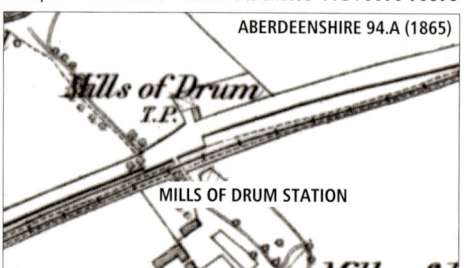

MIRFIELD (1st) (L&YR)
31 March 1845 - 5 March 1866
Line Operational – Demolished – No access **SE20166 19560**

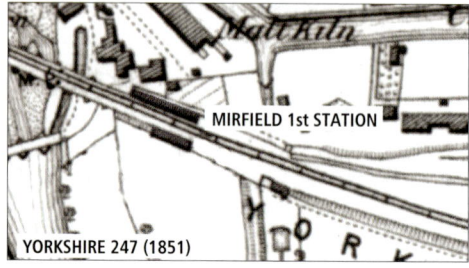

MILVERTON FOR WARWICK (1st) (L&NWR)
9 December 1844 - 13 October 1883
Line Operational – Demolished – No access
SP30516 65992

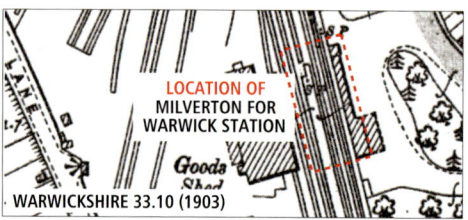

MOAT LANE (L&NR)
August 1859 - 3 January 1863
Line lifted – Demolished – Station building in private use
SO04030 90908

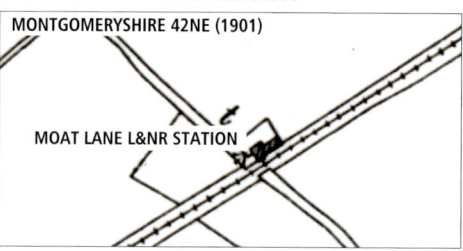

MINIONS (L&CdnR)
1860 - 1886
Line lifted – Demolished **SX26083 71170 (e)**

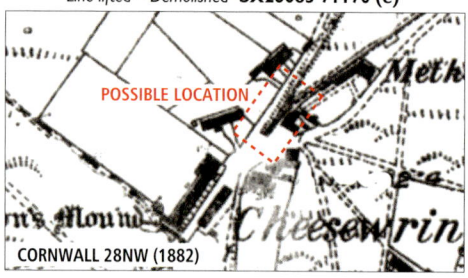

MONTROSE (AbdeenR)
1 February 1848 - 17 September 1849
Line lifted – Demolished – Station site occupied by dwellings
in Railway Place **NO71779 57419**

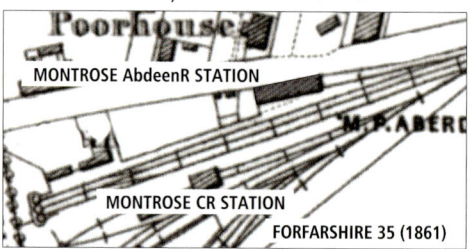

MINORIES (L&BwallR)
6 July 1840 - 24 October 1853
Line Operational – Demolished – No access
TQ33685 80870 (a)

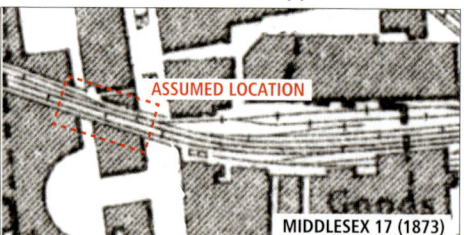

MONUMENT LANE (1st) (L&NWR)
June 1853 - 1886
Line Operational – Demolished – No access
SP05423 87012 (a)

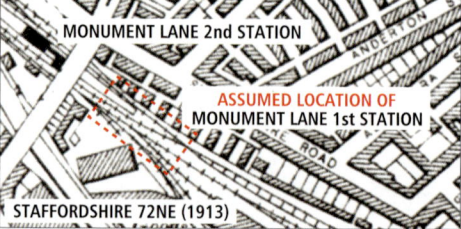

MOOR EDGE (B&TR)
29 June 1864 - ? 1864
Line Operated by Tyne & Wear Metro – Demolished – No access
NZ24952 67165 (a)

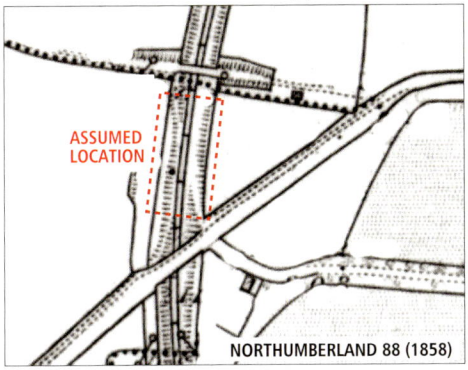
NORTHUMBERLAND 88 (1858)

MORECAMBE POULTON LANE
(L&NWR)
1 November 1870 - 9 May 1886
Line Operational – Demolished – No access
SD44117 64242 (a)

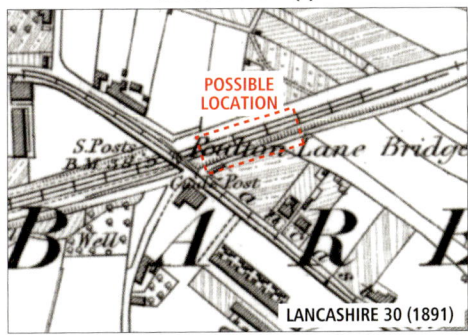
LANCASHIRE 30 (1891)

MORETON [TRAMWAY STATION]
(OW&WR)
c1834 - 4 June 1853
Line lifted – Demolished – Station site occupied by a Co-Op store
SP20589 32795

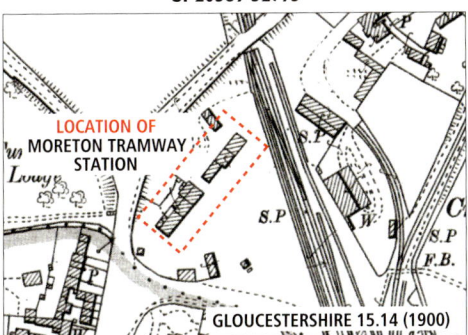
GLOUCESTERSHIRE 15.14 (1900)

MOOR EDGE - MOSSBLOWN JUNCTION HALT

MORFA (C&LR)
1 July 1869 – 5 July 1870
Line lifted – Demolished – Station site unused **SH48327 61659**

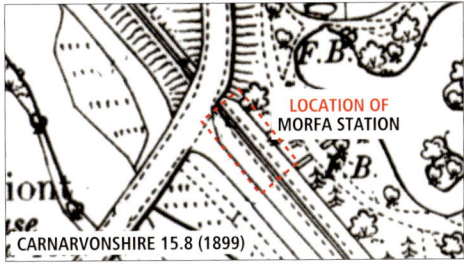
CARNARVONSHIRE 15.8 (1899)

MORNINGSIDE (1st) (CR)
October 1844 - February 1853
Line lifted – Demolished - Station site unused.
NS83259 55094 (a)

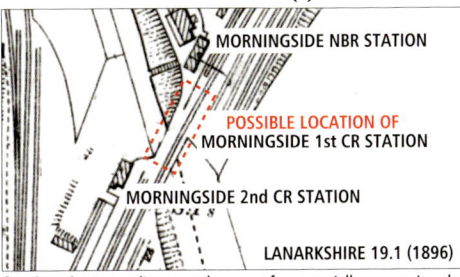
LANARKSHIRE 19.1 (1896)

Sited to the immediate south west of, or partially occupying the site of, Morningside [NBR] (2 June 1845 – 1 May 1930)

MORPETH (2nd) (NER)
1 April 1858 - 24 May 1880
Line lifted – Demolished – Grade II listed station building in private use **NZ20358 85370**

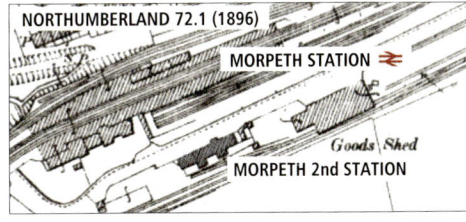

MOSSBLOWN JUNCTION HALT*
(G&SWR)
Not known
Line Operational for Freight – Demolished – No access
NS39286 24641 (a)

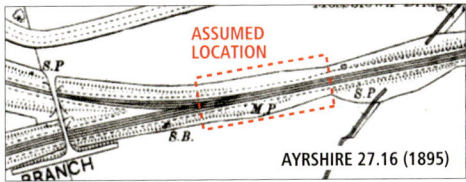
AYRSHIRE 27.16 (1895)

MOSSLEY HILL (1st) – MURIE CROSSING

MOSSLEY HILL (1st) L&NWR)
15 February 1864 - 13 July 1891
Line Operational – Demolished – No access
SJ39185 87355

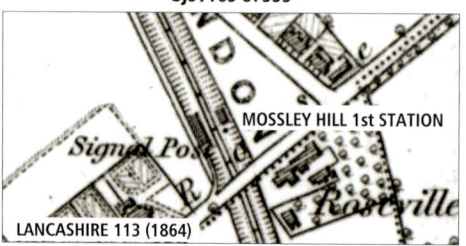

LANCASHIRE 113 (1864)

MOTHERWELL (1st) (CR)
20 March 1841 - 31 July 1885
Line lifted – Demolished – Station site in commercial use
NS75233 57167 (a)

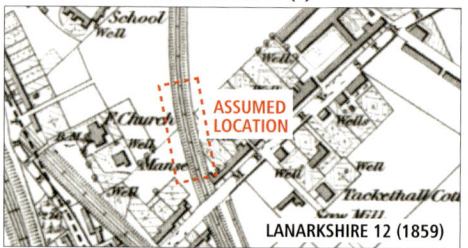

ASSUMED LOCATION

LANARKSHIRE 12 (1859)

MOTHERWELL BRIDGE (CR)
20 March 1841 - 31 July 1885
Line Operational – Demolished – No access
NS75072 56994 (a)

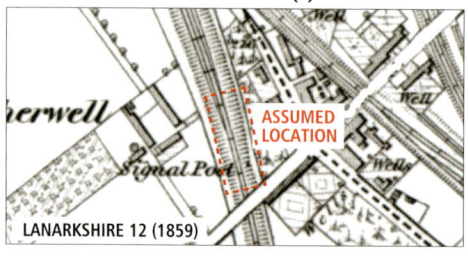

ASSUMED LOCATION

LANARKSHIRE 12 (1859)

MOTHERWELL JUNCTION (CR)
1 June 1849 - 31 July 1885
Line Operational – Demolished – No access **NS75464 56861**

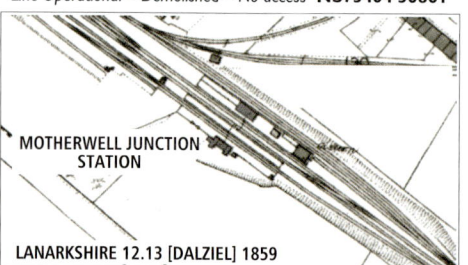

MOTHERWELL JUNCTION STATION

LANARKSHIRE 12.13 [DALZIEL] 1859

MOULSFORD (GWR)
1 June 1840 - 29 February 1892
Line Operational – Demolished – No access **SU59231 85142**

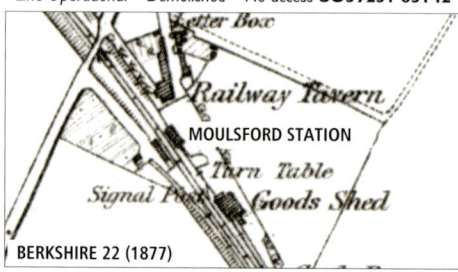

MOULSFORD STATION

BERKSHIRE 22 (1877)

MOUNTAIN ASH (1st) (TVR)
6 August 1846 - 1 January 1857
Line Operational - Demolished – No access
ST04704 99244 (a)

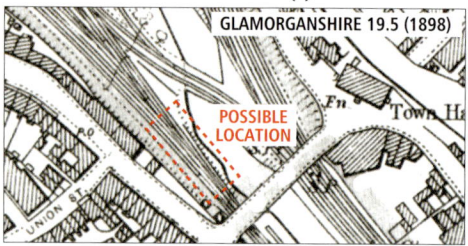

GLAMORGANSHIRE 19.5 (1898)

POSSIBLE LOCATION

MUIRKIRK (1st) (G&SWR)
9 August 1848 - 1896
Line lifted – Demolished – Station House in private use. Station site in use as a car park for "Kames Motorsport Complex"
NS69564 26526

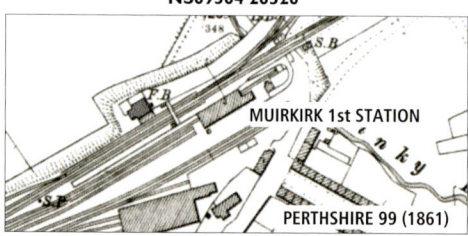

MUIRKIRK 1st STATION

PERTHSHIRE 99 (1861)

MURIE CROSSING* (CR)
10 May 1852 - 1873
Line Operational – Demolished **NO22543 23214**

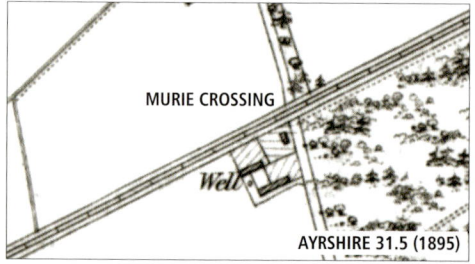

MURIE CROSSING

AYRSHIRE 31.5 (1895)

NEATH (1st) (GWR)
19 June 1850 – July 1865
Line Operational – Demolished – No access
SS75046 97397 (a)

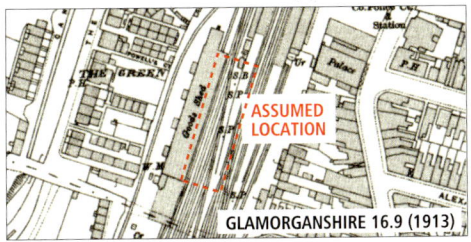

NETHERTON (GWR)
NEATH (1st) (GWR) - NEWBOLD WHARF
20 December 1852 – 1 March 1878
Line Operational for Freight – Demolished – No access
SO94285 89476 (a)

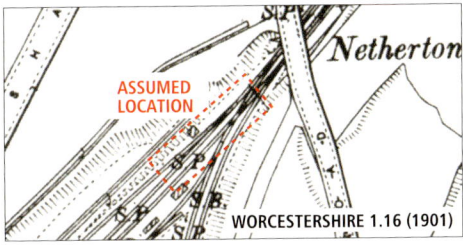

NEATH (2nd) (GWR)
July 1865 – 20 August 1877
Line Operational – Demolished – No access
SS75131 97704 (a)

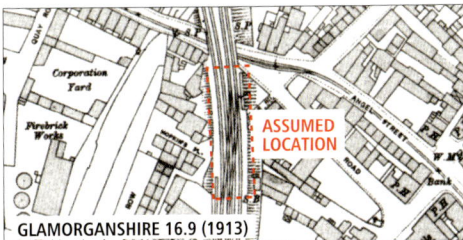

NEWARTHILL (CR)
15 May 1867 – 1 June 1880
Line Operational – Demolished **NS77549 58876**

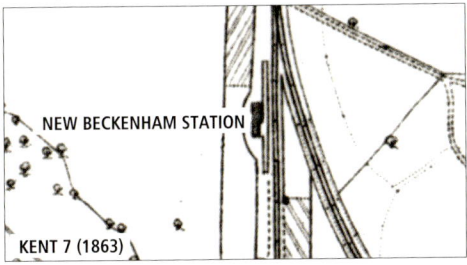

NEATH (N&BR)
1 August 1878 – 1 August 1889
Line lifted – Demolished – Station site in commercial use
SS75103 98125

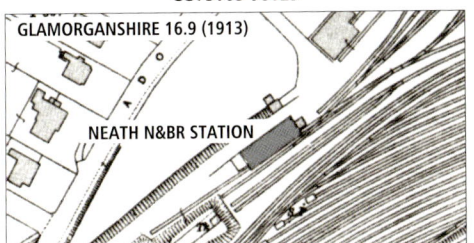

NEW BECKENHAM (SER)
1 April 1864 – 1886
Line Operational – Demolished – No access **TQ36722 70209**

NEILSTON (GB&NDR)
8 October 1855 – 18 April 1870
Line Operational – Demolished – No access **NS47322 57581**

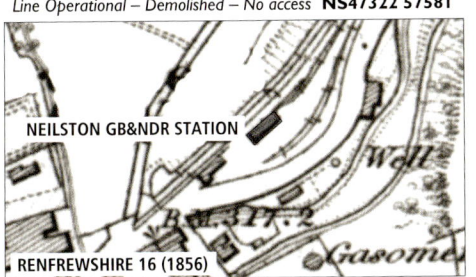

NEWBOLD WHARF (OW&WR)
Prior to 1834 – 30 September 1858
Line lifted – Demolished – Station site in domestic use
SP24426 46823

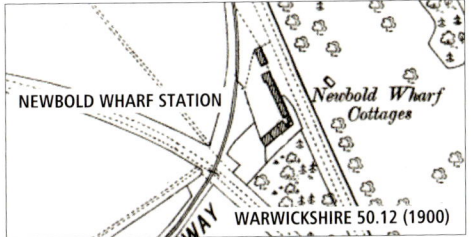

NEWBURGH (1st) - NEW ENGLAND PLATFORM (2nd)

NEWBURGH (1st) (NBR)
17 May 1848 - 12 August 1906
Line Operational – Demolished – No access **NO23501 18122**

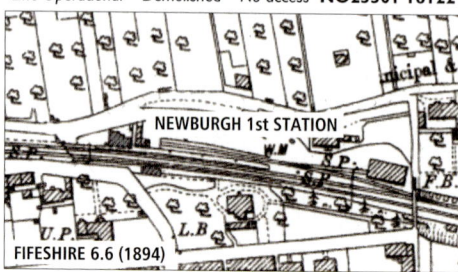
NEWBURGH 1st STATION
FIFESHIRE 6.6 (1894)

NEWCASTLE CARLIOL SQUARE (YN&BR)
20 June 1839 - 30 August 1850
Line lifted – Demolished – The northbound access road to the A167(M) crosses the station site **NZ25209 64252**

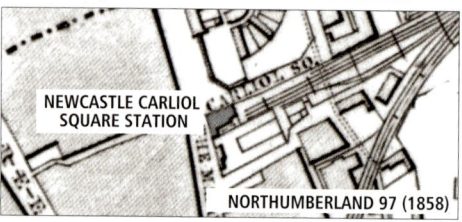
NEWCASTLE CARLIOL SQUARE STATION
NORTHUMBERLAND 97 (1858)

NEWCASTLE FORTH (YN&BR)
1 March 1847 - 1 January 1851
Line lifted – Demolished – Station site incorporated into Newcastle Station **NZ24482 63807**

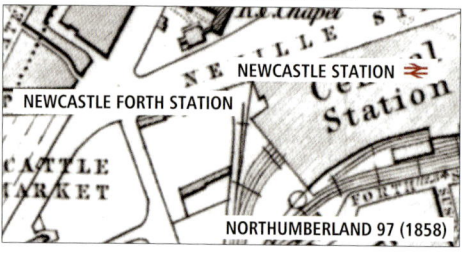
NEWCASTLE STATION
NEWCASTLE FORTH STATION
NORTHUMBERLAND 97 (1858)

NEWCASTLE SHOT TOWER (N&CR)
21 May 1839 - 1 March 1847
Line extant – Demolished **NZ23890 63240 (a)**

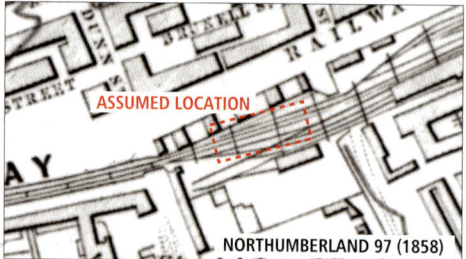
ASSUMED LOCATION
NORTHUMBERLAND 97 (1858)

NEW CROSS (ELR)
7 December 1869 - 1 September 1886
Line lifted – Demolished – Station site partially in commercial use and partially occupied by dwellings in Auburn Close
TQ36212 77086

NEW CROSS ELR STATION
NEW CROSS GATE STATION
LONDON 104 (1903)

NEW DYKES BROW (NBR)
4 October 1856 - October 1866
Line lifted – Demolished – A track passes through the station site
NY24146 57767

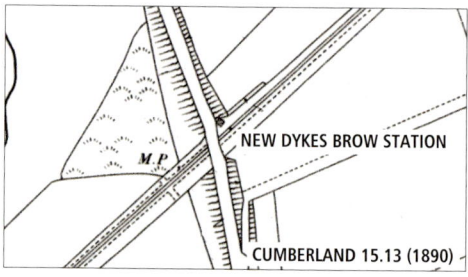
NEW DYKES BROW STATION
CUMBERLAND 15.13 (1890)

NEW ENGLAND PLATFORM* (1st) (GNR)
1856 - 1878
Line lifted – Demolished – Station site in commercial use **TF17980 00775 (a)**

NEW ENGLAND PLATFORM* (2nd) (GNR)
1878 - c1900
Line lifted – Demolished – The A15, Bourgess Boulevard, passes through the station site **TF18182 00728 (a)**

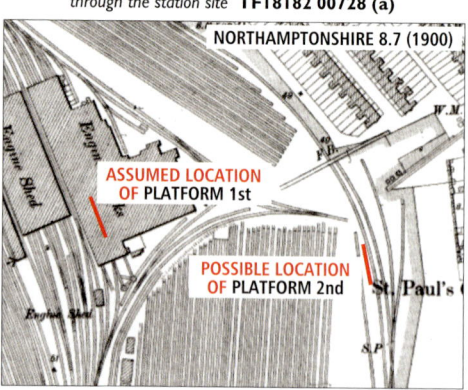
NORTHAMPTONSHIRE 8.7 (1900)
ASSUMED LOCATION OF PLATFORM 1st
POSSIBLE LOCATION OF PLATFORM 2nd

NEW HALLS — NEWPORT MILL STREET

NEW HALLS (NBR)
May 1870 - 1 September 1878
Line lifted – Demolished – Station site unused
NT13723 78228 (a)

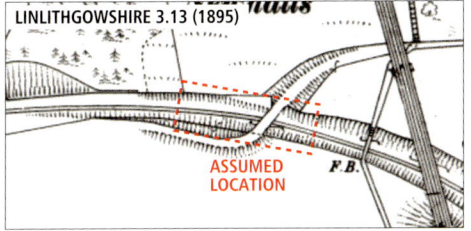

NEW PASSAGE PIER (GWR)
8 September 1863 - 1 December 1886
Line lifted – Station and pier demolished **ST54021 86755**

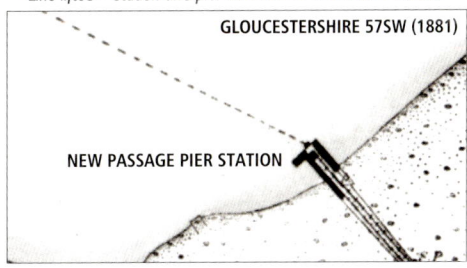

NEWHAM (WCwallR)
16 April 1855 - 16 September 1863
Line lifted – Demolished – Station site occupied by dwellings and a car park **SW82912 44275**

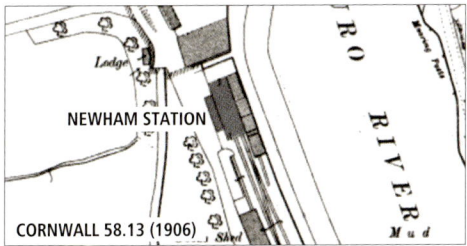

NEWPORT COURT-Y-BELLA (MonmouthsR)
23 December 1850 - 4 August 1852
Line extant – Demolished **ST30770 87034 (a)**

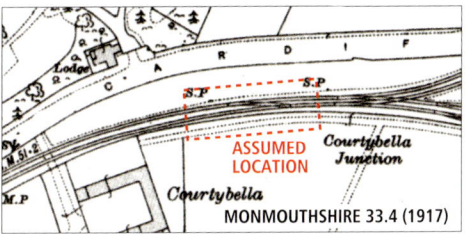

NEWHAVEN WHARF FOR PARIS (LB&SCR)
8 December 1847 - 17 May 1886
Line lifted – Demolished – Station site in commercial use
TQ44970 00821

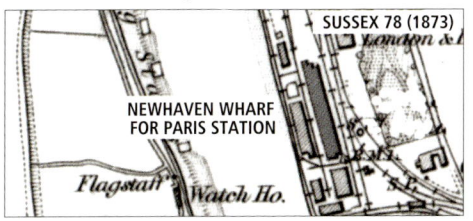

NEWPORT DOCK STREET (GWR)
4 August 1852 - 11 March 1880
Line lifted – Demolished – Station site in commercial use
ST31675 87491

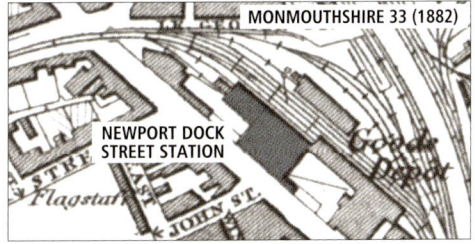

NEW PASSAGE (GWR)
8 September 1863 - 1 December 1886
Line lifted – Demolished – Station site occupied by a dwelling in New Passage Road **ST54377 86350**

NEWPORT MILL STREET (GWR)
9 March 1853 - 11 March 1880
Line lifted – Demolished – The A4042, Heidenhiem Drive, passes through the station site **ST31044 88589**

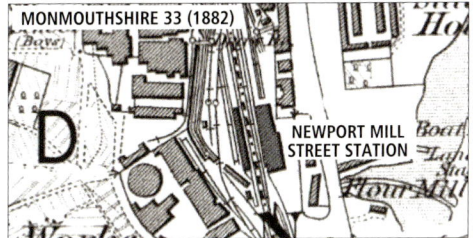

NEWPORT PAN LANE - NEW WANDSWORTH

NEWPORT PAN LANE (IoWR [NJn])
11 August 1875 - 1 June 1879
Line lifted – Demolished – Saint Georges Way passes through the station site **SZ50318 88874**

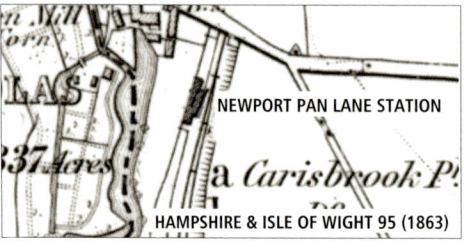

NEWSTEAD (NBR)
November 1849 - October 1852
Line lifted – Demolished – Station site unused
NT56547 34150

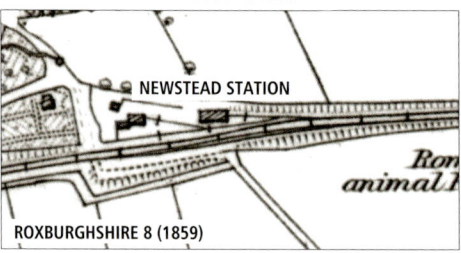

NEWTON (1st) (CR)
November 1852 - 19 December 1873
Line Operational – Demolished **NS66997 60514**

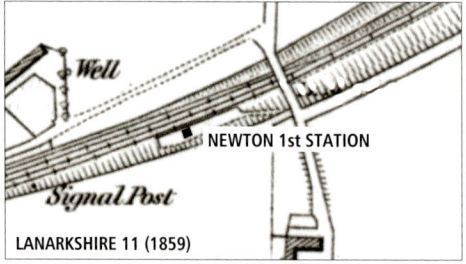

NEWTON RACECOURSE* (L&NWR)
20 June 1832 - ?
Line lifted – Demolished – Station site occupied by housing
SJ56688 95597

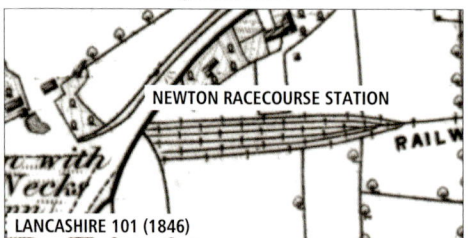

NEWTON ROAD (1st) (L&NWR)
4 July 1837 - 1 March 1863
Line Operational – Demolished – No access
SP02312 93937 (a)

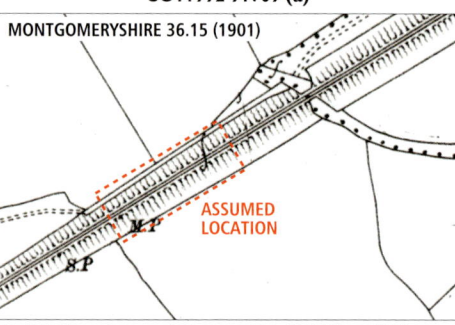

NEWTOWN (L&NR)
11 August 1859 - 10 June 1861
Line Operational – Demolished – No access
SO11992 91709 (a)

Sited 1056 yards east of *Newton [CamR]* (10 June 1861 -)

NEWTYLE (1st) (CR)
3 April 1832 - 31 August 1868
Line lifted – Demolished – Platform and station building extant
NO29966 41364

NEW WANDSWORTH (LB&SCR)
29 March 1858 - 1 November 1869
Line Operational – Demolished – No access
TQ27037 74886
FOR MAP SEE CLAPHAM COMMON, PAGE 37

NIDDRIE (NBR)
1 September 1848 – 1 February 1869
Main Line Operational – Demolished – No access
NT31802 71883

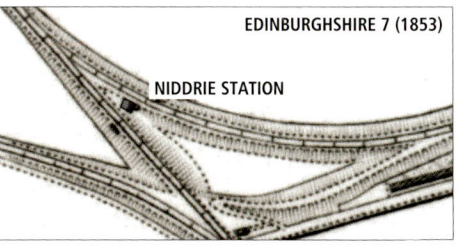

NIDDRIE JUNCTION (NBR)
2 June 1832 – 14 July 1847
Line Operational – Demolished – No access **NT31828 71849**

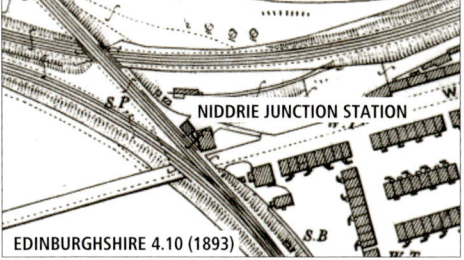

NINE ELMS (L&SWR)
21 May 1838 – 11 July 1848
Line lifted – Demolished – Station site in commercial use
TQ30003 77735

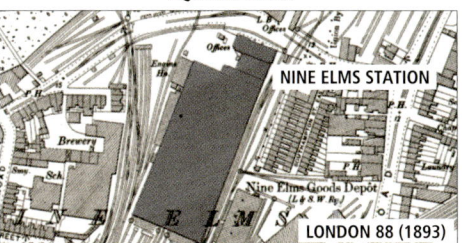

NINE ELMS ROYAL STATION* (L&SWR)
1853 – 1876
Line lifted – Demolished **TQ30091 77539**

NIDDRIE - NORTHAMPTON (1st) (MR)
NINEWELLS JUNCTION (CR)
10 June 1861 – October 1865
Line Operational – Demolished – No access **NO36829 29677**

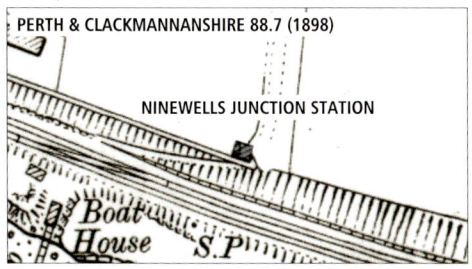

NOOK PASTURE (NBR)
2 January 1864 – 1 January 1874
Line lifted – Demolished – Station site unused
NY44748 79150 (a)

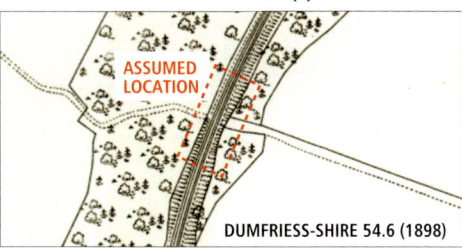

NORTHALLERTON TOWN (NER)
25 May 1852 – 1 January 1856
Line Operational – Station building in commercial use
SE36523 94568

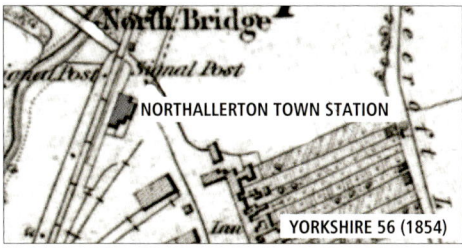

NORTHAMPTON (1st) (MR)
1 October 1866 – 10 June 1872
Line lifted – Demolished – Station site occupied by dwellings
in Henry Bird Way **SP75526 59655**

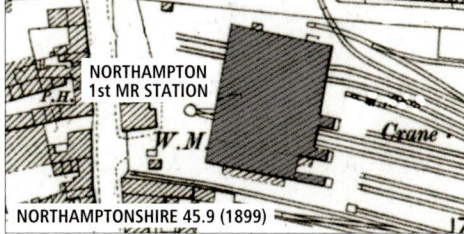

NORTH END – NORTON BRIDGE (1st) (L&NWR)

NORTH END (E&WJnR)
August 1872 – 1 August 1877
Line Operational for Freight – Demolished **SP38948 53090**

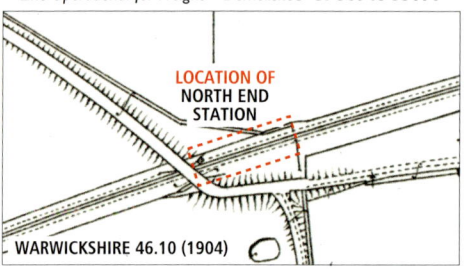

NORTH KENT JUNCTION* (SER)
1 September 1849 – 1 October 1850
Line Operational – Demolished – No access
TQ36123 77959 (a)

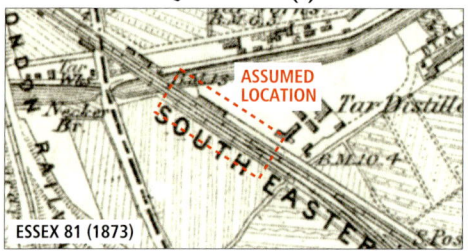

NORTH QUEENSFERRY PIER (NBR)
1 November 1877 – 5 March 1890
Line lifted – Demolished – A track passes through the station site
NT12790 80505

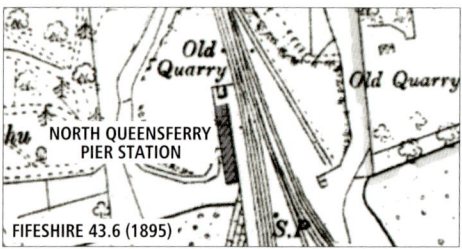

NORTH SHIELDS STATION (NER)
27 June 1864 – 3 July 1882
Line lifted – Demolished – A pathway passes through the station site **NZ36363 69221**

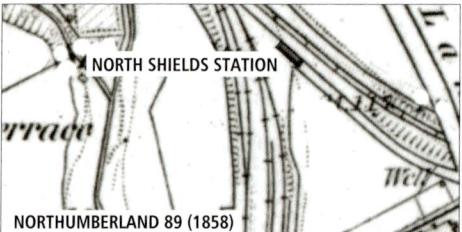

NORTH SHIELDS TERMINUS (NER)
1 April 1861 – 7 July 1882
Line lifted – Demolished – Station site occupied by houses in Hazeldene Court **NZ36352 69032**

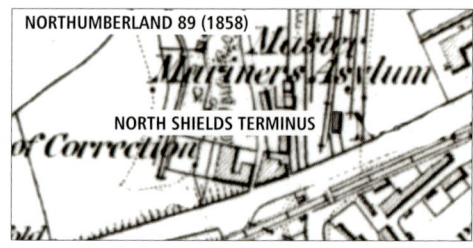

NORTHWICH (1st) (CLC)
1 January 1863 – May 1868
Line lifted – Demolished – Station site occupied by part of car park for a Tesco Superstore **SJ66987 73996**

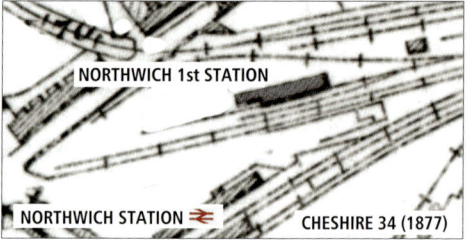

NORTON (MR)
November 1841 – 1 October 1855
Line Operational – Demolished – No access
SO89290 51208 (e)

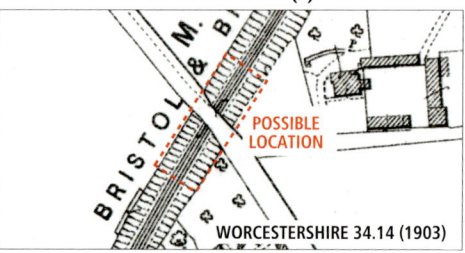

NORTON BRIDGE (1st) (L&NWR)
4 July 1837 – 14 October 1876
Line Operational – Demolished – No access
SJ87122 30069 (a)

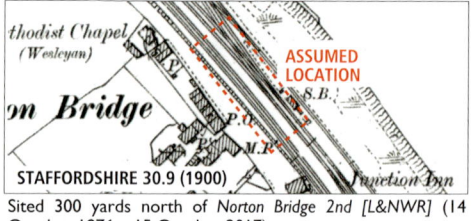

Sited 300 yards north of *Norton Bridge 2nd [L&NWR]* (14 October 1876 – 15 October 2017)

NORTON BRIDGE (NSR)
17 April 1848 - 1850
Line Operational – Demolished – No access
SJ87011 30291 (e)

NORTON JUNCTION (NER)
March 1850 - July 1870
Line Operational – Demolished – No access **NZ42822 22275**

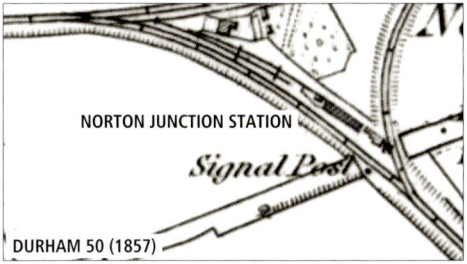

NORWICH THORPE (1st) (GER)
1 May 1844 - 3 May 1886
Line lifted – Demolished - Station Approach and Riverside pass through the station site **TG23809 08317**

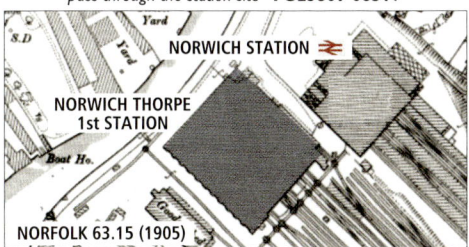

NORWOOD (LB&SCR)
5 June 1839 - 1 June 1859
Line Operational – Demolished – No access
TQ34106 68435 (a)

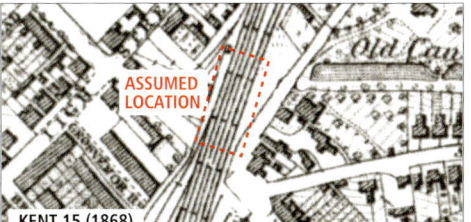

NORTON BRIDGE (NSR) - OAKWELLGATE

NOTTINGHAM THE MEADOWS (MR)
4 June 1839 - 22 May 1848
Line lifted – Station building in use as part of Nottingham Magistrates Court **SK57330 39214**

NUNEATON (1st) (MR)
1 November 1864 - 1 September 1873
Line Operational – Demolished – No access
SP35432 92548 (a)

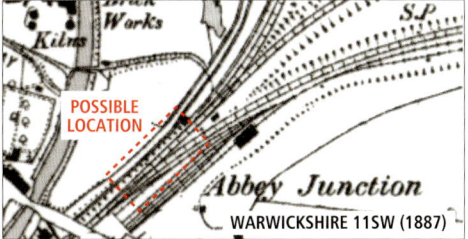

OAKENSHAW (MR)
1 July 1840 - 1 June 1870
Line Operational – Demolished – No access **SE35911 18917**

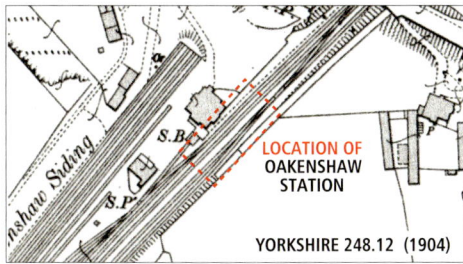

OAKWELLGATE (N&DJnR)
5 September 1839 - 2 September 1844
Line Operational – Demolished – No access
NZ25579 63556 (a)

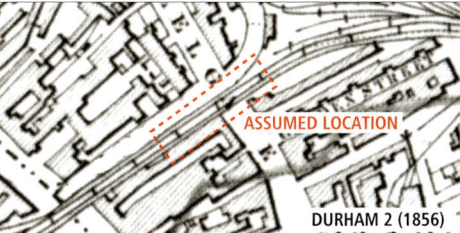

ODDINGLEY - OXFORD (1st) (GWR)

ODDINGLEY (MR)
September 1845 - 1 October 1855
Line Operational – Demolished – No access
SO91657 59043 (a)

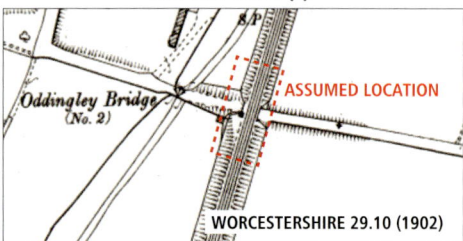

OUSE BRIDGE (GER)
May 1848 - 1 January 1864
Line Operational – Demolished – No access **TL59208 98571**

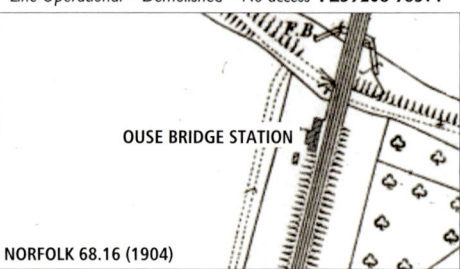

OLDFIELD ROAD (L&YR)
February 1852 - 2 December 1872
Line Operational – Demolished – No access
SJ82486 98281 (a)

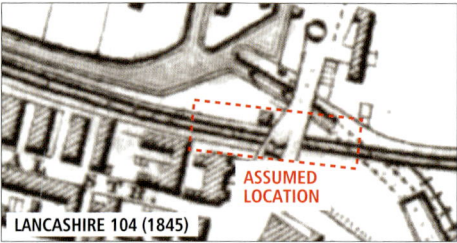

OVERSEAL AND MOIRA (A&NJR)
1 September 1873 - 1 July 1890
Line lifted – Demolished – Station site unused **SK30514 16138**

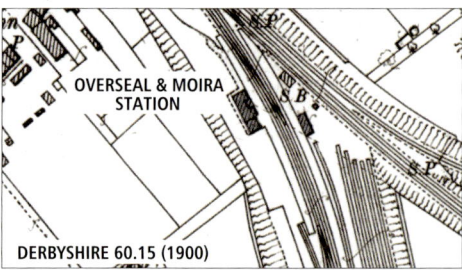

OLDHAM MUMPS (L&NWR)
5 July 1856 - 1 November 1862
Line lifted – Demolished – Station site in commercial use
SD93482 04923 (a)

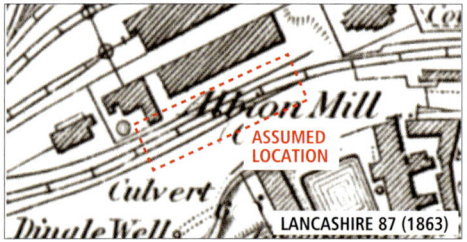

OVERTOWN (1st) (CR)
8 May 1843 - 1 October 1881
Line Operational – Demolished – No access **NS80688 53596**

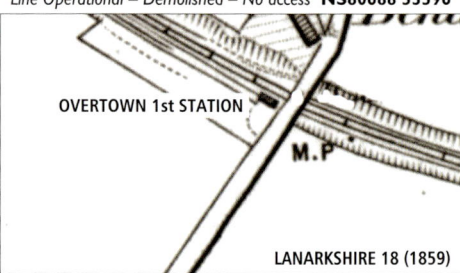

OTNEY (LC&DR)
1 June 1874 - 1 November 1880
Line Operational – Demolished – No access
TQ53305 58430 (a)

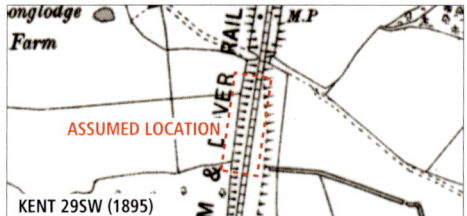

This was an exchange platform

OXFORD (1st) (GWR)
12 June 1844 - 1 October 1852
Line lifted – Demolished – Station site occupied by dwellings
SP51252 05376 (a)

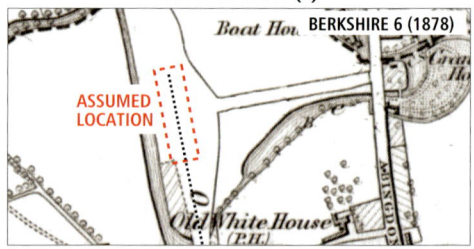

OX HOUSE* (GWR)
20 August 1857 - ?
Line lifted – Demolished – A pathway passes through the station site **SO41710 60954 (a)**

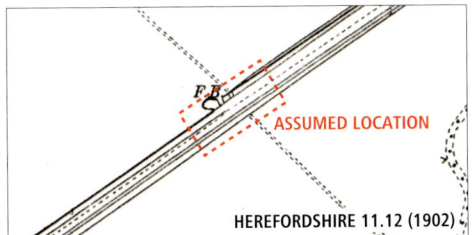

PAISLEY HAMILTON STREET (G&SWR)
3 April 1837 - 1 February 1866
Line lifted – Demolished – Station site unused **NS48554 64516**

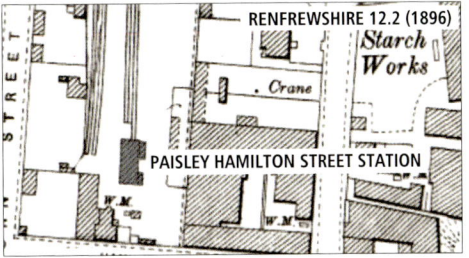

OXSPRING (MS&LR)
? - 1 November 1847
Line lifted – Demolished – A pathway passes through the station site **SE26925 01928**

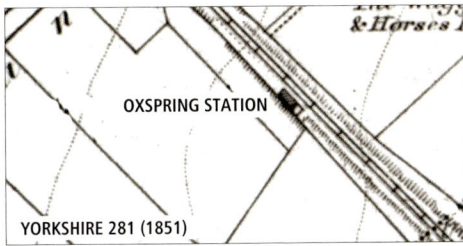

PANDY (TVR)
1 May 1861 - 2 August 1886
Line Operational – Demolished – No access **ST00775 91845 (a)**

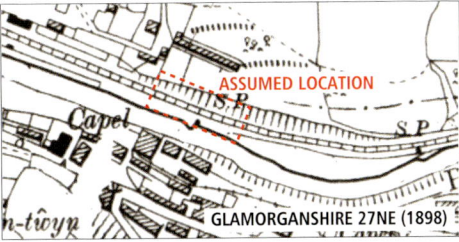

PADDINGTON (1st) (GWR)
4 June 1838 - 29 May 1854
Line lifted – Demolished – Station site in commercial use **TQ26282 81618**

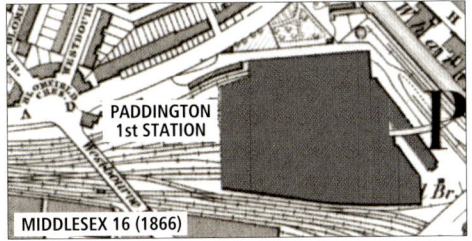

PANT (L&NWR)
1 July 1869 - 5 July 1870
Line Operated by Welsh Highland Railway – Demolished – A path also passes through the station site **SH47953 61167 (a)**

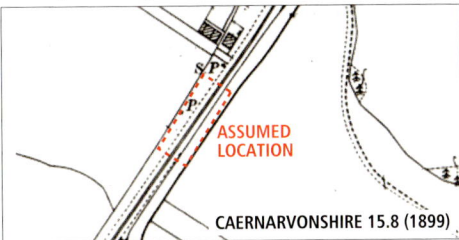

PAINSHAW (1st) (NER)
1841 - 1 July 1881
Line Operational – Demolished – No access **NZ32019 53587**

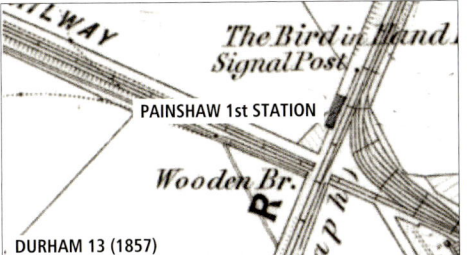

PANTEG (1st) (GWR)
21 December 1874 - July 1880
Line Operational – Demolished – No access **ST29734 98371**

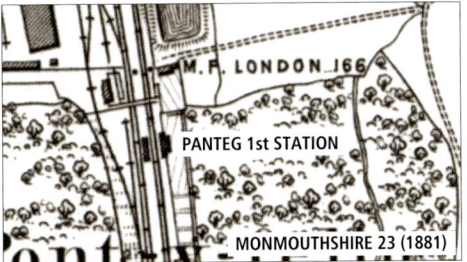

PARK (1st) - PARK VILLAGE

PARK (1st) (L&YR)
26 September 1846 - 1889
Line Operational – Demolished – No access **SJ87467 99548**

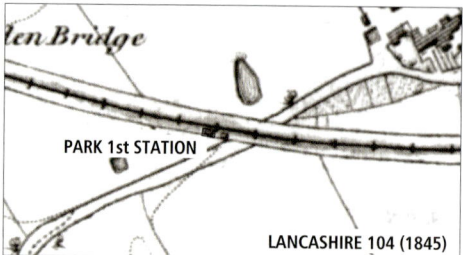

PARKGATE (1st) (BheadR)
1 October 1866 - 19 April 1886
Line lifted – Demolished – Station site occupied by Neston Wirral Way Car Park **SJ28373 77849**

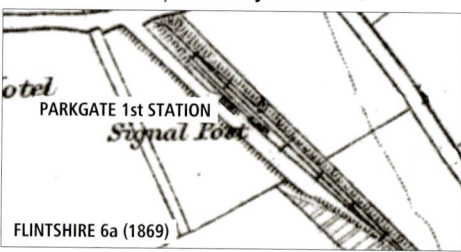

PARKHEAD (W&DwtJnR)
1 September 1845 - December 1846
Line lifted – Demolished – A pathway passes through the station site **NZ00271 43116**

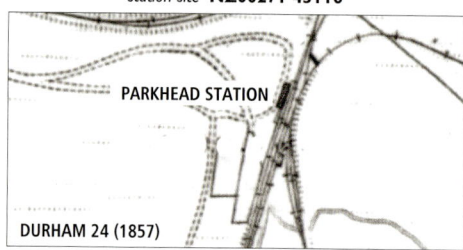

PARKSIDE (L&MR)
17 September 1830 - 1839
Line Operational – Demolished – No access **SJ60546 95522**

PARKSIDE (L&NWR)
1839 - 1 May 1878
Line Operational – Demolished – No access **SJ60836 95595**

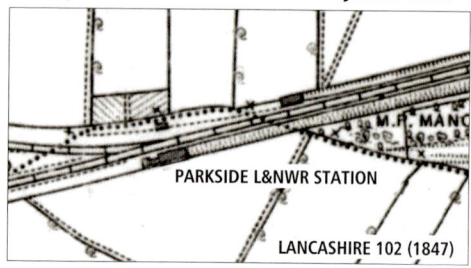

PARK STREET (1st) (L&NWR)
5 May 1858 - 1 June 1858
Line Operational – Demolished – No access **TL14510 03525**

PARK STREET (2nd) (L&NWR)
1 August 1858 - 24 May 1890
Line Operational – Demolished – No access **TL14452 03405**

PARK VILLAGE* (NER)
Not known
Line lifted – Demolished – A pathway passes through the station site **NY68706 61517**

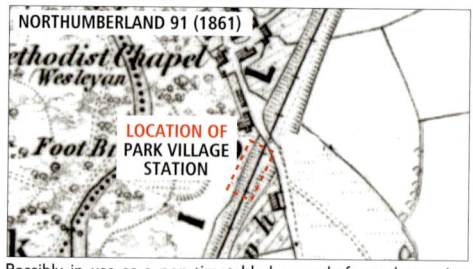

Possibly in use as a non-timetabled, non-platformed stopping place well into the 20thC

PARSLEY HAY (1st) (L&NWR)
June 1833 - 4 August 1899
Line lifted – Demolished – A road leading to the High Peak Trail passes through the station site **SK14731 63682**

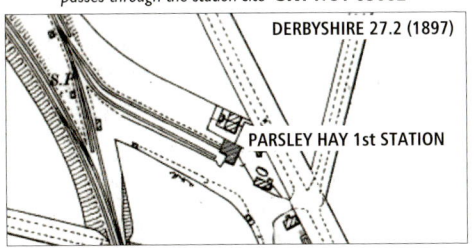

PEEBLES (1st) (NBR)
4 July 1855 - 1 October 1864
Line lifted – Demolished – Station site partially landscaped and partially occupied by housing **NT25144 40858**

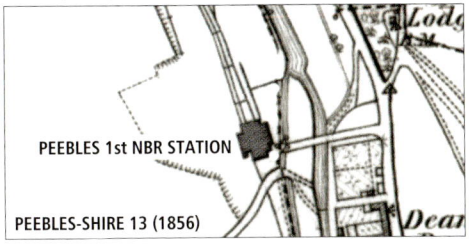

PARTINGTON (1st) (CLC)
1 May 1874 - 29 May 1893
Line lifted – Demolished – A pathway passes through the station site **SJ72413 91736**

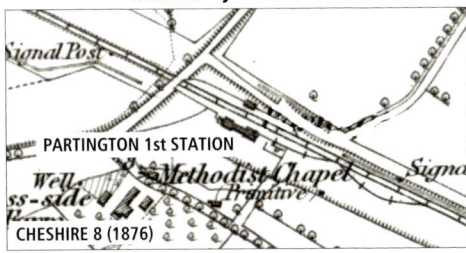

PELAW JUNCTION (1st) (NER)
30 December 1839 - Prior to 1857
Line Operational – Demolished – No access **NZ29558 62141**

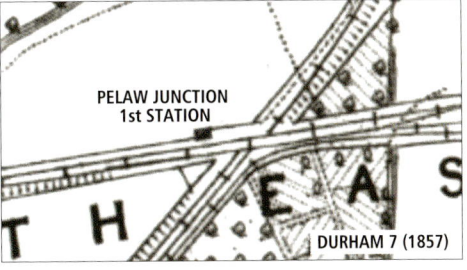

PATCHWAY (1st) (GWR)
8 September 1863 - 10 August 1885
Line Operational – Demolished – No access **ST60784 81531**

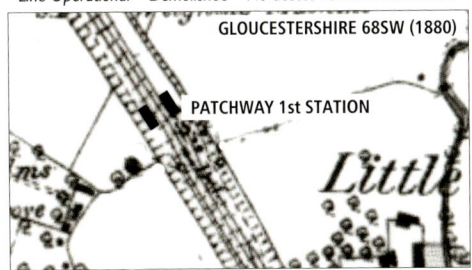

PELAW JUNCTION (2nd) (NER)
Prior to 1857 - 18 November 1896
Line Operational – Demolished – No access **NZ29763 62169**

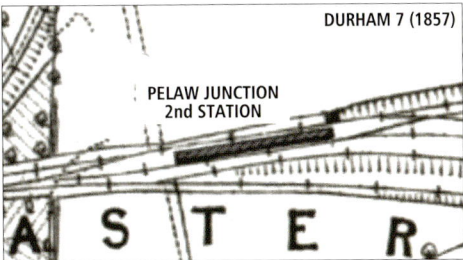

PATNA (1st) (G&SWR)
7 August 1856 - 1897
Line Operational for Freight – Demolished **NS41686 10935**

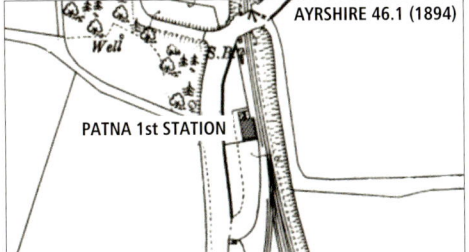

PELTON (1st) (NER)
March 1862 - 1 December 1868
Line lifted – Demolished – Station site occupied by Greenland Mews **NZ25438 51983 (a)**

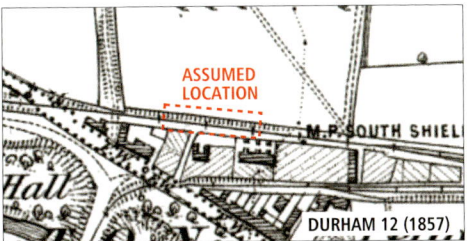

PENCADER JUNCTION - PERCY MAIN (1st)

PENCADER JUNCTION (M&MR)
1 January 1866 – May 1880
Line lifted – Demolished – A track passes through the station site
SN44547 37009 (a)

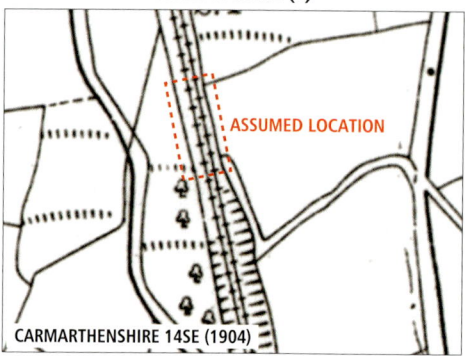

PENPONDS (WCwallR)
23 May 1843 – 16 February 1852
Line lifted – Demolished – Station site occupied by housing in Penware Parc **SW64195 39371 (a)**

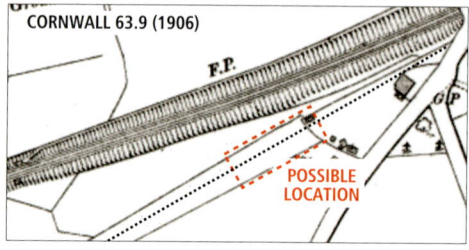

PENGE (L&CrR)
5 June 1839 – 13 June 1859
Line Operational – Demolished
TQ34958 70514

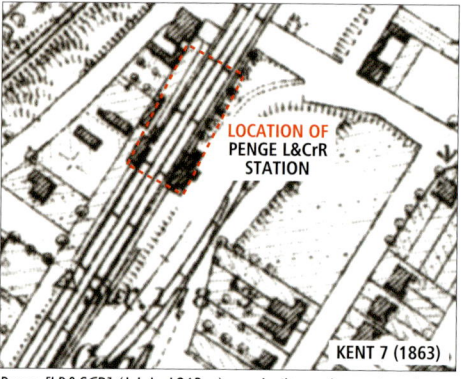

Penge [LB&SCR] (1 July 1863 -) was built on the station site

PENTYRCH (TVR)
8 October 1840 – June 1863
Line Operational – Demolished – Station House in private use
ST12926 81835

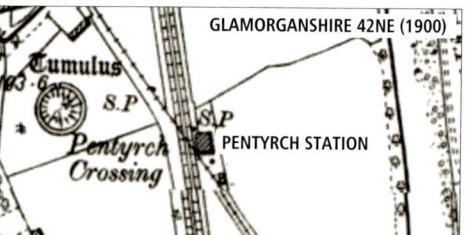

PEN-Y-GROES (NantlleR)
11 August 1856 – 12 June 1865
Line lifted – Demolished – Station site unused
SH46722 52979 (a)

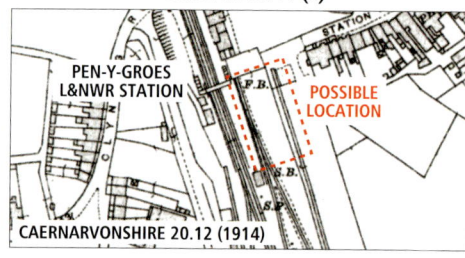

PENISTONE (MS&LR)
14 July 1845 – 1 February 1874
Line lifted – Demolished – The Trans Pennine Trail passes through the station site **SE24445 03416**

PERCY MAIN (1st) (BS&PMR)
28 August 1841 – 25 June 1844
Line lifted – Demolished – Station site unused **NZ33462 67091**

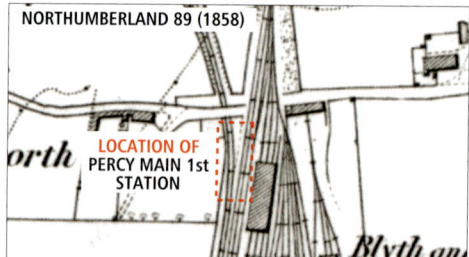

104

PERCY MAIN (2nd) (B&TR)
25 June 1844 - 27 June 1864
Line lifted – Demolished – Station site occupied by housing in
Kilburn Gardens **NZ33641 67396**

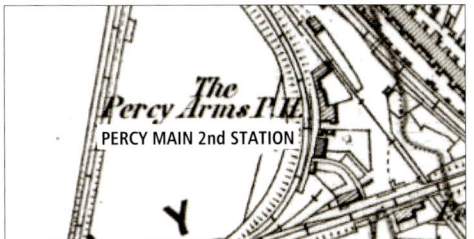

PIMLICO (LB&SCR)
29 March 1858 - 1 October 1860
Line lifted – Demolished – Station site occupied by dwellings in
Queenstown Road **TQ28682 77569**

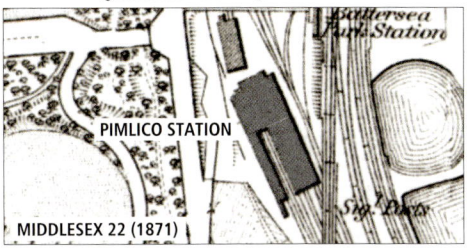

PERTH GLASGOW ROAD (SNER)
8 August 1859 - May 1860
Line Operational – Demolished – No access **NO11094 23553**

PINCHINGTHORPE (1st) (NER)
25 February 1854 - December 1876
Line lifted – Demolished – Station building in private use –
A pathway passes through the station site **NZ58376 15222**

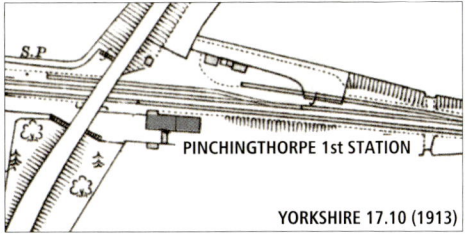

PETERBOROUGH CRESCENT (MR)
February 1858 - 1 August 1866
Line Operational – Demolished – No access **TL18747 98603**

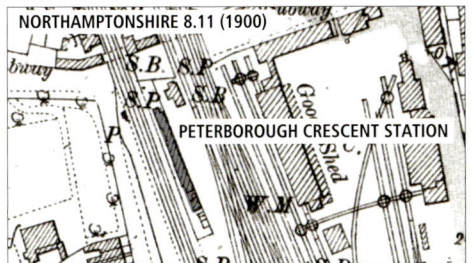

PIRTON (B&GR)
November 1841 - November 1844
Line Operational – Demolished **SO89708 47051 (a)**

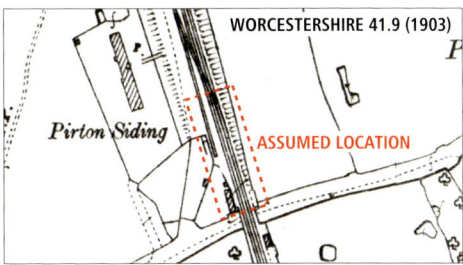

PIEL PIER (FurnR)
24 August 1846 - 1 October 1881
Line lifted – Demolished – Station site partially unused and
partially occupied by a car park **SD23198 64967**

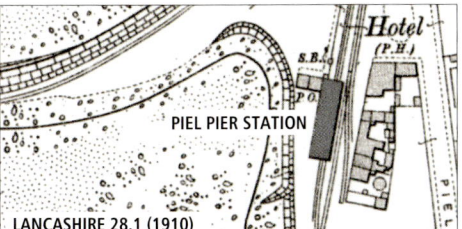

PITSEA (LT&SR)
1 July 1855 - 1 June 1888
Line Operational – Demolished – No access **TQ73714 87544**

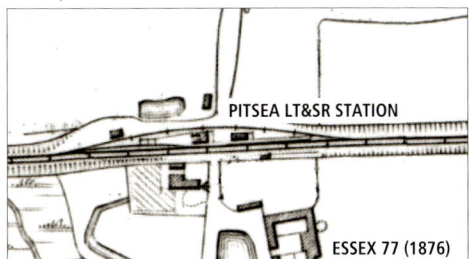

POPLAR (L&BwallR) - PORTSKEWETT (1st)

POPLAR (L&BwallR)
6 July 1840 - c1845
Line lifted – Demolished – Aspen Way crosses the station site
TQ38384 80648

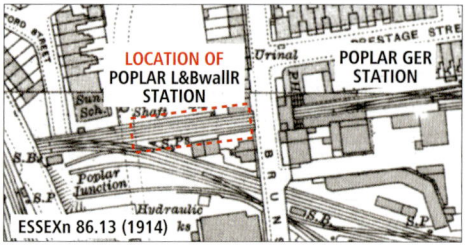
ESSEXn 86.13 (1914)

PORT CARLISLE JUNCTION (NBR)
July 1863 - 1 July 1864
Main line Operational – Demolished – No access
NY39243 56586

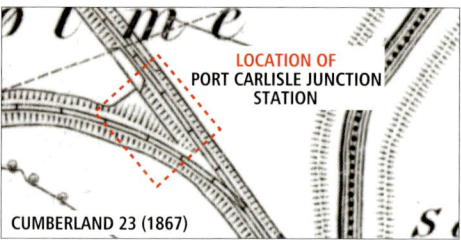
CUMBERLAND 23 (1867)

PORT CLARENCE (1st) (NER)
1835 - 1882
Line lifted – Demolished – Station site unused
NZ50796 21180 (e)

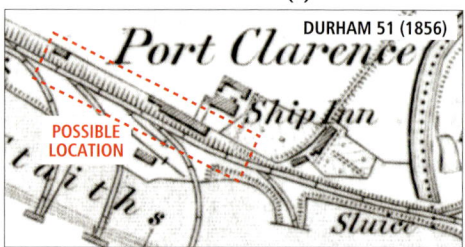
DURHAM 51 (1856)

PORT DINORWIC (1st) (L&NWR)
1 July 1852 - 1873
Line lifted – Demolished – A pathway passes through the station site **SH52916 67857**

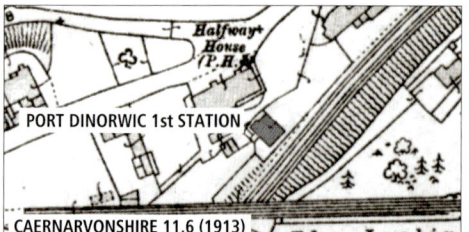
CAERNARVONSHIRE 11.6 (1913)

PORT EDGAR (NBR)
2 September 1878 - 5 March 1890
Line lifted – Demolished – Station site in use for boat storage
NT11758 78754

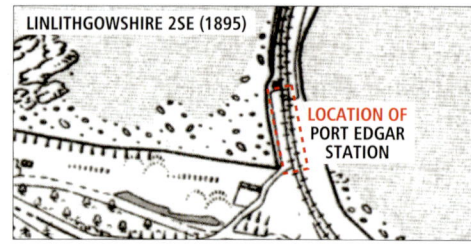
LINLITHGOWSHIRE 2SE (1895)

PORTH (1st) (TVR)
4 February 1861 - 1 July 1876
Line Operational – Demolished – No access **ST02467 91513**

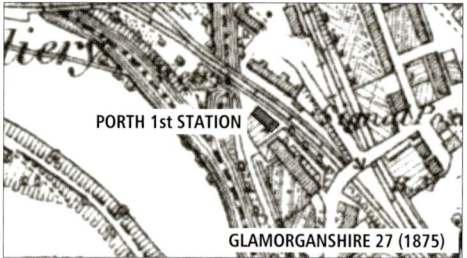
GLAMORGANSHIRE 27 (1875)

PORTOBELLO (L&NWR)
1 October 1854 - 1 January 1873
Line Operational – Demolished – No access
SO95017 98611 (a)

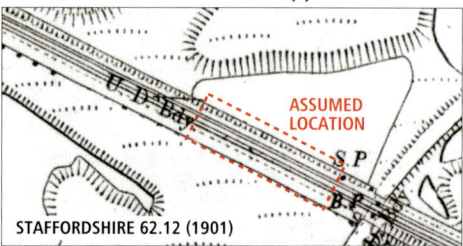
STAFFORDSHIRE 62.12 (1901)

PORTSKEWETT (1st) (GWR)
19 June 1850 - 1 October 1863
Line Operational – Demolished – No access
ST49930 87959 (a)

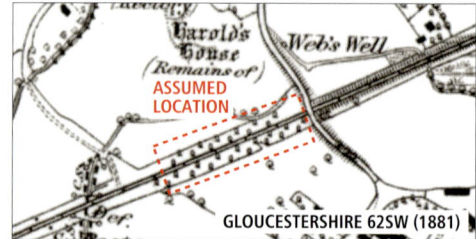
GLOUCESTERSHIRE 62SW (1881)

PORTSKEWETT PIER - POYNTON MIDWAY

PORTSKEWETT PIER (GWR)
1 January 1864 - 1 December 1886
Line lifted – Station and pier demolished **ST51555 87977**

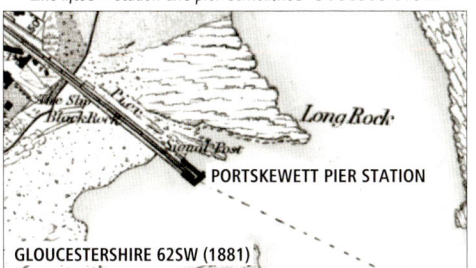

PORTWOOD (CLC)
1 December 1865 - 1 September 1875
Line lifted – Demolished – Station site occupied by part of a Tesco Extra car park **SJ89987 91013**

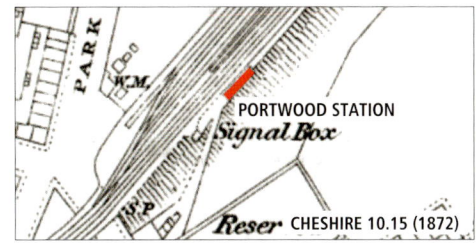

PORTSOY (1st) (GNofSR)
13 July 1859 - 1 April 1884
Line lifted – Demolished – Station site in commercial use
NJ58990 65833

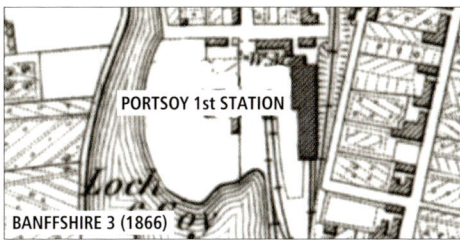

POTTON (1st) (B&CR)
9 November 1857 - January 1862
Line lifted – Demolished – Station site partially unused and partially occupied by dwellings **TL22037 48984**

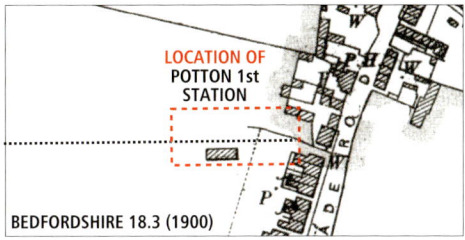

PORTSWOOD (1st) (L&SWR)
1 May 1861 - 5 March 1866
Line Operational – Demolished – No access
SU43227 14132 (a)

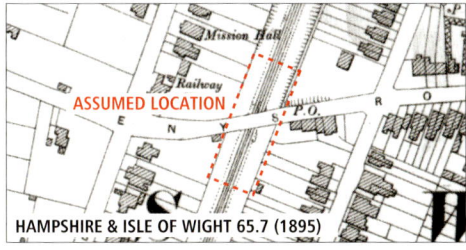

POULTON (1st) (P&WR)
16 July 1840 - 29 March 1896
Line lifted – Demolished – Station site occupied by dwellings in Station Road **SD35103 39871**

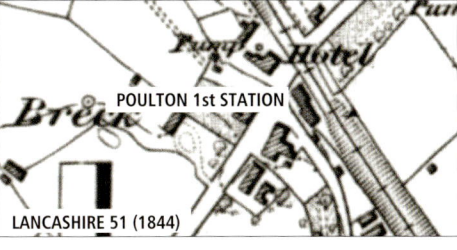

PORT TALBOT DOCKS (R&SBR)
24 August 1891 - 14 March 1895
Line lifted – Demolished – Station site unused **SS75846 89083**

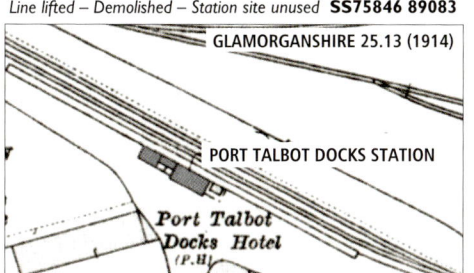

POYNTON MIDWAY (L&NWR)
24 November 1845 - 1 August 1887
Line Operational – Demolished – Station building in private use
SJ91512 82678

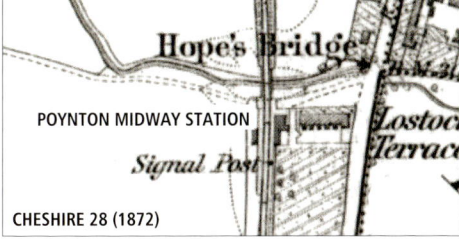

107

PRESTATYN (1st) - **PRINCES RISBOROUGH** (W&PRR)

PRESTATYN (1st) (L&NWR)
1 May 1848 - 28 February 1897
Line Operational – Demolished – Restored station building in commercial use **SJ06489 83098**

PRESTON DOCK STREET JUNCTION (L&PJnR)
26 June 1840 - 12 February 1844
Line Operational – Demolished – No access
SD53421 29314 (a)

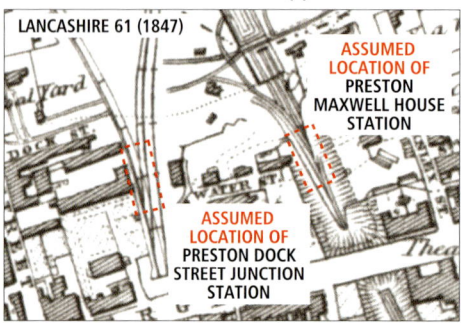

PRESTON MAUDLANDS (P&WR)
16 July 1840 - 11 February 1844
Line lifted – Demolished – Station site occupied by University of Lancaster's Roeburn House **SD53197 29753**

PRESTON MAUDLANDS BRIDGE (P&LR)
1 November 1856 - 1 June 1885
Line lifted – Demolished – A roadway passes through the station site **SD53294 29826**

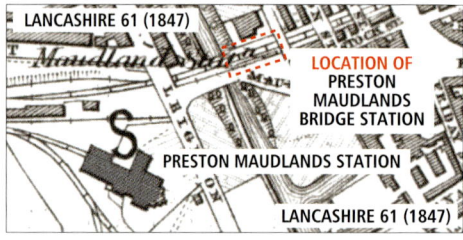

PRESTON MAXWELL HOUSE (NUR)
1 January 1842 - 11 February 1844
Line lifted – Demolished – Station site occupied by sidings
SD53474 29292 (a)
SEE MAP OF PRESTON DOCK STREET JUNCTION (ABOVE)

PRESTON DEEPDALE STREET (FP&WRJnR)
1 May 1840 - 1 November 1856
Line lifted – Demolished – Station site in commercial use
SD54620 29992

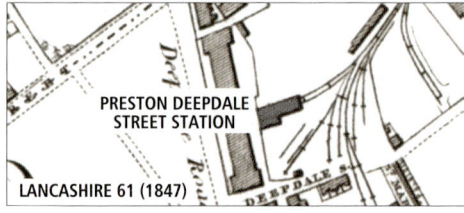

PRESTON-ON-STOUR [TRAMWAY STATION] (OW&WR)
Prior to 1834 - 30 September 1858
Line lifted – Demolished – Station site absorbed into the A3400, Shipston Road **SP21468 50171 (e)**

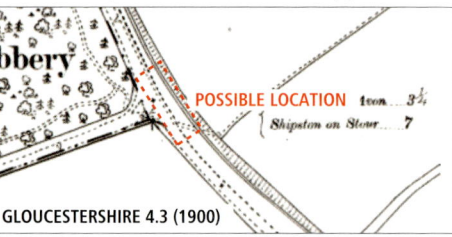

PRICKWILLOW (ECR)
19 January 1850 - October 1850
Line Operational – Demolished – No access **TL59558 82802**

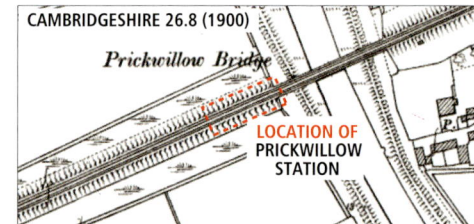

PRINCES RISBOROUGH (W&PRR)
15 August 1872 - 1 July 1883
Line Operated by Chinnor & Princes Risborough Railway – Demolished **SP79952 02733**

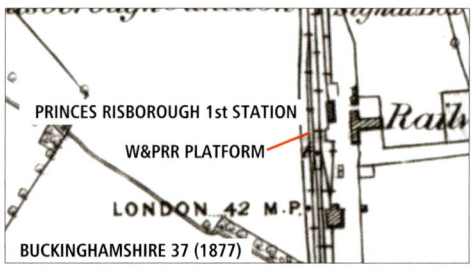

108

PROSPECT HILL (B&TR)
28 August 1841 - 27 June 1864
Line lifted – Demolished – A cycleway passes through the station site **NZ31525 70560**

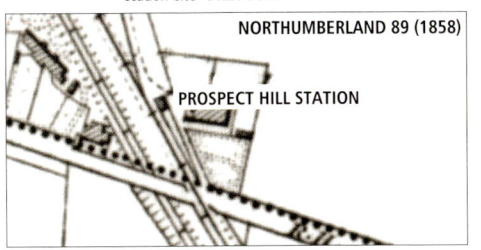

PULFORD (GWR)
4 November 1846 - January 1855
Line Operational – Demolished **SJ36882 59671**

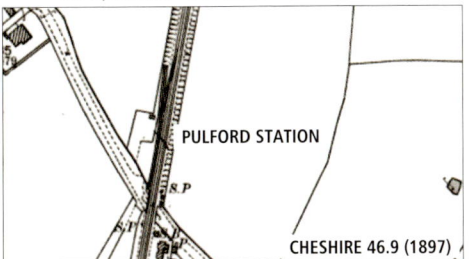

PWLL GLAS (VanR)
1 December 1873 – July 1879
Line lifted – Demolished – Station site in private use
SN97060 89507

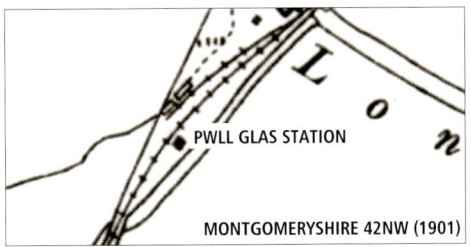

PWLL-Y-PANT (RhyR)
1 April 1871 - 1 March 1893
Line Operational – Demolished – No access **ST14911 88916**

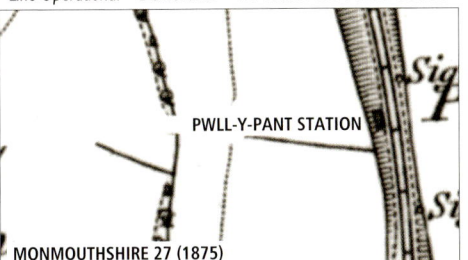

PROSPECT HILL - RAFFORD

PYLE (1st) (GWR)
19 June 1850 - 13 November 1876
Line Operational – Demolished – No access **SS82709 81927**

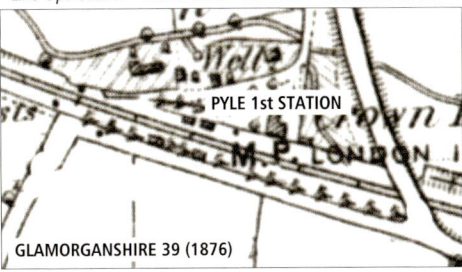

QUAINTON ROAD (MetR)
23 September 1868 - 1896
Line Operational for Freight – Demolished **SP73757 19017**

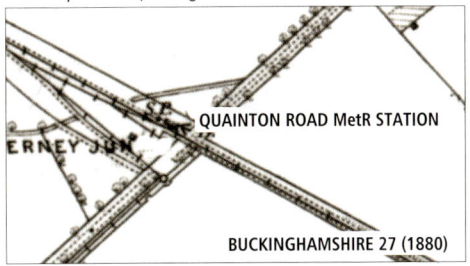

RADFORD (1st) (MR)
2 October 1848 - 10 September 1876
Line lifted – Demolished – Station site occupied by dwellings
SK54927 40154 (a)

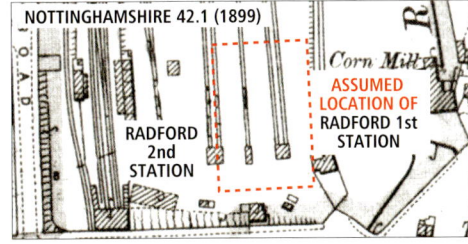

RAFFORD (HR)
3 August 1863 - 31 May 1865
Line lifted – Demolished – The Dava Way passes through the station site **NJ05005 55854 (a)**

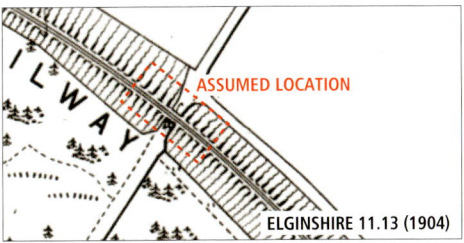

109

RAGLAN FOOTPATH - READING (SER)

RAGLAN FOOTPATH (GWR)
5 October 1857 - 1 July 1876
Line lifted – Demolished – Station site in agricultural use
SO41882 07106

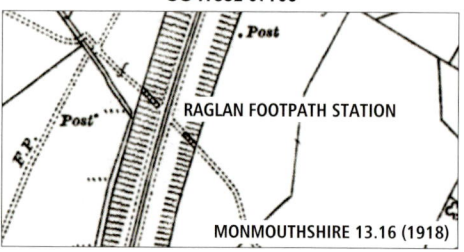

MONMOUTHSHIRE 13.16 (1918)

RAGLAN ROAD (GWR)
5 October 1857 - 1 July 1876
Line lifted – Demolished – The A449 passes through the station site **SO41967 05413**

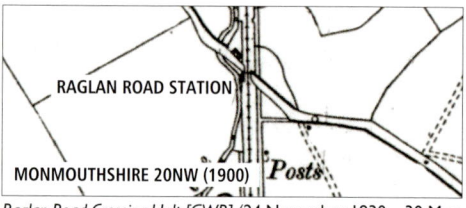

MONMOUTHSHIRE 20NW (1900)

Raglan Road Crossing Halt [GWR] (24 November 1930 – 30 May 1955) was built on the station site

RAILWAY TERRACE* (L&CdnR)
Prior to 1889 - c1896
Line lifted – Demolished – A roadway passes through the station site **SX25829 69380**

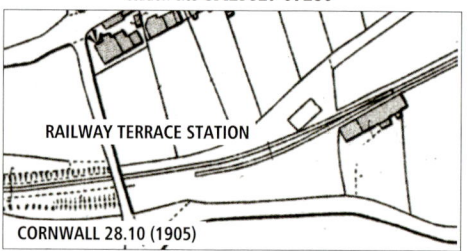

CORNWALL 28.10 (1905)

RAINFORD (1st) (L&YR)
20 November 1848 - 1 February 1858
Line Operational – Demolished – No access
SD46845 02141

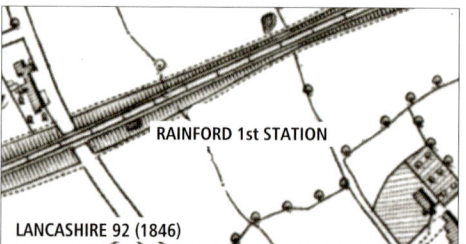

LANCASHIRE 92 (1846)

RAINTON MEADOWS (N&DJnR)
9 March 1840 - 18 June 1844
Line lifted – Demolished – Station site occupied by dwellings in Benridge Bank **NZ32503 47017**

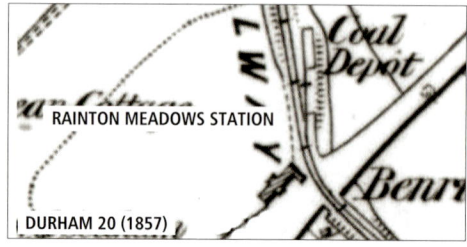

DURHAM 20 (1857)

RAMPER (P&WR)
1842 - April 1843
Line Operational – Demolished – No access
SD34349 42025 (a)

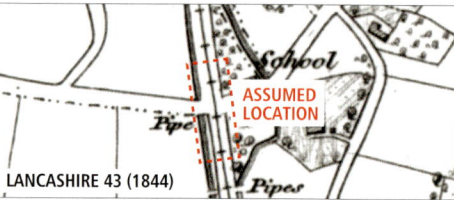

LANCASHIRE 43 (1844)

Cleveleys [P&WR] (April 1865 – 1927) was built on, or adjacent to, the station site

RATBY (1st) (MR)
18 July 1832 - 26 April 1833
Line lifted – Demolished – The Ivanhoe Trail passes through the station site **SK51801 05383 (a)**

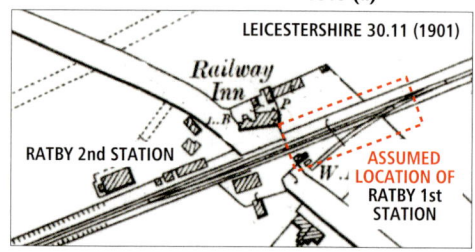

LEICESTERSHIRE 30.11 (1901)

READING (SER)
4 July 1849 - 30 August 1855
Line lifted – Demolished – Forbury Road crosses over the west end of the station site, remainder in commercial use
SU71816 73714 (a)

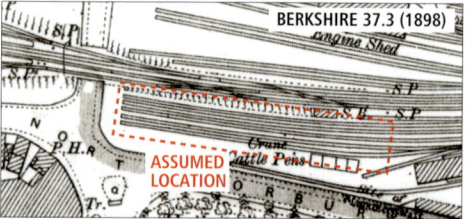

BERKSHIRE 37.3 (1898)

110

REDCAR (S&DR) - REDRUTH

REDCAR (S&DR)
25 June 1847 - 19 August 1861
Line lifted – Demolished – Station site redeveloped
NZ60213 25241

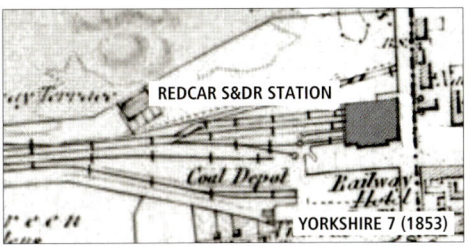

REDDITCH (1st) (MR)
19 September 1859 - 4 May 1868
Line lifted – Demolished – Station site in commercial use
SP03781 67946

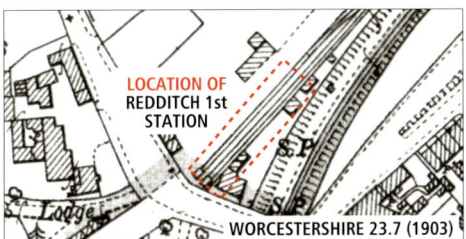

REDENHALL (GER)
2 November 1860 - 1 August 1866
Line lifted – Demolished – Station site unused
TM25792 84354

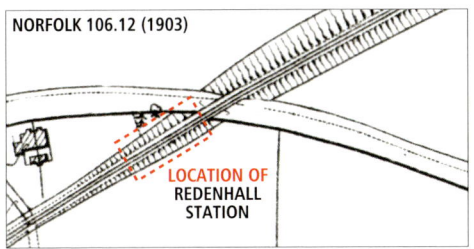

REDHEUGH (YN&BR)
1 March 1837 - May 1853
Line lifted – Demolished – Station site landscaped
NZ24606 63044

RED HILL (PS&NWalesR)
13 August 1866 - 22 June 1880
Line Operational – Demolished – No access **SJ46903 09692**

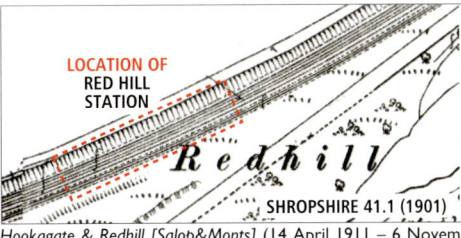

Hookagate & Redhill [Salop&Monts] (14 April 1911 – 6 November 1933) was built on the east end of the station site

REDHILL (SER)
26 May 1842 - 15 April 1844
Line Operational – Demolished – No access
TQ28237 49714 (e)

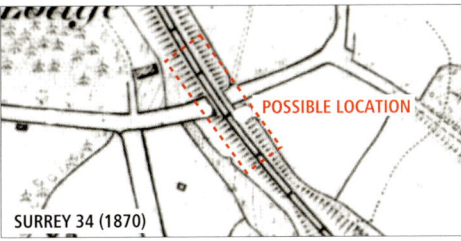

RED HOUSE (VanR)
September 1876 - February 1879
Line lifted – Demolished – Station site in agricultural use
SN99141 90260

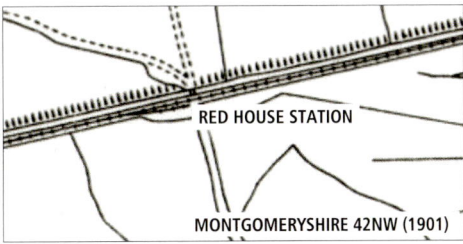

REDRUTH (WCwallR)
23 May 1843 - 25 August 1852
Line lifted – Demolished – Station site occupied by "West End Long Stay Car Park" **SW69404 41832**

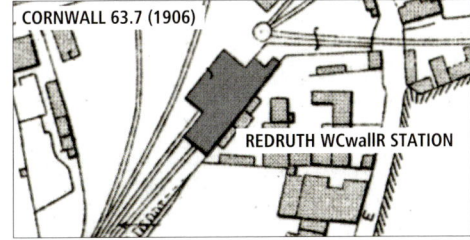

REIGATE (L&BrR) - RIPLEY (1st)

REIGATE (L&BrR)
12 July 1841 - 15 April 1844
Line Operational – Demolished – No access **TQ27878 49667**

RIBBLETON (1st) (P&LR)
June 1863 - September 1866
Line lifted – Demolished – One degraded platform extant – A cycle/footway passes through the station site
SD56086 31303

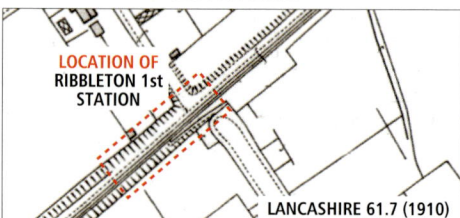

RESPRYN (CwallR)
4 May 1859 - October 1864
Line Operational – Demolished – No access
SX10038 63496 (a)

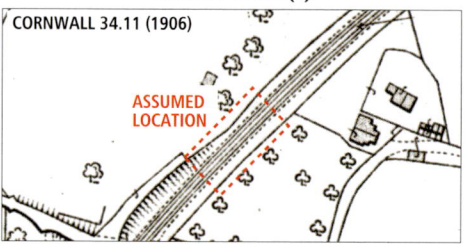

RICHMOND (1st) (L&SWR)
22 August 1848 - September 1849
Line lifted – Demolished – Station site occupied by a car park
TQ18101 75112

RETFORD (MS&LR)
17 July 1849 - 1 July 1859
Line Operational – Demolished – Station House in private use as the "Old Station House B&B" **SK70750 80348**

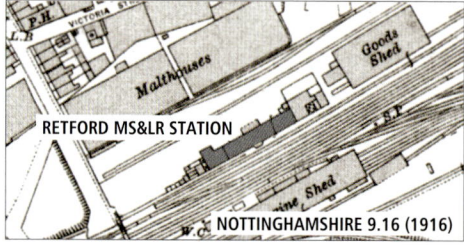

RILLATON BRIDGE* (L&CdnR)
Prior to 1889 - c1896
Line lifted – Demolished – Station site unused **SX26376 71345**

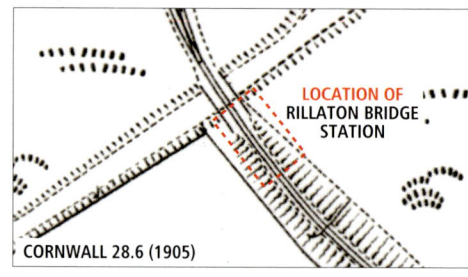

RHOS (1st) (GWR)
14 October 1848 - February 1855
Line Operational – Line lifted – No access **SJ30869 47109**

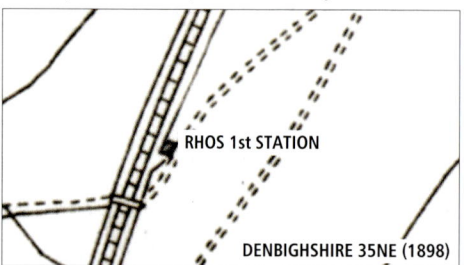

RIPLEY (1st) (MR)
1 September 1856 - 2 September 1889
Line lifted – Demolished – Station site in commercial use
SK40507 49517

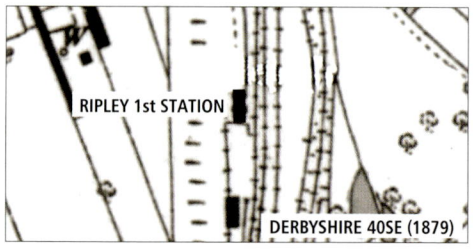

RISHTON (1st) - ROEBUCK

RISHTON (1st) (L&YR)
19 June 1848 - January 1849
Line Operational – Demolished – No access
SD71743 29731 (a)

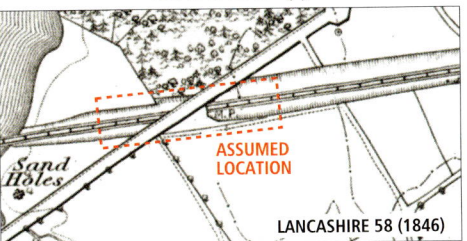

LANCASHIRE 58 (1846)

RIVER DOUGLAS (WLancsR)
1 August 1878 - April 1889
Line lifted – Demolished – Station site in commercial use
SD45001 22799

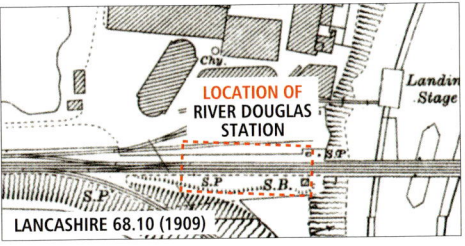

LANCASHIRE 68.10 (1909)

ROADE (1st) (L&NWR)
17 September 1838 - c1881
Line Operational – Demolished – No access
SP75435 51656 (a)

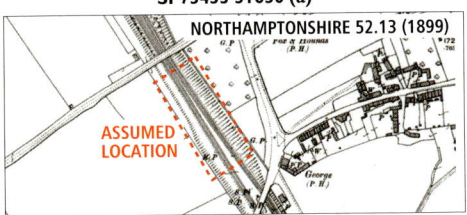

Sited 242 yards north of Roade 2nd [L&NWR] (c1881 - 7 September 1964)

ROADWATER (WSsetMinR)
4 September 1865 - 8 November 1898
Line lifted – Demolished – Station building in private use
ST03225 38235

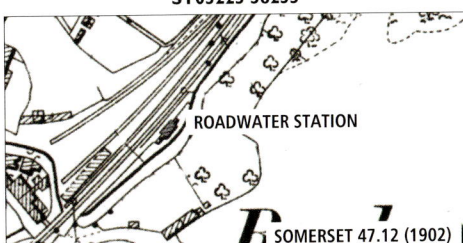

ROCHDALE (1st) (L&YR)
4 July 1839 - 28 April 1889
Line Operational – Demolished – No access **SD90255 12844**

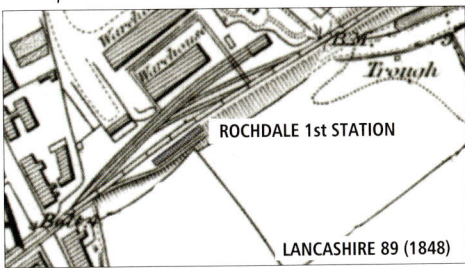

LANCASHIRE 89 (1848)

ROCK FERRY (1st) (L&NWR/GWR)
1 January 1863 - 15 June 1891
Line Operational – Demolished – No access
SJ32894 86584

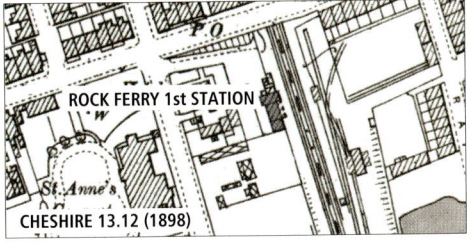

CHESHIRE 13.12 (1898)

ROCK LANE (BheadR)
30 May 1846 - 1 November 1862
Line Operational – Demolished – No access **SJ33019 86140**

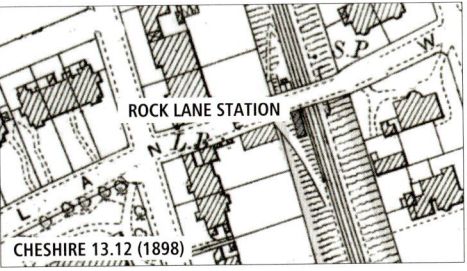

CHESHIRE 13.12 (1898)

ROEBUCK (L&CR)
26 June 1840 - August 1849
Line Operational – Demolished – No access
SD51364 39733 (a)

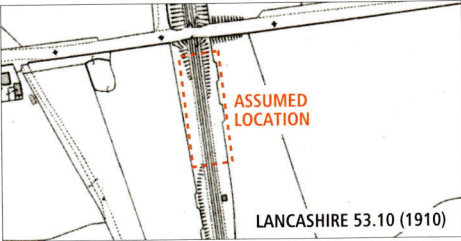

LANCASHIRE 53.10 (1910)

113

ROGERSTONE (1st) - ROTHERHAM (2nd) (GCR)

ROGERSTONE (1st) (GWR)
12 July 1851 - 1900
Line lifted – Demolished – The A467 passes through the station site
ST26690 88400

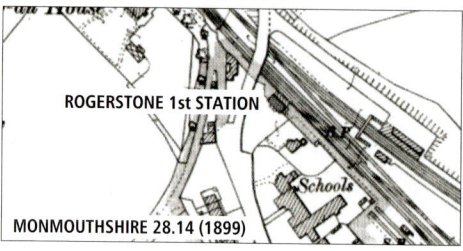

MONMOUTHSHIRE 28.14 (1899)

ROHALLION (I&PJnR)
February 1860 - October 1864
Line Operational – Demolished – No access **NO05985 38941**

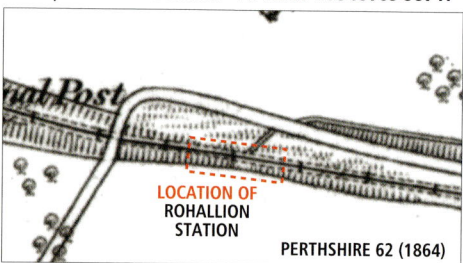

PERTHSHIRE 62 (1864)

ROOD END (GWR)
1 April 1867 - 1 May 1885
Line Operational – Demolished – No access **SP00152 89047**

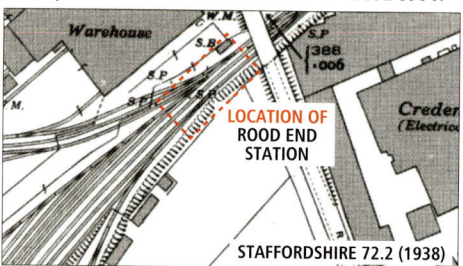

STAFFORDSHIRE 72.2 (1938)

ROOSE GATE (FurnR)
June 1851 - March 1858
Line Operational – Demolished – No access **SD22065 69712**

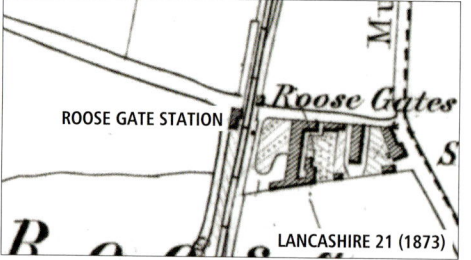

LANCASHIRE 21 (1873)

ROSEHAUGH HALT (HR)
Not known
Line lifted – Demolished – Crossing Keeper's Cottage in private use
NH67602 54614

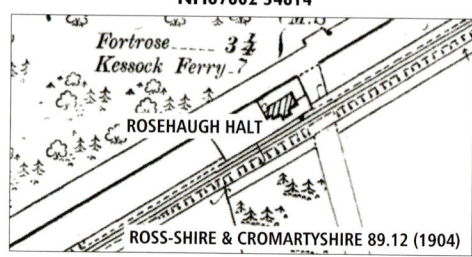

ROSS-SHIRE & CROMARTYSHIRE 89.12 (1904)

ROSEMILL HALT (CR)
Not known
Line lifted – Demolished – Station site in private use
NO36441 35425 (a)

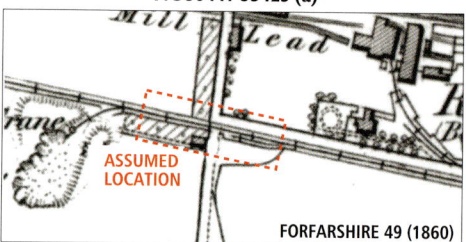

FORFARSHIRE 49 (1860)

ROTHERHAM (1st) (GCR)
1 August 1868 - 1870
Line lifted – Demolished – Station site in commercial use
SK42362 92524 (a)

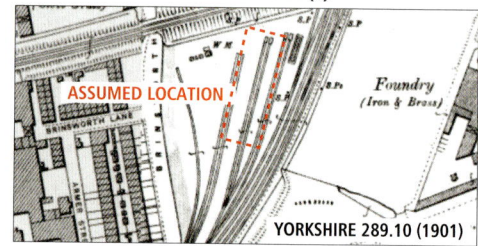

YORKSHIRE 289.10 (1901)

ROTHERHAM (2nd) (GCR)
1870 - 1 February 1874
Line Operational – Demolished – No access
SK42593 93066 (a)

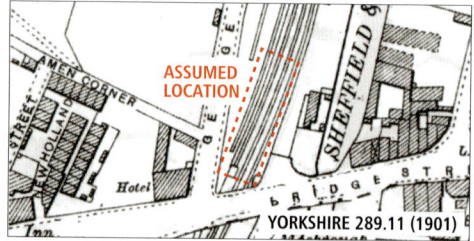

YORKSHIRE 289.11 (1901)

114

ROUND OAK (1st) (GWR)
20 December 1852 - c1894
Line Operational for Freight – Demolished – No access
SO92021 87887 (a)

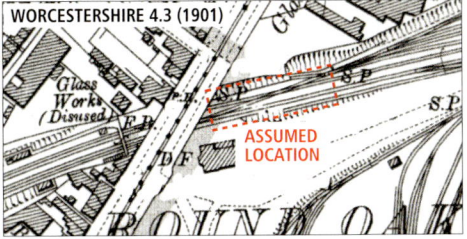

ROYAL GARDENS (NER)
June 1857 - June 1859
Line Operational – Demolished **SE27888 35182**

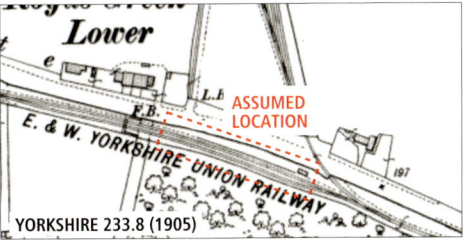

Burley Park [BR] (20 November 1988 -) was built on the station site

ROWSLEY (L&NWR/MR)
4 June 1849 - 1 August 1862
Line lifted – Demolished – Station building incorporated into "Peak Shopping Village" **SK25880 65999**

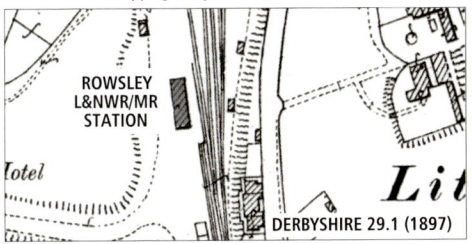

ROYDS GREEN LOWER* (E&WYorksUnR)
Not known
Line lifted – Demolished – Station site unused
SE35106 25777 (a)

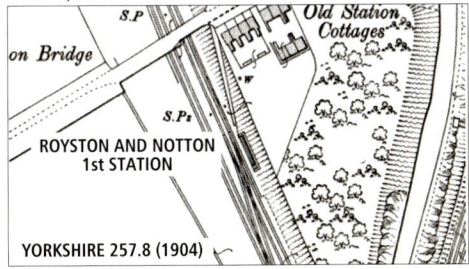

ROYAL ALBERT DOCK GALLIONS
(L&IDJC)
3 August 1880 - 12 December 1886
Line lifted – Demolished – Station site occupied by dwellings in Shackleton Way **TQ44103 80706 (a)**

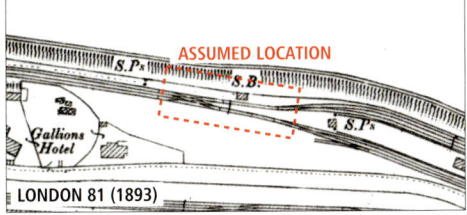

ROYSTON AND NOTTON (1st) (MR)
6 April 1841 - 1 July 1900
Line Operational – Demolished – No access **SE36614 13179**

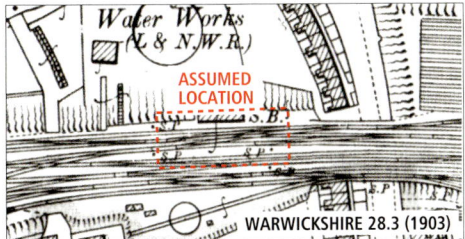

ROYAL ALBERT DOCK MANOR WAY
(L&IDJC)
3 August 1880 - 1887
Line lifted – Demolished – Station site in commercial use
TQ43656 80743 (a)

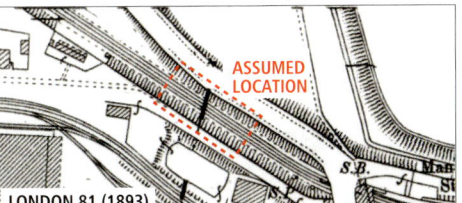

RUGBY (L&BmR)
9 April 1838 - 4 July 1840
Line Operational – Demolished – No access
SP50074 76116 (a)

ROUND OAK (1st) - RUGBY (L&BmR)

RUGBY (1st) (L&NWR) - St ANDREWS (1st)

RUGBY (1st) (L&NWR)
4 July 1840 - 5 July 1885
Line Operational – Demolished – Station site absorbed into
Rugby Station **SP51049 75990**

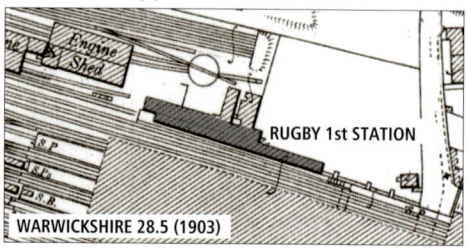
RUGBY 1st STATION
WARWICKSHIRE 28.5 (1903)

RUMBLING BRIDGE (1st) (NBR)
1 May 1863 - 1 October 1868
Line lifted – Demolished – Station site unused
NT01835 99434

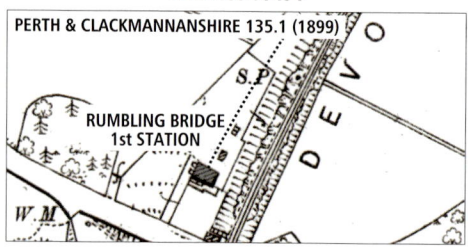
PERTH & CLACKMANNANSHIRE 135.1 (1899)
RUMBLING BRIDGE 1st STATION

RUNCORN GAP (StHC&RC)
21 February 1833 - 1 July 1852
Line lifted – Demolished – The Mersey Gateway Bridge Approach
Road crosses the station site **SJ51572 84720**

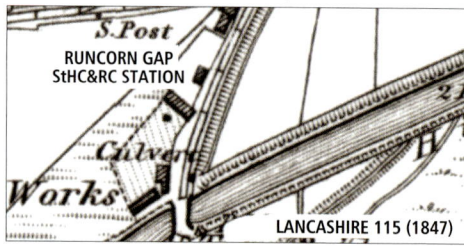
RUNCORN GAP StHC&RC STATION
LANCASHIRE 115 (1847)

RUSHEY PLATT (1st) (M&SWJnR)
18 December 1883 - 2 March 1885
Line lifted – Demolished – Station site in commercial use
SU13300 83847 (a)

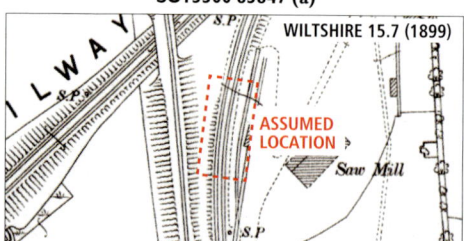
WILTSHIRE 15.7 (1899)
ASSUMED LOCATION

RUSHFORD (M&BR)
4 June 1840 - April 1843
Line Operational – Demolished – No access
SJ87030 95298 (a)

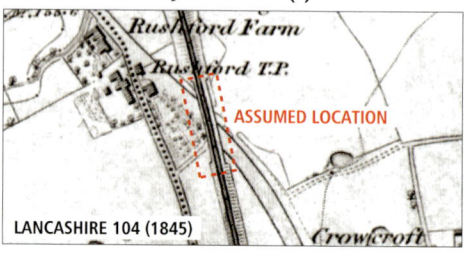
ASSUMED LOCATION
LANCASHIRE 104 (1845)

RUTHERGLEN (1st) (CR)
1 June 1849 - 31 March 1879
Line Operational – Demolished – No access **NS61545 61851**

RUTHERGLEN 1st STATION
LANARKSHIRE 10 (1859)

RYDER'S HAY (SStaffsR)
24 March 1856 - 1 June 1858
Line lifted – Demolished – A pathway passes through the
station site **SK02685 03843**

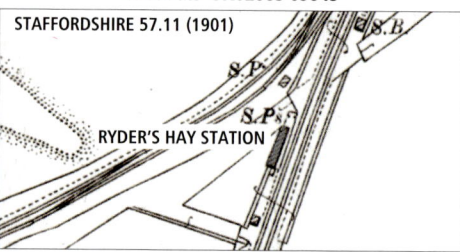
STAFFORDSHIRE 57.11 (1901)
RYDER'S HAY STATION

St ANDREWS (1st) (NBR)
1 July 1852 - 1 December 1867
Line lifted – Demolished – Station site occupied by "Old
Course Hotel" **NO49967 17116**

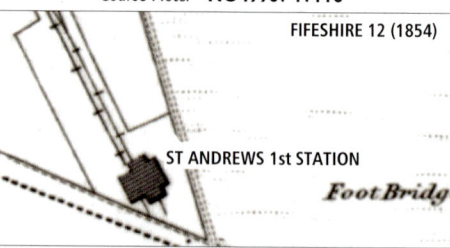
FIFESHIRE 12 (1854)
ST ANDREWS 1st STATION

116

St CLEER* (L&CdnR)
Prior to 1889 - c1896
Line lifted – Demolished – Station site in community use
SX25086 68442

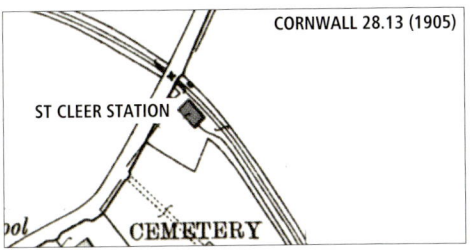

St GERMAIN'S (EAnglianR)
27 October 1846 - October 1850
Line Operational – Demolished **TF61671 13852**

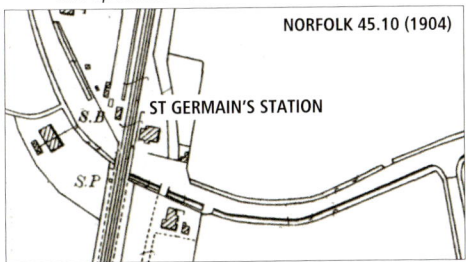

St HELENS (1st) (StHC&RC)
21 February 1833 - June 1849
Line lifted – Demolished – Station site occupied by a wooded area
SJ51717 94863

St HELENS (2nd) (StHC&RC)
June 1849 - 1 February 1858
Line lifted – Demolished – Parr Street crosses the station site
SJ51493 95198

St CLEER - St MARGARET'S (1st)
St HELENS (3rd) (L&NWR)
1 February 1858 - 17 July 1871
Line Operational – Demolished – Station site partially occupied by St Helens Central station forecourt. Remainder unused
SJ51577 95262

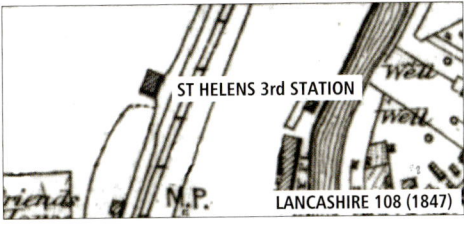

St LEONARDS (NBR)
2 June 1832 - 30 September 1860
Line lifted – Demolished – Station site occupied by dwellings
NT26567 72793 (a)

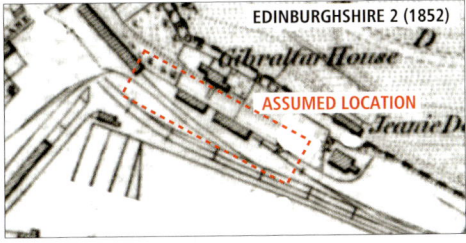

St LEONARDS WEST MARINA (1st) (LB&SCR)
7 November 1846 - 1 June 1889
Line Operational – Demolished – No access **TQ78535 08849**

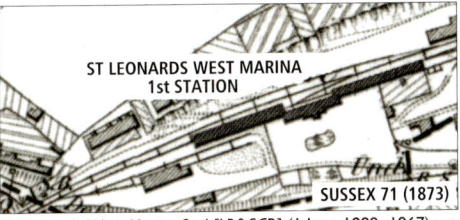

St Leonards West Marina 2nd [LB&SCR] (1 June 1889 -1967) was built on the east end of the station site

St MARGARET'S (1st) (GER)
31 October 1843 - 3 July 1863
Line Operational – Demolished – No access **TL38144 11750**

St QUINTIN PARK AND WORMWOOD SCRUBBS (1st) - SAXBY (1st)

St QUINTIN PARK AND WORMWOOD SCRUBBS (1st) (WLR)
1 August 1871 - 1 November 1893
Line Operational – Demolished – No access
TQ23171 81498 (a)

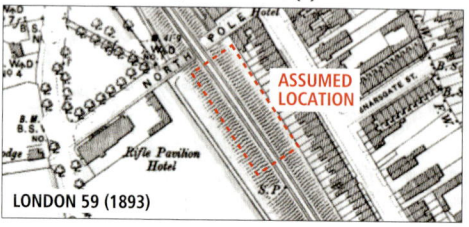

SALTCOATS (2nd) (G&SWR)
1 July 1858 - 1882
Line Operational – Demolished – No access
NS24709 41383 (a)

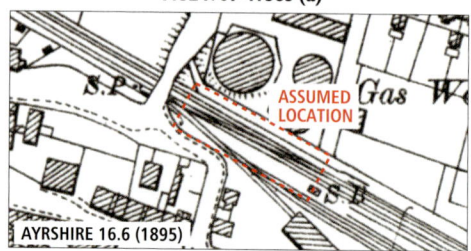

SALISBURY MILFORD (L&SWR)
1 March 1847 - 2 May 1859
Line lifted – Demolished – Station site in commercial use
SU15211 29618

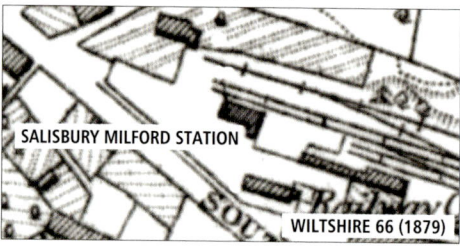

SANDALL (SYorks&RDNR)
April 1857 - September 1859
Line lifted – Demolished – A pathway passes through the station site **SE60891 08216 (a)**

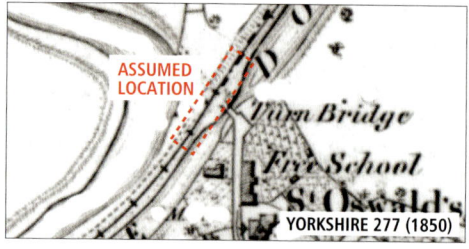

SALCEY FOREST (SuAT&MJR)
1 December 1892 - 30 March 1893
Line lifted – Demolished – Station site unused **SP81290 53607**

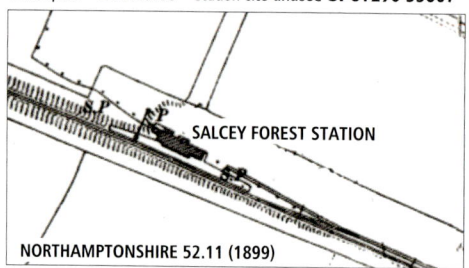

SANDHILLS (1st) (L&YR)
4 July 1854 - Prior to 9 July 1881
Line Operational – Demolished – Degraded platforms partially extant **SJ34239 93116**

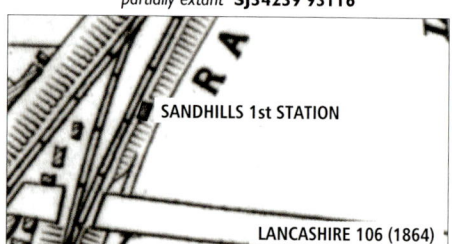

SALTCOATS (1st) (G&SWR)
17 August 1840 - 1 July 1858
Line Operational – Demolished – No access **NS24968 41273**

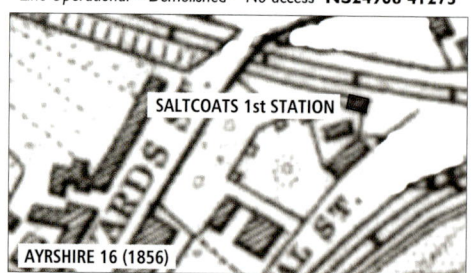

SAXBY (1st) (MR)
February 1849 - 28 August 1892
Line lifted – Demolished – Station building in private use
SK81212 19322

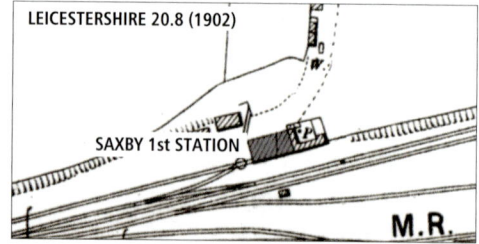

SCARNING (EAnglianR)
11 September 1848 - October 1850
Line lifted – Demolished – The A47 passes through the station site
TF95715 12673 (a)

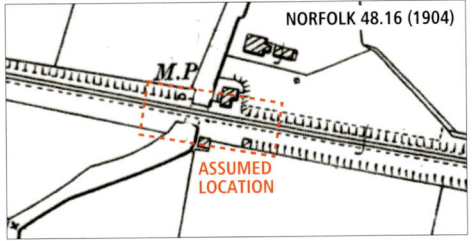

SCROPTON (NSR)
September 1849 - 1 January 1866
Line Operational – Demolished – No access
SK19154 30161 (a)

SCARNING - SERRIDGE PLATFORM

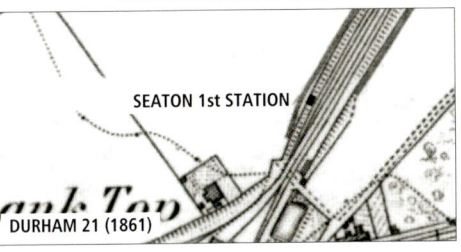

SCOLE* (GER)
c1850 - 1886
Line lifted – Demolished – Station site in agricultural use
TM13749 80185 (a)

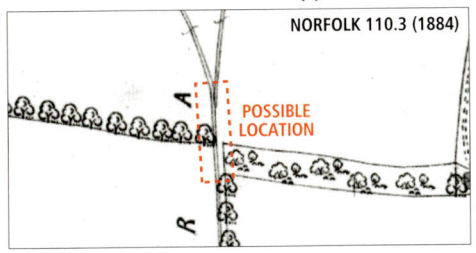

SEATON (1st) (NER)
19 October 1836 - Prior to 1898
Line lifted – Demolished – A pathway passes through the station site **NZ39182 49452**

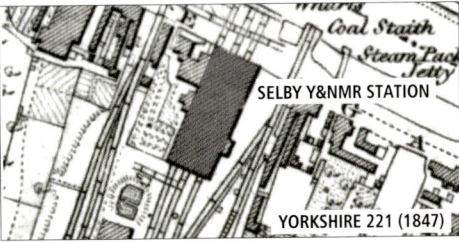

SCORTON (L&PJnR)
26 June 1840 - August 1840
Line Operational – Demolished – No access
SD50087 48265 (a)

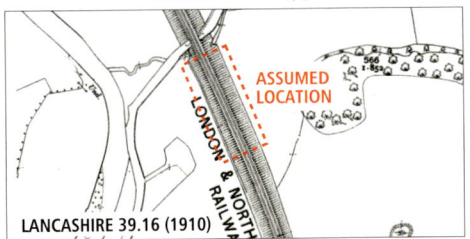

SELBY (Y&NMR)
22 September 1830 - 2 July 1840
Line lifted – Demolished – Station building extant in commercial use **SE61881 32383**

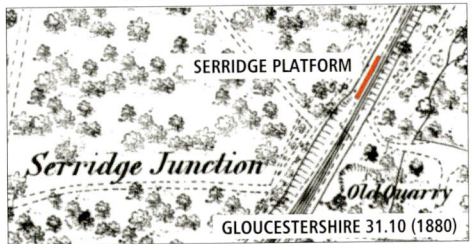

SCOTLAND STREET (NBR)
31 August 1842 - 2 March 1868
Line lifted – Demolished – Station site landscaped as a park
NT25452 74855

SERRIDGE PLATFORM* (S&WyeR)
July 1877 - 1 November 1879
Line lifted – Demolished - The Family Cycle Trail passes through the station site **SO62018 13808**

SETTLE JUNCTION (MR)
2 October 1876 – 1 November 1877
Line Operational – Demolished – No access **SD81403 60325**

SHERBURN HOUSE (1st) (NER)
1837 – 24 July 1893
Line lifted – Demolished – Station site in private use **NZ30460 41755**

SHARPNESS (1st) (MR)
1 August 1876 – 16 October 1879
Line Operational for Freight – Demolished **SO67288 02023**

SHERIFFHALL (NBR)
2 June 1832 – 1849
Line lifted – Demolished – Station site unused **NT32143 67852 (a)**

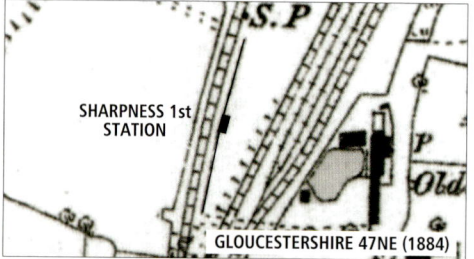

SHEFFIELD BRIDGEHOUSES (MS&LR)
14 July 1845 – 15 September 1851
Line Operational – Demolished – No access **SK35635 88230**

SHERN HALL STREET, WALTHAMSTOW (GER)
26 April 1870 – 17 November 1873
Line Operational – Demolished – No access **TQ38075 89192 (a)**

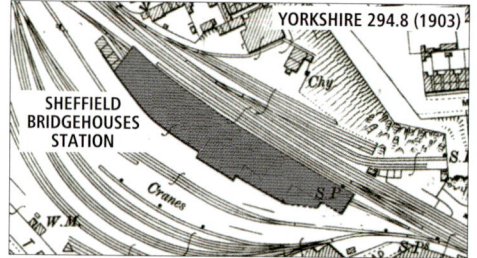

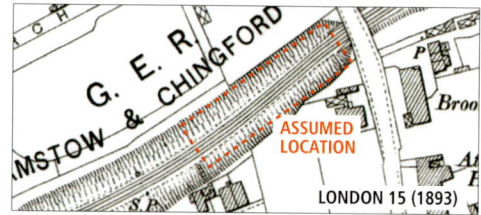

SHEFFIELD WICKER (MR)
1 November 1838 – 1 February 1870
Line lifted – Demolished – Station site in commercial use **SK36050 88182**

SHINCLIFFE TOWN (NER)
28 June 1839 – 24 July 1893
Line lifted – Demolished – Station site occupied by a dwelling **NZ28900 40885**

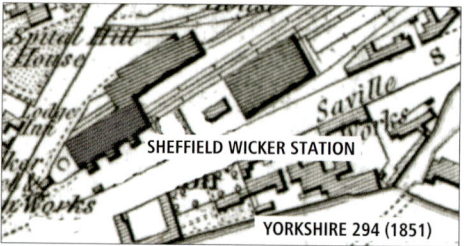

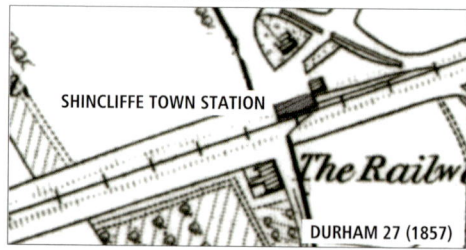

SHIPLEY (1st) (MR)
16 July 1846 - 1849
Line Operational – Demolished – No access **SE14890 37073**

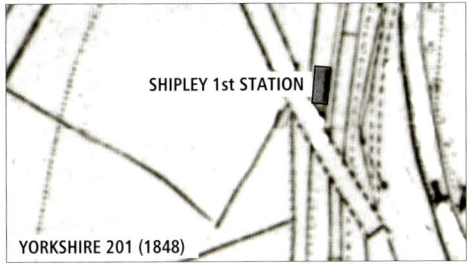

SHIRLEY HOLMES PLATFORM (L&SWR)
10 October 1860 - 6 March 1888
Line Operational – Demolished – No access **SZ30424 98226**

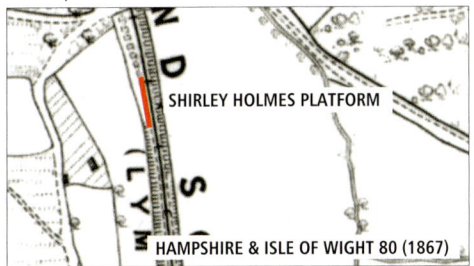

SHORNCLIFFE CAMP (SER)
1 November 1863 - 1 February 1881
Line Operational – Demolished – No access **TR20755 36487**

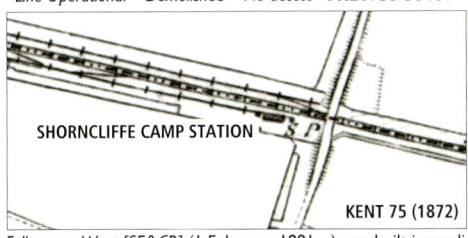

Folkestone West [SE&CR] (1 February 1881 -) was built immediately east of the station site

SHREWSBURY ENGLISH BRIDGE
(S&HR)
2 November 1866 - 2 May 1898
Line Operational – Demolished – No access
SJ49692 12532 (a)

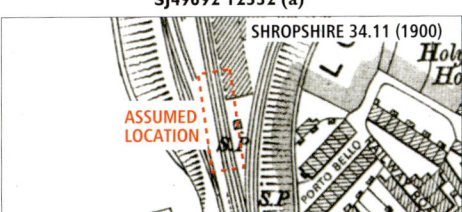

SHIPLEY (1st) - SKIPTON (1st)
SIBSON (GNR)
1 January 1870 - 1 March 1878
Line lifted – Demolished – Station site unused
TL09607 98128 (a)

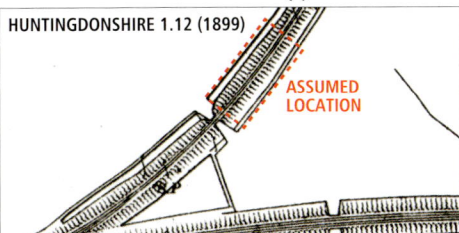

SILVERDALE FOR KNUTTON CLOUD
(NSR)
7 April 1862 - 1 February 1870
Line lifted – Demolished – Station site unused
SJ81761 46746 (a)

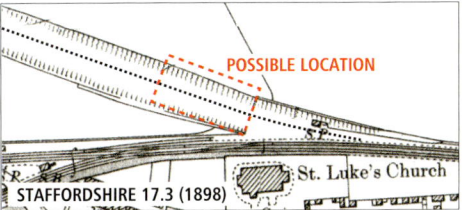

SKELLINGTHORPE (GNR)
2 January 1865 - 1 June 1868
Line Operational – Demolished – No access
SK94163 72696 (a)

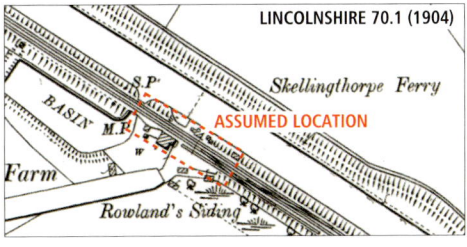

SKIPTON (1st) (MR)
7 September 1847 - 30 April 1876
Line Operational – Demolished – No access **SD98668 51217**

121

SLATEFORD (1st) - SOUTHCOATES (1st)

SLATEFORD (1st) (CR)
1 January 1853 - 1871
Line Operational – Demolished – No access **NT22142 70893**

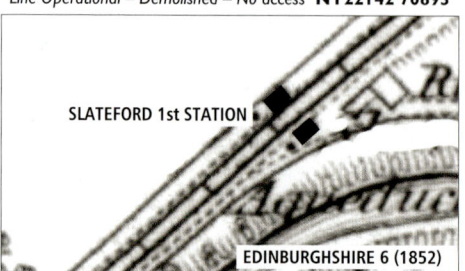

SMALLBERRY GREEN (L&SWR)
22 August 1849 - 1 February 1850
Line Operational – Demolished – No access
TQ15856 76657 (a)

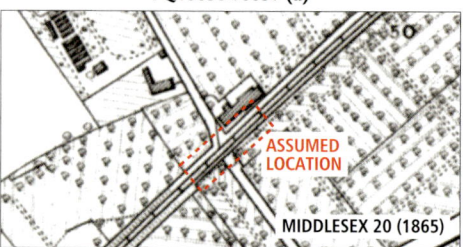

SOHO (1st) (L&NWR)
2 May 1853 - c1886
Line Operational – Demolished – No access
SP03143 88704 (a)

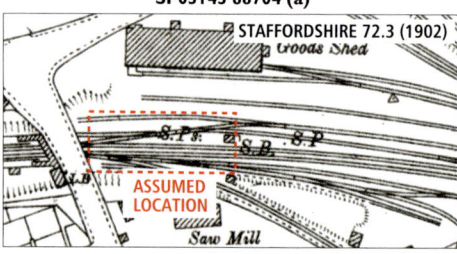

SOURDON (GNofSR)
1 October 1858 - 1 August 1866
Line lifted – Demolished – Station site unused **NJ28929 50830**

SOUTH ALLOA (CR)
12 September 1850 - 1 October 1885
Line lifted – Demolished – Station site in commercial use
NS87835 91786

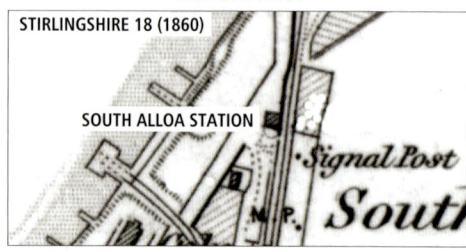

SOUTHAMPTON WEST END (L&SWR)
1 June 1847 - 1 November 1895
Line Operational – Demolished – Part of station site occupied by
Southampton Central Station car park
SU41462 12160

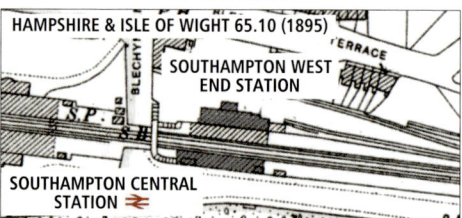

SOUTH CHURCH (S&DR)
19 April 1842 - c1845
Line Operational – Demolished – No access **NZ22093 28594**

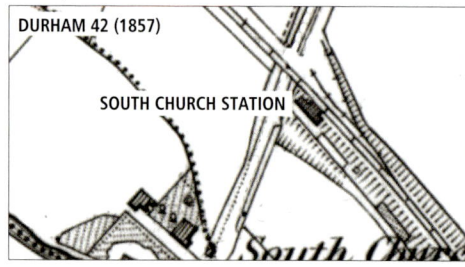

SOUTHCOATES (1st) (NER)
1 June 1853 - November 1854
Line lifted – Demolished – The A1033 passes through the station site. **TA11118 29681**

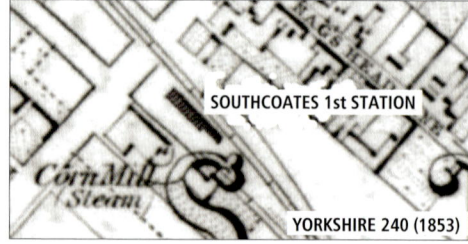

SOUTHPORT EASTBANK STREET - SPA ROAD AND BERMONDSEY (1st)

SOUTHPORT EASTBANK STREET
(LC&SR)
24 July 1848 - 22 August 1851
Line Operational – Demolished – Station Master's House in private use **SD33751 16586**

LANCASHIRE 75 (1846)

SOUTH SHIELDS (1st) (NER)
17 December 1842 - 2 June 1879
Line lifted – Demolished – Station site occupied by a car park **NZ36024 66877**

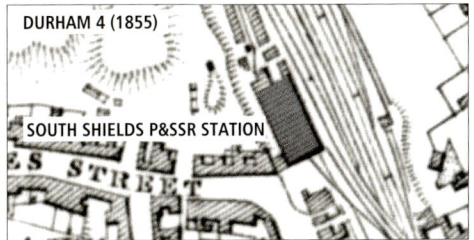

DURHAM 4 (1855)

SOUTHPORT LONDON STREET (L&YR)
9 April 1855 - 1 April 1857
Line lifted – Demolished – Station site occupied by Southport Station car park **SD33897 17117**

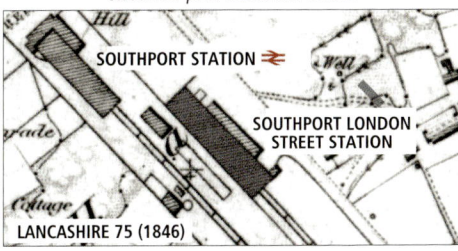

LANCASHIRE 75 (1846)

SOUTH SHIELDS (P&SSR)
16 April 1835 - 19 August 1844
Line lifted – Demolished – Station site occupied by a car park **NZ36250 67372**

DURHAM 4 (1855)

SOUTH QUEENSFERRY (1st) (NBR)
1 June 1868 - 2 September 1878
Line lifted – Demolished – Station site occupied by housing in Plewland Croft **NT12631 78333**

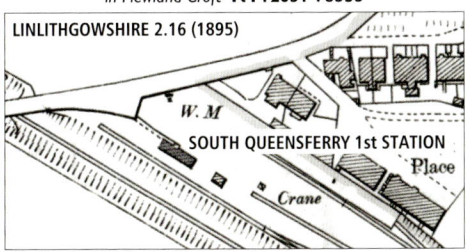

LINLITHGOWSHIRE 2.16 (1895)

SOWERBY BRIDGE (1st) (L&YR)
5 October 1840 - 1 September 1876
Line Operational – Demolished – No access **SE05757 23510 (a)**

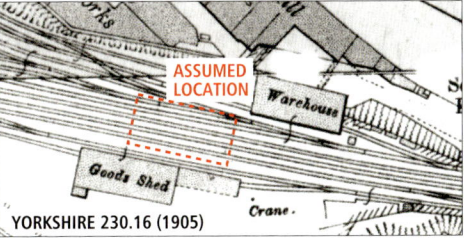

YORKSHIRE 230.16 (1905)

SOUTH SHIELDS (BlingJnR)
19 June 1839 - 17 December 1842
Line lifted – Demolished – Station site landscaped **NZ35739 66356**

DURHAM 4 (1855)

SPA ROAD AND BERMONDSEY (1st) (SER)
8 February 1836 - 1 September 1872
Line Operational – Demolished – No access **TQ34088 79269**

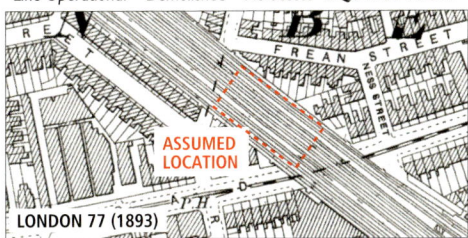

LONDON 77 (1893)

123

SPENNYMOOR (1st) - STAFFORD COMMON (1st)

SPENNYMOOR (1st) (NER)
April 1856 - 1 June 1878
Line lifted – Demolished – Station site occupied by dwellings in Rosa Street **NZ25389 33717**

SPORLE (EAnglianR)
26 October 1847 - October 1850
Line lifted – Demolished – Station site unused **TF84980 12231**

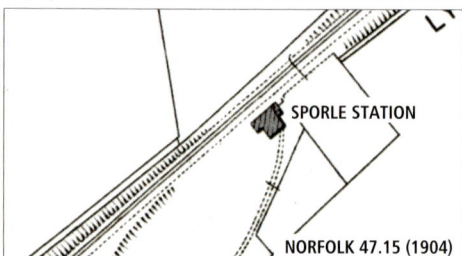

SPETCHLEY (MR)
24 June 1840 - 1 October 1855
Line Operational – Demolished **SO90320 53711**

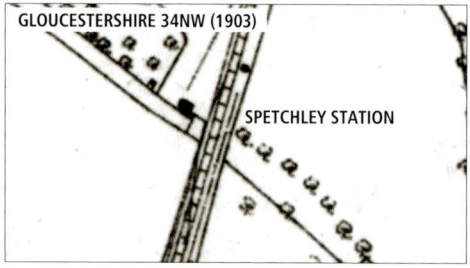

SPRINGWELL (NER)
5 September 1839 - 1 March 1872
Line Operational – Demolished **NZ31087 62380**

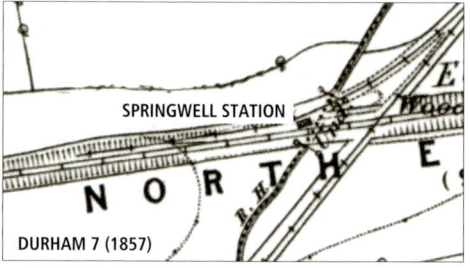

SPINKS LANE (NorfolkR)
30 July 1845 – December 1845
Line Operational - Demolished **TG13158 02165**

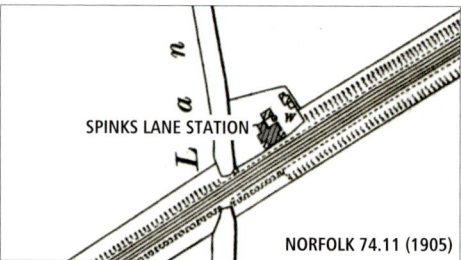

SPROTBOROUGH (MS&LR)
1 February 1850 - 1 January 1875
Line Operational – Demolished – No access **SE54133 00909**

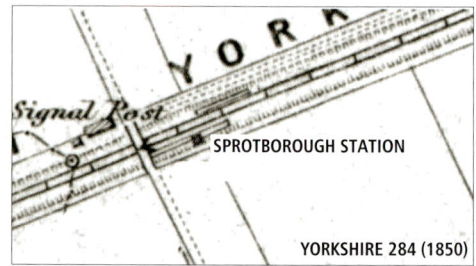

SPITAL (1st) (L&NWR/GWR)
30 May 1846 - c1891
Line Operational – Demolished – No access **SJ33927 82983**

STAFFORD COMMON (1st) (GNR)
1 July 1874 - 1882
Line lifted – Demolished – A pathway passes through the station site **SJ92089 24817**

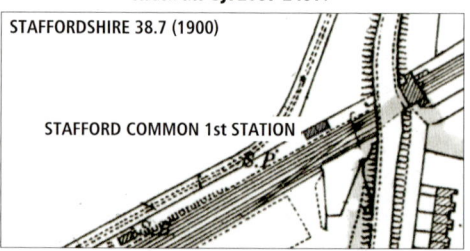

STAINFORTH (MS&LR)
1 July 1856 - 1 October 1866
Line lifted – Demolished – Station site unused SE64155 12108

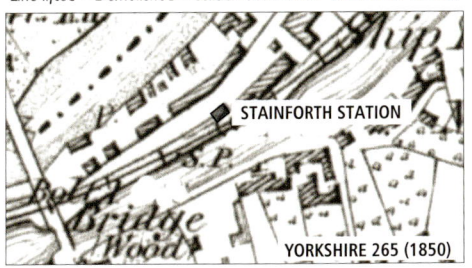

STAINFORTH STATION

YORKSHIRE 265 (1850)

STAIRFOOT (MS&LR)
August 1851 - 1 December 1871
Line lifted – Demolished – A footpath passes through the station site SE37451 05447

STAIRFOOT STATION

YORKSHIRE 275 (1850)

STAMFORD WATER STREET (MR)
2 October 1846 - 19 June 1848
Line Operational – Demolished – No access
TF03475 06861 (a)

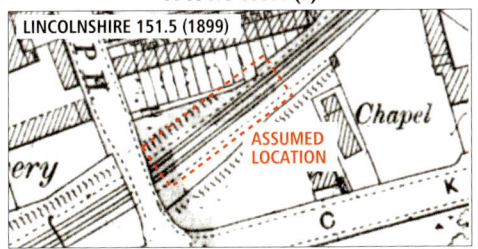

LINCOLNSHIRE 151.5 (1899)

ASSUMED LOCATION

STANHOPE (1st) (NER)
22 October 1862 - 21 October 1895
Line lifted – Demolished – Station site in commercial use
NZ00009 38715

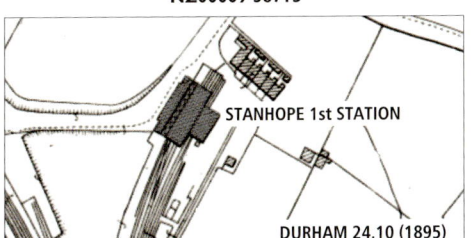

STANHOPE 1st STATION

DURHAM 24.10 (1895)

STAINFORTH - STEEPLE HOUSE AND WIRKSWORTH
STANLEY (CR)
2 August 1848 - 1856
Line Operational – Demolished – No access
NO10509 33018 (a)

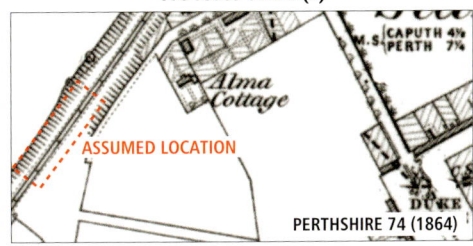

ASSUMED LOCATION

PERTHSHIRE 74 (1864)

STARSTON (GER)
1 December 1855 - 1 August 1866
Line lifted – Demolished – Station House in private use
TM23408 83988

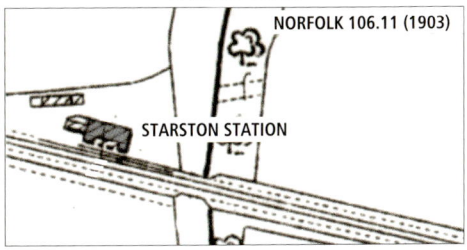

NORFOLK 106.11 (1903)

STARSTON STATION

STECHFORD GATES (L&NWR)
October 1844 - 1 February 1882
Line Operational – Demolished – No access
SP13071 87460 (a)

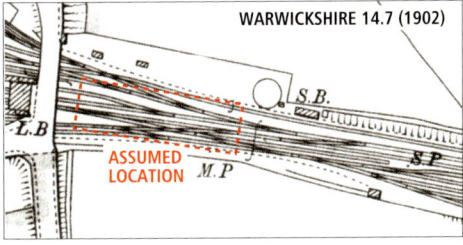

WARWICKSHIRE 14.7 (1902)

ASSUMED LOCATION

STEEPLE HOUSE AND WIRKSWORTH (L&NWR)
June 1833 - December 1877
Line lifted – Demolished – The High Peak Trail passes through the station site SK28837 55447

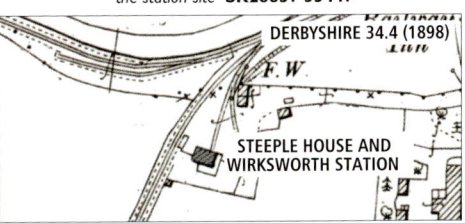

DERBYSHIRE 34.4 (1898)

STEEPLE HOUSE AND WIRKSWORTH STATION

STEETON AND SILSDEN (1st) - STOCKTON (2nd) (S&DR)

STEETON AND SILSDEN (1st) (MR)
December 1847 - 1 March 1892
Line Operational – Demolished – Station House in private use
SE03762 44862

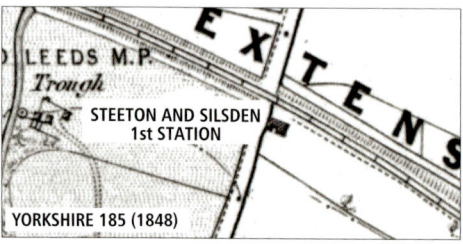
YORKSHIRE 185 (1848)

STEWART'S LANE (LC&DR)
1 May 1863 - 1 January 1867
Line Operational – Demolished – No access
TQ29068 76872 (a)

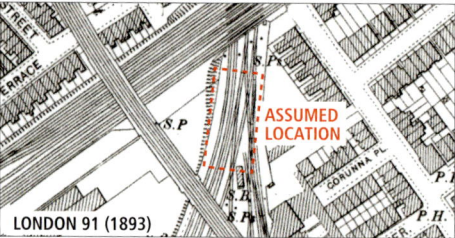
LONDON 91 (1893)

STILLINGTON (1st) (NER)
Prior to 11 October 1842 - July 1856
Line Operational – Demolished – No access **NZ35931 23858**

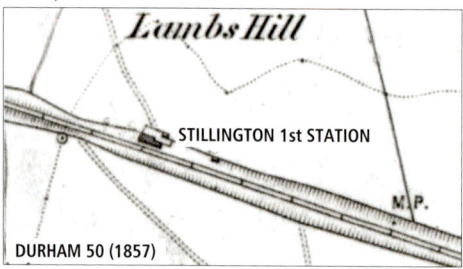
DURHAM 50 (1857)

STOAT'S NEST (LB&SCR)
12 July 1841 - 1 December 1856
Line Operational – Demolished – No access **TQ30449 60109**

SURREY 20 (1867)

STOCKPORT PORTWOOD (CLC)
12 January 1863 - 1 September 1875
Line lifted – Demolished – Station site part of car park for a Tesco Extra Superstore **SJ89993 91022**

CHESHIRE 10 (1872)

STOCKTON (Stktn&HpoolR)
9 February 1841 - 2 June 1852
Line lifted – Demolished – Station site in commercial use
NZ44676 19851

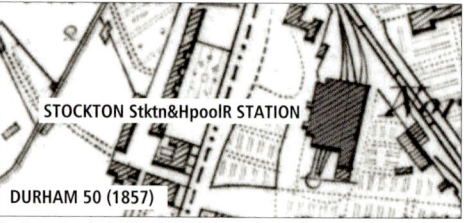
DURHAM 50 (1857)

Stockton 1st [NER] (- 1865) was built on the station site

STOCKTON (1st) (S&DR)
27 September 1825 - 27 December 1830
Line lifted – Demolished – The A1305, Riverside, passes through the station site **NZ44683 19070 (a)**

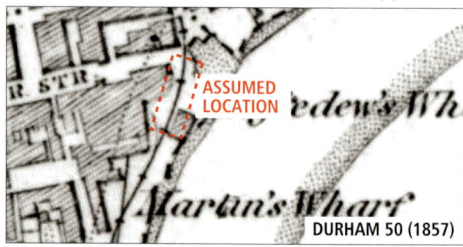
DURHAM 50 (1857)

STOCKTON (2nd) (S&DR)
27 December 1830 - 1 July 1848
Line lifted – Demolished – The Booking Office building is Grade II listed and in community use **NZ44688 18381**

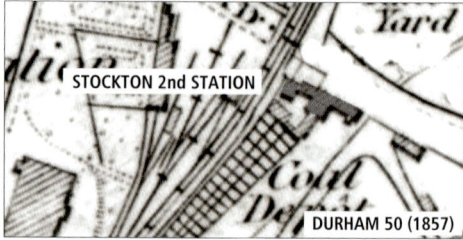
DURHAM 50 (1857)

STOKE BRUERN - STRATFORD-ON-AVON BIRMINGHAM ROAD

STOKE BRUERN (SuAT&MJR)
1 December 1892 – 31 March 1893
Line lifted – Demolished – Station House and platform in private use **SP73621 50508**

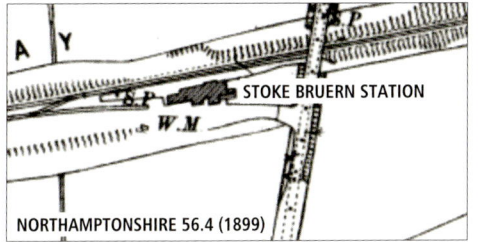

STONY HILL (P&WR)
1 April 1865 - September 1872
Line Operational – Demolished – No access
SD30903 31689 (a)

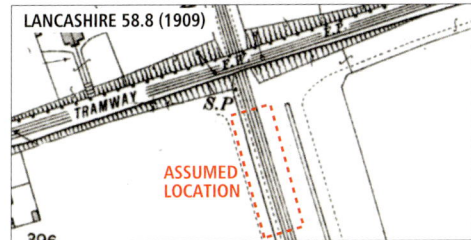

STOKE CANON (1st) (GWR)
13 August 1852 - 2 July 1894
Line Operational – Demolished – No access **SX93679 98008**

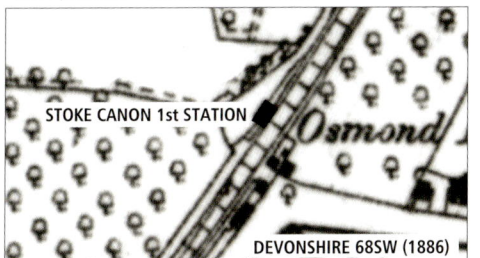

STRATFORD [TRAMWAY STATION] (OW&WR)
Prior to 1834 - 30 September 1858
Line lifted – Demolished – Station site landscaped
SP20436 54944

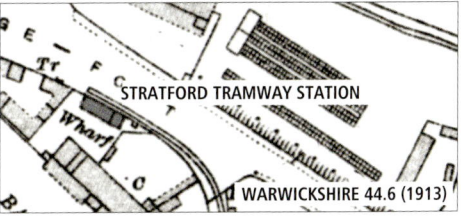

STOKE WORKS (MR)
17 September 1840 - 1 October 1855
Line Operational – Demolished – No access
SO94189 66378 (e)

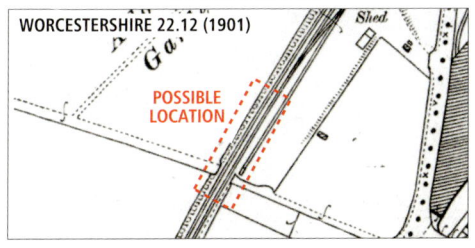

STRATFORD-ON-AVON (WMidR)
12 July 1859 - 1 January 1863
Line lifted – Demolished – Seven Meadows Road passes through the station site **SP19661 54375 (a)**

STONE (1st) (NSR)
17 April 1848 - 1 May 1849
Line Operational – Demolished – No access
SJ89661 34212 (a)

STRATFORD-ON-AVON BIRMINGHAM ROAD (SoAR)
10 October 1860 - 1 January 1863
Line lifted – Demolished – Station site in commercial use
SP19733 55591

STROOD - SWADLINCOTE (1st)

STROOD (SER)
10 February 1845 - 18 June 1856
Line lifted – Demolished – Station site unused **TQ74138 69360**

SUTTON (1st) (GER)
16 April 1866 - 10 May 1878
Line lifted – Demolished – Station site occupied by a car park
TL45300 78663

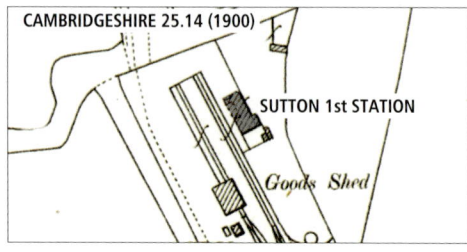

SUDBURY (1st) (GER)
2 July 1849 - 9 August 1865
Line lifted – Demolished – Station site in commercial use
TL87580 41203

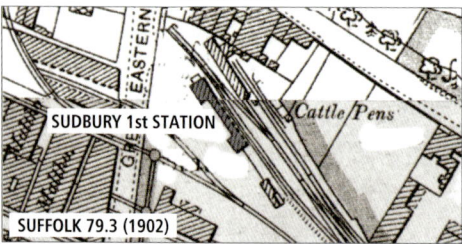

SUTTON BRIDGE (MR)
1 July 1862 - January 1867
Line lifted – Demolished – The A17 passes through the station site
TF48121 21027

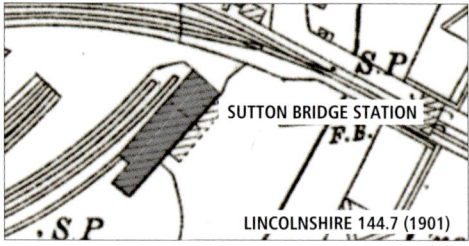

SUNDERLAND FAWCETT STREET (NER)
1 June 1853 - 4 August 1879
Line lifted – Demolished – Station site occupied by a car park
NZ39698 56614

SUTTON COLDFIELD (1st) (L&NWR)
2 June 1862 - 15 December 1884
Line lifted – Demolished – Station site occupied by station car park
SP11923 96358

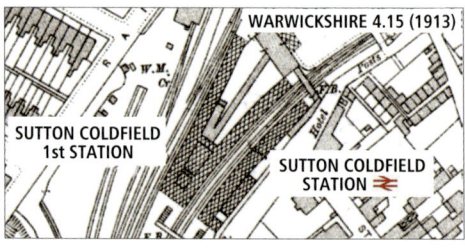

SUNDERLAND MOOR (NER)
19 October 1836 - 1 May 1858
Line lifted – Demolished – Station site unused **NZ40850 57388**

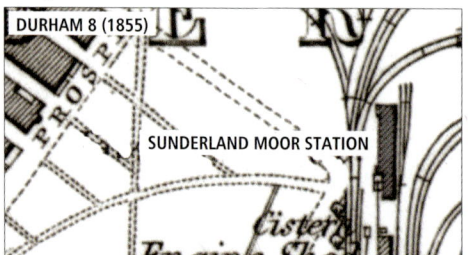

SWADLINCOTE (1st) (MR)
1 March 1849 - 1 May 1883
Line lifted – Demolished – Station site in commercial use
SK30051 19874

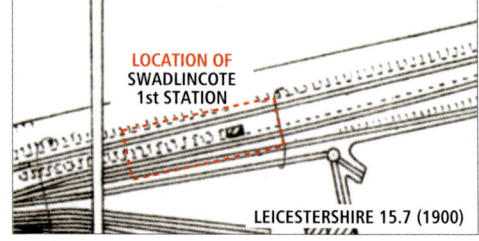

SWALWELL (YN&BR)
August 1850 - May 1854
Line lifted – Demolished – Station site in commercial use
NZ20417 62349

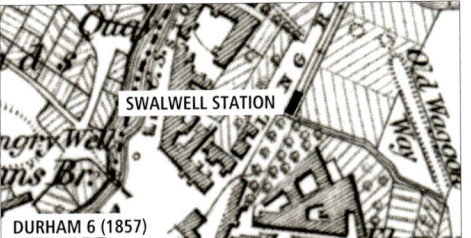

DURHAM 6 (1857)

SWANSEA BAY (1st) (L&NWR)
14 December 1867 - 2 June 1892
Line lifted – Demolished – The westbound carriageway of the A4067, Oystermouth Road, passes through the station site
SS64425 92216 (a)

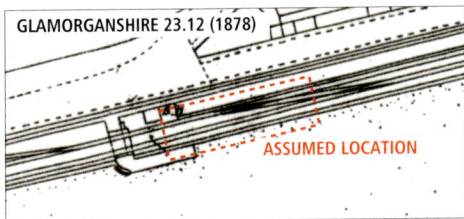

GLAMORGANSHIRE 23.12 (1878)

SWANSEA WIND STREET (GWR)
1 August 1863 - 1 March 1873
Line lifted – Demolished – The A4067, Quay Parade, passes through the station site **SS65918 92973 (a)**

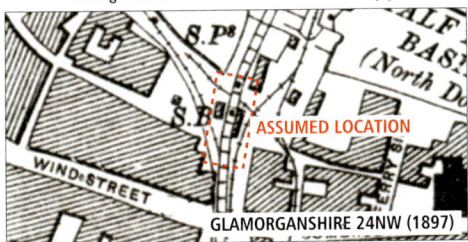

GLAMORGANSHIRE 24NW (1897)

SWAYFIELD* (GNR)
Not known
Line Operational – Demolished – No access
SK99446 23129 (e)

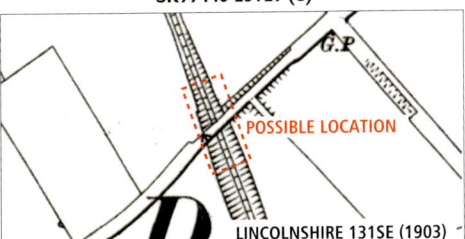

LINCOLNSHIRE 131SE (1903)

SWALWELL - TAFFS WELL (1st)

SWINDON (B&GR)
26 May 1842 - 1 October 1844
Line Operational – Demolished – No access
SO93952 24965 (a)

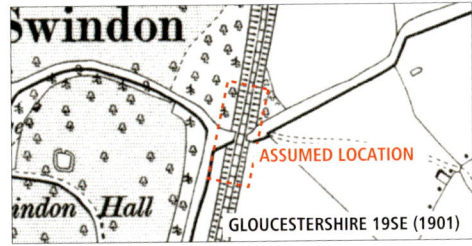

GLOUCESTERSHIRE 19SE (1901)

SWINTON (1st) (MR)
1 July 1840 - 2 July 1899
Line Operational – Demolished – No access **SK46179 99070**

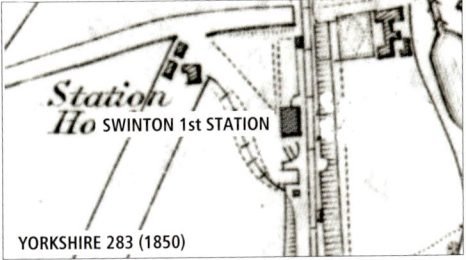

YORKSHIRE 283 (1850)

SYMINGTON (1st) (CR)
15 February 1848 - 30 November 1863
Line Operational – Demolished – No access **NS99130 35781**

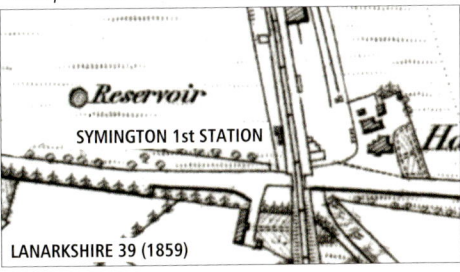

LANARKSHIRE 39 (1859)

TAFFS WELL (1st) (TVR)
8 October 1840 - 22 June 1863
Line Operational – Demolished – No access
ST11955 83905 (a)

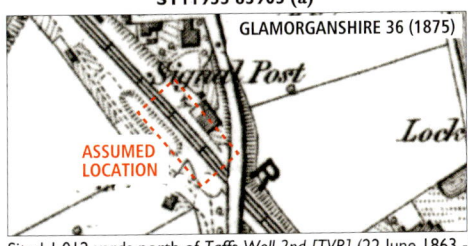

GLAMORGANSHIRE 36 (1875)

Sited 1,012 yards north of *Taffs Well 2nd [TVR]* (22 June 1863 -)

TALYLLYN (MidWR) - TENBY (P&TR)

TALYLLYN (MidWR)
21 September 1864 - 1 October 1869
Line lifted – Demolished – Station site unused
SO11081 27313 (a)

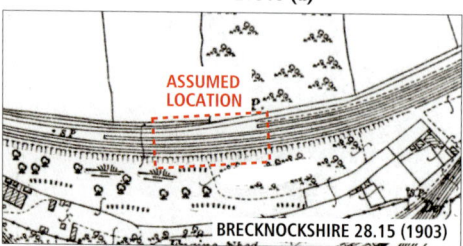
BRECKNOCKSHIRE 28.15 (1903)

TALYLLYN (BRYNDERWEN) (B&MTJnR)
23 April 1863 - 1 October 1869
Line lifted – Demolished – A pathway passes through the station site **SO10725 27416**

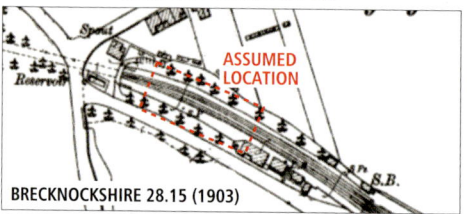
BRECKNOCKSHIRE 28.15 (1903)

Talyllyn Junction [B&MTJnR] (1 October 1869 - 31 December 1962) was built on, or near to, the station site.

TANFIELD LEA (BlingJnR)
16 June 1842 - August 1844
Line lifted – Demolished – New Front Street passes through the station site **NZ19319 54793 (a)**

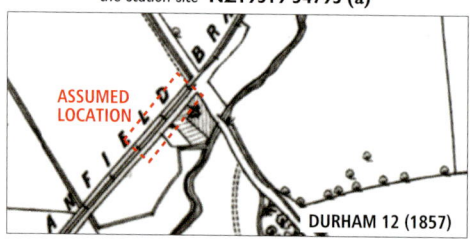
DURHAM 12 (1857)

TAN-Y-MANOD (B&Ff/GWR)
30 May 1868 - 10 September 1883
Line (Standard gauge) Mothballed – Demolished
SH70564 45248 (a)

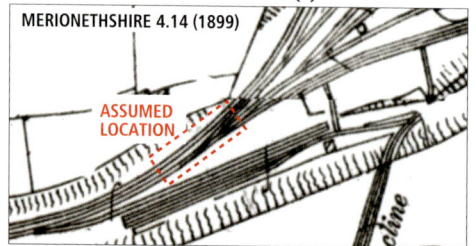
MERIONETHSHIRE 4.14 (1899)

TAPLOW (GWR)
4 June 1838 - 1 September 1872
Line Operational – Demolished – No access
SU90913 81197 (a)

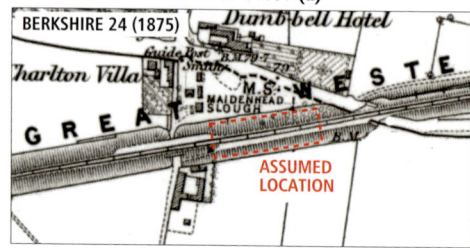
BERKSHIRE 24 (1875)

TEMPLECOMBE LOWER (S&DJtR)
3 February 1862 - 17 January 1887
Line lifted – Demolished – Station site in commercial use
ST70980 22809 (a)

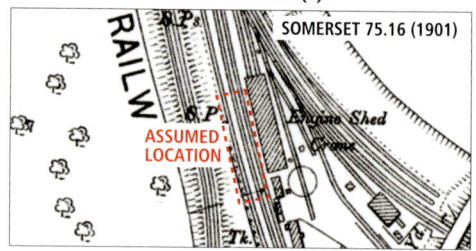
SOMERSET 75.16 (1901)

TENBURY WELLS (1st) (TJR)
1 August 1861 - 13 August 1864
Line lifted – Demolished – Station site in commercial use
SO59169 68905

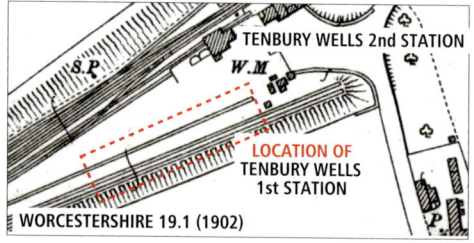
WORCESTERSHIRE 19.1 (1902)

TENBY (P&TR)
6 August 1863 - 4 September 1866
Line lifted – Demolished – Station site occupied by a car park
SN12856 00722

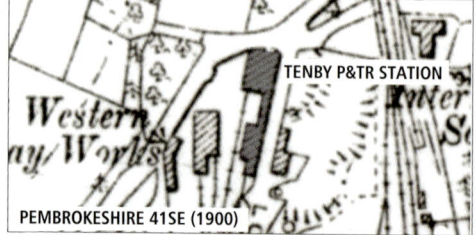
PEMBROKESHIRE 41SE (1900)

TETBURY ROAD (GWR)
12 May 1845 - 1 May 1882
Line Operational – Demolished – No access **ST98151 98796**

GLOUCESTERSHIRE 59 (1882)

TEWKESBURY (1st) (MR)
21 July 1840 - 16 May 1864
Line lifted – Demolished – Station site occupied by a car park
SO89402 32979

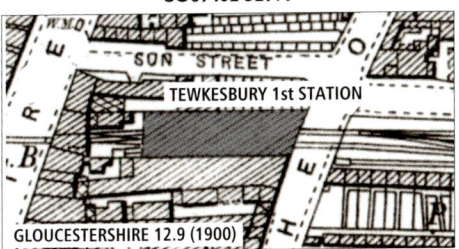
GLOUCESTERSHIRE 12.9 (1900)

THAMES HAVEN (LT&SR)
7 June 1855 – 23 September 1880
Line lifted – Station and pier demolished – No access
TQ74257 81467

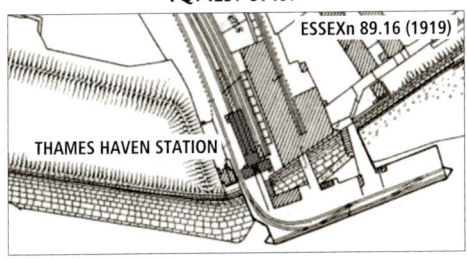
ESSEXn 89.16 (1919)

THE AVENUE (B&TR)
1 April 1861 - 27 June 1864
Line lifted – Demolished – Station site unused
NZ31692 76180 (a)

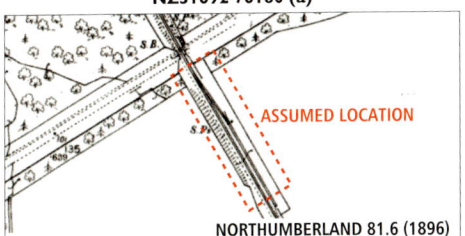
NORTHUMBERLAND 81.6 (1896)

TETBURY ROAD - THORNTON LANE

THIRSK TOWN (NER)
1 June 1848 - December 1855
Line lifted – Demolished – Station site occupied by a Tesco Supermarket **SE42669 81879**

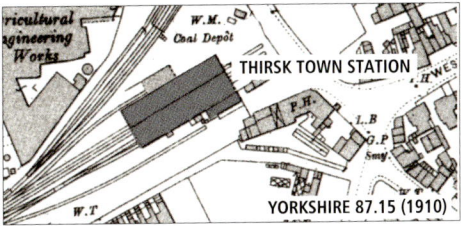
YORKSHIRE 87.15 (1910)

THORNE (SYorks&RDNR)
1 November 1859 - 10 September 1866
Line lifted – Demolished – Station site occupied by housing in Dunstan Drive **SE68528 13089**

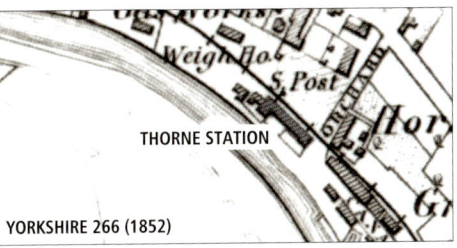
YORKSHIRE 266 (1852)

THORNE LOCK (SYorks&RDNR)
1 July 1856 - 10 September 1859
Line lifted – Demolished – Station site occupied by housing in Union Road **SE68161 13193 (a)**

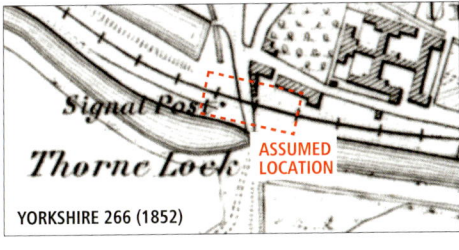
YORKSHIRE 266 (1852)

THORNTON (Lstr&SwngtnR)
18 July 1832 - 1 January 1842
Line lifted – Demolished **SK45745 08059**

THORNTON LANE (MR)
1850 - 1 October 1865
Line Operational – Demolished – No access **SK45733 08054**

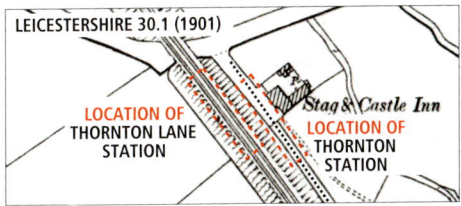
LEICESTERSHIRE 30.1 (1901)

131

THURGOLAND - TOW LAW (1st)

THURGOLAND (MS&LR)
December 1845 – 1 November 1847
Line lifted – Demolished – A footpath passes through the station site **SE29133 00374**

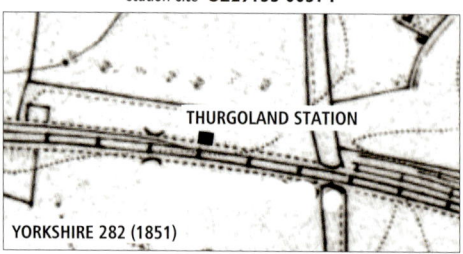
THURGOLAND STATION
YORKSHIRE 282 (1851)

TIVERTON (1st) (GWR)
12 June 1848 – 1 August 1884
Line lifted – Demolished – Station site in commercial use
SS96006 12626

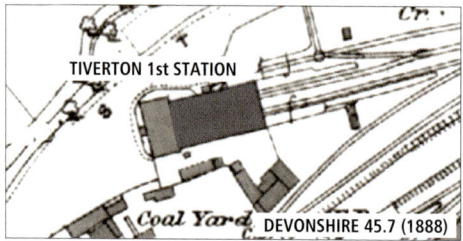
TIVERTON 1st STATION
DEVONSHIRE 45.7 (1888)

TIVOLI, MARGATE* (SER)
20 July 1848 – c1867
Line lifted – Demolished – Station site unused **TR35308 69832**

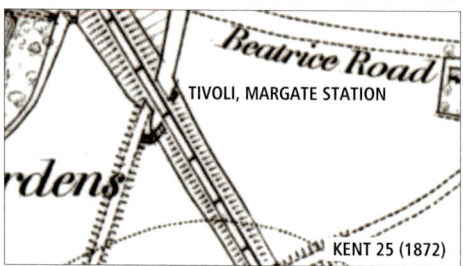
TIVOLI, MARGATE STATION
KENT 25 (1872)

TOD POINT (NER)
January 1873 – December 1873
Line lifted – Demolished – Station site unused **NZ57253 24746**

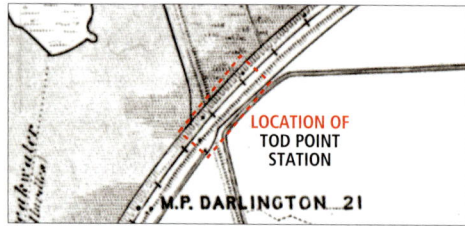
LOCATION OF TOD POINT STATION
M.P. DARLINGTON 21

Warrenby Halt [NER] (October 1920 – 19 June 1978) may have been built on the station site

TOKENBURY CORNER* (L&CdnR)
c1889 – c1896
Line lifted – Demolished – Station site unused **SX28038 69938**

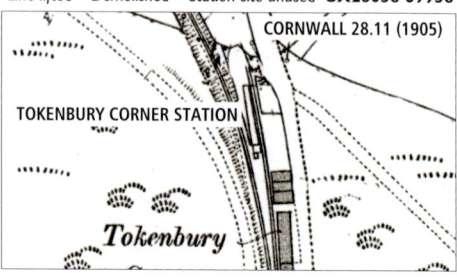
CORNWALL 28.11 (1905)
TOKENBURY CORNER STATION

TOOTING JUNCTION (1st) (TM&WR)
1 October 1868 – 12 August 1894
Main Line Operational – Demolished – Part of degraded platform extant **TQ27828 70585**

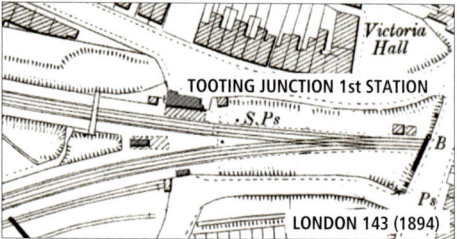
TOOTING JUNCTION 1st STATION
LONDON 143 (1894)

TOWER OF LONDON (MetR)
25 September 1882 – 13 October 1884
Line Operated by LU **TQ33606 80786**

LONDON 5.11 (1914)
TOWER OF LONDON STATION

Tower Hill [LU] (5 February 1967 –) was built on the station site

TOW LAW (1st) (NER)
October 1846 – 2 March 1868
Line lifted – Demolished – Station site in commercial use
NZ12009 39045

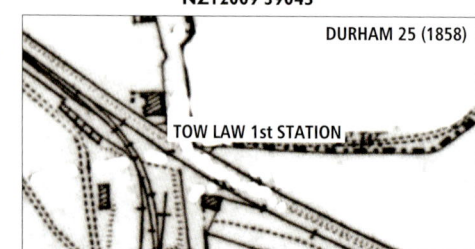
DURHAM 25 (1858)
TOW LAW 1st STATION

TRANMERE (BLcs&CheshJnR)
30 May 1846 - October 1857
Line Operational – Demolished – No access **SJ32755 87049**

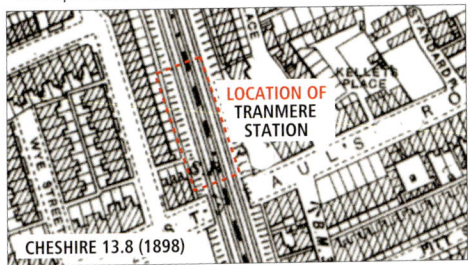

TRIMDON FOUNDRY (NER)
TRANMERE - TROON (1st) (G&SWR)
13 October 1846 - August 1873
Line lifted – Demolished – Station site unused/landscaped
NZ37013 35855

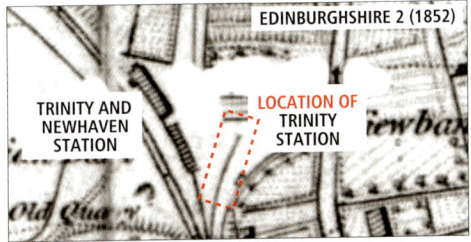

TRAP ROAD (L&NWR)
12 April 1870 - September 1871
Line lifted – Demolished – A footpath passes through the station site **SS59377 97681**

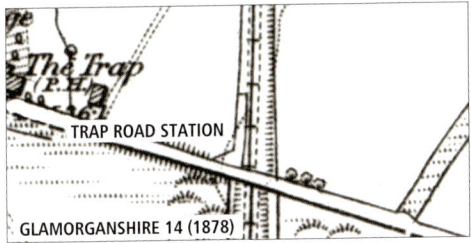

TRINITY (NBR)
31 August 1842 - 19 January 1846
Line lifted – Demolished – Station site occupied by housing
NT24946 76867

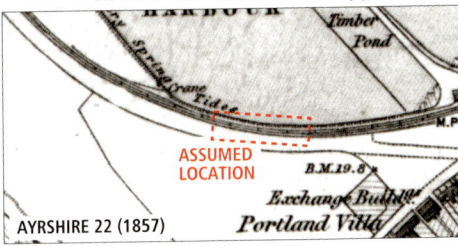

TREAMAN (1st) (TVR)
October 1848 - January 1857
Line Operational – Demolished **SO02378 00788 (e)**

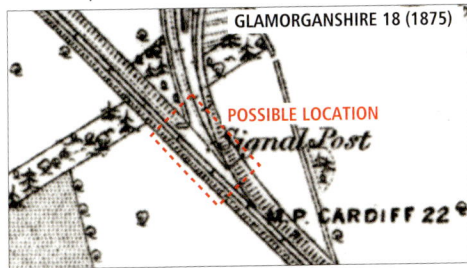

TROON (GPK&AR)
1818 - 28 October 1850
Line lifted – Demolished – Harbour Road passes through the station site **NS31289 31067 (a)**

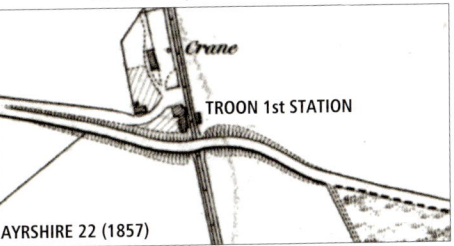

TREORCHY (1st) (TVR)
27 September 1869 – 3 March 1884
Line Operational – Demolished – No access **SS95441 96870**

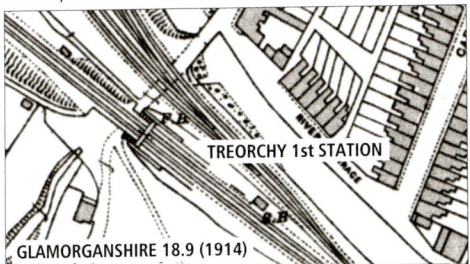

TROON (1st) (G&SWR)
5 August 1839 - 2 May 1892
Line lifted – Demolished – Station site occupied by housing in Old Station Wynd **NS33158 31169**

133

TRURO HIGHER TOWN [TRURO ROAD] - ULVERSTON (U&LR)

TRURO HIGHER TOWN [TRURO ROAD] (WCwallR)
25 August 1852 - 16 April 1855
Line lifted – Demolished – Station site unused
SW81245 44300 (a)

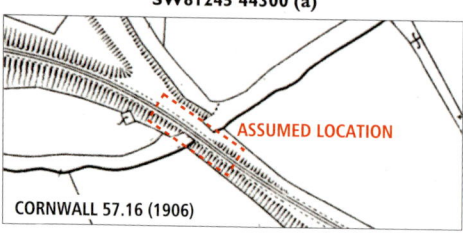

TUNBRIDGE JUNCTION (1st) (SER)
26 May 1842 - 1864
Line Operational – Demolished – No access
TQ59000 45990 (a)

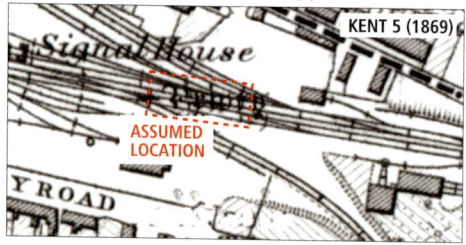

TUNNEL JUNCTION (NER)
13 October 1858 - 1 August 1863
Line Operational – Demolished – No access
NZ22613 27656

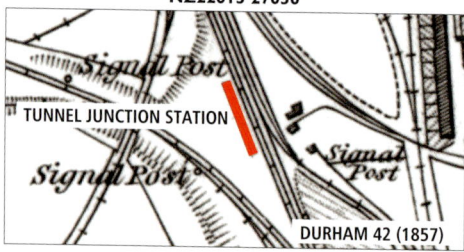

TYDDYN GWYN (B&Ff/GWR)
30 May 1868 - 10 September 1883
Standard Gauge Line Mothballed – Demolished
SH70393 44559

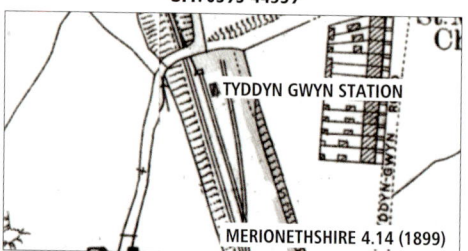

TYNDRUM (1st) (CR)
1 August 1873 - 1 May 1877
Line lifted – Demolished – Station site occupied by dwellings in Lower Station Road **NN32799 30172**

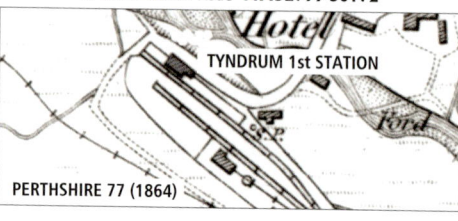

TYNEMOUTH (1st) (NER)
29 March 1847 - 3 July 1882
Line lifted – Demolished – Station site occupied by housing in Oxford Street **NZ36738 69164**

TYNEMOUTH (2nd) (NER)
c1864 - 3 July 1882
Line lifted – Demolished – Station site in commercial use
NZ36703 69195

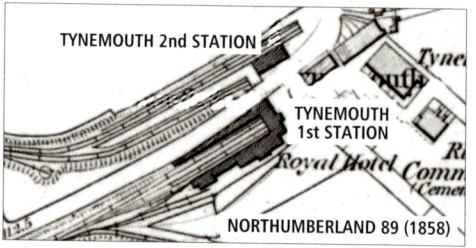

TYWYN (1st) (CamR)
24 October 1863 - c1870
Line Operational – Demolished – No access **SH58538 00446**

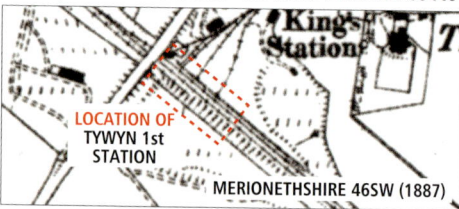

ULVERSTON (U&LR)
7 June 1854 - 26 August 1857
Line lifted – Demolished – Station site in commercial use
SD28520 77929

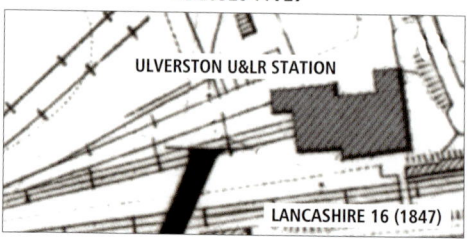

UNDER HILL (W&FJnR)
1 November 1850 - 1 January 1860
Line Operational – Demolished **SD18586 82833**

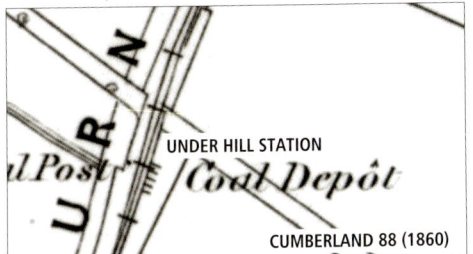

UPHOLLAND (1st) (L&YR)
20 November 1848 - June 1852
Line Operational – Demolished – No access **SD52522 04031**

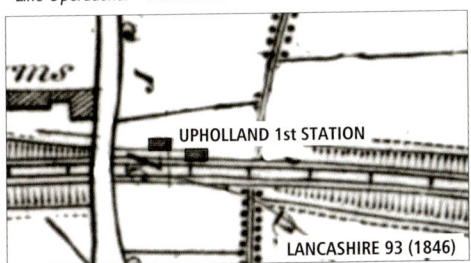

UPPER GREENHILL (NBR)
March 1848 - September 1865
Line Operational – Demolished – No access **NS81496 78642**

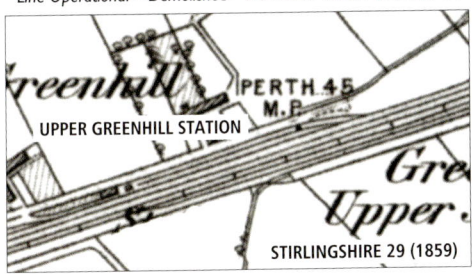

UPWEY (1st) (GWR)
21 June 1871 - 19 April 1886
Line Operational – Demolished – No access **SY67107 84025**

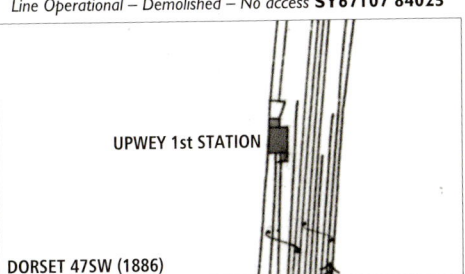

UNDER HILL - VAUXHALL (GJnR)
UTTOXETER BRIDGE STREET (NSR)
7 August 1848 - 22 September 1881
Line Operational – Demolished – No access **SK09476 33215**

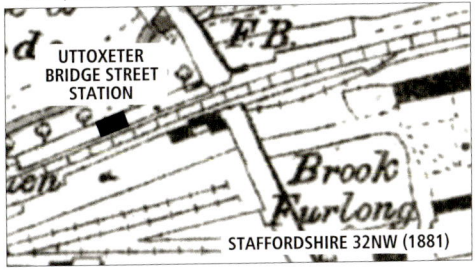

UTTOXETER DOVE BANK (NSR)
13 July 1849 - 22 September 1881
Line lifted – Demolished – Station site occupied by A518, Derby Road and roundabout **SK09476 33855**

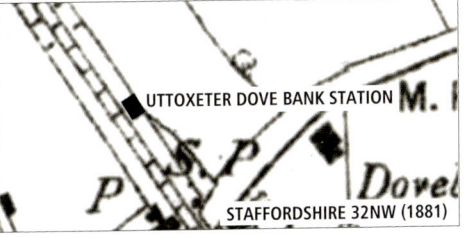

UTTOXETER JUNCTION (NSR)
13 July 1849 - 22 September 1881
One line Operational – Demolished – No access
SK10115 33196

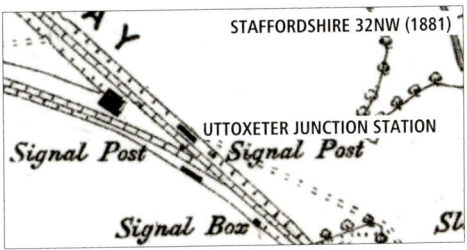

VAUXHALL (GJnR)
4 July 1837 - 19 November 1838
Line Operational – Demolished – No access
SP08385 87209 (a)

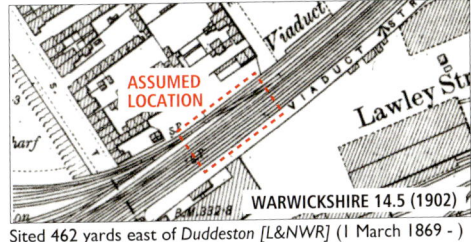

Sited 462 yards east of *Duddeston* [L&NWR] (1 March 1869 -)

VICTORIA PARK (NLR) - WALNUT TREE BRIDGE

VICTORIA PARK (NLR)
14 June 1856 - 1 March 1866
Line Operational – Demolished – No access
TQ36606 84740 (a)

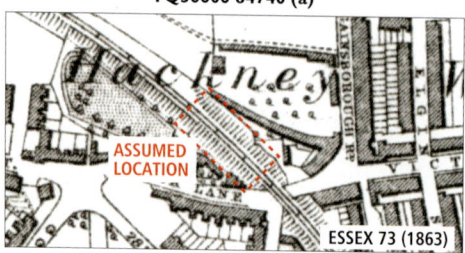

VICTORIA PARK AND BOW
(ECR/L&BwallR)
31 March 1849 - 6 January 1851
Line Operational – Demolished – No access **TQ37326 83149**

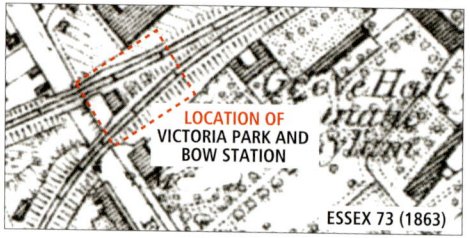

VIGO (NER)
16 April 1835 - December 1853
Line lifted – Demolished – Station site unused
NZ28195 54088 (a)

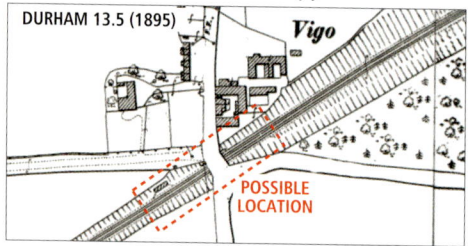

WADEBRIDGE (1st) (L&SWR)
1 October 1834 - 1 November 1886
Line lifted – Demolished – A road passes through the station site
SW99052 72345

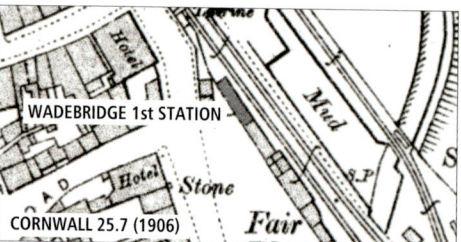

WAKEFIELD WESTGATE (1st) (GNR)
5 October 1857 - 1 May 1867
Line Operational – Demolished – No access **SE32830 20585**

Sited 220 yards south of *Wakefield Westgate 2nd [GNR]* (1 May 1867 -)

WALLACE NICK (NBR)
17 June 1850 - 27 January 1851
Line lifted – Demolished – A cycle/walkway passes through the station site **NT72362 32675 (a)**

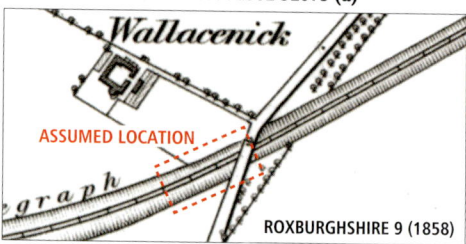

WALLYFORD (NBR)
1 May 1866 - 14 October 1867
Line Operational – Demolished – No access
NT35969 71983 (a)

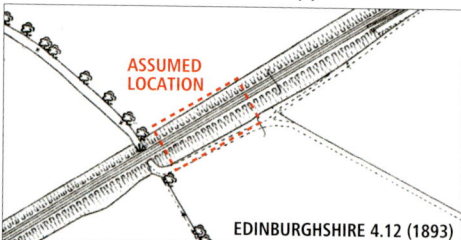

WALNUT TREE BRIDGE (RhyR)
31 March 1858 - December 1871
Line lifted – Demolished – Station site occupied by a car park
ST12491 83217

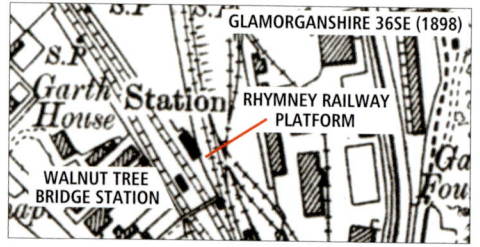

WALSALL BRIDGEMAN PLACE (SStaffsR)
1 November 1847 - 9 April 1849
Line Operational – Demolished – No access
SP00954 98296 (a)

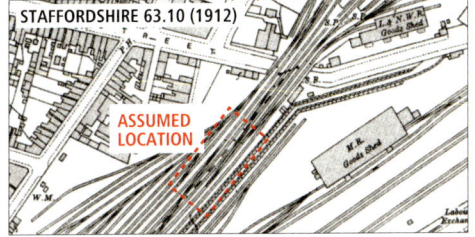

WANDSWORTH COMMON (WEoL&CPR)
1 December 1856 - 1 June 1858
Line Operational – Demolished – No access
TQ27579 73669 (a)

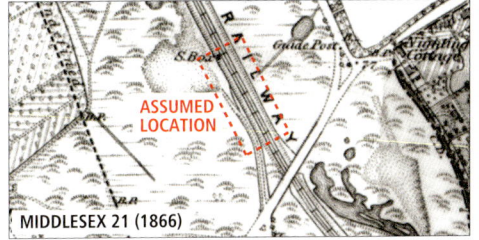

WALSOKEN (ECR)
1 February 1848 - August 1851
Line lifted – Demolished – Station site occupied by houses
in Meadowgate Lane **TF47226 08916 (a)**

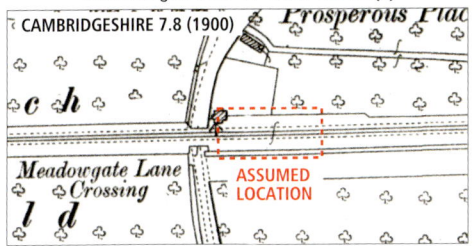

WAREHAM (1st) (L&SWR)
1 June 1847 - 4 April 1887
Line Operational – Demolished – No access
SY92077 88233 (a)

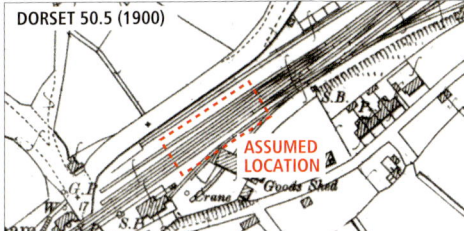

WALTHAM CROSS (1st) (GER)
15 September 1840 - 1885
Line Operational – Demolished – No access **TL36530 00417**

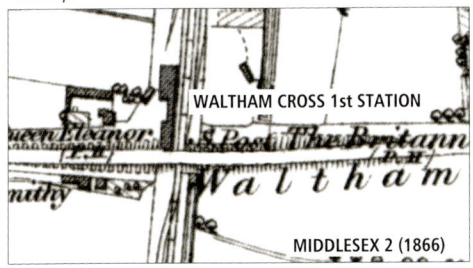

WARRINGTON BANK QUAY (1st) (L&NWR)
4 July 1837 - 16 November 1868
Line Operational – Demolished – No access **SJ59966 88097**

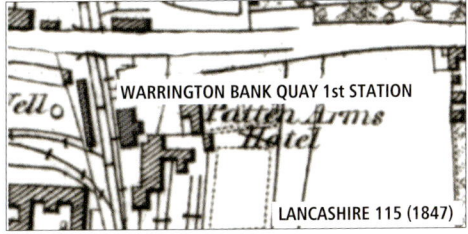

WALTON JUNCTION (BLcs&ChshJnR)
5 May 1857 - 1 September 1858
Line Operational – Demolished – No access **SJ59778 86405 (a)**

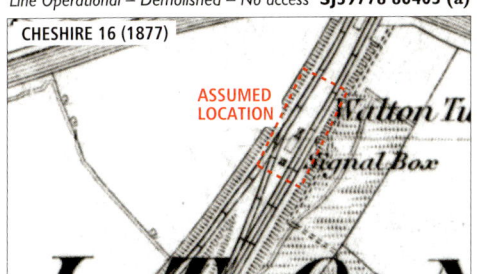

WARRINGTON DALLAM LANE (GJnR)
1832 - 4 July 1837
Line lifted – Demolished – Station building in use as
"The Three Pigeons" pub **SJ60457 88652**

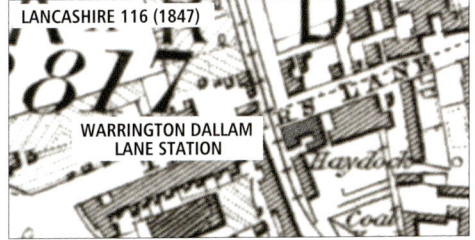

WARRINGTON WHITECROSS - WATERLOO MERSEYSIDE (1st)

WARRINGTON WHITECROSS (L&NWR)
1 February 1853 – 1 May 1854
Line Operational for Freight – Demolished – No access
SJ59423 87904 (e)

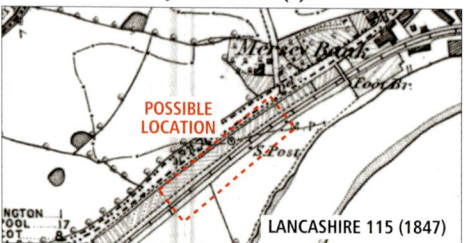

LANCASHIRE 115 (1847)

WARRISTON (NBR)
20 May 1846 – 22 May 1868
Line lifted – Demolished – A pathway passes through the station site **NT25247 75446**

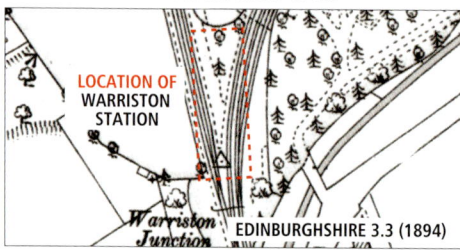

EDINBURGHSHIRE 3.3 (1894)

WARTON (LYTHAM DOCK) (P&WR)
1 June 1865 – 1 May 1874
Line lifted – Demolished – Station site unused
SD38273 28016 (a)

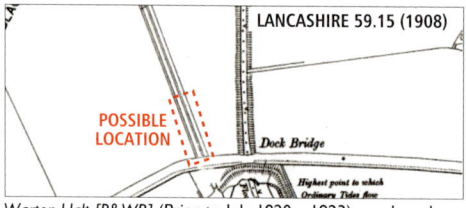

LANCASHIRE 59.15 (1908)

Warton Halt [P&WR] (Prior to July 1920 – 1923) may have been built on the station site

WASHFORD (WSsetMinR)
4 September 1865 – 7 November 1898
Line lifted – Demolished – Station site occupied by a dwelling
ST04880 41158

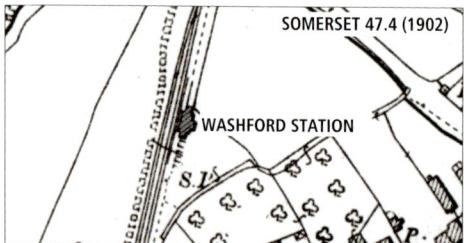

SOMERSET 47.4 (1902)

WASHINGTON (D&PR)
24 February 1837 – 6 September 1847
Line lifted – Demolished – A pathway passes through the station site **NO26637 41905 (a)**

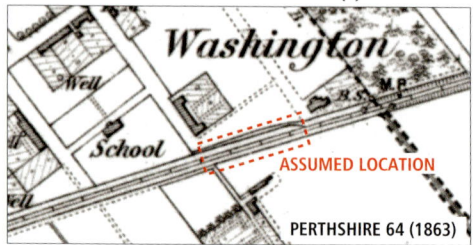

PERTHSHIRE 64 (1863)

WASHINGTON (1st) (NER)
16 April 1835 – December 1853
Line Operational – Demolished **NZ31647 55207**

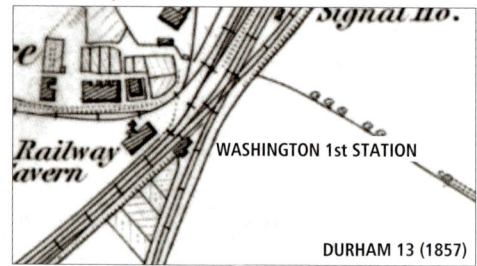

DURHAM 13 (1857)

WATCHET (WSsetMinR)
4 September 1865 – 7 November 1898
Line lifted – Station building and part of one platform in private use **ST06979 43435**

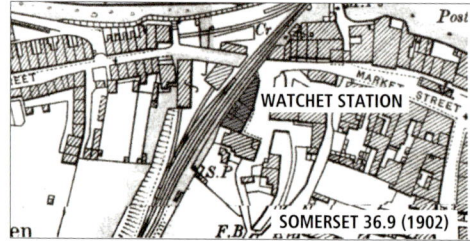

SOMERSET 36.9 (1902)

WATERLOO MERSEYSIDE (1st) (L&YR)
24 July 1848 – 24 July 1881
Line Operational – Demolished **SJ31830 98278**

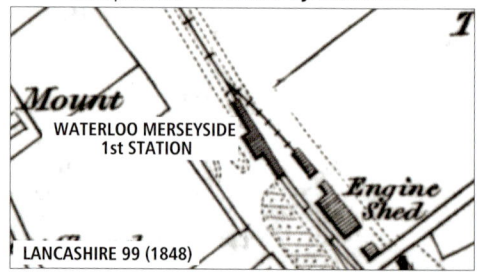

LANCASHIRE 99 (1848)

WATFORD (L&NWR)
20 July 1837 - 5 May 1858
Line Operational – Demolished – Street level Grade II listed station building in commercial use **TQ10806 97593 (a)**

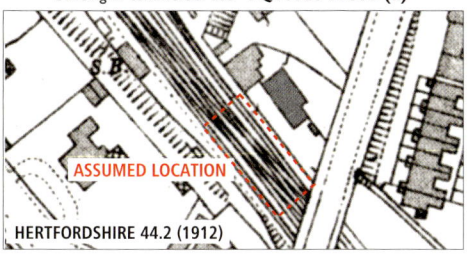

HERTFORDSHIRE 44.2 (1912)

WAVERTON (1st) (L&NWR)
February 1846 - 6 June 1898
Line Operational – Demolished – No access **SJ45522 63120**

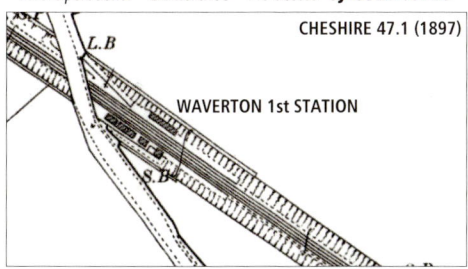

CHESHIRE 47.1 (1897)

WAVERTREE LANE (L&MR)
17 September 1830 - 15 August 1836
Line Operational – Demolished – No access **SJ37632 90035 (a)**

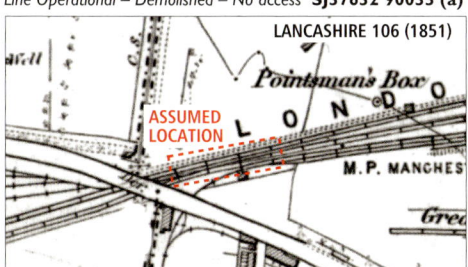

LANCASHIRE 106 (1851)

WEARMOUTH (YN&BR)
19 June 1839 - 19 June 1848
Line lifted – Demolished – Station site in commercial use
NZ39847 58121

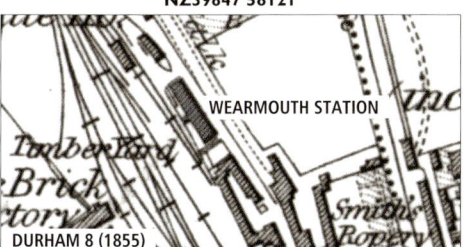

DURHAM 8 (1855)

WATFORD - WELLINGTON COLLEGE

WEDNESFIELD HEATH (L&NWR)
4 July 1837 - 1 January 1873
Line Operational – Demolished – No access **SO92772 99704**

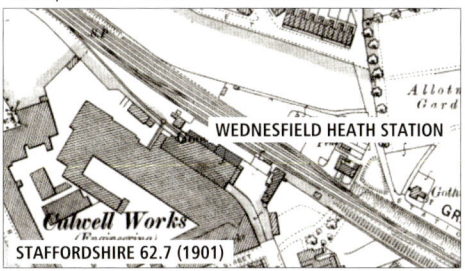

STAFFORDSHIRE 62.7 (1901)

WEEDON (1st) (L&NWR)
17 September 1838 - 18 February 1888
Line Operational – Demolished – No access **SP63017 59788**

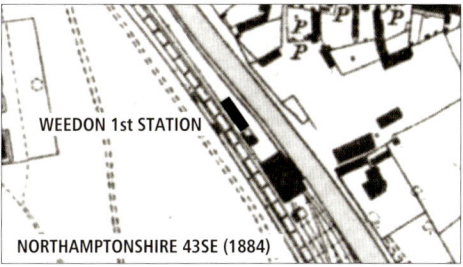

NORTHAMPTONSHIRE 43SE (1884)

WEETON (P&WR)
November 1840 - April 1843
Line Operational – Demolished – No access
SD37716 34534 (a)

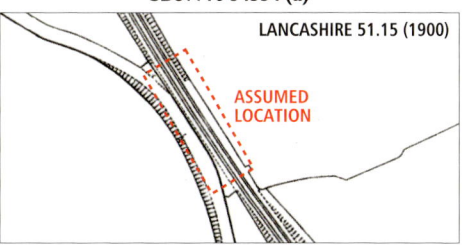

LANCASHIRE 51.15 (1900)

WELLINGTON COLLEGE (SER)
29 January 1859 - c1860
Line Operational – Demolished – No access
SU82562 63023 (a)

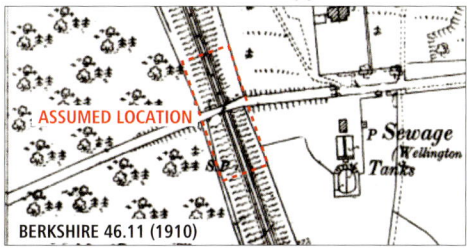

BERKSHIRE 46.11 (1910)

WELLS (1st) (GWR) - WEST HELMSDALE

WELLS (1st) (GWR)
1 March 1862 - 1 January 1878
Line lifted – Demolished – The A371, East Somerset Way, passes through the station site **ST54618 45162**

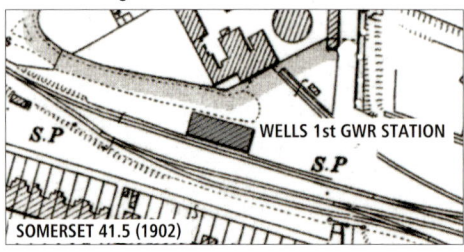

WESTERFIELD (FIxstoweR)
1 May 1877 - 1 September 1879
Line lifted – Station building and platform extant
TM17056 47238

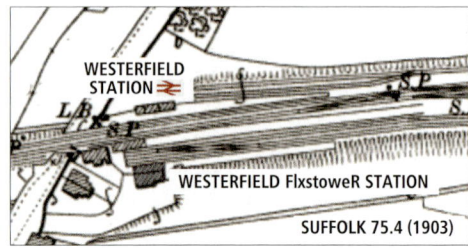

WELWYN JUNCTION (GNR)
1 March 1858 - 1 September 1860
Line Operational – Demolished – No access
TL24026 13115 (a)

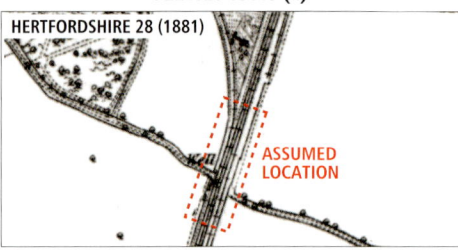

WESTERTON (NER)
11 July 1835 - April 1867
Line lifted – Demolished – Station site in agricultural use
NZ25738 30115 (e)

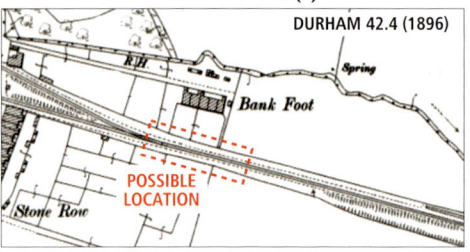

WENFORD BRIDGE (L&SWR)
30 September 1834 - 1 November 1886
Line lifted – Demolished – Station site occupied by a car park
SX08584 75098

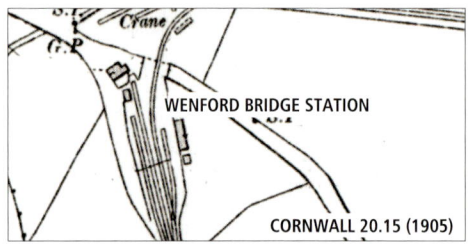

WEST HARTLEPOOL (1st) (NER)
9 February 1841 - 3 May 1880
Line lifted – Demolished – Station site occupied by housing in Britannia Close **NZ51500 32807 (a)**

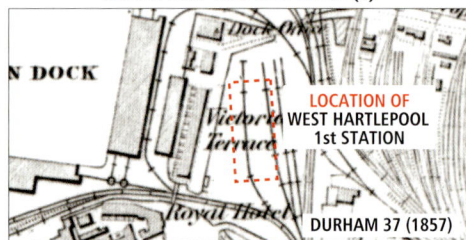

WEST DRAYTON (1st) (GWR)
4 June 1838 - 9 April 1884
Line Operational – Demolished – No access **TQ05944 80102**

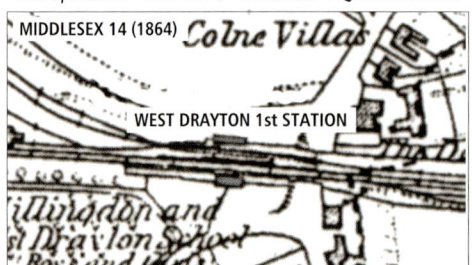

WEST HELMSDALE (HR)
1 November 1870 - 19 June 1871
Line Operational – Demolished – No access
ND01846 14354 (a)

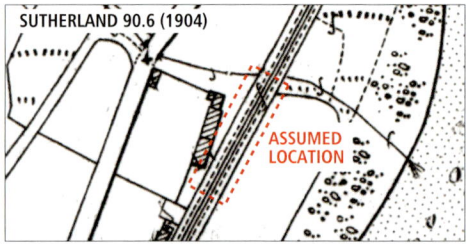

140

WEST HOUSE - WHALEY

WEST HOUSE (MR)
May 1862 - 1 August 1865
Line Operational - Demolished - No access
SK42345 58448 (a)

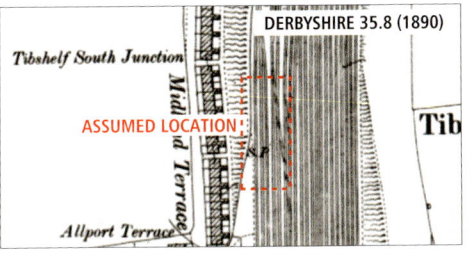

DERBYSHIRE 35.8 (1890)

WESTON-SUPER-MARE (B&ER)
14 June 1841 - 20 July 1866
Line lifted – Demolished – Station site occupied by a garden with a floral clock marking site of station **ST32086 61368**

WESTON-SUPER-MARE (GWR)
20 July 1866 - 1 March 1884
Line lifted – Demolished – Station site in commercial use
ST32158 61271

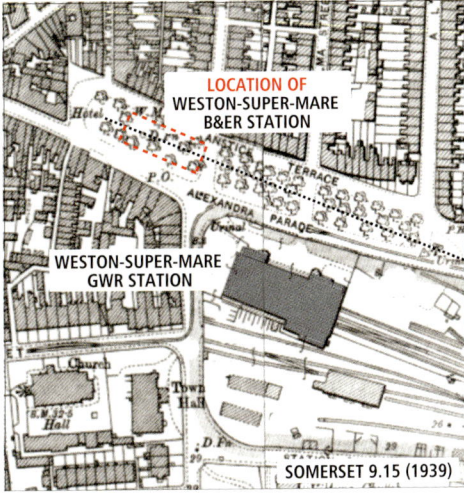

SOMERSET 9.15 (1939)

WEST KIRBY (1st) (WirralR)
1 April 1878 - 30 July 1899
Line lifted – Demolished – Station site in commercial and community use **SJ21381 86938**

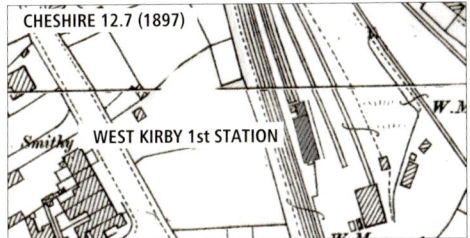

CHESHIRE 12.7 (1897)

WEST LYNN (E&MR)
1 March 1866 - 1 July 1886
Line lifted – Demolished – The westbound carriageway of the A47 passes through the station site **TF60937 18580**

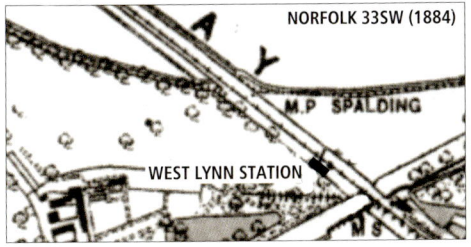

NORFOLK 33SW (1884)

WESTWOOD (MS&LR)
4 September 1854 - 9 October 1876
Line lifted – Demolished – A walkway passes through the station site **SK34218 98548**

YORKSHIRE 282 (1851)

WESTON JUNCTION (GWR)
14 June 1841 - 1 March 1884
Line Operational – Demolished – No access
ST33988 60384 (a)

SOMERSET 16.4 (1902)

WHALEY* (L&NWR)
June 1833 - April 1876
Line lifted – Demolished – Tom Brads Croft passes through the station site **SK01219 81562 (e)**

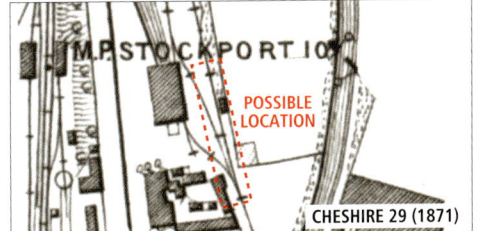

CHESHIRE 29 (1871)

WHATSTANDWELL BRIDGE - WHITEHAVEN

WHATSTANDWELL BRIDGE (1st) (MR)
September 1853 - 11 November 1894
Line Operational – Demolished – No access **SK33197 54417**

WHELLEY (LUR)
1 January 1872 – 1 March 1872
Line lifted – Demolished – A pathway passes through the station site **SD59437 06628**

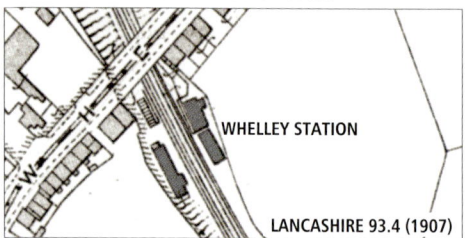

WHIFFLET (CR)
November 1845 - 1 June 1886
Line Operational – Demolished – No access **NS73816 64038**

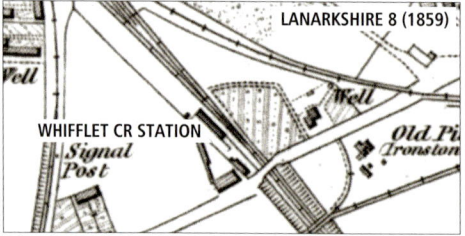

WHIFFLET (1st) (NBR)
26 October 1871 - 26 August 1895
Line Operational – Demolished – No access
NS73536 64410 (a)

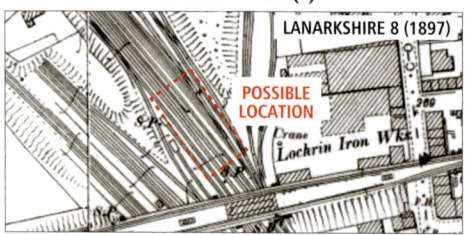

Sited north of Whifflet 2nd [NBR] (26 August 1895 – 22 September 1930) (Precise location unknown)

WHITACRE JUNCTION (1st) (MR)
10 February 1842 - 1 November 1864
Line Operational – Demolished – No access **SP21984 92711 (a)**

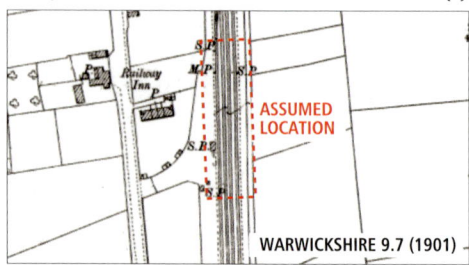

WHITBECK CROSSING HALT (W&FJnR)
1 December 1850 - March 1861
Line Operational – Demolished – No access **SD11588 83889**

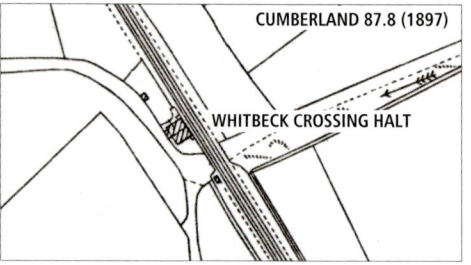

WHITBY (Y&NMR)
8 June 1835 - 1 July 1847
Line lifted – Demolished – Station site occupied by a car park
NZ89908 10696 (a)

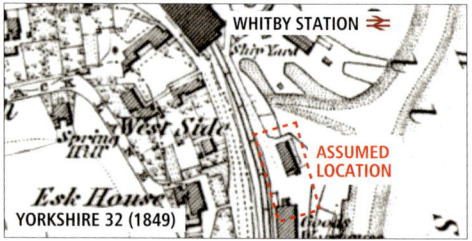

WHITEHAVEN (L&NWR)
19 March 1847 - 24 December 1874
Line lifted – Demolished – Station site in commercial use
NX97423 18580

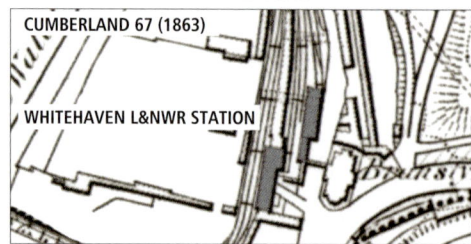

WHITEHAVEN NEWTOWN (W&FJnR)
19 July 1849 - 3 December 1855
Line lifted – Demolished – Station site occupied by a car park
NX97249 17677

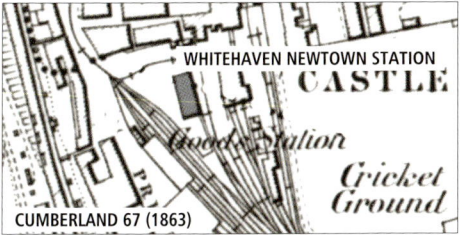

WHITEMILL (LlnyR)
20 July 1866 - 1 November 1870
Line lifted – Demolished – Station site occupied by a filling station
SN46566 21459 (a)

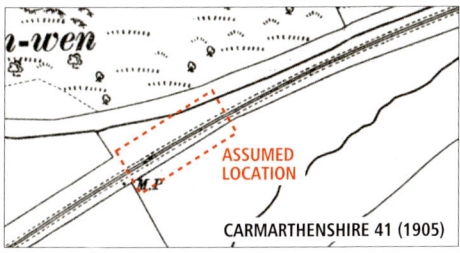

WHITLAND (P&TR)
5 September 1866 - August 1869
Line lifted – Demolished – Station site in commercial use
SN19905 16450

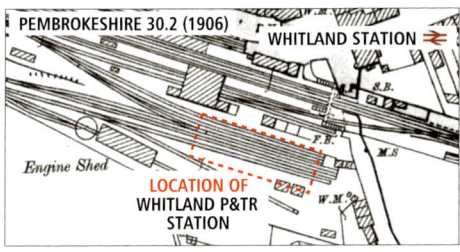

WHITSTABLE (1st) (SER)
4 May 1830 - 4 June 1846
Line lifted – Demolished – Station site in commercial use
TR10944 67098

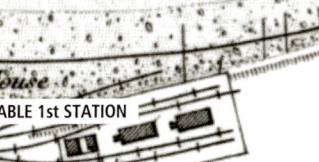

WHITEHAVEN NEWTOWN - WIDNES (1st)
WHITSTABLE (2nd) (SER)
4 June 1846 - 3 June 1895
Line lifted – Demolished – Station site in commercial use
TR10969 67022

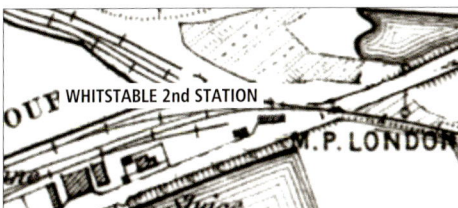

WHITTINGTON (1st) (MR)
1 October 1861 - 9 June 1873
Line Operational – Demolished – No access
SK39901 74879 (a)

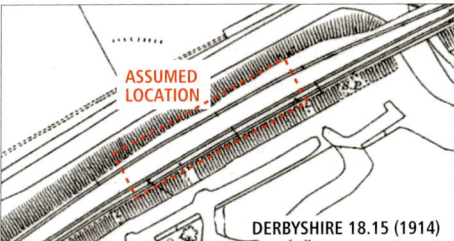

WICHNOR (L&NWR/MR)
2 April 1855 - 1 November 1877
Line Operational – Demolished – No access
SK19529 16233 (a)

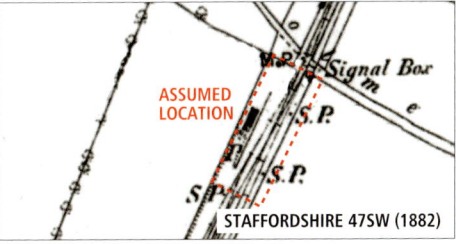

WIDNES (1st) (L&NWR)
1 July 1852 - 1 March 1870
Line lifted – Demolished – The Mersey Gateway Bridge Road crosses the station site **SJ51175 84776**

143

WIGAN (1st) (L&YR) - WILLOUGHBY (1st)

WIGAN (1st) (L&YR)
20 November 1848 - 26 May 1860
Line Operational – Demolished – No access **SD58199 05473**

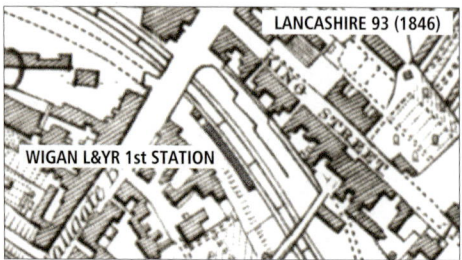

WILDERSPOOL (W&SR)
1 November 1853 - 1 October 1871
Line Operational for Freight – Demolished **SJ60781 87683**

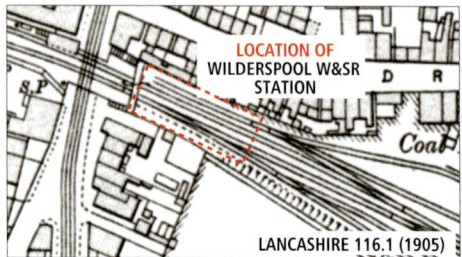

WIGAN (2nd) (L&YR)
26 May 1860 - 2 February 1896
Line Operational – Demolished – Part of station site occupied by west end of Wigan Wallgate Station **SD57947 05611**

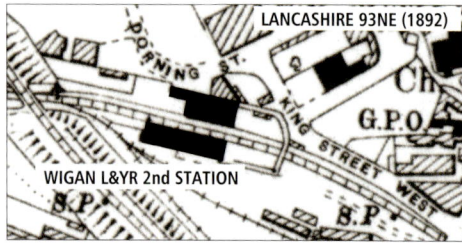

WILLESDEN (L&NWR)
Prior to June 1841 - 1 September 1866
Line Operational – Demolished – No access
TQ20936 83314

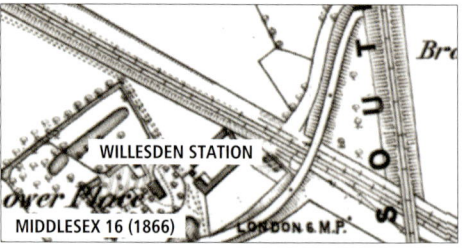

WIGAN CHAPEL LANE (NUR)
3 September 1832 - 31 October 1838
Line lifted – Demolished – Station site in commercial use
SD58348 05180

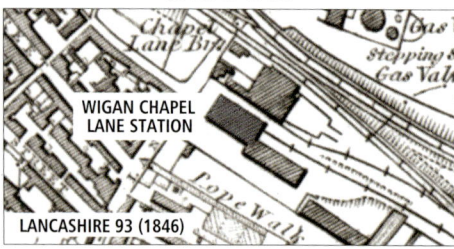

WILLIAMSTON (NBR)
13 August 1849 - 17 June 1850
Line Operational - Demolished - No access
NT54057 84618 (a)

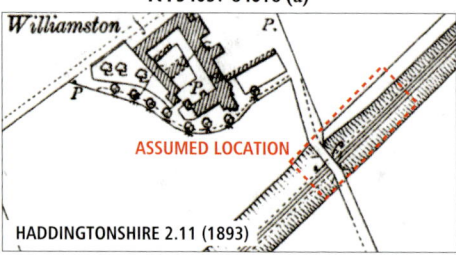

WIGAN DARLINGTON STREET (WigJnR)
1 April 1884 - 3 October 1892
Line lifted – Demolished – Station site in commercial use
SD58821 05275

WILLOUGHBY (1st) (GNR)
4 September 1848 - 4 October 1886
Line lifted – Demolished – Station Master's House in private use - Station site in commercial use **TF46665 71930**

WILSON - WITNEY (1st)

WILSON (MR)
1 October 1869 - 1 June 1871
Line lifted – Demolished – The Cloud Trail Greenway passes through the station site **SK40768 24787 (a)**

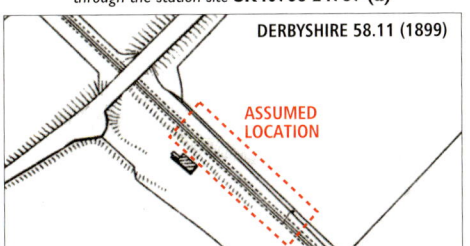
DERBYSHIRE 58.11 (1899)
ASSUMED LOCATION

WINWICK QUAY (GJnR)
Prior to 1837 - 28 November 1840
Line Operational – Demolished – No access **SJ59603 91728**

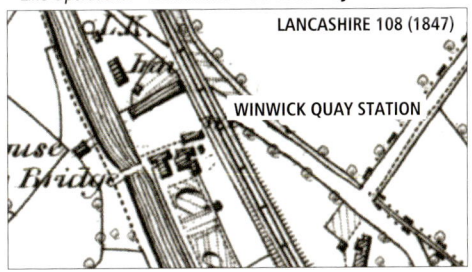
LANCASHIRE 108 (1847)
WINWICK QUAY STATION

WIMBLEDON AND MERTON (L&SWR)
21 May 1838 - 21 November 1881
Line Operational – Demolished – No access **TQ24738 70580**

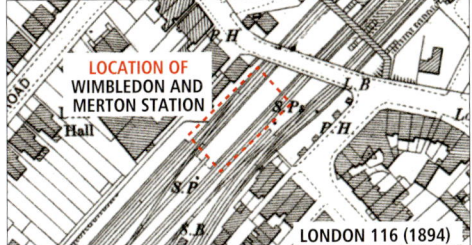
LOCATION OF WIMBLEDON AND MERTON STATION
LONDON 116 (1894)

WISBECH (WStI&CJnR)
3 May 1847 - c1852
Line lifted – Demolished – Station site in commercial use
TF45859 09328 (a)

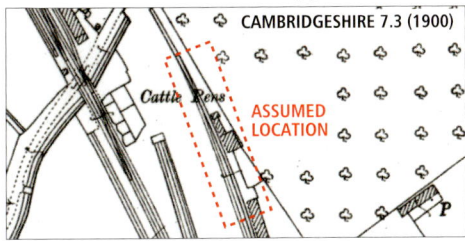
CAMBRIDGESHIRE 7.3 (1900)
ASSUMED LOCATION

WINDSOR BRIDGE, PENDLETON (L&YR)
Prior to October 1839 - June 1856
Line Operational – Demolished – No access **SJ81818 98750 (a)**

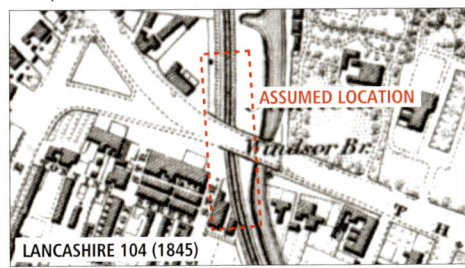
ASSUMED LOCATION
LANCASHIRE 104 (1845)

WITHIN'S LANE (ELancsR)
August 1847 - December 1851
Line Operational – Demolished – No access
SD79098 08150 (a)

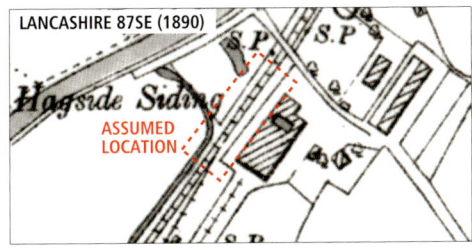
LANCASHIRE 87SE (1890)
ASSUMED LOCATION

WINTHORPE (MR)
Not known
Line Operational – Demolished – No access
SK81024 57252 (a)

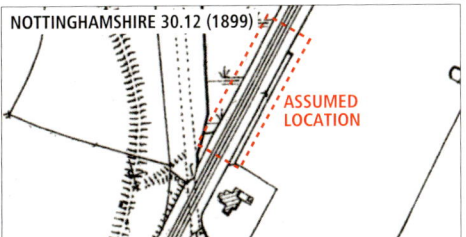
NOTTINGHAMSHIRE 30.12 (1899)
ASSUMED LOCATION

WITNEY (1st) (GWR)
14 November 1861 - 15 January 1873
Line lifted – Demolished – Station site in commercial use
SP35716 09154

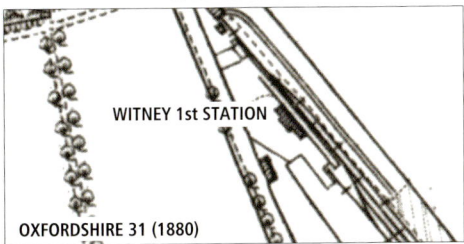
WITNEY 1st STATION
OXFORDSHIRE 31 (1880)

WITTON-LE-WEAR (1st) - WOODLEY

WITTON-LE-WEAR (1st) (NER)
3 August 1847 - c1852
Line Operated by the Weardale Railway Project – Demolished
NZ14729 31085

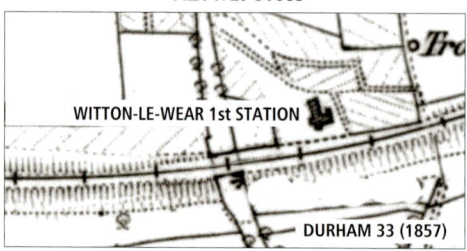

WOLVERTON (2nd) (L&NWR)
c1843 - 1 August 1881
Line extant as access to works – Demolished – Station site
in commercial use **SP81961 41165**

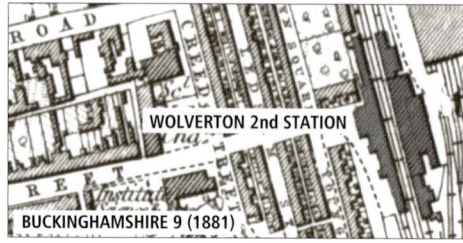

WOLVERHAMPTON (S&BmR)
13 November 1849 - 1 July 1852
Line lifted – Demolished – Station site landscaped
SO91845 98999

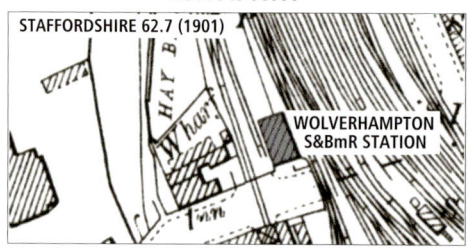

WOODGATE (LB&SCR)
8 June 1846 - 1 June 1864
Line Operational – Demolished – No access **SU93874 04329**

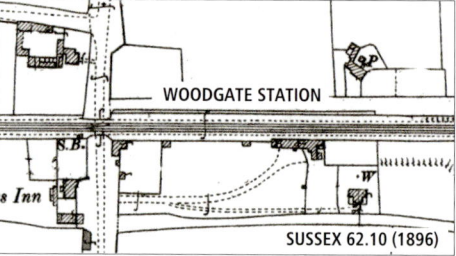

WOLVERHAMPTON STAFFORD ROAD (S&BmR)
October 1850 - July 1852
Line Operational – Demolished – No access **SJ91177 00376**

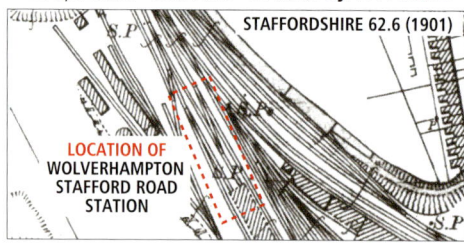

WOODHOUSE JUNCTION (MS&LR)
October 1850 - 11 October 1875
Line Operational – Demolished **SK43228 85108**

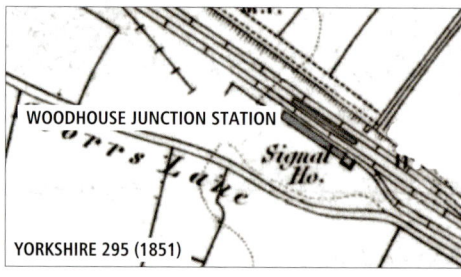

WOLVERTON (1st) (L&NWR)
17 September 1838 - c1843
Line extant – Demolished – Station site in works use
SP81833 41578 (a)

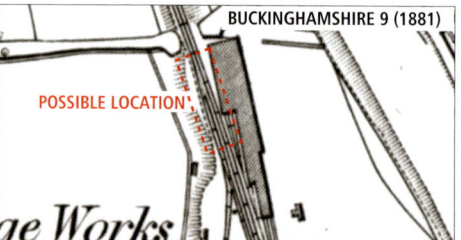

WOODLEY (M&KR)
1 October 1826 - c1830
Line lifted – Demolished – A walkway passes through the
station site **NS66211 72291 (a)**

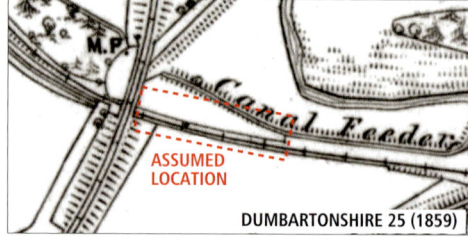

146

WOODVILLE (1st) (MR)
1 April 1859 – 1 May 1883
Line lifted – Demolished – Station site in commercial use
SK31531 19342

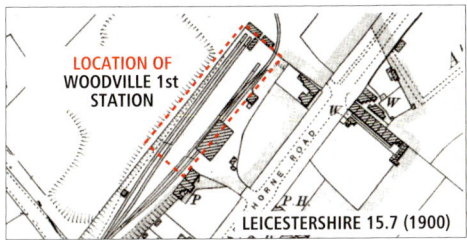

WRAYSBURY (1st) (L&SWR)
September 1848 – 1 April 1861
Line Operational – Demolished – No access **TQ01021 74611**

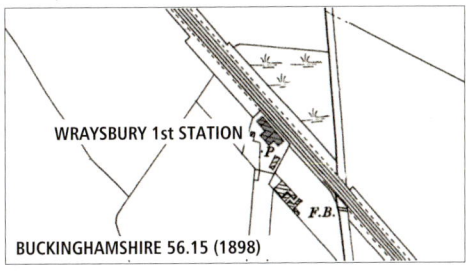

WORTLEY AND FARNLEY (1st) (L&NWR)
8 October 1848 – 1 March 1882
Line Operational – Demolished – No access **SE27449 31860**

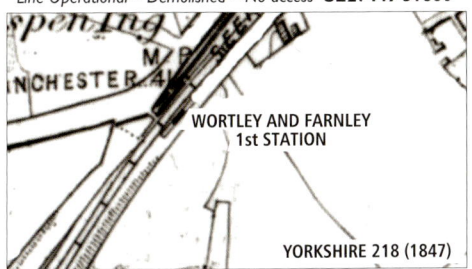

WYKE (L&YR)
7 August 1850 – 23 September 1896
Line Operational – Demolished – No access
SE14572 26644 (a)

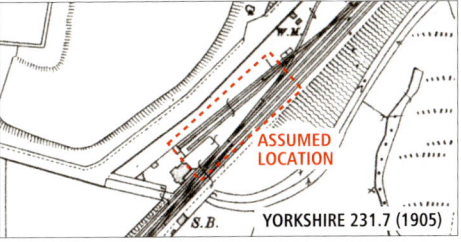

WORTWELL (GER)
2 November 1860 – 1 January 1878
Line lifted – Demolished – The A143 passes through the station site **TM27492 85053**

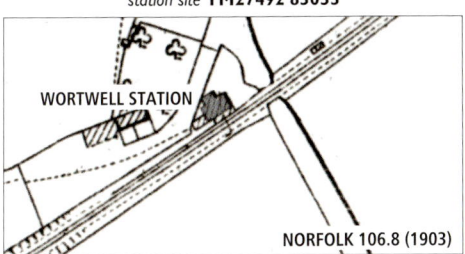

YAPHAM GATE (NER)
February 1855 – 29 April 1865
Line lifted – Demolished – Crossing Keeper's House in private use
SE77350 50870

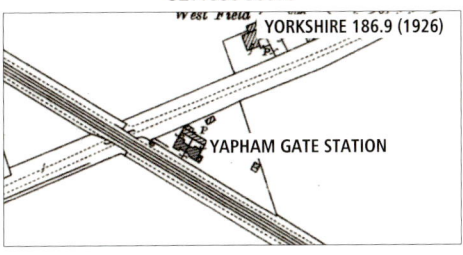

WRAY (NWR)
17 November 1849 – 1 June 1850
Line lifted – Demolished – Station site in agricultural use
SD59706 68284

YAPTON (LB&SCR)
8 June 1846 – 1 June 1864
Line Operational – Demolished – No access **SU98076 04394**

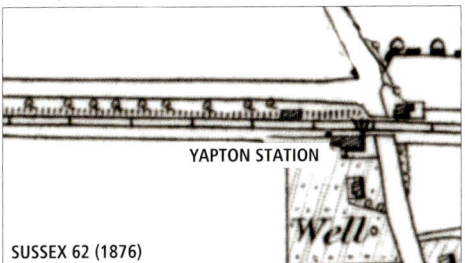

147

YARM DEPOTS (S&DR)
16 October 1826 - 7 September 1833
Line lifted – Demolished – Station site occupied by housing – The A67 passes through the station site **NZ41807 13444**

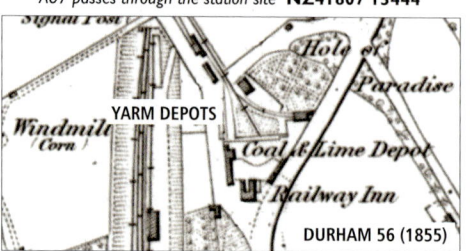

YARM OLD (S&DR)
10 October 1825 - 16 June 1862
Main Line Operational – Demolished – Station site in school use
NZ41413 14535

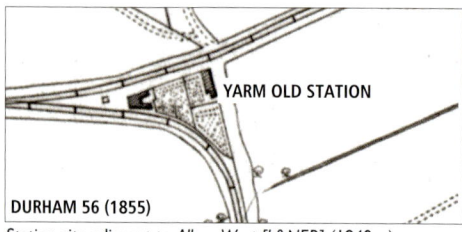

Station site adjacent to *Allens West [L&NER] (1940 -)*

YEARSETT (GWR)
2 May 1874 - 22 October 1877
Line lifted – Demolished – Station site unused
SO70610 53369 (a)

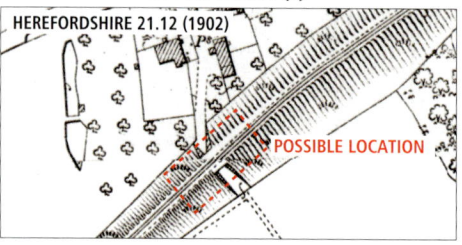

YEOVIL HENDFORD (B&ER)
1 October 1853 - 1 June 1861
Line lifted – Demolished – Station site in commercial use
ST55195 15451

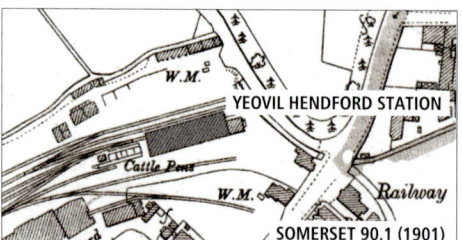

YNISGEINON JUNCTION (N&BR)
December 1873 - June 1874
Line lifted – Demolished – Station site unused
SN76090 07071 (a)

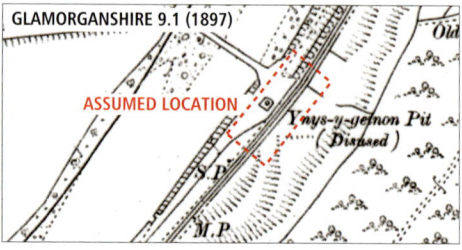

YNYSYGEINON (SwVleR)
21 January 1861 - 1 March 1862
Line lifted – Demolished – Station site unused
SN76503 07623 (a)

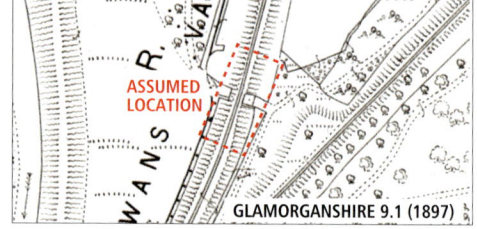

YORK (1st) (NER)
4 January 1841 - 25 June 1877
Line lifted – Demolished – Station building converted into offices for York City Council **SE59799 51713**

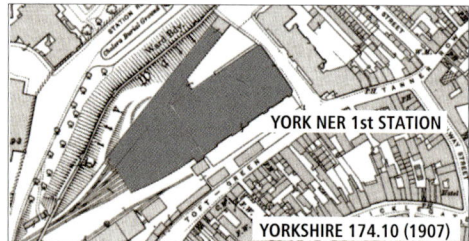

YORK (Y&NMR)
30 May 1839 - 4 January 1841
Line lifted – Demolished – Station occupied by "York Railway Institute" **SE59586 51510**

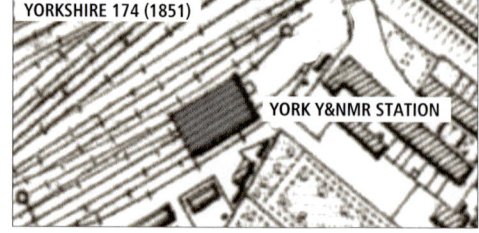

PART TWO
THE INDEPENDENT LINES

These are the stations that, nominally, were on lines that would have retained independence when the railways were "grouped" in the 20thC. Whilst the majority of the smaller lines saw themselves swallowed up or amalgamated with the larger companies that came to dominate the system by the end of the 19thC, there were a number that maintained their independence throughout their existence. In some cases this was involuntary as they were regarded as such a poor proposition that they were not worth taking on and missed out at Grouping and, those that survived long enough, railways nationalisation in 1948.

THE GROUPING OF RAILWAYS 1923

During WWI the railways, which numbered more than a hundred companies, had been run under state control. In retrospect much of the pre-war competition had been considered wasteful with companies vying for business along parallel routes so the government decided to take the opportunity to correct this and amalgamate them into larger entities. The aim was to stem the losses being made by many of the companies, move the railways away from internal competition and retain some of the benefits which the country had derived from the government-controlled railway.

State control continued until 1921 and on 19 August 1921 the Transport Act was passed which, effectively, carved the railway system into four large groups; London Midland & Scottish Railway, London & North Eastern Railway, Southern Railway and Great Western Railway - The Big Four. However it did not embrace all the companies, with those built by a Light Railway Order being given exemption. Joint railways and London suburban railways (London Electric and Metropolitan Railways) were also omitted

The Act took effect 1 January 1923.

THE NATIONALISING OF RAILWAYS 1948

Following the end of WWII the Big Four were effectively bankrupt and the railway system was in a run-down and dilapidated state because of war damage and minimal maintenance. In line with the Labour Government's policy of nationalisation of some of the country's assets the Transport Act 1947 was drawn up and as well as railways it embraced canals, 'bus companies, sea and shipping ports and road haulage.

British Railways came into effect 1 January 1948.

FESTINIOG RAILWAY (1ft 11½in GAUGE) 1865-1946, 1955- (Preserved)

The railway, for transporting slate, was incorporated on 23 May 1832 and the line, between Porthmadoc and Blaenau Ffestiniog, opened on 20 April 1836. Steam-hauled passenger services commenced in January 1865 and these lasted until the outbreak of WWII in 1939. It closed totally in 1946 but from 1949 was revived by groups of railway enthusiasts culminating in its reopening on 23 July 1955. The line is operated by the *Ffestiniog Railway Trust*

DINAS
1865 - August 1870
Line lifted – Demolished - Station site unused **SH69400 46417**

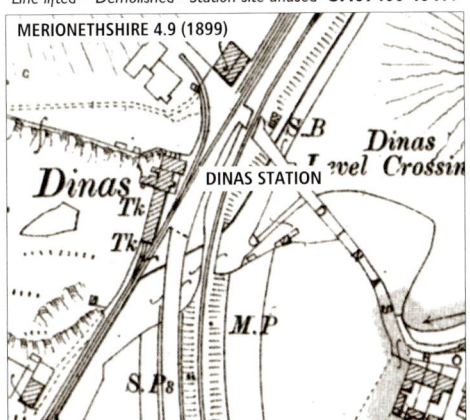

HAFOD-Y-LLYN
1865 - March 1871
Line lifted and subsequently restored by Welsh Highland Railway – Halt rebuilt **SH59702 44876**

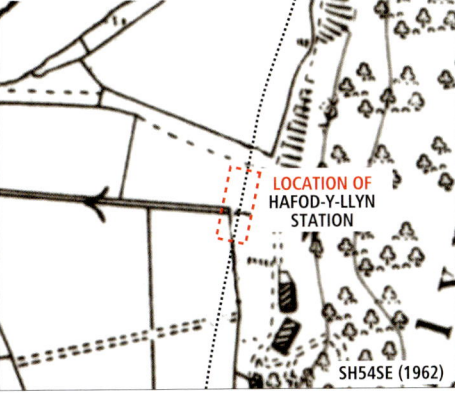

149

GLYN VALLEY TRAMWAY (2ft 4½in GAUGE) 1873-1935

The company was incorporated on 10 August 1870 and the line, between Chirk and Glynceiriog, opened for goods in April 1873 with passenger services commencing 1 April 1874. Carrying passengers continued until road competition forced this to cease 6 April 1933 and it totally closed 6 July 1935 with the track being removed the following year. The *New Glyn Valley Tramway & Industrial Heritage Trust* have established a base and museum at the former engine shed at Glynceiriog.

CASTLE MILL
1 April 1874 - 1 April 1886
Line lifted – Demolished – Station site absorbed into the B4500
SJ26391 37685 (a)

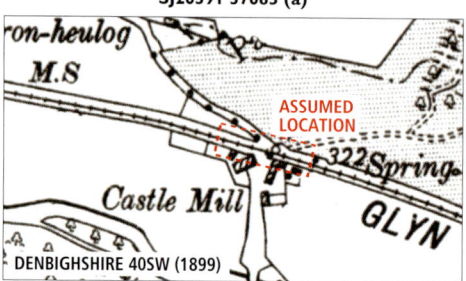

HERBER TOLL GATE
1 April 1874 - September 1883
Line lifted - Demolished **SJ25425 38079**

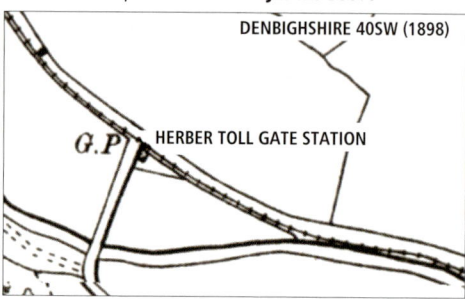

PONTFAEN (1st)
1 April 1874 - 1 April 1886
Line lifted – Demolished – Station site absorbed into the B4500
SJ27982 37091

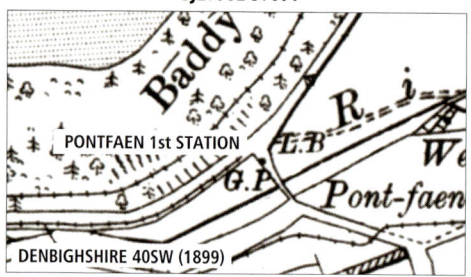

QUEEN'S HEAD INN
1 April 1874 - 1 April 1886
Line lifted **SJ22078 37253**

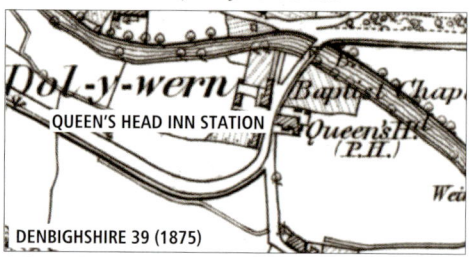

Dolywern (15 March 1891 – 6 April 1933) was subsequently established on the site.

LIVERPOOL OVERHEAD RAILWAY 1893-1956

Incorporated 24 July 1888 the line opened between Herculaneum Dock and Alexandra Dock 6 March 1893, Alexandra Dock and Seaforth Sands 30 September 1894 and Herculaneum Dock and Dingle 21 December 1896. It operated successfully until the post-WWII era when renewals costing in the region of £2m were required. It was felt that the expense was not justified and the 6.5 mile line closed 31 December 1956 with demolition of the piers and infrastructure expedited the following year.

HERCULANEUM DOCK (1st)
6 March 1893 - 21 December 1896
Line lifted – Station and piers demolished – Sefton Street passes through the station site **SJ35406 87446**

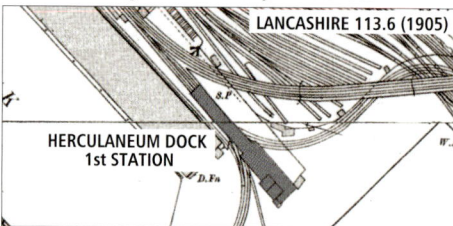

Sited 164 yards south of *Herculaneum Dock 2nd* (21 December 1896 – 31 December 1956).

SANDON DOCK
6 March 1893 - May 1896
Line lifted – Station and piers demolished – Regent Road passes through the station site **SJ33772 92925**

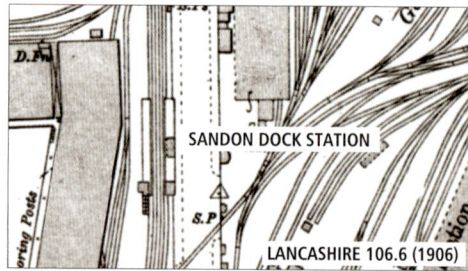

SWANSEA & MUMBLES RAILWAY 1807-1960

The 5.5 miles long railway, from Swansea to Oystermouth, was constructed in 1807 as a 4ft gauge line, converted to standard gauge in 1855 and extended to Mumbles Pier in 1898. It carried passengers from 25 March 1807 (As the first railway in the world to do so), originally horse drawn then by steam locomotives from 1877 and electric trams from 2 March 1929. It was sold to the *South Wales Transport Company* in 1958 who immediately went to Parliament with an Abandonment Bill and despite strong local opposition it was passed as the South Wales Transport Act 1959. The line was closed in two sections, Southend to Mumbles Pier 11 October 1959 and totally 5 January 1960 with the track being promptly lifted.

ARGYLE STREET
August 1878 - 1887
Line lifted – Demolished – Oystermouth Road passes through the station site **SS65039 92417 (a)**

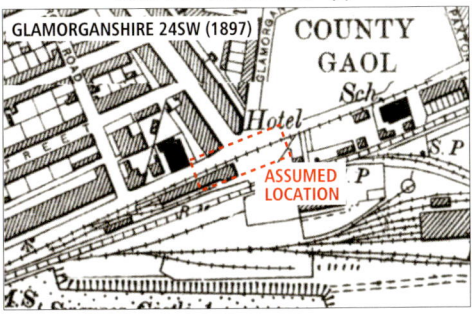

BOND STREET
November 1878 – December 1879
Demolished – The A4067, Mumbles Road, passes through the station site. **SS64695 92289 (a)**

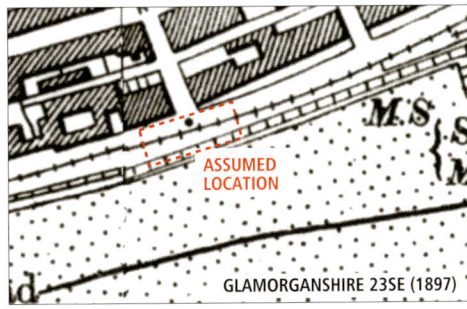

BEECH STREET
May 1882 - c1895
Line lifted – Demolished – Oystermouth Road passes through the station site **SS64804 92323 (a)**

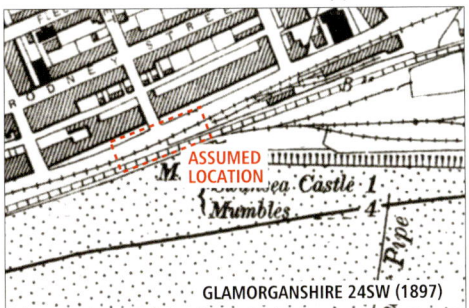

HAROLDS MOOR
December 1878 - May 1896
Line lifted – Demolished – A4067, Mumbles Road, passes through the station site **SS61430 89048 (a)**

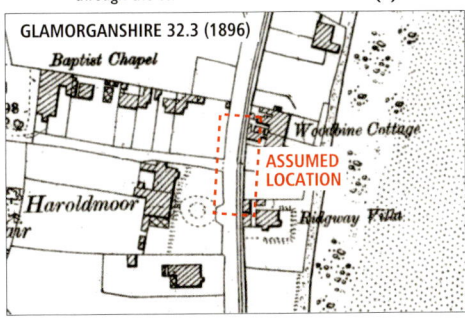

BLACKPILL (1st)
25 July 1860 - 26 August 1900
Line lifted – Demolished – A4067, Mumbles Road, passes through the station site **SS61887 90523**

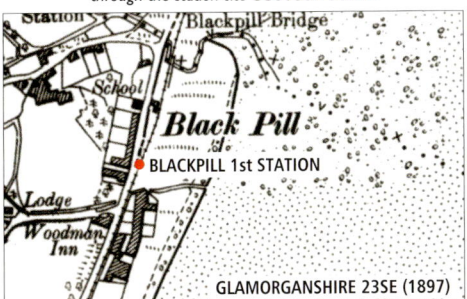

WEST CROSS (1st)
11 November 1860 – 26 August 1900
Demolished – The A4067, Mumbles Road, passes through the station site. **SS61456 89158**

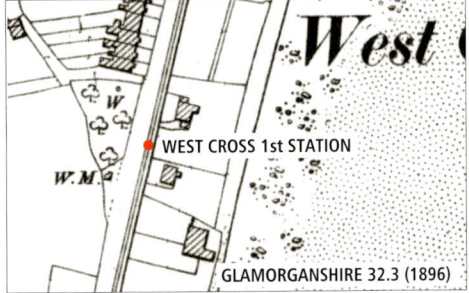

APPENDIX
ADDITIONAL STATIONS

These are some of the stations that are not covered in the main body of the book, due to lack of space or information but are noted here. There are numerous others that have also been recorded, particularly in the very early days, but for which little is known and these have been omitted.

ABBEY HOLME* (M&CR) Opening and closing dates unknown. Existence unclear
ABERCARN (GWR) 23 December 1850 – August 1867. Resited on deviation of line. **ST21426 95268 (a)**
ABERDARE JUNCTION (AR) 6 August 1846 – March 1848. **ST08300 948778 (a)**
ABERKENFIG (Ll&OR) April 1869 - 1 February 1870. Possibly same site as *Sarn* (28 September 1992 -) **SS89863 83373 (a)**
ACHEILIDH CROSSING* (HR) Opening and closing dates unknown. **NC66437 03954 (a)**
AINTREE CINDER LANE* (L&YR) March 1878 – 1881. Temporary station
AIRDRIE LEA END (M&KR) 1828 – 1843. Probably no station **NS74622 65585 (e)**
ALDHAM JUNCTION (SYorks&RDNR) January 1855 – September 1859. **SE39073 04329 (a)**
ALLERWASH (N&CR) 28 June 1836 - January 1837. **NY87593 67228 (a)**
AMBERSWOOD (HINDLEY) (LUR) 1 January 1872 – 1 March 1872. **SD61972 05236 (e)**
AMBLE JUNCTION (NER) 3 November 1855 - 2 April 1859. **NZ22054 98384 (a)**
ANERLEY BRIDGE (L&CrR) 5 June 1839 - 12 June 1839. **TQ34570 69840 (a)**
ANNESLEY COLLIERY SIDINGS PLATFORM* (MR) 1 March 1882 – ? **SK51995 53312 (e)**
APPLEFORD (GWR) 12 June 1844 - February 1849. *Appleford [GWR]* (11 September 1933 – 5 May 1969) was built on the station site. **SU52522 93700**
ARRAM GATE HOUSE (Y&NMR) 2 August 1854 – 6 August 1864. Possibly same site as *Arram [NER]* (September 1855 -) **TA03517 44279**
ASBY* (WC&ER) Opening and closing dates unknown. **NY06482 20611 (a)**
ASHTON MOSS (OA&GBJR) 26 August 1861 – 1 June 1862. On LANCASHIRE 105 (1880) **SJ92574 98673**
AYLESBURY (A&BR) 23 September 1868 – 1 November 1868. Temporary Station closed when line extended to *Aylesbury [GWR]* (1 October 1863 -) following conversion to standard gauge

BAGWORTH INCLINE HOUSE (Lstr&SwngtnR) 18 July 1832 – c1833 **SK44623 09042**
BAGWORTH STAUNTON ROAD (Lstr&SwngtnR) 18 July 1832 – 27 April 1833. Temporary terminus closed when line extended.
BANBURY ROAD (alias OXFORD ROAD) (L&NWR) 2 December 1850 – 20 May 1851. Temporary terminus closed when line extended to *Oxford Rewley Road [L&NWR]* (20 May 1851 – 1 October 1951). **SP50028 11845 (a)**
BAT & BALL (LC&DR) 2 June 1862 – 1 August 1869. Temporary station closed when line extended to *Sevenoaks [SER]* (2 March 1868 -). **TQ53119 56825 (a)**
BEAM BRIDGE (B&ER) 1 May 1843 – 1 May 1844. Temporary terminus between Wellington and Whiteball Tunnel, providing connection with road service to Exeter pending completion of tunnel. **ST10761 19328 (a)**
BEAULIEU ROAD (L&SWR) July 1847 - 1 March 1860. *Beaulieu Road [L&SWR]* (1 November 1895 -) was built on the station site. **SU34943 06276**
BEDLAY (M&KR) 10 December 1849 – 31 December 1849. **NS69597 70098 (a)**
BERMONDSEY STREET (L&GrR) 10 October 1836 – 14 December 1836. **TQ33145 80031 (a)**
BIRKENHEAD DOCKS (H&BheadR&T) 2 July 1866 - 1 April 1878. A tram stop
BIXLADE* (S&WyeR) 1889 – 1894. Siding available for picnic carriage. **SO60858 09996 (a)**
BLACKBOY (S&DR) July 1827 – ? Branch to colliery. No station. **NZ22499 28662 (e)**
BLACKBURN FORGE (S&RR) 1 November 1838 – 25 March 1839. **SK39188 91421 (a)**
BLACKGRANGE (St&DunfR) November 1852 – November 1852. **NS83896 948323**
BLUE ANCHOR LANE* (L&GrR) 9 June 1835 – 12 November 1835. **TQ34447 91421 (a)**
BOURNE (M&ER) 1 August 1866 – 1866. **TF09781 19856 (a)**
BOW (ECR) 14 September 1840 – 1 December 1840. **TQ37380 83194 (a)**
BOW (1st) (NLR) 26 September 1850 - 1 November 1870.**TQ37411 82841 (e)**
BRADWELL WOOD SIDINGS* (NSR) ? - c1900 No station at this location
BRIDGENESS* (NBR) Opening and closing dates unknown. **NT01242 81591 (e)**
BRIDLINGTON QUAY* (NER): Starting and ending dates unknown. **TA18239 66520 (a)**
BROOKFIELD (M&CR) 2 December 1844 – 10 February 1845. Temporary station closed when line extended to *Low Row [M&CR]* (30 November 1844 – 2 February 1848). **NY24143 47926 (a)**

152

BROOKHAY (SStaffsR) 9 April 1849 – December 1849. **SK16024 11783 (a)**
BROUGHTON (L&PJnR) 26 June 1840 – November 1840. *Broughton [L&PJnR]* (November 1840 – 1 May 1939) was built on the station site. **SD51505 36316**
BURGESS HILL (1st) (LB&SCR) 21 October 1841 – 2 October 1843, 1 May 1844 – c1875. **TQ31586 18715**
BURY ST EDMUNDS (1st) (GER) 24 December 1846 – November 1847. Temporary station replaced to the west by *Bury St Edmunds 2nd [GER]* (November 1847 -). **TL85438 65174 (a)**

CADMORE'S LANE, CHESHUNT (N&ER) 22 November 1841 – May 1842. **TL36694 02887**
CAMPERDOWN JUNCTION (D&AR) 1 February 1880 – March 1880. **NO41159 30598**
CAIRNHILL BRIDGE (M&KR) cJuly 1832 - October 1832. **NS74008 64046 (e)**
CALDER IRONWORKS (M&KR) June 1831 - ?. **NS74401 63813 (e)**
CAMBRIAN NAVIGATION COLLIERY* (GWR) c1896 - ? **SS97125 92817 (a)**
CARNOUSTIE (1st) (D&AR) 8 October 1838 – c1900. *Carnoustie [D&AR]* (May 1903 -) was built on the station site. **NO56583 34475**
CASTLEMILK* (CR): c1847 - ? **NY15968 77628**
CHEPSTOW EAST (SWR) 19 September 1851 – 19 July 1852. Temporary station pending completion of the Chepstow Bridge. **ST54843 94622 (a)**
CHEQUERBENT SIDING* (L&NWR) Opening and closing dates unknown. **SD67367 06075 (e)**
CHICHESTER (1st) (LB&SCR) 8 June 1846 – 15 March 1847. Temporary terminus closed when line extended to *Havant [LB&SCR]* (15 March 1847 -). **SU85967 04302 (a)**
CHURCHDOWN (B&GR) 9 August 1842 - 27 September 1842. *Churchdown [GWR/MR]* (2 February 1874 – 2 November 1964) was probably built on the station site. **SO88554 20265 (a)**
CLARKSTON (M&KR) cJune 1832 - mid-October 1832. *Clarkston [NBR]* (11 August 1862 – 9 January 1956) was probably built on the station site.
COFTON FARM (B&GR) 17 September 1840 – 17 December 1840. Temporary terminus. **SP01227 75423 (e)**
COLCHESTER (ECR) 1848 - c1850. Station not completed and not opened
COMELY PARK (NBR) 1 November 1877 - 5 March 1890. *Dunfermline Lower [NBR]* (5 March 1890 -) was opened on the station site. **NT09676 87095**
CORBETT'S LANE (L&GrR) 8 June 1835 – 12 November 1835. *Southwark Park [SE&CR]* (1 October 1902 – 21 September 1925) was subsequently built on the station site. **TQ35211 78564**
CORNBROOK (MSJn&AR) 12 June 1856 – 1 May 1865
CORWEN (DC&RR) 22 September 1864 – 1 September 1865. Temporary terminus until access to *Corwen [GWR]* (8 May 1865 – 14 December 1964) was made available. **SJ07890 43613 (a)**
CRAIGIE (D&AR) 6 October 1838 – 9 June 1839. Temporary terminus closed when line extended to *Roodyards [qv]*. **NO43566 31010 (a)**
CRUMLIN (NA&HR) 20 August 1855 – 1 June 1857. Temporary station pending completion of Crumlin Viaduct **ST21763 98665 (a)**

DALVEY (I&AJR) 22 December 1857 – April 1858. Temporary terminus closed shortly after line extended to *Forres [I&AJnR]* (25 March 1858 – 3 August 1863) [qv] on 25 March 1858. **NJ00078 57789 (a)**
DANBY WISKE (NER) 1 August 1841 - June 1842. **SE34357 98899 (a)**
DARLEY DALE (1st) (MR) 4 June 1849 – c1874. **SK27284 62610**
DENBIGH HALL (L&BmR) 9 April 1838 – 17 September 1838. Temporary terminus closed when Kilsby Tunnel opened. **SP86324 35315 (a)**
DEPTFORD (L&GrR) 8 February 1836 – 24 December 1838. Temporary station closed when line extended to *Greenwich [L&GrR]* (24 December 1838 – 12 April 1840). *Deptford [L&GrR]* (24 December 1838 -) was built on the station site. **TQ37145 77402**
DERBY (B&DJR) 12 August 1839 – 11 May 1840. Temporary station closed when line extended to *Derby [MR]* (11 May 1840 -)
DERBY (MCR) 4 June 1839 – 11 May 1840. Temporary station closed when line extended to *Derby [MR]* (11 May 1840 -)
DOG LANE (MS&LR) 1 May 1846 – 1 November 1847. On, or near, site of *Dukinfield Dog Lane [MS&LR]* (17 November 1841 – 23 December 1845) **SJ93340 97448 (a)** (See page 47)
DOLGELLEY (CamR) 21 June 1869 – 1 August 1869. Temporary terminus closed when line extended to GWR system. **SH72442 18103 (a)**
DONCASTER (1st) (GNR) 7 September 1848 – September 1850. Temporary station
DUDLEY (SStaffsR) 1 November 1849 – 1 May 1850. Temporary station.
DUNHAM (W&SR) June 1854 – April 1855. Temporary station. **SJ73878 88694 (a)**

EARL'S COURT (2nd) (MDR) 30 December 1875 – 1 February 1878. Temporary station whilst 3rd station was being built. **TQ25576 78621 (a)**
EARLYVALE GATE† (PeeblesR) June 1856 – 28 February 1857. **NT24221 50782 (a)**
ECCLESFIELD (SYorks&RDNR) November 1854 - 1856. *Ecclesfield East [MS&LR]* (1 August 1876 – 7 December 1953) was built on the station site. **SK36555 94287**
EDINBURGH (Temporary Station 1) (NBR) 22 June 1846 – 3 August 1846. Temporary station closed upon opening of Temporary Station 2 at east end of site of *Edinburgh Canal Street [NBR]* (17 May 1847 – 2 March 1868) **NT26116 73903 (a)**
EDINBURGH (Temporary Station 2) (NBR) 3 August 1846 – 17 May 1847. Temporary station closed upon opening of *Edinburgh Canal Street [NBR]* (17 May 1847 – 2 March 1868). **NT25882 73851 (a)**
ELSENHAM (1st) (GER) 30 July 1845 – 1846
EXHIBITION (CR) 1 May 1890 – 3 November 1890
EXHIBITION (NBR) 1890 – January 1891

FISHERROW (NBR): 2 July 1846 – 1847 **NT32432 72188 (a)**
FISHPONDS (MR) October 1849 – 1 September 1850. **ST63306 75542 (e)**
FOLKESTONE (1st) (SER) 28 June 1843 – 18 December 1843. Temporary station. *Folkestone East [SER]* (18 December 1843 – 6 September 1965) was built on the station site. **TR23415 36863**
FRIZINGTON HALT (NORTH) (WC&ER) June 1875 – January 1888. Temporary station at north end of a weak bridge **NY03322 15449 (e)**
FRIZINGTON HALT (SOUTH) (WC&ER) June 1875 – January 1888. Temporary station at south end of a weak bridge **NY03322 15449 (e)**

GARLIESTOWN (WigtownshireR) 2 August 1875 – 3 April 1876
GLASGOW SOUTH SIDE (GB&KJR) 29 September 1848 – 1 October 1877. Same station as *Glasgow South Side [CR] [qv]*
GLENBURNIE (Ed&NR) 9 December 1847 – 18 May 1848. Temporary terminus. **NO25113 17139 (a)**
GLENFOOT (St&DunfR) 3 June 1851 – 22 December 1851. Temporary terminus closed when line extended to *Tillicoultry [NBR]* (22 December 1851 – 15 June 1964) **NS90966 96168 (a)**
GRANGE COURT (GWR) 11 July 1853 – 1 June 1855. Temporary exchange station. *Grange Court [GWR]* (1 June 1855 – 2 November 1964) was built on the station site. **SO72601 16152**
GUILDFORD St CATHERINE'S TUNNEL* (L&SWR) 23 March 1895 – 1 April 1895. Temporary station after tunnel collapse. **SU99359 48493 (a)**

HAGGERLEASES (S&DR) April 1859 – August 1859. **NZ11419 25454 (a)**
HAMMERSMITH (1st) (H&CR) 13 June 1864 – 1 December 1868. *Hammersmith 2nd [H&CR]* (1 December 1868 -) was partially built on the station site. **TQ23313 78748**
HARTLEPOOL (Stktn&HpoolR) June 1847 – c1851. Temporary terminus. **NZ51571 32603 (a)**
HATFIELD (ECR) December 1844 - February 1849. *Hatfield Peverel [GER]* (1 March 1878 -) was built on the station site. **TL78917 12227**
HAVANT NEW (L&SWR) 1 January 1859 – 8 June 1859. **SU72659 07050 (e)**
HAYDON BRIDGE (N&CR) 28 June 1836 - 18 June 1838. *Haydon Bridge [NER]* (18 June 1838 -) was built on the station site following extension of the line. **NY842769 64551**
HEAP BRIDGE* (L&YR) 9 September 1874 - ? **SD82870 10543 (a)**
HEMSBY (GY&SLR) 15 July 1878 – July 1879. Temporary station to *Martham [Y&NMR]* (15 July 1878 – 2 March 1959). **TG49474 17516 (e)**
HEREFORD JUNCTION* (GWR) cJanuary 1854 - ? Exchange platform
HIGH ROYDS (SYorks&RDNR) July 1856 – September 1856 **SK35813 01768 (a)**
HINDLOW (1st) (L&NWR) June 1833 – December 1877 **SK08581 69261 (a)**
HOLYTOWN (CR) 6 March 1835 - July 1869. LANARKSHIRE 12 (1859) **NS75051 60285**
HOPTON* (L&NWR) June 1833 – April 1876 **SK25287 54643 (a)**
HORSHAM (1st) (LB&SCR) 14 February 1848 - 10 October 1859. *Horsham [LB&SCR]* (10 October 1859 -) was built on the station site. **TQ17884 30970**
HOWOOD (GPK&AR) 21 July 1840 - 12 August 1840. Temporary terminus. **NS39665 60560 (a)**
HUNTHILL JUNCTION* (CR) Opening and closing dates unknown. Exchange platform. **NS67968 56835 (a)**
HUTTONS LANE (S&DR) 1855 – c1871. **NZ60287 14865 (a)**

IRELAND COLLIERY* (MR) 1885 – 1888. **SK43722 74013 (a)**

JARROW DOCK (NER) August 1856 – cJanuary 1861. **NZ35935 64141 (a)**

KEMPSEY (B&GR) November 1841 - November 1844. **SO89033 49302 (e)**
KENSINGTON (1st) (WLR) 27 May 1844 – 1 December 1844. **TQ24515 78983 (a)**
KETLEY FORGE* (GWR) 1873 – 1889. **SJ67392 11034 (e)**
KILLAMARSH (NMR) 6 April 1841 – c1843. *Killamarsh West [MR]* (21 July 1873 – 1 February 1954) was built on the station site. **SK44697 81303**
KILNHURST (MS&LR) 3 April 1871 – 1 September 1871. **SK46389 97266 (a)**
KILNWICK GATE* (NER) 1877 - ? **TA02613 48634**
KINROSS (KR) 20 June 1860 – 20 September 1860. Temporary terminus closed when line extended to *Loch Leven [NBR]* (20 September 1860 – 1 September 1921)
KIRTLEBRIDGE (1st) (CR) March 1848 – Prior to 1858. **NY23868 72713 (a)**
KNUTSFORD (CMR) 12 May 1862 – 1 January 1863. Closed when line extended to *Northwich [CLC]* (1 January 1863 – 22 June 1870) **SJ75188 78280 (a)**

LEEDS WELLINGTON (1st) (MR) 1 July 1846 - 30 September 1850. *Leeds Wellington [MR]* (30 September 1850 – 2 May 1938) was built on the station site. **SE29888 33325**
LIMPET MILL (AberdeenR) 1 November 1849 – 1 April 1850. Temporary terminus closed when line extended to *Aberdeen Ferryhill [AberdeenR]* (1 April 1850 – 2 August 1854) *[qv]*. **NO88952 88624 (a)**
LLANDAVEL COLLIERY* (GWR) ? – Prior to July 1897. **SO18974 03969 (a)**
LLANGEFNI (ACR) 12 March 1865 – 1 February 1866. Temporary terminus closed when line extended to *Llanerchymedd [ACR]* (1 February 1866 – 7 December 1964) **SH45867 75421 (a)**
LLANVAIR (NA&HR) 2 January 1854 – 1 October 1854. **SH32922 07145 (a)**
LONDON EAST INDIA DOCKS (GER) 1877 – 1890. **TQ38783 80836 (e)**
LUDGATE HILL (LC&DR) 21 December 1864 - 1 June 1865. *Ludgate Hill [SE&CR]* (1 June 1865 – 3 March 1929) was built on the station site. **LONDON 5.10 (1914) TQ31680 81074**

MALTON ROAD (NER) ? – 29 April 1865. **SE64664 56457 (a)**
MANSFIELD (2nd) (MR) 9 October 1849 - 1 March 1872. *Mansfield [MR]* (1 March 1872 – 11 August 1952) was built on the station site. The station was subsequently reopened 20 November 1995. **SK53703 60841**
MARKET HARBOROUGH (L&NWR) 29 April 1850 – 1 September 1884. *Market Harborough [L&NWR/MR]* (1 September 1884 -) was built on the station site. **SP74189 87474**
MARSHES TURNPIKE GATE (MonmouthsR) 1 July 1852 – 9 March 1853. Temporary terminus closed when line extended to *Newport Mill Street [MonmouthsR]* (9 March 1853 – 11 March 1880). **ST30973 88916 (a)**
MEIROS COLLIERY* (GWR) Prior to 1890 – Prior to July 1897. **ST00396 84000 (a)**
MELTON MOWBRAY (1st) (MCR) 1 September 1846 – 1 May 1848. *Melton Mowbray [MR]* (1 May 1848 -) was built on the station site. **SK75286 18741**
MORRISTON EAST (SwVleR) 2 October 1871 – 1 March 1875. Temporary terminus closed when line extended beyond *Clydach-on-Tawe [SwVleR]* (1 March 1875 – 25 September 1950). **SS67399 97786 (a)**
MUCH WENLOCK (1st) (GWR) 1 February 1862 – 1 August 1884. **SJ62087 00020 (a)**
MUIR OF ORD MARKET STANCE PLATFORM* (HR) 1867 – c1898. **NH52801 49348 (a)**

NANTLLE (NantleR) *(3ft 6in gauge)* 11 August 1856 - 12 June 1865. **SH48787 52901**
NETHERSEAL COLLIERY* (MR) June 1877 - ? **SK27608 15426 (a)**
NETLEY HOSPITAL* (L&SWR) 5 March 1866 - 18 April 1900. **SU46442 08526 (a)**
NEWARTHILL (W&CnessR) 6 March 1835 - 1844
NEW BARNET (1st) (GNR) 7 August 1850 – c1890. **TQ26457 96152 (a)**
NORTHAM ROAD (L&SWR) 10 June 1839 – 11 May 1840. Temporary terminus closed when line extended to *Southampton Terminus [L&SWR]* (11 May 1840 – 5 September 1966). **SU42831 12293 (a)**
NORTH CAMP (1st) (SER) August 1857 – Prior to 1871. **SU88586 53792 (a)**
NORTHFIELD (1st) (MR) 1 September 1870 – 1893. *Northfield [MR]* (1893 -) was built on the station site **SP02461 78024**
NORTH SHIELDS (1st) (NER) 20 June 1839 – 1890. *North Shields [NER]* 2nd (1890 – 11 August 1980) was built on the station site. This was rebuilt and reopened as *North Shields Metro* (14 November 1982 -). **NZ35344 68728**

OAK TREE† (NER) 27 September 1825 - 1 July 1887. **NZ35446 13675 (e)**
ORCHARD STREET (SYorks&RDNR) 10 September 1859 – 1 October 1866
ORTON (1st) (HR) 18 August 1858 – 1859. **NJ31208 52244 (a)**
OSWESTRY (1st) (GWR) 1 January 1849 – 1866. *Oswestry 2nd [GWR]* (1866 – 7 July 1924) was built on the station site. **SJ29393 29225**
OXFORD ROAD (GWR) 12 June 1844 – 2 June 1856 (Possibly alternative name for *Oxford 1st [GWR] [qv]*)

PENSHER (1st) (DJR) 9 March 1840 – 1 July 1881. **NZ32014 53577**
PERTH (SCentR) 23 May 1848 - 2 August 1848. Temporary station
PIMHOLE (L&YR) 1 May 1848 – November 1848. **SD81989 10092 (e)**
POKESDOWN (1st) (L&SWR) 1 July 1886 – Prior to 1890. **SZ12577 92421 (a)**
PORTPATRICK HARBOUR†* (PortR) 11 September 1868 – November 1868. **NW99837 54280 (a)**
PRESTON WEST END GATE (H&HR) September 1854 – October 1854. **TA16936 29407 (a)**
PWLLHELI ROAD (Nantlle) (3ft 6in gauge) 11 August 1856 – 12 June 1865. Llanwnda [L&NWR] (2 September 1867 – 7 December 1964) was built on the station site. **SH47279 57723**

RAINTON (N&DJnR) 19 June 1844 – August 1844
RAINTON (NER) c1855 – c1860. **NZ33210 46110**
RAWLINSON BRIDGE (B&PR) 4 February 1841 – 22 December 1841. Temporary terminus closed when line extended to Chorley [B&PR] (22 December 1841 -) **SD59777 14142 (a)**
REEDSMOUTH (1st) (BCR) May 1861 - 1 November 1864. **NY86517 82006 (a)**
REIGATE JUNCTION (SER) 15 April 1844 – August 1858. **TQ28227 49734 (a)**
RHOSYMEDRE (S&CR) 14 October 1848 – June 1849. **SJ28252 42235 (e)**
ROMAN ROAD (L&SR) 22 September 1834 – 10 November 1834. Ridge Bridge [NER] (1913 – c1921) was built on the station site. **SE34101 32795 (a)**
ROODYARDS (D&AR) 9 June 1839 – 2 April 1840. Temporary terminus closed when line extended to Dundee Trades Lane [D&AR] (2 April 1840 – 14 December 1857). **NO41830 30801 (a)**
RUGBY WHARF (MCR) 30 June 1840 – 4 July 1840. Temporary terminus closed when line extended to Rugby [L&NWR/MR] (4 July 1840 – 5 July 1855) [qv]. **SP50050 76708 (a)**

St LEONARDS, BULVERHYTHE (LB&SCR) 27 June 1846 – 7 November 1846. Temporary terminus closed when line extended to St Leonards West Marina 1st [LB&SCR] (7 November 1846 – 1882) [qv]. **TQ76632 08012 (a)**
SANDHURST (1st) (SER) 4 May 1852 - 2 June 1856
SANDIACRE & STAPLEFORD (MR) 6 September 1847 - 1 May 1872. **SK48352 36341 (a)**
SAUNDERSFOOT (1st) (P&TR) 5 September 1866 - June 1868. **SN12354 06032 (a)**
SEAFORTH (LC&SR) 1 October 1850 – 26 December 1866. Seaforth & Litherland [L&YR] (26 December 1866) was built on the station site. **SJ33349 97078**
SEATON SLUICE (B&TR) 3 May 1851 – April 1853. **NZ33797 76637 (a)**
SEDDON'S FIELD BRIDGE (MB&BR) 11 June 1838 – 31 July 1838
SELLY OAK (1st) (MR) 3 April 1876 - 13 April 1885. **SP04423 82665**
SHEIRE HEATH (SER) 20 August 1849 – Prior to January 1850
SHELTON (NSR) January 1862 – 13 July 1864. **SJ87890 47499 (e)**
SHENFIELD (ECR) October 1847 - March 1850. Shenfield and Hutton Junction [GER] (1 January 1887 -) was built on the station site. **TQ61355 94981**
SHEPHERD'S BUSH (WLR) 27 May 1844 – 1 December 1844. Shepherds Bush [LOROL] (28 September 2008 -) was built on the station site. **TQ23782 80034**
SHREWSBURY (S&CR) 12 October 1848 – 1 June 1849. Shrewsbury [S&HR] (1 June 1845 -) was built on the station site. **SJ49467 12955**
SILVERHILL COLLIERY* (GNR) Opening and closing dates unknown. **SK47107 61625 (a)**
SLEIGHTHOLME (C&SBR) 22 August 1856 – June 1857. **NY19527 53675 (a)**
SLOUGH (1st) (GWR) 1 June 1840 - 8 September 1884. Slough 2nd [GWR] (8 September 1884 -) was built on part of the station site. **SU97761 80193**
SOUTHAMPTON DOCKS EMPRESS DOCK* (L&SWR) 26 July 1890 – ?
SOUTHAMPTON OUTER DOCK* (L&SWR) 1 July 1843 - ?
SOUTHAMPTON INNER DOCK* (L&SWR) 1851 - ?
SOUTHPORT WINDSOR ROAD (WLancsR) 10 June 1878 – 4 September 1882. Temporary terminus closed when line extended to Southport Central [L&YR] (4 September 1882 – 1 May 1901). **SD34577 16838 (a)**
SOUTH STOCKTON (S&DR) 27 September 1825 - 1 July 1848. South Stockton 1st [NER] (1 July 1848 – 1882) [qv] was built on the station site. **NZ45080 18311**
SPA ROAD AND BERMONDSEY (L&GrR) 8 February 1836 – 14 December 1836. Temporary station, Spa Road and Bermondsey 1st [L&GrR] (31 October 1842 – 1 September 1873) [qv] was built on the station site **TQ34088 79269**
SPELBROOK (N&ER) 22 November 1841 – 16 May 1842. Temporary terminus closed when line extended to Bishops Stortford [N&ER] (16 May 1842 -). **TL48878 17560 (a)**

SPIERSBRIDGE (GB&KJR) 27 September 1848 – 1 May 1849. **NS54501 58846 (a)**
STAFFORD (GJnR) 4 July 1837 – 1862. **SJ91921 22792 (a)**
STANHOPE† (W&DwtJnR) 1 September 1845 – 1846. **NZ00009 38715 (a)**
STEWART'S LANE (WEoL&CPR) 29 March 1858 – 1 December 1858. **TQ29068 76872 (a)**
STOKE-ON-TRENT (1st) (NSR) 17 April 1848 – 9 October 1848. Temporary station. **SJ88257 44995 (a)**
STRANTON (Stktn&HpoolR) 10 February 1841 – June 1847. Temporary station. **NZ51578 32509 (a)**
STRATFORD MARKET (1st) (EC&TJR) 14 June 1847 – 1892. *Stratford Market 2nd [GER]* (1892 – 6 May 1957) was built on the station site. This was subsequently demolished at track level and replaced by *Stratford High Street [DLR]* (31 August 2011 -) **TQ38762 84020**
SWINDON WORKS* (GWR) c1880 - Prior to July 1897. **SU14305 85158 (a)**

TALK O' TH' HILL†* (NSR) ? – c1900. **SJ82459 52406 (e)**
TALLOW HILL (GWR/MR) ? – 5 October 1850. Temporary station. **SO85826 55085 (a)**
TATHAM BRIDGE (NWR) 17 November 1849 – 2 May 1850. Temporary terminus closed when line extended to *Bentham [NWR]* (1 June 1850 -). **SD61028 69278 (a)**
TAY PORT (EP&DR) 17 May 1850 - 12 May 1879. *Tayport [NBR]* (12 May 1879 – 22 May 1966) was built on the station site. **NO45813 29067**
TEIGNMOUTH (1st) (SDevonR) 30 May 1846 - 25 May 1884. *Teignmouth 2nd [GWR]* (25 May 1884 -) was built on the station site. **SX94217 73125**
THORPE & WHITLINGHAM (NorfolkR) 22 June 1844 - 12 September 1847. **TG27032 08372 (a)**
TIFFIELD (N&BJR) October 1869 – February 1871. **SP69741 52070 (a)**
TOLLERTON (GNofER) 1 August 1841 – c1892. **SE51539 64497**
TREETON (1st) (NMR) 6 April 1841 – c1843. *Treeton 2nd [MR]* (1 October 1884 – 29 October 1951) was built on the station site. **SK42948 87771**
TUNBRIDGE WELLS (JACKWOOD SPRINGS) (SER) 15 September 1845 – 25 November 1846. Temporary terminus closed when line extended to *Tunbridge Wells [SER]* (25 November 1846 -). **TQ58703 40182 (a)**
TWYFORD (L&SoR) July 1839 – September 1839. *Shawford [L&SWR]* (1 September 1882 -) was probably built on the station site. **SU47250 24970**
TWYMYN BRIDGE* (MawddwyR) 9 August 1880 – 10 December 1880. Temporary platform after bridge washed away. **SH82526 04833 (a)**
TY COCH* (L&NWR) 19 August 1879 – 21 August 1879. Temporary station due to flooding. **SJ07848 64909 (a)**

ULVERSTON (2nd) (FR) 26 August 1857 – c1874. **SD28764 77929 (a)**
USK (NA&HR) 2 June 1856 - 28 August 1857. Temporary station. **SO37236 01262 (a)**

WAEN LLWYD COLLIERY* (GWR) c1887 - c1897. **SO17670 06640 (a)**
WARDEN (N&CR) 28 June 1836 – c1837. **NY91032 66140 (e)**
WEDNESBURY (1st) (L&NWR) 1 May 1850 – 1 September 1863
WENNINGTON (1st) (L&NWR) 17 November 1849 – 1 May 1850
WEST HAMPSTEAD (1st) (MetR) 30 June 1879 - 13 June 1897. *West Hampstead [MetR]* (13 June 1897 -) was built on the station site. **TQ25598 84662**
WEST LONDON JUNCTION [with GWR] (WLR) 27 May 1844 – 1 December 1844. **TQ22606 82222 (a)**
WEST LONDON JUNCTION [with L&BmR] (WLR) 27 May 1844 – 1 December 1844. **TQ21967 82818 (a)**
WHIFFLET (MonklandR) 10 December 1849 - 10 December 1851. **NS73771 64140 (a)**
WHITTLESTONE HEAD (BBC&WYorksR) 12 June 1848 – 1 August 1848. **SD72112 19185 (a)**
WINDSOR & ETON RIVERSIDE (L&SWR) 1 December 1849 - 1 May 1851. Temporary station. **SU96905 77282 (a)**
WIVENHOE (W&BR) 1 August 1876 – 1 September 1877. Temporary station used during a dispute with the GER **TM03802 21664 (a)**
WOODFIELD (L&YR) 1 June 1874 – 1 July 1874. **SE12743 14459 (a)**

YEALAND (L&CR) 1848 – November 1852. **SD51271 73940 (e)**
YNYSYGEINON JUNCTION (MR) December 1873 – 1874. **SN76119 07109 (a)**

ABBREVIATIONS USED

A&BR; Aylesbury & Buckingham Railway
A&NJR; Ashby & Nuneaton Joint Railway
AberdeenR; Aberdeen Railway
AN&B&EJnR; Ambergate, Nottingham & Boston & Eastern Junction Railway
ACR; Anglesey Central Railway
AR; Aberdare Railway
B&CR; Bedford & Cambridge Railway
B&DJR; Birmingham & Derby Junction Railway
B&ER; Bristol & Exeter Railway
B&Ff; Bala & Ffestiniog Railway
B&GR; Birmingham & Gloucester Railway
B&MTJnR; Banff, Macduff & Turriff Junction Railway
B&PR; Bolton & Preston Railway
B&TR; Blyth & Tyne Railway
BBC&WYorksR; Bolton, Blackburn, Clitheroe & West Yorkshire Railway
BCR; Border Counties Railway
BheadR; Birkenhead Joint Railway
BLcs&ChshJnR; Birkenhead, Lancashire & Cheshire Junction Railway
BlingJnR; Brandling Junction Railway
BP&GVR; Burry Port & Gwendraeth Valley Railway
BR; British Railways
BS&PMR; Blyth, Seghill & Percy Main Railway
C&BheadR; Chester & Birkenhead Railway
C&DumbtnJR; Caledonian & Dumbartonshire Junction Railway
C&HR; Chester & Holyhead Railway
C&LR; Carnarvon & Llanberis Railway
C&SBR; Carlisle & Silloth Bay Railway
C&SLR; City & South London Railway
CLC; Cheshire Lines Committee
ClevelandR; Cleveland Railway
CMR; Cheshire Midland Railway
CofGUR; City of Glasgow Union Railway
CR; Caledonian Railway
CamR; Cambrian Railway
CwallR; Cornwall Railway
D&AR; Dundee & Arbroath Joint Railway
D&NR; Dundee & Newtyle Railway
D&PR; Dundee & Perth Railway
DC&RR; Denbigh, Corwen & Ruthin Railway
DJR; Durham Junction Railway
DLR; Docklands Light Railway
DP&AJnR; Dundee, Perth & Aberdeen Junction Railway
DsetCR; Dorset Central Railway
DsideR; Deeside Railway
E&BR; Edinburgh & Bathgate Railway
E&GR; Edinburgh & Glasgow Railway
E&LBR; Edenham & Little Bytham Railway
E&LR; Epsom & Leatherhead Railway
E&MR; Eastern & Midlands Railway
E&WJnR; East & West Junction Railway

E&WYorksUnR; East & West Yorkshire Union Railway
EAnglianR; East Anglian Railway
EC&TJR; Eastern Counties & Thames Junction Railway
ECR; Eastern Counties Railway
Ed&NR; Edinburgh & Northern Railway
ELancsR; East Lancashire Railway
EP&DR; Edinburgh, Perth & Dundee Railway
EUnionR; Eastern Union Railway
FestiniogR; Festiniog Railway
FlxstoweR; Felixstowe Railway
FP&WRJnR; Fleetwood, Preston & West Riding Junction Railway
FurnR; Furness Railway
G&SWR; Glasgow & South Western Railway
GB&KJR; Glasgow, Barrhead & Kilmarnock Joint Railway
GB&NDR; Glasgow, Barrhead & Neilston Direct Railway
GD&CR; Glasgow, Dumfries & Carlisle Railway
GER; Great Eastern Railway
GJnR; Grand Junction Railway
GlVyT; Glyn Valley Tramway
GNofER; Great North of England Railway
GNofSR; Great North of Scotland Railway
GPK&AR; Glasgow, Paisley, Kilmarnock & Ayr Railway
GWR; Great Western Railway
GY&SLR; Great Yarmouth & Stalham Light Railway
H&BheadR&T; Hoylake & Birkenhead Railway & Tramway
H&CR; Hammersmith & City Railway
H&HR; Hull & Holderness Railway
HH&BR; Hereford, Hay & Brecon Railway
HR; Highland Railway
I&AJnR; Inverness & Aberdeen Junction Railway
I&PJnR; Inverness & Perth Junction Railway
IoWCR; Isle of Wight Central Railway
IoWR [NJn]; Isle of Wight Railway [Newport Junction]
KR; Kinross-shire Railway
L&BmR; London & Birmingham Railway
L&BrR; London & Brighton Railway
L&BwallR; London & Blackwall Railway
L&CdnR; Liskeard & Caradon Railway
L&CR; Lancaster & Carlisle Railway
L&CrR; London & Croydon Railway
L&GrR; London & Greenwich Railway
L&IDJC; London & India Docks Joint Committee
L&MR; Liverpool & Manchester Railway
L&NER; London & North Eastern Railway
L&NR; Llanidloes & Newtown Railway
L&NWR; London & North Western Railway
L&PJnR; Lancaster & Preston Junction Railway
L&SoR; London & Southampton Railway

L&SR; Leeds & Selby Railway
L&SWR; London & South Western Railway
LC&DR; London, Chatham & Dover Railway
LC&SR; Liverpool, Crosby & Southport Railway
LderryS&SR; Londonderry, Seaham & Sunderland Railway
Ll&OR; Llynvi & Ogmore Railway
LlnyR; Llanelly Railway
LOR; Liverpool Overhead Railway
LOROL; London Overground Rail Operations Ltd
Lstr&SwngtnR; Leicester & Swannington Railway
LT&SR; London, Tilbury & Southend Railway
LU; London Underground
LUR; Lancashire Union Railway
M&BR; Manchester & Birmingham Railway
M&CR; Maryport & Carlisle Railway
M&ER; Midland & Eastern Railway
M&KR; Monkland & Kirkintilloch Railway
M&LR; Manchester & Leeds Railway
M&MR; Manchester & Milford Railway
M&SWJnR; Midland & South Western Junction Railway
MaccCteeR; Macclesfield Committee
MB&BR; Manchester, Bolton and Bury Railway
MawddwyR; Mawddwy Railway
MCR; Midland Counties Railway
MDR; Metropolitan District Railway
MetR; Metropolitan Railway
MidWR; Mid Wales Railway
MonklandR; Monkland Railway
MonmouthsR; Monmouthshire Railway
MorayshireR; Morayshire Railway
MR; Midland Railway
MS&LR; Manchester, Sheffield & Lincolnshire Railway
MSJn&AR; Manchester South Junction & Altrincham Railway
NA&HR; Newport, Abergavenny & Hereford Railway
NantleR; Nantlle Railway
N&BJR; Northampton & Banbury Junction Railway
N&BR; Neath & Brecon Railway
N&CR; Newcastle & Carlisle Railway
N&DJnR; Newcastle & Darlington Junction Railway
N&ER; Northern & Eastern Railway
NBR; North British Railway
NER; North Eastern Railway
New&BR; Newcastle & Berwick Railway
NewmarketR; Newmarket Railway
NLR; North London Railway
NMR; North Midland Railway
NorfolkR; Norfolk Railway
NSR; North Staffordshire Railway
NUR; Northern Union Railway
NWR; North Western Railway
OA&GBJR; Oldham, Ashton & Guide Bridge Junction Railway
OW&WR; Oxford, Worcester & Wolverhampton Railway

OystermouthR; Oystermouth Railway
P&LR; Preston & Longridge Railway
P&SSR; Pontop & South Shields Railway
P&TR; Pembroke & Tenby Railway
P&WR; Preston & Wyre Joint Railway
PeeblesR; Peebles Railway
PortR; Portpatrick Railway
PS&NWalesR; Potteries, Shrewsbury & North Wales Railway
R&SBR; Rhondda & Swansea Bay Railway
RhyR; Rhymney Railway
S&CR; Shrewsbury & Chester Railway
S&BmR; Shrewsbury & Birmingham Railway
S&DJtR; Somerset & Dorset Joint Railway
S&DR; Stockton & Darlington Railway
S&HR; Shrewsbury & Hereford Joint Railway
S&RR; Sheffield & Rotherham Railway
S&WyeR; Severn & Wye Railway
SAuL&MR; Sheffield, Ashton-under-Lyme & Manchester Railway
St&DunfR; Stirling & Dunfermline Railway
StHC&RC; St Helens Canal & Railway Company
Salop&Monts; Shropshire & Montgomeryshire Railway
SirhowyR; Sirhowy Railway
SDevonR; South Devon Railway
SER; South Eastern Railway
SCentR; Scottish Central Railway
SMJR; Scottish Midland Junction Railway
SNER; Scottish North Eastern Railway
SoAR; Stratford on Avon Railway
SStaffsR; South Staffordshire Railway
Stktn&HpoolR; Stockton & Hartlepool Railway
SuAT&MJR; Stratford-upon-Avon, Towcester & Midland Junction Railway
Sw&MblesR; Swansea & Mumbles Railway
SWR; South Wales Railway
SwVleR; Swansea Vale Railway
SYorks&RDNR; South Yorkshire & River Dun Navigation Railway
TJR; Tenbury Joint Railway
TM&WR; Tooting, Merton & Wimbledon Railway
TVR; Taff Vale Railway
U&LR; Ulverstone & Lancaster Railway
VanR; Van Railway
VoCR; Vale of Clwyd Railway
VoNR; Vale of Neath Railway
W&BR; Wivenhoe & Brightlingsea Railway
W&CnessR; Wishaw & Coltness Railway
W&DwtJnR; Wear & Derwent Junction Railway
W&FJnR; Whitehaven & Furness Junction Railway
W&PRR; Watlington & Princes Risborough Railway
W&SR; Warrington & Stockport Railway
WC&ER; Whitehaven, Cleator & Egremont Railway
WCwallR; West Cornwall Railway
WEoL&CPR; West End of London & Crystal Palace Railway

WigJnR; Wigan Junction Railway
WigtownshireR; Wigtownshire Railway
WirralR; Wirral Railway
WLR; West London Railway
WLancsR; West Lancashire Railway
WM&CR; Wilsontown, Morningside & Coltness Railway
WM&CQR; Wrexham, Mold & Connahs Quay Railway

WMidR; West Midland Railway
WrVyR; Wear Valley Railway
WStl&CJnR; Wisbech, St Ives & Cambridge Junction Railway
WSsetMinR; West Somerset Mineral Railway
Y&NMR; York & North Midland Railway
Y&NNR; Yarmouth & North Norfolk Railway
YN&BR; York, Newcastle & Berwick Railway

WITH THANKS TO

Bernard Anderson *(Great Eastern Railway Society)*, Geoff Burton *(Great Central Railway Society)*, Tom Burnham, Nick Fleetwood, Ian Mitchell, Richard Pulleyn, Keith Richardson and Richard Lacey *(North Eastern Railway Association)*, Chris Leach *(Lancashire & Yorkshire Railway Society)*, David Patrick *(London & North Western Railway Society)*, Jim Summers, Niall Ferguson and Roger Pidgeon *(Caledonian Railway Association)*, Dave Harris *(Midland Railway Society)* David Jones *(Great Western Railway Society)*, Tim Owen *(Furness Railway Trust)*, Tony Riley *(South Eastern & Chatham Railway Society)*, Dave Searle *(London, Brighton & SCR)*, Jim Lindsay, Nick Pigott, Phil Mackie, Keith Turner and Peter Waller.

BIBLIOGRAPHY

RAILWAY ATLAS, THEN & NOW by Paul Smith & Keith Turner. Ian Allan Publishing Second Edition. ISBN 978 0 7110 3833 2 (2015)

RAILWAY PASSENGER STATIONS IN GREAT BRITAIN: A CHRONOLOGY by Michael Quick. Railway & Canal Historical Society ISBN 978 0 901461 57 5 (2009)

ENCYCLOPÆDIA OF BRITISH RAILWAY COMPANIES by Christopher Awdry. Guild Publishing CN8983

ATLAS OF THE GREAT WESTERN RAILWAY AS AT 1947 by RA Cooke. Wild Swan Publications. ISBN 0 906867 65 7 (1988)

CLINKER'S REGISTER OF CLOSED PASSENGER STATIONS & GOODS DEPOTS IN ENGLAND, SCOTLAND AND WALES 1830-1980 by CR Clinker. Avon Anglia Publications. Second Edition. ISBN 0 905466 91 8 (1988)

THE DIRECTORY OF RAILWAY STATIONS by RVJ Butt. Patrick Stephens Ltd. ISBN 1 85260 508 1 (1995)

COMPLETE BRITISH RAILWAYS MAPS & GAZETTEER 1825-1985 by CJ Wignall. Oxford Publishing Company. ISBN 0 86093 294 X (1985)

LONDON RAILWAY ATLAS by Joe Brown. Ian Allan Publishing. Fourth Edition. ISBN 978 0 7110 3819 6

SCOTTISH RAILWAY ATLAS, THEN & NOW by Paul Smith & Paul Jordan. Crécy Publishing Ltd. ISBN 978 1 80035 034 2 (2021)

BIRMINGHAM & WEST MIDLANDS RAILWAY ATLAS by Joe Brown. Crécy Publishing Ltd. Second Edition. ISBN 978 1 80035 146 2

EARLY RAILWAY PRINTS - A SOCIAL HISTORY OF THE RAILWAYS FROM 1825 TO 1850 by Gareth Rees. Phaidon Press Ltd. ISBN 0 7148 2039 3 (1980)

WEBSITES ACCESSED

DISUSED STATIONS: http://disused-stations.org.uk/
ENGINE SHED SOCIETY: www.engineshedsociety.co.uk
GREAT NORTH OF SCOTLAND RAILWAY ASSOCIATION: http://www.gnsra.org.uk/
NATIONAL LIBRARY OF SCOTLAND: https://maps.nls.uk/
ORDNANCE SURVEY: https://www.ordnance survey.co.
RAIL MAP ONLINE: https://www.railmaponline.com/UKIEMap.php
RAIL SCOT: https://www.railscot.co.uk/
UK GRID REFERENCE FINDER: https://gridreferencefinder.com/
WIKIPEDIA: https://en.wikipedia.org/